DAVID W. BLIGHT

Beyond the Battlefield

Race, Memory, & the American Civil War

University of Massachusetts Press *Amherst & Boston*

Copyright © 2002 by
University of Massachusetts Press
All rights reserved
Printed in the United States of America
LC 2002000560
ISBN 1-55849-344-1 (library cloth ed.); 361-1 (paper)
Designed by Richard Hendel
Set in New Baskerville and Monotype Clarendon
Printed and bound by The Maple-Vail Book Manufacturing Group

Library of Congress
Cataloging-in-Publication Data

Blight, David W.
Beyond the battlefield : race, memory, and the American Civil War / David W.
Blight.
   p. cm.
Includes bibliographical references and index.
ISBN 1-55849-344-1 (alk. paper) — ISBN 1-55849-361-1 (pbk. : alk. paper)
1. United States—History—Civil War, 1861–1865—Influence.
2. United States—History—Civil War, 1861–1865—African Americans.
3. United States—History—Civil War, 1861–1865—Monuments.
4. United States—Race relations. 5. Memory—Social aspects—United States.
I. Title
E468.9 .B57 2002
973.7′1—dc21

                              2002000560

British Library Cataloguing in Publication
data are available.

To James G. Blight and janet Lang,

for their inspirations over many years,

and to

the memory of Nathan Irvin Huggins

Contents

Preface

During the past decade and a half, academic and public historians have become increasingly concerned with the relationship of history to memory. Indeed, "memory studies" has emerged as a subfield in American history. One of the most important subjects for Americanists, certainly the one that has occupied me, is the memory of the Civil War in American life and culture. This book brings together twelve essays and lectures that represent my own contribution to this field over approximately fifteen years. In the essays as a whole I explore the three primary concerns of my scholarly life: the meaning of the causes, course, and consequences of the Civil War; the nature of African American history and the significance of race in American history generally; and the character and purpose of the study of historical memory.

The introduction, "The Confluence of History and Memory," is intended as a primer about the theoretical relationship of these two essential dimensions of the historian's craft and our relationship to the vast marketplace of historical consciousness. The four chapters in part 1 examine prewar or wartime questions of autobiography, Civil War causation, soldiers' experiences, and the leadership and relationship of Frederick Douglass and Abraham Lincoln. The next six chapters, which compose part 2, deal directly with problems in Civil War memory; in each case the tangled relationship between the memory of the war itself and the memory of black emancipation forms a layered central theme. The final two pieces are reflections on meaning and memory in African America history; they represent research and commentary about two twentieth-century African Americans and the significance of race in American history. One these men, Nathan Irvin Huggins, I knew well, if too briefly; the other, W. E. B. Du Bois, was a major actor in that history.

Collecting such writings into a single volume allows authors to trace the archaeology of their own work over time, an endeavor both revealing and humbling. So much seems unexplored, unsaid. But I offer these pieces, knit together by their common threads, as the residue of an unfinished fascination with the meaning of the Civil War "beyond the battlefield" (as Douglass challenged his generation and us to think about it), with why America is so vexed by the problem of race, and with why we must understand the relationships between history and memory. What happened on battlefields in the Civil War is very important to know and understand. The legions of readers for Civil War military history should continue to hear the bugle call to knowledge of how the war was fought, which leaders were most pivotal in outcomes and why, which factors led to Union victory and Confederate defeat, and the values and motivations of soldiers and civilians in waging such a fundamental struggle for America's national existence. But the boundaries of military history are fluid; they connect with a broader social, cultural, and political history in myriad ways. In the long run, the meanings embedded in those epic fights are what should command our greatest attention. The "war of ideas," as Douglass aptly called it, has never completely faded from our nation's social condition or historical memory. Suppress it as we may, it still sits in our midst, an eternal postlude playing for all who deal seriously with America's past and with our enduring predicaments with race, pluralism, and equality.

The research and writing of these essays date back to at least 1987 when I first wrote about Frederick Douglass and the memory of the Civil War. The people who have influenced or helped me produce this book number more than I can name. But I owe special debts that I gratefully acknowledge here. First and foremost is to Clark Dougan at the University of Massachusetts Press, whose patience, friendship, and commitment to this book, and my work generally, were above and beyond the call of duty. Clark, and his colleague Bruce Wilcox, helped me understand how to have the audacity to assemble my collected essays in one place with reasonable coherence. I benefited greatly from having two superb readings of the entire manuscript, by John David Smith and Scott Sandage. Both offered splendid criticisms and suggestions. For their permission to republish essays often in slightly revised form, I thank the *Journal of American History, Slavery and Abolition, Reviews in American History,* Oxford University Press, Kent State University Press, University of Massachusetts Press, Marquette University Press, and the National Park Service. For their many readings, their colleagial support, and influences too many to name, I thank the following: Gabor Boritt, Fitzhugh Brundage, Randall Burkett, Christopher Clark, Catherine Clinton, Kathleen Dalton,

David Brion Davis, Robert Gooding-Williams, Hugh Hawkins, James Horton, Lois Horton, Jeffrey Ferguson, Michael Kammen, Edward Linenthal, James Marten, William McFeely, Peter Pouncey, Richard Rabinowitz, Lisa Raskin, Ronald Rosbottom, Martha Sandweiss, Richard Sewell, Nina Silber, Brooks Simpson, Werner Sollors, Robert Sutton, Howard Temperly, and Donald Yacovone. I give enormous thanks to Nancy Board for reformatting and helping me reproduce these essays in consistent form. At the University of Massachusetts Press, Carol Betsch helped bring this work to publication with an expert hand. Laura Gottlieb produced a marvelous index. And finally, for helping me in the arduous task of reading the proofs and in many other tasks of life, I am deeply grateful to Karin Beckett.

David W. Blight
Amherst, Massachusetts

Beyond the Battlefield

Introduction

The Confluence of History and Memory

The concepts of history and memory can be conflated, or they can be discretely preserved in both use and meaning. They represent two attitudes toward the past, two streams of historical consciousness that must at some point flow together. For professional historians a separation is often important; for the general public and for history's enormous audience of readers and enthusiasts the two terms frequently mingle in common usage. Historians are custodians of the past; along with our colleagues in archives, libraries, and publishing, we have a great deal to do with the shape and content of the history that becomes part of public and social memory. We are preservers and discoverers of the facts and the stories out of which people in general imagine their civic lives. But as John Lukacs wrote in 1968, "what historians ought to consider are not only increasing varieties of records but a deepening consciousness of the functions of human memory." We need a sense of both humility and engagement in the face of public memory. "The remembered past," warned Lukacs, "is a much larger category than the recorded past . . . and this is especially important in the democratic age in which we live."[1] In the intensive quietude of research and in the creative tensions of writing narrative, historians both record and remember, for ourselves and our readers, and we can hope, for that vast public engaged every day in some form of remembrance.

In this book I assess individual memories (actual remembered experience)—in letters, memoirs, speeches, debates, and autobiography. But my primary concern is with collective memory—the ways in which groups, peoples, or nations remember, how they construct versions of the past and employ them for self-understanding and to win power and place in an ever-changing present. These essays are studies of memory as an instrument of power.

Establishing some differences between history and memory as working terms is important. *History*—what trained historians do—is a reasoned reconstruction of the past rooted in research; it tends to be critical and skeptical of human motive and action, and therefore more secular than what people commonly refer to as memory. History can be read by or belong to everyone; it assesses change and progress over time, and is therefore more relative, more contingent upon place, chronology, and scale. *Memory,* however, is often treated as a sacred set of potentially absolute meanings and stories, possessed as the heritage or identity of a community. Memory is often owned; history, interpreted. Memory is passed down through generations; history is revised. Memory often coalesces in objects, sacred sites, and monuments; history seeks to understand contexts and the complexity of cause and effect. History asserts the authority of academic training and recognized canons of evidence; memory carries the often more powerful authority of community membership and experience. Or as the French historian Pierre Nora put it, "memory dictates, while history writes."[2]

Such separations are not to suggest that these two attitudes toward the past are everywhere distinct; in the expanding marketplace of public history and in the often warring national and ethnic memories that shape so much of the domestic and international culture of our time, history and memory must be treated as unsteady, conflicted companions in our quest to understand humankind's consciousness of the past. In the confluence of history and memory, we will find much of what is exciting and troubling about how nations and communities use the past.

The concept of individual memory is easier to grasp than that of collective memory. In one of the oldest but deepest reflections on the subject, Saint Augustine, in the *Confessions,* was awed by memory. "Great is the power of memory," he wrote, "a fearful thing, O my God, a deep and boundless manifoldness; and this thing is the mind, and this am I myself."[3] In a real sense, we are our individual memories; we cannot function effectively without them. But we also know that nations and other human groups devise, however illusively, collective memories and transmit them through myths, traditions, stories, rituals, and formal interpretations of history. Indeed, what scholars used to call and examine as *myth* transformed in the 1980s and 1990s into the study of *memory.*

Everyone who studies the relationship between history and memory does so largely because of the politics of memory. Social history has also led historians to social memory. The study of social classes, communities, structures, and heretofore underrepresented groups inevitably drew some historians to a fascination with social remembering and forgetting. The history of the twentieth century, moreover, has made us increasingly concerned with how nations organize their pasts, and with how and why great violence can be committed in the name of memory. Modern nations have taken their very sustenance at times from the pasts upon which they are built or imagined. In his classic study *The Collective Memory*, the sociologist Maurice Halbwachs's analysis of the relationship of individual and collective memory (what he preferred to call "autobiographical" and "historical" memory) was very much aimed at how historians think. Whether writing biography or broad social histories of forces at work over the long duration, historians seek to know the relationship between the individual and society. Halbwachs's insights into how we remember in groups, associations, frameworks, communities, and institutional spaces serve historians who seek to know how historical consciousness is forged or diminished in any given culture.[4] What historians studying memory have come to understand is simply that the process by which societies or nations remember collectively itself has a history, and that by writing those histories we enrich our understanding of the very idea of the past and our relationships to it. We need, therefore, studies of memory that are rooted in deep research, sensitive to contexts and to the varieties of memory at play in any given epoch.

Many historians are not fully comfortable with the philosopher Walter Benjamin's challenge: "To articulate the past historically does not mean to recognize 'the way it really was' (Ranke). It means to seize hold of a memory as it flashes up at a moment of danger." Benjamin's insight is that there are great stakes in struggles over rival versions of the past—often long epochs of development and conflict rather than merely flashpoints. But there is no need to abandon Otto von Ranke's famous dictum of the historian's craft—the historian's concern with memory should be no less devoted to evidence and the search for reality than the study of elections, diplomacy, or any other subject. Among American historians, Michael Kammen has led the way in the study of memory, investigating what he calls "the phenomenon of a society becoming its own historian—for better and for worse." This means we are often studying a process of forgetting as much as remembering; we are examining conscious and unconscious "distortions" of the past in the name of causes, both lost and won. Kammen cautioned those engaged in memory studies to be careful in our use of terms such as "collective" and "popular" memory, to remember that dominant (official) memories are not as static and controlling as we sometimes think, and that all assessment of historical memory must be keenly attuned to historical particularities. Kammen urged all students of memory to treat it as the politics of culture. In other words, scholars and public historians should go ahead and investigate myth, ritual, and tradition, the vernacular and the official, but we should be good historians and watch our abstractions—we should seize those times when memory conflicts were acute, but always with our time-honored methods of understanding, as best we can, "the way it really was."[5]

There are, of course, risks as historians shift their gaze on to matters of social and public memory. We could become servants of the very "culture wars" that have given rise to so many struggles over memory in our time. Memory is usually invoked in the name of nation, ethnicity, race, religion, or someone's felt need for peoplehood. It often thrives on grievance and on the elaborate invention of traditions; its lifeblood is mythos. Like our subjects, we can risk thinking *with* memory rather than *about* it. Indeed, the study of memory may itself be fueled at times by its salience in the world's post-Holocaust and post–Cold War need to assess the stories of survivors of genocide, trauma, or totalitarian control over historical consciousness. While I agree that the world is riven with too much memory and that its obsessions can paralyze whole peoples and stifle democratizing and universalizing principles, it is precisely because of this dilemma that we must study historical memory. We must know its uses and perils, its values and dark tendencies. People will develop a sense of history by one means or another. The greatest risk, wrote Cynthia Ozick, is that they will derive that sense of the past only from the "fresh-hatched inspiration" of their "Delphic priests." History is often weak in the face of the mythic power of memory and its many oracles. But we run the greatest risk in ignoring that weakness, wishing that the public would adopt a more critical, interpretive sense of the past. "Cut off from the uses of history, experience, and memory," Ozick cautioned, the "inspirations" alone of any culture's Delphic priests "are helpless to make a future."[6] As historians, we are bound by our craft and by our humanity to study the problem of memory, and thereby help make a future.

We must respect the poets and priests, honoring them by studying and learning from them. We should study and understand the power of the myths that define societies and cultures. But then, standing at the confluence of the two streams, we should write the history of memory, observing and explaining the turbulence we find. In "To a Historian,"

Walt Whitman invited us to mingle our best skills with his own in this exciting task:

> You who celebrate bygones
> Who have explored the outward, the surfaces of the races, the life that has exhibited itself,
> Who have created of man as the creature of politics, aggregates, rulers and priests,
> I, habitan of the Alleghanies, treating of him as he is in himself in his own rights,
> Pressing the pulse of the life that has seldom exhibited itself, (the great pride of man in himself,)
> Chanter of Personality, outlining what is yet to be,
> I project the history of the future.[7]

Neither poets nor historians can stand alone in using and explaining the past. Since all memory is in some way prelude, we have to chant together.

NOTES

1. John Lukacs, *Historical Consciousness or the Remembered Past* (1968; reprint, New York: Schocken Books, 1985), 33.

2. One of the best discussions of the differences between history and memory, a condensation of his multivolume study of *places* in memory, is Pierre Nora, "Between Memory and History: Les Lieux de Memoire," *Representations,* no. 26 (spring 1989): 7–25. The literature on historical memory is vast. For the best over-all treatment of memory and tradition in America, see Michael Kammen, *Mystic Chords of Memory: The Transformation of Tradition in American Culture* (New York: Knopf, 1991). For a series of essays by historians assessing the phenomenon of memory studies, see Susan A. Crane, "Writing the Individual Back into Collective Memory"; Alon Confino, "Collective Memory and Cultural History: Problems of a Method"; and Daniel James, "Meatpackers, Peronists, and Collective Memory: A View from the South," all in *American Historical Review* 102 (December 1997): 1371–412. On the significance of memory and popular culture, see Roy Rosen-zweig and David Thelen, *The Presence of the Past: Popular Uses of History in American Life* (New York: Columbia University Press, 1998); Raphael Samuel, *Theaters of Memory: Past and Present in Contemporary Culture,* vol. 1 (London: Verso, 1994); An-dreas Huyssen, *Twilight Memories: Marking Time in a Culture of Amnesia* (London: Routledge, 1995); and Tony Horwitz, *Confederates in the Attic: Dispatches from the Unfinished Civil War* (New York: Pantheon, 1998). Of particular use to me have also been *Memory and American History,* ed. David Thelen (Bloomington: Indiana University Press, 1990); Paul Connerton, *How Societies Remember* (Cambridge, Eng.: Cambridge University Press, 1989); *Memory: History, Culture, and the Mind,*

ed. Thomas Butler (Oxford: Basil Blackwell, 1989); *Commemorations: The Politics of National Identity,* ed. John R. Gillis (Princeton: Princeton University Press, 1994); David Lowenthal, *The Past Is a Foreign Country* (New York: Cambridge University Press, 1985); David Lowenthal, *Possessed by the Past: The Heritage Crusade and the Spoils of History* (New York: Free Press, 1996); Edward T. Linenthal, *Sacred Ground: Americans and Their Battlefields,* 2d ed. (Urbana: University of Illinois Press, 1993); Edward T. Linenthal, *Preserving Memory: The Struggle to Create America's Holocaust Museum* (New York: Viking, 1995); Sanford Levinson, *Written in Stone: Public Monuments in Changing Societies* (Durham: Duke University Press, 1998); James E. Young, *The Texture of Memory: Holocaust Memorials and Meaning* (New Haven: Yale University Press, 1993); Marita Sturken, *Tangled Memories: The Vietnam War, the AIDS Epidemic, and the Politics of Remembering* (Berkeley: University of California Press, 1997); Patrick H. Hutton, *History as an Art of Memory* (Hanover, N.H.: University Press of New England, 1993); *Bonds of Affection: Americans Define Their Patriotism,* ed. John Bodnar (Princeton: Princeton University Press, 1996); Jacques Le Goff, *History and Memory,* trans. Steven Rendall and Elizabeth Claman (New York: Columbia University Press, 1992); Jeffrey Herf, *Divided Memory: The Nazi Past in the Two Germanys* (Cambridge: Harvard University Press, 1997); Jay Winter, *Sites of Memory, Sites of Mourning: The Great War in European Cultural History* (Cambridge, Eng.: Cambridge University Press, 1995); Michael S. Roth, *The Ironist's Cage: Memory, Trauma, and the Construction of History* (New York: Columbia University Press, 1995); Patrick J. Geary, *Phantoms of Remembrance: Memory and Oblivion at the End of the First Millennium* (Princeton: Princeton University Press, 1994); and Christopher Lasch, *The True and Only Heaven: Progress and Its Critics* (New York: Norton, 1991). All scholars of memory benefit from rereadings of Friedrich Nietzsche, *The Use and Abuse of History,* trans. Adrian Collins (New York: Liberal Arts Press, 1949).

3. Saint Augustine, *Confessions,* trans. Edward Bouverie Pusey (New York: Book-of-the-Month Club, 1996), 240.

4. Maurice Halbwachs, *The Collective Memory* (New York: Harper and Row, 1950), 52. Histories of memory, and its many mediums, have appeared in waves in scholarly literature. Another good example is *American Historical Review* 106 (June 2001): 804–64, a forum in which four historians treat the question of the memory of World War II as represented by film in Britain, the United States, and the Soviet Union. The pieces include John Bodnar, "*Saving Private Ryan* and Postwar Memory in America"; Geoff Eley, "Finding the People's War: Film, British Collective Memory, and World War II"; Denise J. Youngblood, "A War Remembered: Soviet Films of the Great Patriotic War"; and Jay Winter, "Film and the Matrix of Memory."

5. Walter Benjamin, *Illuminations: Essays and Reflections,* ed. Hannah Arendt (1955; reprint, New York: Schocken Books, 1969), 255; Kammen, *Mystic Chords of Memory,* 3–14. For Ranke, see Leopold von Ranke, "The Ideal of Universal History," excerpted in *The Varieties of History: From Voltaire to the Present,* ed. Fritz Stern (New York: Vintage, 1973), 54–62. On "distortions," see Michael Kammen, "Some Patterns and Meanings of Memory Distortion in American History," in

Kammen, *In the Past Lane: Historical Perspectives on American Culture* (New York: Oxford University Press, 1997), 199–212. For one of the best studies of the relationship between vernacular and official memories, see John Bodnar, *Remaking America: Public Memory, Commemoration, and Patriotism in the Twentieth Century* (Princeton: Princeton University Press, 1992).

6. Cynthia Ozick, "Metaphor and Memory," in Ozick, *Metaphor and Memory: Essays* (New York: Vintage International, 1991), 281. On invented traditions, see *The Invention of Tradition,* ed. Eric Hobsbawm and Terrance Ranger (Cambridge, Eng.: Cambridge University Press, 1983). On the problem of excessive memory consciousness, see Charles S. Maier, "A Surfeit of Memory? Reflections on History, Melancholy, and Denial," *History and Memory: Studies in the Representations of the Past* 5 (fall–winter 1993): 136–52; Peter Novick, *The Holocaust in American Life* (Boston: Houghton Mifflin, 1999); and a special issue of *Representations,* particularly Thomas Laqueur, introduction, and Kerwin Lee Klein, "On the Emergence of Memory in Historical Discourse," in *Representations* no. 69 (winter 2000): 1–8, 127–50. On the history wars, especially in museum controversies, see *History Wars: The* Enola Gay *and Other Battles for America's Past,* ed. Edward T. Linenthal and Tom Englehardt (New York: Henry Holt, 1996).

7. Walt Whitman, "To a Historian," in *Leaves of Grass,* ed. Emory Holloway (Garden City, N.Y.: Doubleday, 1926), 3.

Preludes

Several Lives in One
Frederick Douglass's
Autobiographical Art

*Memory was given to man for some wise purpose. The past
is . . . the mirror in which we may discern the dim outlines of
the future and by which we may make them more symmetrical.*
　—*Frederick Douglass*

In 1980, when I was a struggling graduate student
and launching an unformed dissertation on Frederick Douglass, I had
the good fortune to meet the late Dickson Preston, journalist, historian,
resident of Maryland's Eastern Shore, and author of *Young Frederick Douglass: The Maryland Years.* I was spending a week or two in Washington,
D.C., on research. Preston agreed to meet me in a parking lot of a community college near Easton. I crawled into his station wagon, and to my
surprise he said, "Before we do anything, let me show you a great tree."
We spent the first half hour observing the great Wye Oak. What followed
next was an unforgettable trek around the back roads of the Eastern
Shore, to some old streets in Easton, the Auld house in Saint Michaels,
the Wye plantation (what Douglass called "the Great House farm"), and
the sites of Edward Covey's and William Freeland's farms where Frederick Bailey had been a slave. Finally, Dick took me out to the bend in
Tuckahoe Creek to the likely site of Betsy Bailey's cabin and Frederick
Douglass's birthplace. I will never forget our walk along the edge of a
muddy cornfield down to the creek. As we retreated toward the bay and
back to the Wye plantation, Preston did his best to retrace the route
Douglass's mother, Harriet, might have taken on her visits to see her
son. The whole experience put me into that mysterious and real world
of Douglass's slave youth, within some of the sites and scenes of the famous autobiographies that many of us teach and read. But as yet, I had
not taken Douglass's autobiographies seriously enough. At that time I
was about the business of imagining a work on Douglass as a thinker, as

an interpreter of the Civil War in the national as well as his own experience. Preston and I talked all day about Douglass's ideas about every imaginable subject. Later, at a long lunch, he gave me some mature advice: he said, whatever you do with Douglass, whatever sources you explore, "go back and read those autobiographies, especially the first two." He left me with the direct admonition: "Douglass really does reveal himself there."[1]

It is intriguing to imagine a day when the National Park Service might find a way to acquire, commemorate, and interpret some of these Douglass sites on Maryland's Eastern Shore. As Americans continue to struggle to face the story of slavery in their past, as we try in faltering ways to have "conversations about race," where better to begin some of these discussions than with Douglass's own tale of bitter complaint and personal triumph? The story Douglass immortalized in his autobiographies is only one small, yet exceptional, part of the larger story of slavery. But as young Americans by the hundreds of thousands now grow up reading Douglass's *Narrative,* how remarkable it would be to take them to Tuckahoe Creek, to the Wye House, to the ridge overlooking Chesapeake Bay, where young Frederick suffered under Edward Covey's cruelty. How effective it would be to have well-trained Park Service personnel read excerpts of the *Narrative* to schoolchildren at specific stops on the Frederick Douglass Trail. In one day's journey, a family could follow the young Douglass from a richly imagined cabin on Tuckahoe Creek, through the allowance day gathering of slaves at the Wye House where Douglass seems to have gathered his most compelling recollections of slave music, all the way to Fells Point in Baltimore, where the twelve-year-old discovered *The Columbian Orator.* It is a long way from Betsy Bailey's cabin in 1818 to the Cedar Hill house (a National Park Service site) in Washington, D.C., in the 1880s. The story just does not flow the right direction gazing only out from Douglass's veranda overlooking Washington. Young people need to know this story as well as they learn any other American story, and they need to see it, as young Frederick would have seen it, from the other side of the Chesapeake. This is not an Underground Railroad tale per se, but it is surely a great story of the descent into slavery and the ascent toward freedom. In his autobiographies, Douglass left many enduring invitations to engage in a conversation about slavery and race, about oppression and its transcendence. With his books in hand, we ought to return to the Eastern Shore, physically and imaginatively, and take him up on the invitation.

American culture has always had a fascination for autobiography: from the Puritan conversion narratives to Benjamin Franklin, on down through the many transformations of the genre, a society that came to exalt the individual—individual rights and the individual's voice—needed, created, and even understood itself at times through the stories we tell each other about ourselves. Obviously, this was not unique with America. At least since Saint Augustine's *Confessions* we have had a model for the sublimity of a Douglass or a Vladimir Nabokov, as well as, I suspect, for the current craze of personal improvement or personal descent stories in our talk show culture (or even the trend toward autobiography among scholars).[2] The bothersome smugness (to some readers) of Ralph Waldo Emerson's "Self Reliance" or Henry David Thoreau's *Walden* do not, when they are read charitably, diminish their central insight: the idea or at least our need to believe in the idea that we can re-create ourselves, that we can make and remake our lives, that our futures are not wholly determined. How precious was that faith to an American slave in the 1820s and 1830s? Frederick Douglass, the autobiographer, endures for many reasons, but not least because his writing represents both the brilliant complaint and the audacious hope of the slave who mastered language and reimagined himself. We should read Douglass's autobiographies not for their "accuracy" but for their "truth."

In an essay she wrote while finishing the novel *Beloved,* called "The Site of Memory," Toni Morrison identified the slave narratives as a large part of her "literary heritage." She described her own creative process as a "kind of literary archeology," journeys to sites where she finds "images" to rework, imagining herself into and out of the lives of a Douglass or a Harriet Jacobs. The truths she finds in the narratives are not always the same ones scholars may find. Her only lament about ex-slave autobiographies, she said, is that the authors were so controlled, so protective in not exposing more of their "interior life." This she takes, of course, as her imaginative challenge. "Like Frederick Douglass talking about his grandmother," wrote Morrison, "and James Baldwin talking about his father, and Simone de Beauvoir talking about her mother, these people are my access to me; they are my entrance into my own interior life. Which is why the images that float around them—the remains, so to speak, at the archeological site—surface first, and they surface so vividly and so compellingly that I acknowledge them as my route to a reconstruction of a world, to an exploration of an interior life that was not written and to the revelation of a kind of truth." I think in Douglass's case, he exposed more of that interior life than Morrison implies. But she surely speaks for all of us—readers, public historians, teachers, and scholars—in helping us understand how we remember, learn, or find access to our own or anyone else's past. And, of course, no work in our literature exposes the double burden of memory quite like *Beloved:* the great peril and the absolute necessity of remembering. In *Beloved,* as Sethe is about to give birth to her baby (Denver) on the banks of the Ohio River, Amy Denver, the southern white woman and midwife says to the suffering Sethe: "it's gonna hurt now; anything coming back to life hurts."[3] In such a simple line Morrison may have captured the meaning of slavery in American memory. No matter how painful slavery is to recollect and confront today, nor how difficult it was for the slave narrators to write about, like the birth of a child, it will come. Douglass and others have been there all along reminding us of this lesson.

In the *Narrative* and in *My Bondage and My Freedom* Douglass saw to the core of the meaning of slavery, for individuals and for the nation. Moreover, his greatest theme of all was the meaning of freedom—as idea and reality, of mind and body, and of the consequences of its denial. Some of the most honest aspects of Douglass's autobiographies are his meditations on the meaning of literacy, on his seizure of language, and about knowledge beyond the borders of slavery. But these were no up . . . up . . . from slavery platitudes; they are statements of fear, anguish, and determination—"soul devouring" thoughts as he put it, visions of an often terrifying future observed through the glass of memory. After his life-changing discovery of *The Columbian Orator* and reading newspapers about "abolitionism" in the North, he nevertheless left this forthright admission in the *Narrative:* "The more I read, the more I was led to abhor and detest my enslavers. . . . As I read and contemplated the subject, behold! that very discontent which Master Hugh had predicted would follow my learning to read had already come, to torment and sting my soul to unutterable anguish. As I writhed under it, I would at times feel that learning to read had been a curse rather than a blessing. It had given me a view of my wretched condition, without a remedy. . . . In moments of agony, I envied my fellow slaves for their stupidity. I have often wished myself a beast. . . . Anything, no matter what, to get rid of thinking! It was this everlasting thinking of my condition that tormented me." Knowledge, awareness of the broader world can be frightful in its unfocused or unreachable stages. "The silver trump of freedom" Douglass continued, "had roused my soul to eternal wakefulness. Freedom now appeared, to disappear no more forever. It was heard in every sound, seen in every thing. It was ever present to torment me with a sense of my wretched condition. I saw nothing without seeing it, I heard nothing without hearing it, and felt nothing without feeling it. It looked from every star, it smiled in every calm, breathed in every wind, and moved in every storm."[4]

The slave narratives are often judged to be significant because they "existed at all," as the novelist and critic Daryl Pinckney wrote in a series on black autobiography in the *New York Review of Books*. But our beleaguered search for the "universal" in literature and history these days need look no further than that previous passage by Douglass about the meaning of literacy. Moreover, if the crisis of the Union brewing during the years Douglass crafted his first two autobiographies was a struggle over conflicting visions of the future, then for black folks, it was a crisis over whether they had a future in America at all. In *Bondage* Douglass offered this timeless explanation of his hatred of slavery and his desire for freedom: "The thought of only being a creature of the *present* and the *past,* troubled me, and I longed to have a *future*—a future with hope in it. To be shut up entirely to the past and present is abhorrent to the human mind; it is to the soul—whose life and happiness is unceasing progress—what the prison is to the body." This passage comes in the midst of an extended demolition of the notion of the "contented slave," a favorite abolitionist theme. But it also demonstrates Douglass's struggle, as writer, to universalize his experience, to probe and recapture portions of his memory, and to achieve recognition and renewal in his reader. Douglass's wonderful story of the slave who would struggle out of his past to some kind of safe landing in a present—to see a future—had much to do with why the *Narrative* became a best-seller, and why, as critic William Andrews has shown, *Bondage and Freedom* belongs along side Walt Whitman, Margaret Fuller, Herman Melville, Thoreau, and Emerson as a great text of the American Renaissance.[5]

We still read Douglass, in part, because he left so many meditations on the meaning of life, the meaning of manliness, the meaning of memory, on just what the weight of the past is over anyone's present. *Bondage and Freedom* may read at times like a melodramatic novel, but it is also a commentary for all time on the idea of resistance, on the right of revolution, on irony and contradiction as values rather then merely obstacles, and on how the quest for a meaningful future is everyone's defense against social death. Douglass dearly needed to escape his past, but he also never stopped probing and reshaping it, ascending from and looking for himself in that past. He knew that both sides of his life could only be explained on both sides of Chesapeake Bay.[6]

Douglass's two antebellum narratives appealed to readers in his own time for many reasons. His story, like American history itself, is both inspiring and terrible. He combined experience with the music of words to make us see America's deepest contradictions, the tragedy and necessity of conflict between slavery and freedom in a republic. Mid-nineteenth-century readers were very familiar with jeremiads that reminded them of America's divinely appointed mission and of such betrayals of that mission as slavery. They were probably both troubled by and attracted to narratives about true and false Americanism. Douglass's autobiographies were not only songs of himself; they were songs of abolitionism, arguments with America's conscience, appeals by the risen slave testifying to his own sufferings and making witness to the crimes of a guilty land, all done in an oratorical, platform style that made them read like extended sermons. But as Vernon Loggins observed in 1931, autobiography and abolitionist propaganda were not antithetical: Douglass "possessed the ability to bring out his sermon without destroying his story."[7] His narratives were political documents written by a black man—the slave become author—allowing access to the sectional crisis on a personal, authentic level. Readers were also drawn to escape and captivity narratives, to tales of self-made men and self-liberation. And perhaps most of all, readers were at home with spiritual autobiographies—ritualistic testimonies about the trial of the soul as well as the body, journeys from mental and spiritual darkness through severe tests to the light of regeneration.

Douglass's writing fit all these literary conventions and more. But he reached readers, and still does, deep in their humanity. In one of the most memorable passages in the *Narrative,* and certainly a reach for the universal, Douglass remembers the terrible year he lived as a sixteen-year-old under the wrath of the slave breaker Edward Covey: it was his "dark night of slavery," a time when he often felt "transformed into a brute," and when he spent whole days "mourning" over his condition. But all this frames a story of resurrection through violence and an unforgettable image of freedom. The Covey farm was only a short distance from Chesapeake Bay, and on its banks Douglass places himself, changing voice to the nearly suicidal sixteen-year-old slave, pouring out his "soul's complaint" in a psalm-like prayer of deliverance. The white-sailed vessels on the bay are "shrouded ghosts" that torment him one moment and become the dreamlike objects of his lonely prayer the next: "You are loosed from your moorings, and are free," Douglass wrote; "I am fast in my chains and am a slave! You move merrily before the gentle gale, and I sadly before the bloody whip! You are freedom's swift-winged angels, that fly round the world; I am confined in bands of iron!" Here Douglass revealed a mind and soul made captive, but through moral imagination and belief in "a better day coming," he keeps faith and seems to will his own freedom. In this famous passage Douglass reached an early height in his craft as a writer. Appealing for deliverance from enemies and testifying to tattered but refurbished faith, Douglass wrote what might be best called his own psalm, or a prose poem, about the meaning of freedom.[8] In the decade before the Civil War, as well as now in our own time of absent heroes and diminished expectations, readers of the *Narrative* can sit with Douglass in the dark night of his soul along their own Chesapeakes and sense the deepest of human yearnings in their own souls.

Douglass's autobiographies appeal to us for another reason: they are, all three of them, the private story converted to public purposes, and they are, despite our appropriate skepticism about autobiography, access to a larger past; they are sources of history. As many critics have said, the best autobiographies reach the standard of great art when the writer treats his or her memory as both source and subject, as recollection transformed in story and metaphor about a world larger than themselves. "A good memoir," wrote William Zinsser, "is also a work of history, catching a distinctive moment in the life of both a person and a society." Ralph Ellison wrote compellingly about how autobiographical works emerge from history and allow us access to it. "One of the reasons we exchange experiences," said Ellison, "is in order to discover the repetitions and coincidences which amount to a common group experience. We tell ourselves our individual stories so as to become aware of our *general* story." And Annie Dillard, another marvelous memoirist, said, "literary nonfiction" is always about two things: the writer's "interior life" and the "vast setting of our common history." We should demand to learn about broad contexts from autobiography, said Dillard. "I admire artists," she said, "who succeed in dividing my attention more or less evenly between the world of their books and the art of their books."[9] This, I think, Douglass accomplished. We learn a good deal of history, a good deal about his world, from Douglass's autobiographies. We are also escorted into that world by a young self-conscious artist determined to exercise control over the chaos of his past by transforming it into the magic of words.

Well into the twentieth century, slave narratives were not considered proper historical sources. They were deemed inauthentic and biased by Ulrich B. Phillips, the first major professional historian of slavery to make extensive use of plantation records. The idea that no fugitive slave could ever have written his or her own narrative persisted well into this century and has by no means died. Phillips and his generation of historians did not acknowledge that slaves left any legitimate testimony on the character and meaning of their own lives.[10] This "plantation legend"—an Old South living a kind of golden age in which the masters provided and the slaves labored in relative contentment—died hard in American historiography and may never die in popular culture.

But the revolution of interest in black history, which coincided with the modern Civil Rights movement in the 1950s and 1960s, brought a renewed attention to the use of the slave narratives. Douglass's autobiographies had been out of print for nearly a century when the first modern edition of the *Narrative* was published by Harvard University Press in 1960 and introduced by the distinguished African American historian Benjamin Quarles. In the 1960s and 1970s historians began to make careful use of the slave narratives as sources of historical information and, perhaps most important, as guides to the slaves' own felt experience. The slave narratives emerged from obscurity and became a major tool by which historians were able to open the world the slaves made—their folk life, religious expression, modes of resistance, and psychological survival.[11]

In this major shift in methodology, the use of previously suspect sources, and the rich analysis that flowed from it, we can see a prime example of how perceptions of historical truth can markedly change. No amount of nostalgia for the great texts of our civilization, no exhortation that we should be uplifted or pleased by our history can ever change this fundamental of the process by which we gain historical understanding. For so long there was much that we did not know about slavery, or that seemed inaccessible, or that we simply did not want to know because scholars ignored a major set of sources. But the questions we choose to ask of the past change with time, and they always will. From the 1960s on the old neglected slave narratives, Douglass's and Harriet

Jacobs's in particular, became sources of all kinds of new questions and interpretations.[12]

What was it like to be a slave? What were the slaves' daily feelings, yearnings, crises, and hardships? The best of the slave narratives offer complex answers to these questions. Although Douglass's autobiographies manipulate readers with the language of the self-made hero ascending to his destiny, their principal historical value may be the access they allow to the psychological world of a slave who had determined to be free. His descriptions of the loving bonds he shared with his pupils at the Sabbath school on Freeland's farm and his romantic but altogether believable images of the fears he and his fellows faced in plotting their escape serve as examples of the self-conscious artist struggling to recapture real experience. Douglass converted the memory of their contemplated escape plan into a mixture of metaphors and terrible opposites: "At every gate through which we were to pass, we saw a watchman—at every ferry a guard—on every bridge a sentinel—and in every wood a patrol. We were hemmed in on every side. Here were the difficulties, real or imagined—the good to be sought, and the evil to be shunned. On the one hand, there stood slavery, a stern reality, glaring frightfully upon us,—its robes already crimsoned with the blood of millions, and even now feasting itself greedily upon our own flesh. On the other hand, away back in the dim distance, under the flickering light of the north star, behind some craggy hill or snow-covered mountain, stood a doubtful freedom—half frozen—beckoning us to come and share its hospitality."[13] Thus could knowledge about the difference between slavery and freedom manifest in the ex-slave's imagination and, in turn, in that of his readers. Slavery, like all historical experience, must be imagined before it can be understood.

Alternating between parody and condemnation, one of the most persistent themes in Douglass's *Narrative* is his portrait of slaveholders. A striking feature of the book is the sheer range of slaveholders Douglass presents. Examples of unmitigated evil and depravity include Covey, Andrew Anthony (Master Andrew), and Orson (called Austin) Gore. Thomas Auld, both cruel and incompetent, is distinguished for his "meanness" but disrespected for his haplessness. At the other end of the human scale, though, we meet William Freeland, a master Douglass seems to have respected because he was educated, sought no religious sanction for slavery, and ran an economically efficient plantation where work expectations and treatment seemed in rational relationship. And, finally, there is Sophia Auld, Douglass's "kind and tender-hearted" mistress in Baltimore who first taught him to read. She becomes Douglass's principal example that slaveholding is learned behavior and presumably can therefore be unlearned. In a document so full of antislavery propaganda, physical violence, and suffering, it may come as some surprise that Douglass could conclude that, for Sophia, "slavery proved as injurious to her as it did to me."[14] But such is the complex picture Douglass creates of a world that not only involved dehumanization but also operated by the cunning and negotiation of human relationships. Indeed, writing became one way Douglass found to process the hatred he harbored for his former masters and for slaveholders in general.

This was, in part, the point of Douglass's famous public letter to Thomas Auld in 1848. The letter, written after Douglass's freedom had been purchased for him by his British antislavery friends, is a highly polemical, at times factually inaccurate attack on Auld as a prototypically evil slaveholder. The highly personal charges Douglass made against Auld do not mask his honest admission at the end of the letter. In words so many slaves must have dreamed they could one day say as freedpeople to their masters, Douglass announced that "I intend to make use of you as a weapon with which to assail the system of slavery . . . and as a means of bringing this guilty nation with yourself to repentance."[15] Again Douglass mingled his personal story, its villains and its self-made hero, with his claims of national birthright. Art, combined with individual grievance, made for effective political activism.

Douglass's autobiographies, understandably, have one primary character—himself. The autobiographical Douglass is a self-made hero, refashioned and reinvented out of his many trials. Born in part out of the genre in which he wrote, but also perhaps out of his own psychological needs, Douglass was remarkably silent about the women in his life. He wrote compassionately about his grandmother and his mother, but they linger in the books only as memories. Anna Murray, who became his wife shortly after his escape from slavery and, indeed, helped him plot his journey to freedom, hardly receives the attention one might expect, especially by the mid-1850s in the second telling of the life's story. By then, Anna had borne four children, endured many of her husband's long absences on speaking tours in both Great Britain and the United States, and held their family together. The critic Mary Helen Washington fairly asked in 1980: "While our daring Douglass . . . was heroically ascending freedom's arc . . . who . . . was at home taking care of the children?" And as critic Deborah McDowell has shown, a "politics of gender" may, indeed, have been at work over the years in anointing Douglass's *Narrative* as the original, or "first," text in the African American tradition. Douglass's use of the concept of manhood, his struggle through violence to overcome Covey and slavery itself, represents masculine expectations of how men thwart oppression or power. Douglass did not allow the many women who influenced his life and mind into his story. He revealed virtually nothing about his many friendships and working relationships with white abolitionist women. Troublesome as this may be to our sensibilities, these silences should not surprise us. Douglass had one story to tell, and as an orphaned fugitive slave who felt compelled to explain his ascendance, he told that story in a gendered, protective, and heroic mode—perhaps the only way he could. His self-created hero is the romantic individualist, resurrected through violence. As Douglass wrote in the sentence announcing his bloody encounter with Covey: "You have seen how a man was made a slave; you shall see how a slave was made a man."[16] But we do need to be careful not to allow our twenty-first-century categories to overwhelm our understanding of Douglass's art. No conspiracy of publishers, editors, or critics alone has pushed Douglass into the American canon. His autobiographies, especially the first two, tell a universal human story, at once so readable among young people and so replete with messages about repression, power, faith, honesty, language, imagination, fear, friendship, and freedom of mind and body. If we manage to read Douglass's texts within their historical contexts, we may glean what he revealed and did not reveal about himself, but we may also understand just a little better the society and the political crises that slavery fomented in America.

Although the slave narratives have limitations as sources for the daily, material lives of slaves, as well as for the socioeconomic structure of the antebellum South, Douglass's account is a window into slave work and culture. He allows us to observe the huge Wye plantation—"the Great House Farm"—in operation. We can almost see its bustling "business-like aspect," hear the "driver's horn" and the profanity of an overseer's voice in the field. Slaves are shown to be the essential laborers at the center of southern economic production, but their work is framed and overwhelmed by the larger story of the potentially total power of masters and overseers. The overseer Austin Gore appears as a kind of absolute creation of the slave system—a grave, humorless man who performed all his duties, including the murder of insubordinate slaves, with military precision.[17] Douglass strove to describe the most terrible meanings of slavery—its existence outside any law or social control and its capacity to render African American life of no value. This is art and history; it has characters, an argument, and a good deal of verifiable evidence.

There are many other examples of how Douglass's autobiographies are historical sources. He may have anticipated modern historians' treatment of slave culture most directly in his discussion of slave music. He portrays the slave songs as primarily expressions of sorrow and lament, but he also indicates the inseparability of the sacred and the secular in black folk music, of everyday life mixed with appeals for deliverance in the most deeply spiritual tones. The slaves, wrote Douglass, "would sometimes sing the most pathetic sentiment in the most rapturous tone, and the most rapturous sentiment in the most pathetic tone." And "into all of their songs they would manage to weave something of the Great House Farm." The scene in which Douglass discusses music is that of a mass of slaves walking toward the Great House Farm on "allowance day." The "dense old woods . . . reverberate" with song as groups of selected slaves congregate at Colonel Lloyd's mansion for their periodic allotments of food and clothing. Here Douglass remembers in telling opposites: the dehumanizing power structure of slavery with the slaves' own best means of inner relief and self-expression, their material sustenance with their spiritual sustenance. And he leaves his invitation to historians and folklorists: "If anyone wishes to be impressed with the soul-killing effects of slavery, let him go to Colonel Lloyd's plantation, and, on allowance day, place himself in the deep pine woods, and there let him, in silence, analyze the sounds that shall pass through the chambers of his soul." *Analyze the sounds.* Since the 1960s this is precisely what a host of scholars have done with the lyrics and forms of slave music, as well as other forms of expressive culture. Scholars have found various ways to gain access to the piney woods, to listen to the slaves' own voices as they created an inner moral order out of potential chaos. But Douglass's invitation, of course, was not to a concert, nor to any sort of celebration of folklife, nor in this case to the romantics in search of authentic culture. Embedded in an abolitionist polemic, this was an invitation to antislavery voters and eventually to historians who might be willing or able to listen for the sheer range of ironic twists in the slaves' manipulation of hope and despair, to feel in their own souls, as Douglass put it, "the highest joy and the deepest sadness."[18] The best work of the revisionist "culture as resistance" school of slavery historiography has come from just such efforts.

It might be said that the Douglass of 1845, who was already becoming the bourgeois man of letters and affairs, distanced himself from the "folk" in his comments on slave music and other subjects. "I did not, when a slave," wrote Douglass, "understand the deep meaning of those rude and apparently incoherent songs." But even as he separated himself from the "wild songs," he admired his fellow slaves' spontaneous ability to "compose and sing as they went along, consulting neither time nor tune." Why should such ambivalence surprise us? Just as Douglass had learned to negotiate the mine field of slavery's human relationships on the Great House Farm and in the different environment of the streets of Baltimore, so too as an autobiographer he negotiated his way into the consciences of different audiences. Nowhere did he describe the slave songs as unworthy of attention or study. Quite the contrary, to the songs he traced his own "first glimmering conception of the dehumanizing character of slavery." Moreover, in those songs, slaves fashioned an art form out of daily life, and "breathed the . . . complaint of souls boiling over with the bitterest anguish." A slave song, said Douglass, was a "prayer to God for deliverance from chains."[19] Such, precisely, was the nature of the slave narratives themselves: ex-slaves using the music of words to issue their moral indictments and to tell their stories.

These are only a few reflections on how Douglass's first two autobiographies are sources of historical understanding. His third autobiography, *The Life and Times of Frederick Douglass,* is a much longer, some say tedious, less literary summing up of an eventful public life. *Life and Times* is a storehouse of information about Douglass's associations and travels, as well as his contributions to events and ideas about the great issues of the Civil War, Reconstruction, and the Gilded Age. One critic called it "iconographic." Beware writing a late memoir, if you have already written an earlier, more poignant one, for you may have, said William Zinsser, "cannibalized your remembered truth and replaced it with a new one." Or as Daryl Pinckney said of how the early part of Malcolm X's autobiography reads better than the later (postreligious conversion) and might have said of the slave narratives against late nineteenth-century autobiographies in the black tradition: "hell has more details."[20]

But some of the writing in *Life and Times* is riveting and revealing, despite its function more as reminiscence than as a personal story of liberation. There are many examples, but I will cite only two. The way Douglass remembered the shared sense of anguish with his fellow citizens in Rochester at the time of Abraham Lincoln's assassination speaks volumes about something he had been seeking all his adult life. "We shared in common a terrible calamity," he wrote, "and this 'touch of nature made us' more than countrymen, it made us Kin.'" Kinship, a sense of belonging, human recognition, citizenship, a country that was home—all these had been some of the deepest yearnings in the "interior life " of this private and public man. And in the next chapter, called "Vast Changes," Douglass left this revealing comment on how he felt at the end of the Civil War, that moment of triumph through tragedy. "A strange and, perhaps, perverse feeling came over me," he wrote. "My great and exceeding joy over these stupendous achievements, especially over the abolition of slavery (which had been the deepest desire and the great labor of my life), was slightly tinged with a feeling of sadness. I felt I had reached the end of the noblest and best part of my life; my school was broken up, my church disbanded, the beloved congregation dispersed, never to come together again. The antislavery platform had performed its work, and my voice was no longer needed. 'Othello's occupation was gone.' The great happiness of meeting with my fellow-workers was now to be among the things of memory."[21] Indeed it would; and Douglass would do some of his best work in the latter part of his life trying to structure a national historical memory of emancipation and the Civil War—one that increasingly the nation did not embrace in the process of sectional reconciliation.

Life and Times is a source, a travelogue, a narrative of events—an aging, dignified, Victorian gentleman's struggle to reinvent himself yet again as the orator-writer and representative man. And, perhaps most of all, it is a fascinating source of meditations on the meaning of individual and social memory. It is Douglass's final, revised trip to the well of memory. Like those of all interesting autobiographers, his motives for continuing to write his story were personal and social. He had one great story to tell, and he had not survived his travails without an expansive ego. He also believed he was "called" to represent and carry the race in history. But he also needed simply to understand himself within the world that had so controlled him and that he had sought so dearly to change. Apparently, even to his final days, Douglass had to keep asking: how did I get from there to here?

Near the end of *Life and Times* Douglass declared that he had "lived several lives in one: first, the life of slavery; secondly, the life of a fugitive from slavery; thirdly, the life of comparative freedom; fourthly, the life of conflict and battle; and fifthly, the life of victory, if not complete, at least assured." With an autobiographer's self-indulgence, Douglass wanted here to demonstrate the struggle and achievement in his life. He had suffered and overcome, we are told. He had persevered through hopelessness, led his people through a trial, and in the end reached at least a personal victory. These are the images of the aging man, attempting to preside over his biographers, control his historical reputation, and shape how we would understand his rites of passage. In Douglass's categories we see his self-image as the fugitive slave risen to racial and national leader, the person and the nation regenerated. Like all autobiographers, Douglass was trying to order, even harness, the passage of time itself. We must read and use this man's autobiographical imagination with caution. But the stages Douglass gave his life are instructive. They do represent turning points that define his career, but no chronology can convey the deeper meanings in such an eventful life. Douglass may have said this best himself in a speech entitled "Life Pictures," delivered first in 1861. The final lines of that speech represent perhaps his most humanistic, if indirect, autobiographical statement: "We live in deeds, not years, in thoughts, not breaths, in feeling, not fingers on a dial. We should count time by heartthrobs; he most lives who thinks the most, feels the noblest, acts the best."[22]

NOTES

This piece was originally delivered as a lecture during a centennial observance of Douglass's death at the Library of Congress in February 1995. Published here with revisions for the first time, it also includes echoes of my introduction, "A Psalm of Freedom," to the Bedford/St. Martin's edition of Douglass's *Narrative* (1993).

1. See Dickson J. Preston, *Young Frederick Douglass: The Maryland Years* (Baltimore: Johns Hopkins University Press, 1980).

2. Saint Augustine, *Confessions,* trans. Edward Bouverie Pusey (New York: Book-of-the-Month Club, 1996). For Augustine's remarkable reflection on the nature of memory, see 230–50. Vladimir Nabokov, *Speak, Memory: An Autobiography Revisited* (New York: G. P. Putnam's, 1947).

3. Toni Morrison, "The Site of Memory," in *Inventing the Truth: The Art and Craft of Memoir,* ed. William Zinsser (Boston: Houghton, Mifflin, 1987), 104, 112–13, 115; Toni Morrison, *Beloved* (New York, Knopf, 1987), 35.

4. Frederick Douglass, *Narrative of the Life of Frederick Douglass, an American*

Slave, Written by Himself, ed. David W. Blight (1845; reprint, Boston: Bedford Books, 1993), 61–62; all citations in this essay are to this edition.

5. Daryl Pinckney, *New York Review of Books,* April 6, 1995, 41; Douglass, *My Bondage and My Freedom,* ed. William L. Andrews (1855; reprint, Urbana: University of Illinois Press, 1987), 197, xi–xxvi. Andrews's introduction to this edition of *My Bondage and My Freedom* is one of the most insightful commentaries on Douglass's second autobiography. See also William L. Andrews, *To Tell a Free Story: The First Century of Afro-American Autobiography, 1760–1865* (Urbana: University of Illinois Press, 1988).

6. On Douglass's search for his patrimony and his need to understand his youth and family ties, see Peter F. Walker, *Moral Choices: Memory, Desire, and Imagination in Nineteenth-Century American Abolition* (Baton Rouge: Louisiana State University Press, 1978), 207–61.

7. Vernon Loggins, *The Negro Author and His Development in America* (New York: Columbia University Press, 1931), 138.

8. Douglass, *Narrative,* 74–75. See my introduction to the 1992 edition, "Psalm of Freedom," 1–23.

9. William Zinsser, "Writing and Remembering," and Annie Dillard, "To Fashion a Text," in *Inventing the Truth,* ed. Zinsser, 22, 56, 72; Ralph Ellison in a 1978 interview, quoted in Charles T. Davis and Henry Louis Gates Jr., *The Slave's Narrative* (New York: Oxford University Press, 1985), xviii–xix.

10. Ulrich B. Phillips, *American Negro Slavery* (New York: Appleton, 1918). On Phillips, see Merton L. Dillon, *Ulrich Bonnell Phillips: Historian of the Old South* (Baton Rouge: Louisiana State University Press, 1985); and John David Smith, *An Old Creed for the New South: Proslavery Ideology and Historiography, 1865–1918* (Athens: University of Georgia Press, 1991), 240–44, 255–67.

11. Douglass, *Narrative of the Life of Frederick Douglass, an American Slave, Written by Himself,* ed. Benjamin Quarles (Cambridge: Harvard University Press, 1960). For a sampling of the most pivotal works on slavery in the 1970s, see John W. Blassingame, *The Slave Community: Plantation Life in the Antebellum South* (New York: Oxford University Press, 1972); Eugene D. Genovese, *Roll, Jordan, Roll: The World the Slaves Made* (New York: Random House, 1976); Herbert Gutman, *The Black Family in Slavery and Freedom* (New York: Random House, 1976); and Lawrence W. Levine, *Black Culture and Black Consciousness: Afro-American Folk Thought from Slavery to Freedom* (New York: Oxford University Press, 1977).

12. See Harriet A. Jacobs, *Incidents in the Life of a Slave Girl, Written by Herself,* ed. Jean Fagan Yellin (Cambridge: Harvard University Press, 1987). For a collection of slave documents, see *Slave Testimony: Two Centuries of Letters, Speeches, Interviews, and Autobiographies,* ed. John W. Blassingame (Baton Rouge: Louisiana State University Press, 1977).

13. Douglass, *Narrative,* 86.

14. Ibid., 59.

15. See letter, Frederick Douglass to Thomas Auld, September 3, 1848, reprinted in *Narrative,* 134–41, quote on 140–41.

16. Mary Helen Washington, "These Self-Invented Women: A Theoretical

Framework for a Literary History of Black Women," *Radical Teacher* (1980): 4; Deborah E. McDowell, "In the First Place: Making Frederick Douglass and the Afro-American Narrative Tradition," in *Critical Essays on Frederick Douglass,* ed. William L. Andrews (Boston: G. K. Hall, 1991), 192–214; Douglass, *Narrative,* 75. On the ways Douglass reconstructs the images of his mother and grandmother from the 1845 to the 1855 autobiographies, see Cynthia S. Hamilton, "Frederick Douglass and the Gender Politics of Reform," in *Liberating Sojourn: Frederick Douglass and Transatlantic Reform,* ed. Alan J. Rice and Martin Crawford (Athens: University of Georgia Press, 1999), 73–92.

17. Douglass, *Narrative,* 45–46, 50–52.

18. Ibid., 46–47. See David W. Blight, "Analyze the Sounds: Frederick Douglass's Invitation to Modern Historians of Slavery," in *Slave Cultures and Cultures of Slavery,* ed. Stephan Palmie (Knoxville: University of Tennessee Press, 1996).

19. Douglass, *Narrative,* 46–47.

20. Eric J. Sundquist, introduction to *Frederick Douglass: New Literary and Historical Essays,* ed. Sundquist (New York: Cambridge University Press, 1990), 1; Zinsser, "Writing and Remembering," in *Inventing the Truth,* ed. Zinsser, 27; Pinckney, *New York Review of Books,* April 6, 1995, 42.

21. Douglass, *The Life and Times of Frederick Douglass* (1892; reprint, New York: Collier, 1962), 370–73.

22. Ibid., 479; Frederick Douglass, "Life Pictures," speech delivered in Syracuse, N.Y., November 14, 1861, Frederick Douglass Papers, Library of Congress, reel 14, 28.

They Knew
What Time It Was
African Americans
and the Coming of the
Civil War

*One-eighth of the whole population were colored slaves, not
distributed generally over the Union, but localized in the Southern
part of it. These slaves constituted a peculiar and powerful
interest. All knew that this interest was, somehow, the cause
of the war.*

—Abraham Lincoln, Second Inaugural Address

*However much they who marched South and North in 1861 may
have fixed on the technical points of union and local autonomy
as a shibboleth, all nevertheless knew, as we know, that the
question of Negro slavery was the real cause of the conflict.*

—W. E. B. Du Bois, The Souls of Black Folk

From different experiences and perspectives nearly
forty years apart, Abraham Lincoln and W. E. B. Du Bois expressed the
same truths about American history: that the Civil War would never have
occurred without sectional conflict over slavery and that the fate of four
and a half million African Americans, slave and free, was inextricably
tied to the fate of the nation in the 1860s. Exactly when and how "all
knew" that slavery was the cause of the war, and just how Americans
came to understand, or deny, emancipation and the promise of black
equality as central legacies of the war remain questions open to debate.
Just how much we "all know" or understand today of the active role of
blacks themselves in the coming of the Civil War—what sectional strife,
the lived experience of slavery, the war, and emancipation meant to
black people—remains a rich field of inquiry. Indeed, in popular understandings of what caused the Civil War and in the broad field of
public history, the place of slavery in this story is very much still a contested matter in America. A consensus in scholarship about slavery's
central place in Civil War causation, as well as about the agency of blacks

themselves in the coming of disunion and emancipation, does not necessarily convert into popular consensus. Such circumstances make it all the more imperative to take a close look at the actual history of African American perspectives and participation in the road to war during the 1850s.

These questions are at the center of an ongoing exploration of the place of the black experience within the fabric of American history. The opening lines of Benjamin Quarles's *Negro in the Civil War* are as good a starting point now as when he wrote them in 1953. "What is America?" asked Quarles. His answer reflected his own era's search for an identifiable national character, and yet, after decades of remarkable development in historiography, especially in African American history, Quarles draws us back to the challenge of generalization amid our rich, new particularism. "A clue to a nation's character is revealed when a crisis comes," wrote Quarles, "in a time of troubles, a nation's culture crops out. Certainly during that fateful span of the Civil War—the only great war in the hundred year period in world history from Waterloo to Sarajevo—this query received an illuminating answer."[1] For blacks, the coming of the Civil War would be more than the nation's culture cropping out; the test of America's national existence would determine if African Americans had a future at all, with human rights and secure social identities, on the North American continent.

Blacks were both direct participants in, as well as historical recipients of, what many historians now refer to as the "Second American Revolution." In its fundamental causes, its scale, and certainly its results, the Civil War era was a revolutionary turn in the course of American history. As much recent scholarship has demonstrated, emancipation was something both seized as well as given. By probing the meaning of the coming of the war to blacks, in free black communities, among fugitive slaves, and on southern plantations, we might yet harvest new fruit in these old vineyards. Moreover, as long as the question of whether the Civil War was "irrepressible" persists as an integral part of pedagogical and scholarly considerations of the coming of the conflict, then we can still learn much by examining both the meaning of America and the war's inevitability through the eyes of antebellum black leaders and from the experience of slaves. To most blacks, slavery was self-evidently a world of brutal contradiction, a system of human and inhuman relationships that operated daily on an assumption of irrepressible conflict. Neither slaves nor black abolitionists were any more prescient than their white fellow Americans about just how and when a war would result from conflict over slavery. But that, as Kenneth Stampp put it, "the issues dividing North and South were genuine and substantial and that conflict between them was natural" were assumptions about which most blacks harbored no doubts.[2]

Although African Americans could not know the course of the revolution they were about to experience when secession and war came in 1861, it may safely be said that among their leaders, "all knew" in their own ways what had caused the conflict. Their greatest leader, Frederick Douglass, spoke for the vast majority of blacks in the summer of 1861 when he declared slavery the "primal cause" of the war. Earlier, during the emotion and confusion of the secession winter, Douglass wrote worried editorials in which he feared "peaceful disunion," but resolved to make the best of it. Writing at least a month before Fort Sumter, Douglass envisioned a future where abolitionists might become guerrilla agitators attacking slavery in a separate country. "Hereafter, opposition to slavery will naturally take a new form," announced Douglass. "The fire is kindled, and cannot be extinguished. The 'irrepressible conflict' can never cease on this continent." Abolition might be postponed and its methods could change, reasoned Douglass. "But it cannot be prevented. If it comes not from enlightenment, moral conviction and civilization, it will come from the fears of tyrants no longer able to hold down their rising slaves."[3] Faith in an inexorable logic of conflict born of the inherent injustices of slavery in the South and racial caste in the North, and of a disinherited people's essential belief in permanent struggle, sustained most black leaders both before and after the outbreak of the war. The process by which emancipation would, in time, emerge out of total war was something black abolitionists could only begin to imagine in the crisis of 1860–61. But as Douglass and many others had already surmised, the course of the war, like its causes, would be driven by a combination of fear, ideology, and the force of events, by human will and military necessities. The logic and the expectation of such a conflict, if not its inevitability, was something blacks had contemplated and analyzed for at least two generations.

As early as the late 1820s and early 1830s, black abolitionists organized, both with their white counterparts and separate from them, to improve their lives and attack slavery. They founded their own churches, newspapers, and moral reform societies, and forged their own protest and self-improvement strategies through black conventions at the state and national levels. Although militant, even revolutionary, stances emerged before the 1840s, especially in such writings as David Walker's *Appeal to the Colored Citizens of the World* (1829), most black leaders devoted themselves to a self-improvement formula based on the guiding assumption that "condition and not color" was the principal dilemma blacks faced. If they could socially elevate themselves through education and employment, and by embracing middle-class values, then racial prejudices among white Americans would erode. By 1840 northern free blacks had founded hundreds of mutual aid societies, schools, orphanages, lyceums, library companies, and the like. In 1832, in one of the first public lectures by an American woman, Bostonian Maria Stewart called her fellow blacks to self-reliance. "O do not say, you cannot make anything of your children," said Stewart, "but say, with the help and assistance of God, we will try. . . . [L]ay the cornerstone for the building of a high school . . . unite and build a store of your own." In a society where slavery rapidly expanded westward, however, where the peculiar institution's philosophical and political defenders became ever more intransigent, and where racism became an increasingly rigid barrier to even the most highly talented blacks, the self-improvement doctrine lost viability.[4]

Changing contexts forced new strategies upon black abolitionists. In the discriminatory world of antebellum northern cities, where they enjoyed no civil or political rights, scrambled for decent housing and schooling, and where their children were discouraged from high aspirations, black leaders could ill afford adherence to abstract principles of antislavery reform. Given the emergencies of their lives, black abolitionists became increasingly pragmatic activists; no single strategy characterized their work by midcentury. Moreover, during the 1840s a new generation of black abolitionists came on the scene. Many of them, like Henry Highland Garnet, William Wells Brown, James W. C. Pennington, Samuel Ringgold Ward, Henry Bibb, and Frederick Douglass, were fugitive slaves whose formative years and antislavery educations were spent on southern plantations, and not in organizations dedicated to moral suasion. By the 1850s the roles of black women in the movement expanded, and such activists as Harriet Tubman, Sojourner Truth, Mary Ann Shadd, Francis Ellen Watkins Harper, and Sarah Parker Remond became professional abolitionists (as orators, writers, and Underground Railroad operatives) in their own right.

What emerged was what numerous historians have referred to as "two abolitionisms," one white and one black, the latter characterized by racial independence and strategic pragmatism, and the former, though still committed to antislavery principles, increasingly divided over doctrines such as political action or evangelical reform. Black abolitionists would themselves engage in a great deal of in-fighting, but generally over basic ends as much as over doctrinal means. Many were also repelled by the racism they encountered from some of their white associates within the movement. The inability of many white abolitionists to comprehend the world in other than moral absolutes, as well as their unwillingness to confront issues of racial prejudice and poverty in the North, drove many black abolitionists toward independent action. A certain logic of responsibility, as well as bitterness toward the behavior of their white colleagues, lay at the root of such separatism. "It is emphatically our battle," declared the highly educated physician-reformer James McCune Smith in 1848; "no one else can fight for us."[5] The two abolitionisms educated each other and were deeply interdependent during the antebellum era. Indeed, many black abolitionists proudly claimed their organizational and ideological roots among the followers of the Massachusetts radical William Lloyd Garrison. But by a combination of moral commitment, a growing political consciousness, and sheer necessity, black abolitionists entered the crucial decade before the Civil War with a deepening sense of how long and complex their "battle" would be.

For antebellum black leaders, the coming of the Civil War would mean the fulfillment of a long-imagined prophecy, but only after a period of crushed hopes. The 1850s were simultaneously a decade of heightened activism and deepening despair among northern blacks. After lifetimes of struggle against slavery and racism, and in the wake of setbacks on the national scene like the Fugitive Slave Act (1850), the Kansas-Nebraska Act (1854), the Dred Scott decision (1857), and southern attempts to reopen the foreign slave trade, northern black leaders suffered both a crisis of faith in America and internal ideological division. By the mid- to late 1850s African American intellectuals had reached a crossroads. Ironically, on the eve of revolutionary changes in their own lives and in American race relations, most black leaders saw a future for their people as dismal as it had ever been. Had disunion and war not come when it did in 1861, it is difficult to know how much longer the bulk of antebellum black leaders could have sustained confidence about their future in America. They had to find their own place on the road to disunion, sustaining themselves through revitalized re-sistance, spiritual wellsprings they shared with the slaves, and from events that both spurned and inspired them. In summing up the politi-cal crisis over slavery expansion as the crux of Civil War causation, Eric Foner concluded that "what was at stake in 1860, as in the entire sec-tional conflict, was the character of the nation's future."[6] For no people was this more true than African Americans. At stake for them were not only worldviews based on slave labor or free labor, but whether they even had a place in that future where one or the other worldview might prevail.

During the 1850s warring temperaments, conflicted and strained priorities, impatience, and a growing sense of powerlessness made black abolitionists as a whole a divided people in a dividing country. They struggled over several fundamental issues: the potential uses of violence as a tactic against slavery and slave catchers; whether black liberation could be achieved within existing American political structures; and em-igration from America as an ultimate solution to the burden of future-lessness. Yet their leadership was almost always without traditional polit-ical sanction since they served a constituency that, by and large, could not vote. They labored heroically with the weapons of language—through oratory and their own press. Especially through best-selling slave narratives and through their presence on countless platforms, black abolitionists were the best living challenges to the American para-dox of slavery and freedom. Some of them did change their world through their voices, but they also discovered the limits imposed by racism, symbolism, and moral suasion. Frederick Douglass described the ironic dilemmas African Americans faced in the nation's impending crisis. In 1853 he complained that the black intellectual was "isolated in the land of his birth—debarred by his color from congenial associations with whites . . . equally cast out by the ignorances of the blacks." Doug-lass spoke for most when he concluded that a pragmatic and increas-ingly radical path was the only alternative for black leadership. "Right antislavery action," wrote Douglass in 1856, "is that which deals the . . . deadliest blow upon slavery that can be given at that particular time. Such action is always consistent, however different may be the forms through which it expresses itself."[7]

Many black leaders insisted that the future of all Americans would be determined by the crisis over slavery and race. The minister and orator Samuel Ringgold Ward aptly asserted that the great question of the

1850s was not "whether the black man's slavery shall be perpetuated, but whether the freedom of any Americans can be permanent." Ward identified a grinding truth that would lie at the root of the Republican party's free labor ideology, the successes of which would begin to lead the country toward disunion and provide a new kind of political hope for northern blacks. He also anticipated by seven years Abraham Lincoln's haunting claim on the eve of emancipation, in December 1862, that "in *giving* freedom to the slave, we *assure* freedom to the free."[8] The future was, indeed, at stake in the crises of slavery and the Union, and black abolitionists provided a huge body of arguments (to the nation and among themselves) to fuel the debate. Just how the two causes— abolition and preserving or reinventing the Union—would ever coalesce in the interest of black freedom was the central challenge of the 1850s for blacks. It was the subject of both great expectation and great discouragement, appeals to revolution against and reform within the American political system, as well as appeals to abandon America altogether.

This dialectic between hope and despair, past and future, took on a new urgency with the passage of the Fugitive Slave Act in 1850. As a response to longstanding southern demands for more stringent federal enforcement of the return of escaped slaves to their owners, this law provided for speedier adjudication of fugitive slave cases and stripped an ill-fated captive of all legal safeguards, such as jury trial or even a judicial hearing. Accepted by some northern political leaders as part of the sectional truce forged in the Compromise of 1850, the Fugitive Slave Act struck fear into northern black communities and enraged antislavery activists of all kinds. Between 1850 and 1860, an estimated twenty thousand blacks fled to Canada to escape capture and reenslavement. The threat was real; during the first six years of enforcement, more than two hundred alleged fugitives were arrested, with only approximately twelve successfully defending their claim to freedom. Perhaps most important in the long run, the Fugitive Slave Act stimulated an organized and often violent resistance to slave catchers and to the entire legal and institutional structure that upheld such a law. This law, and resistance to it, forced the wrongs of slavery and repression into northern consciousness in a more palpable way than ever before. No longer would fugitive slaves be the "invisible men" of the nineteenth century. The fears and aspirations of the runaway who risked all things mortal to achieve freedom, increasingly immortalized in the slave narratives and in Harriet

Beecher Stowe's *Uncle Tom's Cabin* (1852), now conditioned a black and white antislavery community for a struggle that would require new weapons.[9]

Numerous fugitive slave rescues had occurred during the 1830s and 1840s, especially through the work of vigilance committees. Such urban organizations as those led by David Ruggles in New York and Robert Purvis and William Still in Philadelphia harbored runaways, fought their legal battles, and engaged in a wide variety of civil disobedience and violent action to protect and spirit fugitives to freedom. American textbooks and folklore know these networks of resistance as the Underground Railroad.[10] After 1850 many operatives, as well as people freed by this system, would call their work by that famous name as well.

The anger and panic that hit northern black communities after 1850 gave a new spirit to antislavery resistance. Henry Bibb, himself a fugitive with family still enslaved in Kentucky, spoke more than hyperbole when he reacted to the new law. "If there is no alternative but to go back to slavery, or die contending for liberty," said Bibb, "then death is far preferable." Resolutions condemning the law and appealing for resistance to slave catchers poured from meetings across the North. In Providence, Rhode Island, blacks pledged to "sacrifice our lives and our all upon the altar of protection to our wives, our children and our fellow sufferers in common with us." In Philadelphia, blacks passed ten resolutions, concluding with an appeal that demonstrates the decline of moral suasion in the face of new realities. They preferred "only those moral means of truth," said the Philadelphia gathering. But the Fugitive Slave bill was an "unheard of" level of injustice; so they swore to "resist to the death any attempt to enforce it upon our persons." Thus the rhetoric of righteous violence, the art of war propaganda, and the claims for retributive justice that would explode among blacks after the outbreak of the Civil War received a full-throated rehearsal during the resistance to the Fugitive Slave Act of the early 1850s. William P. Powell, an aggressive activist who had protested Jim Crow before the Massachusetts legislature and labored for women's rights and black self-reliance from a pacifist perspective, found the Fugitive Slave Act more than he could bear. By such legislation, Powell concluded, the federal government had "declared war" upon blacks, free and slave, a sentiment shared widely in abolitionist communities. Concerned about the law, and worried about the education of his seven children, Powell moved to Liverpool, England, for ten years, returning to America only when the secession crisis in 1860 prompted new hope.[11]

In America, rhetoric and reality met in numerous actual rescues of fugitive slaves. Among the most celebrated were the successful rescues of Shadrach Minkins in Boston, in February 1851; Jerry McHenry in Syracuse, New York, in September 1851; and the Christiana, Pennsylvania, "riot," also in September 1851, in which a Maryland slave owner, Edward Gorsuch, sought to retrieve four of his escaped bondsmen. In a pitched battle fought between a large crowd of blacks armed with clubs and guns, Gorsuch was killed and his son gravely wounded. The four fugitives, hidden by abolitionists, disappeared into freedom in Canada.[12]

Less celebrated, though equally important, was the unsuccessful effort to free Anthony Burns in Boston in May 1854. Burns was a thirty-year-old fugitive slave who had recently escaped from Virginia. Burns was seized and jailed by the local Fugitive Slave Law commissioner, and his case became the subject of an intensive legal and, finally violent, effort to free him. After all legal means were quickly exhausted, including a countersuit entered against Burns's Virginia owner by black community leader Lewis Hayden, an interracial mob killed one guard in an unsuccessful attempt to break the fugitive out of jail. Boston became an armed camp for a week and a half as President Franklin Pierce ordered federal troops with artillery into the city, making a test case of enforcement of the Fugitive Slave Act. Burns was escorted to the docks by a corps of U.S. Marines and shipped back to slavery in Virginia, where he would spend four months in a slave pen before being sold. Throughout the ordeal in Boston, hundreds of blacks from that city and surrounding towns kept a vigil around the building that housed Burns. "Through that long week of agony," wrote one observer, "the vicinity of the slave pen [the Boston jail] was thronged by colored men and women, watching from dawn till eve, and some of them the long night through, patiently awaiting the fate of their poor brother in bonds; seeking in every way in their power to show their sympathy for him, and hoping and praying, to the last moment, for his deliverance from the hand of the kidnapper."[13] Such a description demonstrates the circumstances for northern blacks in the mid-1850s: they had experienced a new level of militance and resistance, but in the face of state power, they were left in helpless frustration.

More than a "spirit" of resistance was at work in the black response to the crises of the 1850s. Both in rhetoric and reality, the uses of violence and legal defiance had fostered immense experience with what David Ruggles, in one of the founding documents of the New York Vigilance Committee, had called "*practical* abolition." The multitude of letters written to William Still (the Philadelphia leader of the Underground Railroad) during the 1850s by fugitive slaves after they had reached relative safety in the North or in Canada attest to the meaning of freedom to so many ordinary folk. "I hear that the yellow fever is very bad down south," wrote Mary D. Armstead from New Bedford, Massachusetts, in 1855; "now if the underground railroad could have free course the emergrant would cross the river of gordan rapidly [.] I hope it may continue to run and I hope the wheels of the car may be greesed with more substantial greese so they may run over swiftly." That system never ran by a "free course"; it always operated by a combination of intricate planning, courage, and fear. But Mary Armstead's homespun "greese" metaphor nicely complements the hope embedded in the refrain of the famous Negro spiritual: "Many thousands rise and go, many thousands crossing over. " By 1863 the wheels of the car would be running in ways that thousands of Mary Armsteads had spent lifetimes contemplating. With unending gratitude, another fugitive, John H. Hill, wrote Still in 1853 to inform him of his arrival and safety in Toronto, attaching a postscript to one letter: "If you know anyone who would give me an education write and let me know for I am in want of it very much."[14] "Practical abolition," indeed.

Moreover, in their resistance to the fugitive issue (revived and fueled by John Brown's raid on Harper's Ferry in 1859), black intellectuals forged a body of protest thought that, though not altogether new, has in its urgency and radicalism reverberated down through African American history ever since. They appealed with scorching irony to the first principles of the Declaration of Independence, especially to the right of revolution. They invoked Patrick Henry's choice between life and death in the face of tyranny, called for days of fasting and prayer in one breath and the killing of kidnappers in the next, and they made the fullest possible use of the natural rights tradition to justify defiance of unjust laws. Above all, they believed they were replenishing a great tradition, not inventing one; they found deep in the bitter well of American irony their own deepest claims to citizenship, in the denial of their freedom a renewed fervor to assert it. Such resistance congealed into arguments so often made that it prompted Benjamin Quarles to conclude that more than anyone else, it was antebellum black abolitionists who refused to allow the United States to ever "derevolutionize the Revolution."[15]

Many black abolitionists took heart from the emerging political antislavery movement, participated in the Liberty and Free-Soil parties in the 1840s, and entered an ambivalent but significant relationship with the Republican party in the 1850s. They also found a storehouse of political hope in the antislavery interpretation of the U.S. Constitution. By the mid-1850s political abolitionists had advanced the theory by which, at the very least, slavery was judged to be a "local" and not a "national" institution, thereby giving the federal government the authority to abolish human bondage wherever it had exclusive jurisdiction (the District of Columbia, the western territories). Following the lead of white abolitionist Gerrit Smith, many black abolitionists went further, pointing to constitutional guarantees of habeas corpus and a "republican form of government" for every state, as well as the Fifth Amendment's declaration that no person could "be deprived of life, liberty, or property without due process of law" as proof that the federal government was constitutionally obligated to abolish slavery everywhere. All knew, no doubt, that constitutional theory would itself never be enough to rid America of slavery. But in trying to imagine a future where blacks would become an equal part of the polity, the antislavery reading of the Constitution and the Republican party's genuine hostility to slavery's expansion were rays of hope in a darkening night of despair in the 1850s. If the Constitution enshrined slavery and made American citizens "mere bodyguards and human fleshmongers," argued Frederick Douglass in 1851, "then we freely admit that reason, humanity, religion and morality alike demand that we do fling from us with all possible haste that accursed Constitution, and that we labor for revolution, at whatever cost and at whatever peril." The political crisis over slavery forced a choice: either America's creeds were a "warrant for the abolition of slavery in every state in the union," as Douglass put it, or the only alternative was violent revolution. Some black leaders (David Walker in 1829 and Henry Highland Garnet in 1843) had for years suggested that the latter path might be the only recourse.[16] But this contrast of extreme alternatives became clearer and not merely rhetorical in the 1850s, and it compelled an awareness among black leaders that desperation can be the seedbed of both revolution and a hard-earned political realism.

Perhaps nothing symbolized the plight of blacks in the 1850s so completely nor caused so much desperation as the words of Chief Justice

Roger B. Taney in the Dred Scott decision of 1857. Black people were "beings of an inferior order," said Taney, "so far inferior, that they had no rights which the white man was bound to respect."[17] Coming from the high court, the denial of black citizenship—which was really the denial of a future in America—had a disturbing air of finality. One black abolitionist said the Dred Scott decision had made slavery "the supreme law of the land and all descendants of the African race denationalized." Mary Ann Shadd Cary, by then leading an emigration movement to Canada, advised her fellow blacks: "Your national ship is rotten and sinking, why not leave it?" Deeply angry, Robert Purvis addressed the annual meeting of the American Anti-slavery Society in New York City shortly after the Scott decision in May 1857. Purvis had "no patience" with any "newfangled doctrine of the anti-slavery character of the American Constitution." He declared himself fed up with "a government that tramples me and all that are dear to me in the dust." Purvis took heart only in "a prospect of this atrocious government being overthrown, and a better one built up in its place." Such rhetoric of revolution among blacks became their best means of understanding the road to disunion that the Dred Scott decision helped so much to build. Writing just after the Scott decision and evoking the economic anxieties that would soon explode in the Panic of 1857, the freeborn poet Frances Ellen Watkins Harper wished Americans would have a deeper moral reaction to slavery. Thousands of lives ruined by unrequited physical toil "should send a thrill of horror through the nerves of civilization and impel the heart of humanity to lofty deeds," claimed Harper. "So it might," she said, "if men had not found out a fearful alchemy by which this blood can be transformed into gold. Instead of listening to the cry of agony, they listen to the ring of dollars and stoop down to pick up the coin."[18] Karl Marx could hardly have said it more poignantly. In this case, the poet understood the political economy; the country was about to experience both a moral and an economic panic in the last years before disunion.

Despair infested black communities in the wake of Dred Scott, but many black abolitionists found in such discouragement the motivation for greater exertions and even more militant rhetoric. J. Sella Martin, the pastor of Joy Street Baptist Church in Boston, drew large audiences with a prepared address on Nat Turner's insurrection, and William J. Watkins, formerly an assistant editor on Frederick Douglass's newspaper, toured the abolitionist circuit with a speech entitled "Irrepressible Conflict." John Rock, the young Boston lawyer, speaking at an anniversary observance of the Boston Massacre in March 1858, announced that he spoke "not simply to honor those brave men who shed their blood for freedom, or to protest the Dred Scott decision," but to "enter into new vows of duty." "Sooner or later," warned Rock, "the clashing of arms will be heard in this country, and the black man's services will be needed." It is easy today to see a clear line of continuity between Rock's rhetoric and the recruitment of black soldiers for the Union army, as well as the war's fortunate ruin of the Dred Scott decision less than five years later. But in those agonizing years, such clarity was as difficult to achieve in black communities as it was in the larger American political culture. By the end of 1858, Frederick Douglass could only counsel his people to "walk by faith, not by sight."[19]

For some antebellum blacks, the despair of the 1850s found release in the alternative of emigration. In the search for a place where they might find a true sense of belonging, some leaders turned to Canada, the Caribbean, or to West Africa. Several significant movements of black emigrationism emerged in the 1850s. The first, beginning in 1852, was led by Martin R. Delany, a physician and antislavery author and editor from Pittsburgh. In 1854 Delany wielded great influence over the National Emigration Convention that met in Cleveland, Ohio, denouncing all cooperation with white abolitionists and advocating mass emigration to the Caribbean or South America. By 1859 Delany shifted his interest to Africa. He made friendly overtures to Liberia, sought money from white colonizationists (an old movement by then that could date its origins from 1816), and led the celebrated Niger Valley Exploring Party into West Africa. Delany was intensely race conscious, and after his conversion to emigrationism in 1852, he saw no prospect for blacks, free or slave, overcoming what he persistently called their "degradation" within American society. As a thinker, Delany helped some blacks imagine, if not create, a black "nation" beyond the pressures and realities of their American lives. As for so many others, the Civil War would be a major turning point in Delany's career; by 1865, he would be the first black commissioned field officer in the Union army.[20]

A second emigration movement was led by Mary Ann Shadd Cary, the eldest of eighteen children of Abraham Shadd, a prominent black shoemaker and abolitionist in Wilmington, Delaware. As a child, Mary Ann Shadd moved to Pennsylvania where she was educated in a Quaker school. She eventually took up residence in Canada in 1850, and with Samuel Ringgold Ward founded the newspaper the *Provincial Freeman*.

Shadd was a tireless advocate of women's rights and education, and through her long lecture tours of the North, as well as her newspaper, she became the most persistent voice of Canadian emigration, a cause spurred by events and geography in the 1850s, as well as by arguments.[21]

A third movement appeared with the African Civilization Society in 1858, led by Presbyterian minister Henry Highland Garnet. As early as 1850 Garnet, a former fugitive slave from Maryland and an eloquent participant in the black convention movement, developed ties to the English free-produce movement. He modeled his own organization on the plan to develop West Africa's economic potential, especially through cotton production. The African Civilization Society was biracial, closely linked to white philanthropy, and very controversial among free blacks. Beginning in 1859 a fourth phase of emigrationism focused on Haiti. With Christian missionary zeal, the Haitian Emigration Bureau was led by the black Episcopalian James T. Holly of New Haven, Connecticut, and the Scottish-born journalist from Boston, James Redpath. In 1860–61 the bureau had several agents working in cities across the North, published its own newspaper, the *Pine and Palm,* and stirred considerable interest among free blacks.[22]

Emigration schemes caused great rancor among black leadership by the eve of the Civil War. The majority of black abolitionists, often led by James McCune Smith and Frederick Douglass, had either denounced or ignored Delany's plans from their inception. Garnet's organization was especially controversial; opposition meetings were held all over the North in 1859–60, some collapsing into bitter exchanges and even fist-fights. The bitterness of the debate over emigration was a measure of the fundamental commitments on both sides and the sheer frustration blacks faced in the 1850s. In whatever form this debate took—claims to "birthright" as American citizens, the "redemption" of Africa, the reinforcement or overcoming of white racism, or simply the individual emigrant's desire to make a new start in life—it was always a struggle to imagine a future, a place where black folk could find livelihood and secure social identities. Typical of black opposition to emigration was an 1853 Illinois state convention that denounced "all attempts to expatriate us from the land of our birth," yet went on to write more than thirty resolutions condemning slavery, calling for self-reliant uplift, and demanding full political and civil rights.[23] However divisive, black responses to the crises of the 1850s were driven both by strife and expectation.

The role the slaves themselves played in causing the Civil War can never be precisely determined. But collectively, by both their mere presence and their concerted actions, they exerted enormous pressure on the sectional conflict of the 1850s. Through a combination of peasant patience, daily resistance, and occasional overt rebellions, slaves became participants in the political crisis surrounding their fate. From Nat Turner's insurrection in 1831 through the frenzied aftermath of John Brown's raid in 1859, white southerners could never really contemplate the slavery question—its existence or expansion—without considering the potential of violent unrest in their midst. The political stakes for slaveholders grew in proportion to their deepening economic commitment to slave labor, but the stakes also increased in relation to their declining sense of physical security. Proslavery ideology became increasingly intransigent, as well as more radical in its suppression of civil liberties and its quest for self-protection, as white southerners felt threatened by a combination of alleged northern "abolition emissaries" and by their own insubordinate slaves.[24]

As many white southerners found public and private ways to admit, the fear of insurrection and general insecurity in the slave regime were not merely abolitionist literary inventions. As early as 1832 in Virginia's harrowing debate over emancipation conducted in the wake of Nat Turner's rebellion, James McDowell asked the unpopular question: "Was it the fear of Nat Turner, and his deluded, drunken handful of followers, which produced such effects?" "No sir," answered McDowell, "it was the suspicion eternally attached to the slave himself—the suspicion that a Nat Turner might be in every family, that the same bloody deed might be acted over at any time and in any place." Similarly, in January 1859 a South Carolina judge, while sentencing a man convicted of aiding a slave's escape, provided a revealing insight into the fundamental insecurity at the base of proslavery ideology. After declaring slaves to be a "description of property" that government was bound to "protect," Judge Francis Withers lectured the defendant: "Slaves are capable of being seduced . . . capable of evil purposes as well as good. They are, to a certain extent, free agents. They have brains, nerves, hands, and thereby can conceive and execute a malignant purpose. When, therefore, you succeed in corrupting a slave, in swerving him from allegiance, what have you done but turn loose an enemy to society in its very bosom."[25] Even before John Brown touched off a wave of southern hysteria in the fall of 1859, the image of Nat Turner had never left the white southern psyche. Neither had the nameless "free agents." Something in the slaves themselves, and in the contradictions of the system that controlled their "brains," "nerves," and "hands," left many slaveholders with what historian Steven Channing has called an "undiminished anxiety," a psychological disposition that transformed a desperate need for *race control* into a political movement for secession.[26]

Put simply, the potential of slave unrest in relation to political crisis had a good deal to do with why the war came. In the late 1850s, especially during election seasons, white southerners became increasingly concerned about the level of political awareness among their slaves. The extraordinary intensity and sectional hostility of the 1856 presidential election, the first such canvass in which the antislavery Republican party made a bid for power with the candidacy of John C. Frémont, caused widespread insurrection rumors and some bloody reprisals against alleged slave rebels in Tennessee and other states.[27] In the sectional crisis over slavery, perception was becoming reality for many Americans. As southern editors increasingly condemned the alleged "secret missionaries" sent by the Republicans to inform the slaves "that Fremont's election would be the signal of their liberation," the slaves were listening. Few slaves may have ever known or met an abolition emissary, but that their masters could not stop talking about or preparing for such specters was exciting, if unsettling, news in the quarters and the fields of slaves' daily lives. Sectional fear had become racial fear for white southerners. And slaves themselves could hardly avoid noticing that the world of politics—its rallies and rituals—had become the place where white folks debated the fate of black folks. Sarah Fitzpatrick, an ex-slave born in 1847 in Alabama, recalled the late 1850s as a time of fear mixed with knowledge. "I 'member fo' de war," said Fitzpatrick, "us chillun use'ta go out in de evenin' an' watch de white fo'ks drill. Dey thought 'Niggers' didn't un'erstand whut wuz gwin' on, but dey knowed whut it meant, dey wuz jes' scaid to say anythin' 'bout it."[28]

Of even greater significance was the wave of slave insurrection panics and reprisals that swept the South in 1859 and 1860 after the Harper's Ferry raid. As Clarence Mohr has carefully demonstrated for the state of Georgia, John Brown laid bare the deepest racial fears and social insecurities of white southerners. Widespread reports of slave arson and broader insubordination, suppression of free speech and attacks on northern salesmen and travelers, and a general "mob psychosis" took over the political and social lives of Georgians during the election year of 1860. Such hysteria was fueled even more by the Texas insurrection panic of the summer of that year, in which approximately fifty blacks and whites died in vigilante violence.[29]

Historians continue to debate whether actual slave conspiracies caused such eruptions in the southern social fabric in 1860. But politics, as we continue to learn, is a process of warring perceptions rooted very often in real ideas. Then as now, John Brown, as well as the numerous alleged slave "ringleaders" of revolts who were executed during the year before secession, were far more important as symbols than as realities. What is certain is that white southerners were deeply worried about maintaining a social order under great duress. Southern editors especially warned about the presence of blacks at political meetings in 1860. A Rome, Georgia, editor tellingly cautioned against the "loose and unguarded discussion before negroes, of the political excitement of which they are the cause." In the cotton belt, the *cause* seemed to be everywhere. A Macon, Georgia, white resident described the problem as many must have seen it by September 1860. "Every political speech" in the presidential campaign, he said, "attracted a number of negroes, who without entering the Hall, have managed to linger around and hear what the orators say until the bell rings, when they leave. They do not congregate in sufficient numbers to make an unlawful assembly, but scatter themselves around—some at the hall door and some in the streets."[30] Slaveholders continued to assure themselves that theirs was a system based on familial relationships, white paternalism and black loyalty, at the same time they described a world teeming with thinking, breathing rebels from within and without. Civil wars are always, perhaps, rooted in the deepest and most tragic of contradictions. In towns and on plantations, the South's racial order, as well as its political economy, was fundamentally threatened in 1860, whether the Republican party intended it in quite such a combination or not.

The manner in which two generations of fugitives pushed their way into freedom and into the political center of the national "house divided" may demonstrate even more how slaves themselves anticipated the war or at least envisioned the political strife at its core. That story was told over and again in the slave narratives, which were testimonies to the romantic travail of escape, a genre the nineteenth century cherished. Former slave autobiographies were also the foundation of an African American literary tradition; they were demonstrations of the will to be known, and the will to be free, through the power of language. The best of the slave narratives were jeremiads, warnings about the impending doom of American society because of the evil of slavery; at the same time they were anguished appeals to the American creeds of liberty and justice. The slave narratives were testaments about the meaning of freedom and the consequences of its denial. They garnered a wide readership in the 1850s, and in their antislavery shock effect, their content became more severe as the sectional crisis deepened. The narratives were in many ways political sermons, chastising the South for its crime of slavery, while also calling the nation back to its promises and insisting that Americans as a whole listen to the pleadings of ordinary slaves. Those who would understand the problem of slavery, wrote Solomon Northrup, must empathetically "toil" with the slave "in the field—sleep with him in the cabin—feed with him on husks . . . know the *heart* of the poor slave—learn his secret thoughts . . . sit with him in the silent watches of the night—converse with him in trustful confidence, of 'life, liberty, and the pursuit of happiness.'"[31] Black abolitionism, especially through the stories told in the slave narratives, had tried to enter American hearts and minds in just such a way for two decades before Fort Sumter. Moreover, Solomon Northrup and that Rome, Georgia, editor, who felt the *cause* of political excitement all around him, would probably have understood, if not appreciated, each other's use of irony. The first principles of the Declaration of Independence were precisely where all sides would eventually look in attempting to understand or avoid the causes of war.

The role slave narratives played in Civil War causation will remain part of the illusive question of the place of abolitionism itself in bringing on the conflict. But as critic William L. Andrews has argued, slave narrative writers were "guerrilla" soldiers "of the pen," analyzing their own alienation from America, while simultaneously demanding a home within it. Their argument with America, their persistent exposure of the evil of slavery, their search for order amid the potential chaos of broken lives, and their preservation of a sense of irony in the face of oppression tell us much about what the coming of the Civil War and emancipation would mean to blacks. In his 1855 autobiography *My Bondage and My Freedom*, Frederick Douglass left the following timeless explanation of his hatred of slavery and desire for freedom: "The thought of only being a creature of the *present* and the *past*, troubled me, and I longed to have a *future*—a future with hope in it. To be shut up entirely to the past and present is abhorrent to the human mind; it is to the soul whose life and happiness is unceasing progress—what the prison is to the body."[32] In his yearning to have a future, Douglass captured the collective mood of his people on the eve of the Civil War. His prison metaphor might be applied both to the social condition of African Americans and to the political condition of the United States. A thoroughly tragic but new future—one with hope in it—was about to emerge.

The conflict that would bring that new future was part of a culture of expectation in black communities, slave and free, during the prewar era. American slaves fashioned a culture that, at its religious and folk foundations, was a means to manipulate and survive in a world of irrepressible strife. Nineteenth-century American slaves conducted their lives without any modern distinction between sacred and secular; they worked, loved, hated, and dreamed in a universe of song, folktales, and religious metaphor, not transmitted merely in otherworldly terms. Their culture was, as historian Lawrence Levine has put it, "forged on the hard rock of racial, social, and economic exploitation and injustice." But how hard was the rock? How movable or unmovable in different contexts? Did the slaves pound on that rock with their labor by day, at most chipping away at the infinity of its weight, while walking around it by night living in an inner world of folk belief that allowed them to sustain their dignity and sense of a future? How many found "a home in that rock," and how many were crushed by it? The study of slave culture as resistance has been an attempt to evaluate the shape and weight of that rock. Slave songs, as well as slave narratives, are replete with the idea of a quest for a sense of "home," a world where power relationships might be reversed, where the slaves' God might enter history and overturn its injustice. "Going home" to the slaves was not only a religious metaphor for death and heaven fatalistically expressed but also a way of imagining how the temporal world might be different. In its broadest terms the coming of the Civil War needs to be seen against this backdrop: a "theater," if you will, as William H. Seward described the country in his famous "Irrepressible Conflict" speech, but one where the slaves were not merely a chorus singing mood music, but people who had thought seriously about a coming catastrophe.[33]

Drawing upon the prophetic books of the Old Testament, Christian slaves were able to invent their own alternative history, to weave Moses and a sense of chosenness, Daniel and the lion's den, Joshua at the battle of Jericho, and a host of other stories into countless visions of deliverance. The time and location of such deliverance were, of course, never really the point. Sorrow and joy marched together in the same cadences of transcendence; the coming might be here, or it might be in a hereafter. Harriet Beecher Stowe once heard Sojourner Truth sing "There Is a Holy City" and remarked that her performance possessed an otherworldly "fervor of Ethiopia, wild, savage, hunted of all nations." But Stowe was also amazed at how real Sojourner's "burning after God" appeared, how compelling was her "stretching her scarred hands towards the glory to be revealed." The belief structure of antebellum African American religion must be taken seriously; it was one way blacks improvised and found a place in the land of the Dred Scott decision. As historian Albert Raboteau aptly wrote, "the story of Israel's exodus from Egypt helped make it possible for the slaves to *project a future* radically different from their present."[34] Slaves had rejected Justice Taney's opinion long before he wrote it. They had sung, chanted, stomped, and written of a future that no Supreme Court, collapsing second American party system, or even the armies of 1861 could avert. The temporal freedom that the coming of the war would seem to make possible only meant that their faith had served them well. When the war came, white Americans in the North and South would harken to a millennial faith and a religious view of history, not unlike that of the slaves, in order to understand the scope of their conflict.

When blacks, slave and free, imagined the possibility of their emancipation, they did so with a combination of millennial expectation and considerations of everyday life. Slaves often feared their would-be liberators, such as John Brown, because no one knew better than they the bloody results of insurrections. A combination of a peasant sense of fear, cunning, and self-protection guided the vast majority of slaves through their daily lives. They were about the business of preserving their own bodies and souls, and learned, in historian Nathan Huggins's telling phrase, that "fear could be managed." But they had real expectations of what freedom would mean when it did arrive. As the emancipation process during the war would reveal, the ex-slaves seized upon the chance to control their own labor, their own persons, and the integrity of their own families. Temporal control and spiritual sustenance were the companion elements of black life that had always been difficult to obtain, but were absolutely crucial to survival. Spiritual and sociopolitical life were not separate matters to most antebellum blacks. "The idea of a revolution in the conditions of the whites and blacks," wrote slave narrator Charles Ball, "is the cornerstone" of black religion. And, as the sectional crisis reached the breaking point in the late 1850s, one of William Still's Underground Railroad correspondents wrote to him from Baltimore asking "what time was it when israel went to Jerico i am very anxious to hear for thare is a mighty host will pass over and you and i my brother will sing hally luja i shall notify you when the great catastrophe shal take place."[35] As the war came, blacks from all backgrounds seemed to know what time it was.

As several historians have portrayed it, the secession crisis of 1860–61 was a time of great fear. The deepest anxieties of northerners and southerners were at stake, as both sections came to view each other in conspiratorial terms. By this time, the notions of a "slave power" conspiracy in northern minds and a "black Republican" conspiracy in southern minds each had long histories. The political process that had produced such conspiratorial consciousness, in its rational and irrational dimensions, was something that blacks, slave and free, had observed, interpreted, and helped to shape. Frederick Douglass remembered the secession winter as an example of the "depths" to which a "noble people can be brought under the sentiment of fear."[36] White fears, born of irreconcilable visions of the future, mingled now with black fears of whether there was a future, in the same tragic story.

After the attack on Fort Sumter, black leaders in the North responded in a variety of ways. Some urged immediate support for war; others favored caution or outright resistance in the face of the Lincoln administration's refusal to accept black enlistments. A few maintained that the hostilities would never be more than a quarrel between white men that would not free any black people. But amid uncertainty, all were deeply interested, and most knew that somebody was going to Jericho. By late summer 1861, James McCune Smith captured decades of expectation as well as the meaning of the moment. "We are concerned in this fight and our fate hangs upon its issues," said Smith. "The South must be subjugated, or we shall be enslaved." Whatever the current policies, Smith asserted, "circumstances have been so arranged by the decrees of Providence, that in struggling for their own nationality they [white northerners] are forced to defend our rights." The conflict, the level of political disorder, the break with the past, and the chance to imagine a new, reinvented American republic that so many black abolitionists had come to desire, whatever the consequences, was now at hand. "At last our proud Republic is overtaken," wrote Frederick Douglass immediately after the bombardment of Fort Sumter. Douglass spoke to the past, present, and future. "Now is the time," he announced, "to change the cry of vengeance long sent up from the toiling bondsmen, into a grateful prayer for the peace and safety of the Government." Black abolitionists had rarely spoken of the United States government in such warm terms. But in spite of untold "desolations" he feared the war would bring, Douglass now saw the hope of "armed abolition" conducted in a sanctioned war against the South. Above all, he saw the central meaning of the war for all Americans in a crisis that, willed or not, "bound up the fate of the Republic and the fate of the slave in the same bundle."[37] Comprehending the full meaning of that mutual fate and understanding why it took war on such a horrible scale to make African Americans free have been the central legacies of the conflict ever since.

NOTES

This a slightly revised version of an essay published in *Why the Civil War Came*, ed. Gabor S. Boritt (New York: Oxford University Press, 1996).

1. Benjamin Quarles, *The Negro in the Civil War* (Boston: Little Brown, 1953), ix.

2 . On the notion of the Civil War as a "Second American Revolution," see, for example, James M. McPherson, *Abraham Lincoln and the Second American Revolution* (New York: Oxford University Press, 1991); Eric Foner, *Reconstruction: America's Unfinished Revolution, 1863–1877* (New York: Harper and Row, 1988); and Bruce Levine, *Half Slave and Half Free: The Roots of Civil War* (New York: Hill and Wang, 1992). Kenneth M. Stampp, "The Irrepressible Conflict," in *The Imperiled Union: Essays on the Background of the Civil War* (New York: Oxford University Press, 1980), 191. On the debate over emancipation as both seized and given, see James M. McPherson, "Who Freed the Slaves?" and Ira Berlin, "Emancipation and Its Meaning in American Life," both in *Reconstruction* 2, no. 3 (1994): 35–44.

3. *Douglass Monthly,* July, April 1861.

4 . Maria Stewart, a speech in Boston's Franklin Hall, September 21, 1832, quoted in *We Are Your Sisters: Black Women in the Nineteenth Century,* ed. Dorothy Sterling (New York: Norton, 1984), 154.

5. *Report on the Proceedings of the Colored National Convention, Held at Cleveland, Ohio, on Wednesday, September 6, 1848* (Rochester, 1848), 19, quoted in *The Black Abolitionist Papers,* ed. C. Peter Ripley et al., 5 vols. (Chapel Hill: University of North Carolina Press, 1985–92), 3:24. On "two abolitionisms," see Jane H. Pease and William H. Pease, *They Who Would Be Free: Blacks' Search for Freedom, 1830–1861* (New York: Atheneum. 1974), 3–16.

6. Eric Foner, "Politics, Ideology, and the Origins of the Civil War," in *Nation Divided: Problems and Issues of the Civil War and Reconstruction,* ed. George M. Fredrickson (Minneapolis: Burgess Publishing, 1975), reprinted in *The Coming of the American Civil War,* ed. Michael Perman, 3d ed. (Lexington, Mass: D.C. Heath, 1993), 186.

7. *Frederick Douglass' Paper,* March 4, 1853, August 15, 1856.

8. Samuel Ringgold Ward, *Autobiography of a Fugitive Negro* (1855; reprint, New York: Arno Press, 1968), 77; Abraham Lincoln, "Annual Message to Congress," December 1, 1862, in *The Collected Works of Abraham Lincoln,* ed. Roy P. Basler, 9 vols. (New Brunswick: Rutgers University Press, 1953–55), 5:537.

9. Leon F. Litwack, *North of Slavery: The Negro in the Free States, 1790–1860* (Chicago: University of Chicago Press, 1961), 248–50; and James Oliver Horton and Lois E. Horton, *In Hope of Liberty: Culture, Community, and Protest among Northern Free Blacks, 1700–1860* (New York: Oxford University Press, 1997), 203–68.

10. See Larry Gara, *Liberty Line: The Legend of the Underground Railroad* (Lexington: University Press of Kentucky, 1961). On vigilance committees, see Pease and Pease, *They Who Would Be Free,* 207–12; Horton and Horton, *In Hope of Liberty,* 229–30, 234–35.

11. Bibb in *Liberator,* April 12, 1850; Providence meeting quoted in Pease and Pease, *They Who Would Be Free,* 217; Philadelphia resolutions in *Witness for Freedom: African-American Voices on Race, Slavery, and Emancipation,* ed. C. Peter Ripley (Chapel Hill: University of North Carolina Press, 1993), 182; Powell, in *Liberator,* October 11, 1850.

12. Pease and Pease, *They Who Would Be Free,* 219–32. On Minkins, see Gary Collison, *Shadrach Minkins: From Fugitive Slave to Citizen* (Cambridge: Harvard University Press, 1997). Three of the fugitives who fought off their pursuers at Christiana fled to Canada via Frederick Douglass's home in Rochester, New York. After having been fed and sheltered by Douglass and then taken by carriage to the Genessee River where they departed for Canada, one of the fugitives gave the abolitionist a revolver as a token of gratitude. See David W. Blight, *Frederick Douglass' Civil War: Keeping Faith in Jubilee* (Baton Rouge: Louisiana State University Press, 1989), 94.

13. *Liberator,* July 7, 1854. On Burns and his rescue, see *Black Abolitionist Papers,* ed. Ripley, 4:395–97. In February 1855 members of the black Twelfth Baptist Church in Boston, of which Burns had been a member, purchased his freedom. A Boston woman sponsored Burns's education at Oberlin College through 1857. He eventually settled in Saint Catherines, Canada West, where he died in 1862. On the Burns case, see Albert J. Von Frank, *The Trials of Anthony Burns: Freedom and Slavery in Emerson's Boston* (Cambridge: Harvard University Press, 1998).

14. Ruggles, in *Black Abolitionist Papers,* ed. Ripley, 3:172; Mary Armstead to William Still, August, 26, 1855, and John H. Hill to William Still, October 30, 1853, in *The Mind of the Negro as Reflected in Letters Written during the Crisis, 1800–1860,* ed. Carter G. Woodson (Washington: Association for the Study of Negro Life and History, 1926), 566, 583.

15. Benjamin Quarles, "The Revolutionary War as a Black Declaration of Independence," in *Black Mosaic: Essays in Afro-American History and Historiography* (Amherst: University of Massachusetts Press, 1988), 57. See the resolutions of a Philadelphia meeting in October 1850 in *Witness for Freedom,* ed. Ripley, 179–83.

16. *Frederick Douglass' Paper,* July 21, 1851, in *The Life and Writings of Frederick Douglass,* ed. Philip S. Foner (New York: International Publishers, 1950), 5:192–93.

17. Quoted in Don E. Fehrenbacher, *The Dred Scott Case: Its Significance in American Law and Politics* (New York: Oxford University Press, 1978), 347.

18. *Provincial Freeman*, April 25, 1857, quoted in *Black Abolitionist Papers*, ed. Ripley, 4:362; Shadd Cary quoted in Quarles, *Black Abolitionists*, 231; speech by Purvis, in City Assembly Room, New York, May 12, 1857, in *Black Abolitionist Papers*, ed. Ripley, 4:363–64; and Frances Ellen Watkins Harper, speech printed in *National Anti-Slavery Standard*, May 23, 1857, quoted in *We Are Your Sisters*, ed. Sterling, 162. Watkins Harper married in 1860. I have used her married name because that is how she is best known, especially during her literary career.

19. Quarles, *Black Abolitionists*, 235; Rock, address in Faneuil Hall, Boston, *Liberator*, March 12, 1858, reprinted in *Afro-American History: Primary Sources*, comp. Thomas R. Frazier, shorter ed. (New York: Harcourt Brace, 1971), 73–74; *Douglass Monthly*, January 1859.

20. Martin R. Delany, *The Condition, Elevation, Emigration, and Destiny of the Colored People of the United States* (1852; reprint, New York: Arno Press, 1968), 199; Nell Irvin Painter, "Martin R. Delany: Elitism and Black Nationalism," in *Black Leaders of the Nineteenth Century*, ed. Leon Litwack and August Meier (Urbana: University of Illinois Press, 1988), 149–71.

21. Jason H. Silverman, "Mary Ann Shadd and the Search for Equality," in *Black Leaders*, 87–100; and *We Are Your Sisters*, ed. Sterling, 165–75.

22. Floyd J. Miller, *The Search for a Black Nationality: Black Emigration and Colonization* (Urbana: University of Illinois Press, 1975), 192–93, 228–49; Horton and Horton, *In Hope of Liberty*, 191–96.

23. *Proceedings of the First Convention of the Colored Citizens of the State of Illinois, Convened at the City of Chicago, October 6–8, 1853*, in *Proceedings of the Black State Conventions, 1840–1865*, ed. Philip S. Foner and George E. Walker (Philadelphia: Temple University Press, 1980), 60–62. Pease and Pease, *They Who Would Be Free*, 267–72.

24. Eugene D. Genovese, *From Rebellion to Revolution: Afro-American Slave Revolts in the Making of the New World* (Baton Rouge: Louisiana State University Press, 1979), 106–17. I take my use of the term "abolition emissaries" (constantly used by white southerners in the late 1850s) from Steven A. Channing, *Crisis of Fear: Secession in South Carolina* (New York: Simon and Schuster, 1970), 38–57; and Clarence L. Mohr, *On the Threshold of Freedom: Masters and Slaves in Civil War Georgia* (Athens: University of Georgia Press, 1986), 8, 28.

25. McDowell quoted in Genovese, *From Rebellion to Revolution*, 116. Withers quoted from *Charleston Courier*, January 30, 1859, in Channing, *Crisis of Fear*, 39 n. 38.

26. Channing, *Crisis of Fear*, 50.

27. Kenneth M. Stampp, *America in 1857: A Nation on the Brink* (New York: Oxford University Press, 1990), 35–36; Genovese, *From Rebellion to Revolution*, 128–29.

28. *New Orleans Picayune*, January 2, 1857, quoted in Stampp, *America in 1857*, 36; Sarah Fitzpatrick, interviewed in 1938, quoted in *Slave Testimony: Two Centuries of Letters, Speeches, Interviews, and Autobiographies*, ed. John W. Blassingame (Baton Rouge: Louisiana State University Press, 1977), 640.

29. Mohr, *On the Threshold of Freedom,* 3–40, "mob psychosis" quotation on 35. Donald E. Reynolds, *Editors Make War: Southern Newspapers in the Secession Crisis* (Nashville: Vanderbilt University Press, 1970), 97–117.

30. Rome and Macon, Georgia, quotations in Mohr, *On the Threshold of Freedom,* 36–37.

31. Solomon Northrup, *Twelve Years a Slave,* quoted in *Slave Testimony,* ed. Blassingame, lxiv.

32. William L. Andrews, *To Tell a Free Story: The First Century of Afro-American Autobiography, 1760–1865* (Urbana: University of Illinois Press, 1986), 172; Frederick Douglass, *My Bondage and My Freedom* (1855; reprint, New York: Dover, 1969), 272.

33. Lawrence W. Levine, *Black Culture and Black Consciousness: Afro-American Folk Thought from Slavery to Freedom* (New York: Oxford University Press, 1977), xi; William H. Seward, "The Irrepressible Conflict," speech in Rochester, New York, October 25, 1858, reprinted in *The Causes of the American Civil War,* ed Edwin C. Rozwenc (Boston: Heath, 1961), 11.

34. Stowe, quoted in Eugene D. Genovese, *Roll, Jordan, Roll: The World the Slaves Made* (New York: Pantheon, 1972), 249; Albert J. Raboteau, *Slave Religion: The Invisible Institution in the Antebellum South* (New York: Oxford University Press, 1978), 312, emphasis added.

35. Nathan Irvin Huggins, *Black Odyssey: The African-American Ordeal in Slavery* (New York: Vintage, 1990), 182. On slave expectations of emancipation, see *Freedom: A Documentary History of Emancipation, 1861–1867,* series 1, vol. 3, *The Wartime Genesis of Free Labor,* ed. Ira Berlin et al. (New York: Cambridge University Press, 1990), 7–9. Ball quoted in Raboteau, *Slave Religion,* 291. "N. I. J." to William Still, April 16, 1859, in *The Mind of the Negro,* ed. Woodson, 563.

36. Channing, *Crisis of Fear,* 17–57; Mohr, *On the Threshold of Freedom,* 3–67. Frederick Douglass, *The Life and Times of Frederick Douglass* (1881; reprint, New York: Collier, 1962), 332.

37. Smith, in *Weekly Anglo-African,* August 24, 1861, in *The Negro's Civil War: How American Negroes Felt and Acted during the War for the Union,* ed. James M. McPherson (New York: Pantheon, 1965), 31; *Douglass Monthly,* May 1861, in *Life and Writings of Frederick Douglass,* ed. Foner, 3:98–99.

No Desperate Hero

Manhood and Freedom in a Union Soldier's Experience

*The soil of peace is thickly sown
with the seeds of war.*
—*Ambrose Bierce*

With the First World War as his model, Paul Fussell wrote that "every war is ironic because every war is worse than expected." As national calamity and as individual experience, certainly this was the case with the American Civil War. That slavery could be abolished only by such wholesale slaughter and that national unity could be preserved only through such fratricidal conflict provide some of the most tragic ironies of American history. On a grand scale, such ironies are easily summarized, but as Fussell observes, all "great" wars consist of thousands of "smaller constituent" stories, which are themselves full of "ironic actions."[1] One of those stories is recorded in the more than two hundred Civil War letters of Charles Harvey Brewster of Northampton, Massachusetts. As Bell Wiley first observed in the 1940s and 1950s, the letters of Civil War soldiers are an extraordinary source for the social history of nineteenth-century America. Brewster's single cache of letters illuminates a remarkable range of attitudes and experience of an ordinary American man caught up not only in the sweeping events of the war but also in the values of his age and the challenge of his own self-development. The emotions and ideas he expressed range from naiveté to mature realism, from romantic idealism to sheer terror, and from self-pity to enduring devotion.[2]

Born and raised in Northampton, Brewster was a relatively unsuccessful, twenty-seven-year-old store clerk and a member of the local militia when he enlisted in Company C of the Tenth Massachusetts Volunteers in April 1861. Companies of the Tenth Massachusetts were formed from towns all over the western section of the state. The citizens of

Northampton embraced the war fever that swept the land in the spring and summer of 1861. On April 18, only three days after the surrender of Fort Sumter, the first meeting of the Company C militia (a unit chartered in 1801) turned into a large public rally where forty new men enlisted. By April 24 seventy-five Northampton women rallied and vowed to sew the uniforms of the local company. As the cloth arrived, some women worked at home and others sewed publicly in the town hall. Local poets came to the armory to recite patriotic verses to the would-be soldiers. Yesterday, farmers, clerks, and mechanics; today they were the local heroes who would "whip secesh." On May 9 Company C marched some seven miles for an overnight encampment in Haydenville, passing through the towns of Florence and Leeds on the way. In each village a brass band, an outdoor feast, and a large crowd cheered them. War was still a local festival in this first spring of the conflict. By June 10 the seventy or so members of the company attended a farewell ball, and four days later they strode down Main Street through a throng so large a corridor could hardly be formed. Flags waved everywhere, several brass bands competed, and Brewster and his comrades joined two other companies of the Tenth on a train for Springfield. En route the soldiers continued the joyous fervor of the day by singing "patriotic airs" to the accompaniment of a lone accordion.[3] Like most of his comrades, Brewster had enlisted for three years, never believing the war would last that long.

After a three-week encampment in Springfield, the Tenth Massachusetts again departed with great ceremony. As was the case in so many American towns that summer, the "ladies of Springfield" formally presented the regimental colors to Col. Henry S. Briggs, commander of the regiment. It was a time, said the women's announcement, for "reverence" to flags, and they urged the men to "defend them to the death." The spokeswoman, a Mrs. James Barnes, assured these young warriors that "the heart of many a wife and mother and child and sister, will beat anxiously for your safety, but remember, no less anxiously for your honor." In Palmer, on the way to Boston, several hundred women gathered at the station to bid the soldiers goodbye, some with bouquets of flowers. The regiment would camp ten more days in Medford, next to Charlestown, on the banks of the Mystic River. Before boarding transports for the voyage to Washington, D.C., the Tenth stood for one more ceremony, this time addressed by former Massachusetts governor George N. Briggs, father of the commander. In a message fathers have for centuries passed to their sons, but rarely so explicitly, Briggs called upon farmboys and clerks to "show yourselves to be men and New England men." He urged them to be gallant and fierce, but always kind to their wounded or captured enemy. He then concluded with a flourish: "When the army of an ancient republic were going forth to battle a mother of one of the soldiers said to him: 'My son, return home with your shield or on your shield.' Adopting the sentiment of the noble mother, let me say . . . bring back those beautiful and rich colors presented you by the ladies of Springfield, the emblems of your country's power and glory, waving over your heads, unstained, or return wrapped in their gory folds."[4] One can never know how closely soldiers listened to such rhetoric in that romantic summer of 1861. The fathers' and mothers' call to war and manliness, in the war they were soon to fight, would indeed become for some men an exhilarating and ennobling challenge, while for others it would become disillusioning or unbearable. For Brewster, it became all those things.

The Tenth Massachusetts spent the rest of 1861 and the winter of 1862 in Camp Brightwood, on the edge of the District of Columbia. There they joined the Seventh Massachusetts, the Thirty-sixth New York, and the Second Rhode Island as part of Couch's Brigade. For three years, Brewster shared the same brigade and battle experiences as Second Rhode Island private, ultimately colonel, Elisha Hunt Rhodes, whose diary became famous as part of a 1990 PBS television documentary on the Civil War.[5] The Tenth participated in almost every major battle fought by the Army of the Potomac, beginning with the Peninsula campaign through Antietam and Fredericksburg in 1862, Chancellorsville, Gettysburg, Bristow Station, and Rappahannock Station in 1863, and the Wilderness, Spotsylvania, and Cold Harbor in 1864. By the time the survivors of the Tenth were mustered out at the end of their three-year enlistment in June 1864, they had witnessed the transformation of their summer outing into the bloodiest war in history, seen thousands die of disease, practiced war upon civilians and the southern landscape, loyally served the cause as variously defined, and tried their best to fulfill their communities' expectations. They returned, in the words of their last commander, Col. Joseph B. Parsons, a "shattered remnant" of "mourners."[6]

Brewster's father, Harvey Brewster, had died in 1839 when Charles was only five years old, leaving Martha Russell Brewster a widow with three small children, including two daughters, four-year-old Martha and two-month-old Mary. Brewster's wartime letters, virtually all of which were written to his mother and two sisters, clearly reflect a background of family financial distress, at the same time they exhibit deep affection. His wartime adventures and sufferings would compel Brewster to expose his self-estimation as a frustrated, if not failed, provider in his capacity as the sole male member of his family. Nevertheless, for Brewster, as has been true for men throughout the ages, war became an ordinary man's opportunity to escape from the ordinary.[7]

Brewster came to loathe war itself; after imagined and romantic warfare gave way to real battle in 1862, he would describe it in honest and realistic terms. Brewster came to understand that in war, perhaps even more than in civilian life, fate was often indifferent to individual virtue, however much he wished it were otherwise. Educated in the Northampton public schools, sensitive and remarkably literate, Brewster was no natural warrior. But he aspired to leadership and craved recognition. The army, and his incessant desire for status within its ranks, became for Brewster the source of community and vocation that he had never achieved.

Brewster survived more than three years of battle, hardship, sickness, and boredom by a combination of devotion, diminished alternatives, self-righteous ambition, and a sense of irony. Like literate soldiers in all ages, or like anyone undergoing loneliness and stress, letters became for Brewster both monologues of self-discovery and dialogues with home. Letters were a humanizing element in a dehumanizing environment, evidence that however foreign civilian life might come to appear, something called "home" still existed. Lying in a rifle pit in June 1862, having experienced his first major battle at Fair Oaks during the Peninsula campaign, Brewster scolded his mother for not writing more often. "It is the little common place incidents of everyday life at home which we like to read," Brewster declared. "It is nothing to the inhabitants of Northampton that the beans are up in the old garden at home; or that Mary has moved her Verbena bed into the garden, but to me, way off here in the swamps, and woods, frying in the sun, or soaking in the rain, it is a very important thing indeed. You do not realize how everything that savors of home relishes with us." Brewster wrote out of self-pity and as a means of feeling alive. In a volatile letter, where he wrote matter-of-factly about the prospect of his own death, he informed his mother that her letters were like "Angels' visits." But sleeping in the mud made even letters sometimes inadequate to the task of sustaining hope and self-respect. "I think it is too bad," said Brewster from the Peninsula, "when letters are the only thing that makes existence tolerable in this God forsaken country."[8]

Letters were a soldier's means of expressing and understanding the absurdity of war, as well as a way of reaffirming a man's commitment to the enterprise. But nothing threw this paradox into greater relief than letters to and from dead men. In the immediate aftermath of the battle of Gettysburg, Brewster lifted three letters from "a dead Rebel's cartridge box, written to his mother and sisters." He sent them to his sister Mary as a souvenir. "Poor fellow," Brewster remarked, "he lay upon the field with his entrails scattered all about by a cannon shot, I cannot help pity him although as you see he expresses no very kindly intentions towards poor us." Backhandedly, Brewster expressed a sense of kinship with his dead enemy. "The mother & sisters will look in vain in the far off Florida for his return," wrote the New Englander, "or even his grave among the green hills of Penn, where his body probably lies in a pit with lots of his comrades." Brewster maintained a certain emotional distance from his unnamed foe in an unmarked grave. But the symbol of the confiscated letters to "mother & sisters" could only have made him and his loved ones back home wonder about the "pit" beneath some "green hills" where Brewster might soon find oblivion. Letters represented the continuity of life, even when they were to or from the dead.[9]

To a significant degree Brewster's war was one man's effort to compensate for prior failure and to imagine a new career within the rigid and unpredictable strictures of the army. Brewster yearned for a "chance" to "better" himself, for the respect of his fellow soldiers, and for the symbols of authority and rank. He entered the service disappointingly as a noncommissioned first sergeant and spent the first summer and autumn of the war pining for the status of a commission. Put simply, Brewster had a chip on his shoulder about the hand that life had dealt him. He frequently referred to a prewar pattern of bad luck as he gossiped about those who got promotions, resented perceived slights, desperately relished compliments about his performance, and moaned to his mother that it was "hope deferred that maketh the heart sick." Brewster constantly measured himself against his fellow soldiers and calculated his chances of promotion against their character and health. His relations with his comrades were a typical combination of male bonding and competition, and he was motivated by a workingman's sense of practical self-interest. "A fellow can sleep very warm in the woods," he told his mother in December 1861, "with a commission in his pocket."[10]

Brewster received his much-coveted commission and promotion to second lieutenant in December 1862. He sent a detailed description of the sword, sash, belt, and cap purchased for him as gifts at considerable cost by members of his company. His letter reads like a description of an impending graduation or a wedding night. "My heart is full to overflowing tonight," Brewster informed his sister. All pettiness and resentment vanished as he realized the "evidence of my standing in the affections of the men." His comrades pooled more than fifty dollars to buy the officer's accoutrements, and Brewster confessed to feeling "wicked" over his good fortune while his comrades in the ranks honored him. The army in winter quarters had become a society of men living together, developing their own rituals and conventions of domestic relations. On the eve of a ceremony that would recognize his new rank, Brewster prepared for a rite of passage and new living arrangements. "I am writing in my tent," he told his sister. "I have not slept in it yet but am going to tonight. Lieut. Weatherill and I have been arranging things all day." There were "new bunks" in his "future home," and he informed Mary that he would be ready to entertain her when she visited. Brewster made the most of this milestone in his life, and a certain tenderness crept into his language as he marveled at the "spontaneous outbreak of feeling" among the men.[11]

Brewster learned what war has often taught us: that men frequently find love and respect for each other more readily in warlike activities than in civilian pursuits. After first wearing his "new uniform," Brewster declared that he felt "quite like a free man once more, now that I am a commissioned officer, it is wonderful what a difference two little straps on the shoulder make." Once again, he recognized his own aims as practical and personal. "Before I had lots of work and very little pay," he wrote, "and now I have very little work and lots of pay."[12] To Brewster freedom meant increased wages, status, and independence in controlling his own labor. But Brewster's new status also represented some ideals in the relations among men that only the army seemed to provide: loyalty, respect, and the burdens and joys of leadership. Brewster would have been deeply heartened by a September 1861 letter written by Henry W. Parsons, a twenty-two-year-old private in his company. "In reguard to Charley Brewster," wrote Parsons to his aunt, "he improves every day he is the best officer in the company that we have had with us yet you will find a large heart beneth his coat." Within a month of writing this tribute to his favorite officer, Parsons died of disease at Camp

Brightwood, but not before informing his aunt that Brewster was "a gentleman to all and will do all for the men that lays in his power—his friends may feel proud of him . . . let me tell you Aunt that this is the place to find out mens disposition one can soon tell a man from a knave or coward." Deeply affected by the loss of such a friend so early in the war, Brewster told his mother that he could not "get over Henry Parsons' death. it came so sudden and he was a particular friend of mine, and he and myself had many a confidential talk together."[13] The quest for status, the love and respect of friends, and the sheer struggle for physical survival all became part of a young officer's daily existence.

As soldiers like Brewster developed their military identities, they were readily reminded of the radical disjuncture between their precarious existence and that of the community left behind. "How I wish some of the stay at homes could enjoy one winter campaign with us," Brewster complained in 1862. "I fancy we should hear less of 'onward to Richmond.'" Once fully initiated to war and to its psychological shocks, a soldier's misery found expression in his contempt for civilians. "People at the North do not realize at all what a soldier's life is," Brewster wrote in 1863; "a soldier has more misery in one day than occurs in a lifetime of a civilian ordinarily and their greatest comforts would be miseries to people at home." Brewster developed a veteran volunteer's increasing estrangement from civilians in a prolonged war. "It is the general feeling among the old regiments, the real volunteers," he said, "that the generality of the citizens loathe and hate them."[14]

By 1864 Brewster was disaffected from his hometown and homesick at the same time. Conscription laws exacerbated such ambivalence, drawing a greater distance between the original volunteers—who by 1863–64 had constructed a self-image as suffering victims—and the draftees from their hometowns. As Northampton strained to fill a draft quota in February 1864, Brewster declared that he did not "believe in drafted patriotism." Brewster worried about what would become of him once his war was over. "This military is a hard worrying and at the same time lazy miserable business," he wrote in April 1864, "but it pays better than anything else so I think I had better stick to it as long as I can." In words representative of Everyman's lament, Brewster declared that he had done his "share of campaigning but somebody must campaign and somebody else must have all the easy money making places and as the harder lot was always mine in civil life I suppose I must expect the same in the military."[15]

Brewster's sentiments toward civilians, as well as his fears of making a living after the war, are reminiscent of dilemmas faced by veterans of other American wars. "I don't know what I am going to do for a living when I come home," Brewster wrote in his last letter from the front in June 1864. "As the end of my service grows near," he said, "I cannot but feel rather bad to leave it for all its hardships and horrors & dangers it is a fascinating kind of life, and much freer from slander jealousy & unkindness than civil life which I almost dread to come back to." Brewster groped to explain why the joy of going home should be so tarnished by fear of civilian livelihood. Suddenly, the army seemed an island of clarity, honesty, and genuineness in a laissez faire sea of treachery. "The Veterans," he said, "wear long faces." He spoke for the veterans in warning that "those who will welcome them with such apparent joy" will be "ready to do them any injury for the sake of a dollar." His fears of civilian life and nostalgia for the comradeship of the army already made him a candidate for the cycles of selective memory that would both plague and inspire Civil War veterans.[16]

Brewster, like most men of his generation, was deeply imbued with the Victorian American values of "manhood" and "courage." He perceived war as the test of his courage, and he constantly sought reassurance that he could meet the challenge. He aspired to the individualized and exemplary conception of bravery, where officers especially had to exhibit their courage to the rank and file. "Courage was the cement of armies," wrote historian Gerald Linderman, in the best study of this concept among Civil War soldiers.[17] Especially in the early stages of the war, there is no question that fear of personal dishonor, so rooted in social constructions of masculinity and in American culture, provided the motivation and much of the discipline of Civil War armies.

But the social expectations of manliness in the face of modern war and the degradation of disease almost overwhelmed Brewster, though he only guardedly admitted it. He was both a victim and a perpetrator of these values. His letters are full of observations about the endless struggle between courage and cowardice, his own and that of his comrades. Like most young men who went to war in the nineteenth century (and in the more violent twentieth century as well), Brewster followed a destructive quest for manhood, fashioned a heroic self-image at every chance, and marveled at the capacity of war to subdue the environment. He also wrote of camp life and war itself as places strictly separating men from women, all the while imagining their scenes and horrors for his female correspondents. Such sentiments, of course, are not merely stored away in the nineteenth century to be unpackaged for modern boyhood fantasies or the mythic uses of the vast Civil War literature. Readers of great memoirs from later wars, like William Manchester's *Goodbye Darkness: A Memoir of the Pacific War,* may find certain echoes in Brewster's letters. When Manchester, the son and grandson of soldiers, wrote of his withdrawal from Massachusetts State College and enlistment in the marines in 1942, "guided by the compass that had been built into me," he represented a male tradition deeply ingrained in American society, and one that common and less literary-inclined men like Brewster had helped to cultivate.[18] Brewster's own manly compass sent him irresistibly off to war, however unprepared or ill equipped for what it would do to his body or his imagination.

In May 1862, just before the battle of Fair Oaks, Brewster wrote daily, dramatic accounts of the impending battle, but even more so, he chronicled his desperate struggle with dysentery and "terrible exposure" while sleeping nightly in the mud. At one point he declares himself so sick that he will have to resign and go home; to fall back now to some makeshift hospital, he believed, would surely mean a hideous and ignoble death. Courage in this instance, Brewster learned, merely meant endurance and a little luck. He could "give up" and seek a furlough, he reasoned, but he feared that the "brave ones that staid at home would call me a coward and all that so I must stay here until after the fight at any rate." In a despairing letter two months later Brewster described "burying comrades who die of disease" as the "saddest thing in the service." Wondering what he would write to a dead comrade's parents, he took heart at how well the man had performed in battle: "thank the lord I can tell them he was brave."[19]

Unable to walk and humiliated by his chronic diarrhea, Brewster spent the battle of Fredericksburg in December 1862 five miles behind the lines where he could only hear that desperate engagement. "I never felt so mean in my life," he wrote. "I lie here like a sculking coward and hear the din of battle but cannot get there it is too bad." The situation is reminiscent of the scene in Stephen Crane's *Red Badge of Courage* when Henry Fleming, tormented by the sounds of battle—"the crackling shots which were to him like voices"—feels "frustrated by hateful circumstances." Henry and Brewster had different burdens to bear; the latter had not run from battle. But a week later Brewster demonstrated his ambivalence about the vexing concept of courage, hoping that the sickness would not seize him again "when there is a battle in prospect, for it lays me open to the imputation of cowardice, which I do not relish at all, although I don't claim to be very brave."[20]

In the boredom, frustration, and danger of three years at the front, sometimes Brewster asserted his own manhood only by attacking that of others. But with time he became a realist about the meaning of courage. On the eve of the Wilderness campaign in April 1864, Brewster hoped that his corps would be held in reserve in the impending fight. "I suppose you will call that a cowardly wish," he told Mary, "but although we see a great many in print, we see very few in reality of such desperate heroes that they had rather go into the heat of battle than not, when they can do their duty just as well by staying out." Having just lived through the worst combat of the war in late May 1864, he could write about courage without pretension. "You are mistaken about their being nothing cowardly about me," Brewster informed Martha. "I am scared most to death every battle we have, but I don't think you need be afraid of my sneaking away unhurt."[21] When introspection overtook the need for camaraderie and bravado, as it frequently did in the last months of his service, Brewster found the moral courage to speak honestly about physical courage.

Brewster kept his women correspondents informed but probably full of tension as he encountered real war. His letters allow us to follow a young man's romantic anticipation of battle through the experience of pitilessly realistic warfare. Upon seeing the aftermath of a battlefield for the first time at Williamsburg, Virginia, he described it as a "fearful, fearful sight." "The ground was strew with dead men in every direction," he told his mother. "But language fails me and I cannot attempt to describe the scene. if ever I come home I can perhaps tell you but I cannot write it." Brewster would see much worse yet, and he would continue to write it into and out of his memory. But he was caught in that dilemma of literate soldiers in all modern wars: the gruesomeness of battlefields seemed, as Fussell put it, "an all-but-incommunicable reality" to the folks back home. Brewster's letters seem to have anticipated what Alexander Aitken wrote about his own rendering of the battle of the Somme in 1916: "I leave it to the sensitive imagination; I once wrote it all down, only to discover that horror, truthfully described, weakens to the merely clinical."[22] Brewster had a sensitive imagination, and he did try to write it all down; one wonders, though, if after the war, looking back at his letters, he might not have felt the same way Aitken did. In its own historical moment the obscenity of war, it seems, begs description; whereas in retrospect, it often must be repressed from memory as people confront the tasks of living.

During Brewster's first major campaign (the Peninsula and the Seven Days, April to July 1862), he expressed virtually every emotion that battle could evoke. At the battle of Fair Oaks Brewster's regiment lost one of every four men engaged (killed, wounded, or missing), and with good reason, the young officer wondered why he was still alive. He tried to describe the sounds and the stench of the battlefield, and the excitement and pulse of the fighting. He also began to demonize the enemy at every turn. In surviving such madness Brewster felt both manly exhilaration and dehumanization. The "life" the soldiers sustained, he said, "would kill wild beasts," and the farmers of Northampton, he maintained, "would call it cruelty to animals to keep their hogs in as bad a place as we have to live and sleep." Most of all Brewster coped with fear and loaded up on opium to command his bowels. Anticipating the great battle for Richmond, he said he could only "dread it," as he had already "seen all I want to of battle and blood."[23] But he had two more years of this to endure; his demeanor and his language would both harden and expand with the experience.

While squatting in a field or brooding in a trench, Brewster sketched battle and its aftermath from a soldier's interior perspective rather than from the sanitized vantage point of headquarters. He rarely wrote about generals and grand strategy, providing an example, as John Keegan put it, of how very different the "face of battle" is from the "face of war."[24] Although he had no serious literary pretensions, Brewster's horror-struck depictions of battle scenes are sometimes similar to the agonizing ironies and relentless realism of Ambrose Bierce's short stories. After Gettysburg he described the endless corpses of dead men and horses as if they were macabre monuments. At Spotsylvania in 1864 the "terrors" he witnessed had become so common that he sometimes worried about his own lack of "feeling," and other times just lost himself in grim details. Describing one trench with dead and wounded Confederates piled "3 or 4 deap," he saw "one completely trodded in the mud so as to look like part of it and yet he was breathing and gasping." In the next letter came the vision of "the most terrible sight I ever saw," a breastwork fought over for twenty-four hours with the dead "piled in heaps upon heaps." As Brewster gazed over the parapet at dawn, "there was one Rebel sat up praying at the top of his voice and others were gibbering in insanity others were whining at the greatest rate." Stealing his nerves, preparing himself to continue this "terrible business," and ever the partisan, Brewster took an awkward solace that he had not, he claimed, heard any wounded Union soldiers "make any fuss."[25]

As he self-consciously became part of a machine of total war Brewster justified the pillaging of southern civilians, supported the execution of deserters, and in his harshest moments advocated the killing of Confederate prisoners. Yet through nature's diversions and a healthy sense of irony, he preserved his humane sensibilities. Brewster nurtured a life-long interest in flowers, gardening, and the natural landscape, and he was an astute observer of the beauty and the strangeness of the Virginia countryside. Ever on the watch for the contrast of peace with war, many a "beautiful morning" in Brewster's letters provided a pastoral backdrop for the dullness of camp or the terror of battle. "I wish you could see what a splendid morning this is," he said to his mother while seated on an oak log at Chickahominy Creek in the spring of 1862. "The trees are in full foliage and the Birds are singing and the water ripples and sparkles at my feet with the sun shining gloriously over all, and if it were not for the Regt I see before me each with his deadly Enfield rifle on his shoulder I could hardly imagine that there was war in the land." Brewster savored opportunities to tell his womenfolk about wild roses and a host of other flower species he observed on the march. In a field near Cold Harbor in May 1864, "magnolias in full bloom" made him reverently grateful, for "their perfume is very refreshing," he said, "after the continued stench of the dead bodies of men and horses which we have endured for the last 19 days." Every war brings these contrasts of ugliness with beauty, images of life next to death, a single poppy blooming in no-man's-land, visions of nature that somehow survive the worst of human nature. Sentimentalized blossoms so often outlast and even replace the stench of the dead and the vileness of war.[26]

One of the most intriguing themes revealed in Brewster's letters is his attitudes and actions regarding race and slavery. Brewster had voted for Abraham Lincoln in 1860 and embraced the Republican party's free labor and antislavery ideology. He had lived all his life in reform-minded Northampton and believed from the first giddy days of the war that he was fighting to save the Union and free the slaves. But Brewster was no radical abolitionist (their ranks were very small in the Union army), and he enjoyed mocking the piety and earnestness of reformers. His racial views were those of a sardonic, white workingman who believed that blacks were a backward if not an inferior race. As historians Bell Wiley and Joseph Glatthaar have shown, use of such terms as "nigger" and "darky" were very common in the letters of Union soldiers, making Brewster's language typical rather than exceptional in this regard.[27] But at the same time Brewster believed that slavery was evil, that a war against secession was inherently a war against racial bondage, and that out of the bloodshed would come a different society. Moreover, he seemed to have held these views earlier than most Union troops. Although his estimations of black character did not change much, wartime experience forced an interesting evolution in Brewster's attitude toward blacks.

During the autumn and winter of 1861–62 the status of slaves who escaped into Union lines remained ambiguous. Contradictory policies toward fugitive slaves were the cause of considerable controversy in the Union ranks, and Brewster's regiment was no exception. The insistence of Generals George B. McClellan and Henry W. Halleck that fugitive slaves be returned to their owners, as well as President Lincoln's pragmatic ambiguity on the issue, were rendered unworkable with time. Very early in the war, at Fortress Monroe, Virginia, Gen. Benjamin F. Butler declared the slaves who escaped to his lines "contraband of war," treating them as confiscated enemy property. The idea caught on as a moral and military imperative.[28]

Yet the slaves themselves were forcing a clearer settlement of this issue by their own courage and resolve. The Civil War was a conflict of such scale that its greatest lessons, collectively and individually, were being learned on the ground where abstractions must be converted into daily decisions. From Camp Brightwood on the outskirts of Washington, D.C., Brewster learned firsthand that many slaves were freeing themselves and converting the war's purpose. Slaves took "leg bail," Brewster wrote approvingly in November 1861. And in language that might have been fitting of a small-town, wartime abolitionist rally, he declared that "this war is playing the Dickens with slavery and if it lasts much longer will clear our Country's name of the vile stain and enable us to live in peace hereafter."[29] In such passages Brewster represented an attitude among white Northerners that, driven by the exigencies of war against the South, prompted Congress and Lincoln eventually to commit the nation to the reality of emancipation.

By December 1861 the Lincoln administration's policy toward blacks remained limited and conflicted. The president's annual message offered little hope to friends of the "contrabands"; he proposed only a plan to colonize escaped slaves and free blacks outside the country. From winter quarters, Brewster offered his own crude antislavery assessment of the situation. "We have got the President's message," he told his mother, "but I don't think it amounts to much he don't talk nigger enough, but its no use mincing the matter. Nigger has got to be talked and thoroughly talked to and I think niggers will come out of this scrape free."[30] In the common coin of camp and apparently back in Northampton as well, Brewster provided an example of the way in which racist language and antislavery ideology combined in the hearts and minds of Yankee soldiers. Brewster lacked eloquence when it came to the question of race, but in language that that great ironist in the White House would have fully understood, he argued unequivocally that the war should be prosecuted more vigorously against slavery.

Brewster spent his first winter at war intensely interested in the "contraband" issue. In January 1862, frustrated by how "slow" the war progressed, he complained that "it seems to be a war for the preservation of slavery more than anything else." Shortly after receiving his commission and setting up his new domestic quarters, Brewster took a seventeen-year-old runaway slave named David as his personal servant. Proud and possessive, he treated his "contraband" with a gushing paternalism. The young lieutenant took pride in relieving the Confederacy of this lone asset. "He was the only slave his master had," said Brewster, "and his master never will have him again if I can help it."[31] During the long winter months, the clandestine protection of his contraband from the former master's clutches became for Brewster the only war he had. But the contraband issue bitterly divided the Tenth Massachusetts, causing by March 1862 what Brewster called nearly "a state of mutiny" in the regiment. Brewster and his antislavery cohort (six contrabands were harbored in Company C alone) would lose this dispute to the proslavery officers in the regiment who determined to enforce a policy of exclusion. Some fugitives were tearfully returned to their waiting owners, while still others were spirited away toward Pennsylvania to an ambiguous fate. Brewster himself believed at one point that he would be charged and court-martialed for his resistance, and at another juncture claimed he was prepared to "resign." "I should hate to have to leave now just as the Regiment is going into active service," he wrote in March, "but I will never be instrumental in returning a slave to his master in any way shape or manner, I'll die first."[32] As Brewster describes this three-month-long dispute at Camp Brightwood, it has both the quality of tragic farce and of high seriousness. This little war within a war reveals in microcosm the much larger social revolution American society was about to undergo, whether it was prepared to confront it or not.

A self-described "free man" with a commission, the recognition-starved Brewster now saw himself as a liberator of his fellow man. As a soldier he was well trained in tactical maneuvers and eager for a taste of battle. As a man he had a yearning to belong to some kind of community. In his contraband Brewster may also have found a need to give and a form of companionship he could truly control. But Brewster and his contraband may have mutually gained a sense of freedom from their short relationship. The same letter that begins with Brewster appearing in his "new uniform" for the first time ends with his asking his mother to help him outfit his servant. "I wish I could get some of my old clothes to put on him," Brewster wrote, "especially my old overcoat. I do not suppose you will have any chance to send them, but if you should I wish you would . . . make a bundle of coat Pants O Coat and vest . . . send them along, and then I could rig him up so his master would hardly know him." Rejoicing in his acquisition of the contraband in another letter, Brewster described David as "quite smart for a nigger though he is quite slow." But he "is willing," Brewster continued, "and I think has improved a good deal since I got him. I have not heard anything of his master, and if I do I shan't give him up without a struggle." Out of sheer self-interest as well as moral concern, Brewster objectified and coddled his contraband. But one is reminded here of the relationship between Huck and Jim in *Huckleberry Finn*. Like Huck, Brewster ultimately had a "sound heart" when it came to the right of a slave to his freedom, and he too decided to "go to hell" rather than return fugitive slaves to bondage. "Without the presence of blacks," Ralph Ellison aptly wrote, Mark Twain's classic "could never have been written." Without "Nigger Jim," Huck's commitment to freedom could never have developed into the "moral center" of that novel. On a simpler and hidden level, without his "right smart nigger," Brewster might never have developed or even understood his own commitment to freedom. Brewster's struggle to free his "contraband" has the same ironic pattern as Huck's: acts of conscience mixed with adventure, moral revolt interrupting a life on a raft moving south. He never matched Huck's revelation that "you can't pray a lie," but Brewster's experience had forced him to clarify his beliefs and to understand much of what the war was about. In his own crude way, Brewster would grasp the meaning of Lincoln's haunting claim at the end of

1862 that "in giving freedom to the slave, we assure freedom to the free." Although much of his prejudice would remain intact, the former store clerk from Northampton had learned something valuable from his "contraband."[33]

After the Tenth Massachusetts returned home in June 1864, Brewster, anxious about civilian life, reenlisted under the auspices of the State of Massachusetts to be a recruiter of black troops in Norfolk, Virginia. Away from the front, living in a boarding house from July to November, Brewster could observe the war and society from a new perspective. He was merely one among a horde of recruiters who descended upon eastern Virginia and other parts of the upper South in 1864. Brewster quipped in frustration that "there are two agents to every man who will enlist." He frequently denigrated the very blacks he sought to recruit, commenting on their alleged propensity to "lie and steal" and their "shiftless" attitude toward work. But he seemed delighted at the presence of a black cavalry regiment that made the local "secesh" furious, and after holding back judgment, he finally praised the black troops who had "fought nobly" and filled the local hospitals with "their wounded and mangled bodies."[34] In Brewster's mind, like that of most white Americans, a full recognition of the dignity of blacks awaited their battlefield sacrifice. Brewster had come to know the folly of desperate heroism, but precisely such an expectation became the test of manhood for the black men he helped to recruit in that last anguished year of the war.

Unhappy and shiftless in his own way, feeling as though he were "living among strangers," and deeply ambivalent about what to do with the rest of his life, Brewster went about his business with an element of greed and very little zeal.[35] He boarded with a southern woman named Mrs. Mitchell, who had just taken the oath of allegiance to the Union. Her husband and one brother were in the Confederate army, while a second brother served in the Union navy. All the servants at the house, of course, were black and now "free." When Brewster, the Yankee conqueror and occupying officer, was not trying to find and spirit black men into the army, he spent time playing with Mrs. Mitchell's three small children or going to the market with his landlady's mother and a "darky girl." Such bizarre domestic tranquility in the midst of catastrophic civil war makes an unforgettable image. Moreover, images of death and maiming frequently appear in Brewster's last letters from the war; he writes of street "murders" committed in Norfolk contrasted with the killing in war, and his only use of the concept of "courage" was applied either to black troops or to the surgeons who volunteered to go fight a yellow-fever epidemic in North Carolina.[36] Living among a subdued enemy and quietly observing the revolution that Confederate defeat and black emancipation might bring, Brewster sat in a recruiting office reading and writing "love letters" for black women to and from their husbands at the front. This is what remained of his job and his war, and it was a remarkable vantage point.

Still patronizing toward the freedpeople, he nevertheless acknowledged their humanity and their influence. "We have to read thier [sic] letters from and write letters to thier husbands and friends at the front daily," Brewster observed, "so that I expect I shall be adept in writing love letters, when I have occasion to do so on my own account. they invariably commence (the married ones) with 'my dear loving husband,' and end with 'your ever loving wife until death.'" If we can imagine Brewster, sitting at a table with a lonely freedwoman, swallowing his prejudices toward blacks and women, and repeatedly writing or reciting the phrases "give my love to . . ." and "you Husband untall Death . . ." we can glimpse in this tiny corner of the war the enormous potential of the human transformations at work in 1864. Thousands of such quiet ironies—the Northampton store clerk turned soldier, recruiter, and clerical conduit for the abiding love among black folks that slavery could not destroy—helped produce what Lincoln referred to in his second inaugural address as the result so "fundamental and astounding."[37]

Brewster left the war for good in November 1864, and for a while he returned to working in a store. But by 1868 he must have written some love letters of his own, for he married Anna P. Williams, the sister of one of his friends in the Tenth. Charles and Anna would eventually have six children, some of whom achieved local prominence in western Massachusetts. By the mid-1870s Brewster had turned his prewar sense of failure into a steady sash, door, and paint business. By 1880 he bought one of the finest residences in Northampton, built three greenhouses, and opened a successful year-round florist business. Local friends remembered him as a man "of great independence of character." He remained an active Republican until the election of 1884 when, for reasons unknown, he supported the Democrat Grover Cleveland rather than James G. Blaine. Brewster became a financially successful Gilded Age businessman. The disdainful, insecure, ambitious soldier of the war letters became the old veteran and family man who grew flowers, speculated in land and other property, made a comfortable living, and actively participated in the GAR (the Grand Army of the Republic, the Union veterans organization). The soldier of 1864 who so feared civilian life had married well and done all right after all.[38]

By the 1880s, like most veterans, Brewster was ready for reconciliation with Confederate veterans. He seemed to love regimental reunions and other GAR activities. In October 1886 he attended Blue-Gray reunions at Gettysburg and Fredericksburg, writing to his children that "papa has had the grandest time he ever had in his life." Of the Confederate veterans, he could only marvel at how they "seem as glad to see us as though we were brothers or cousins at least." The tour of the Gettysburg battlefield "brings the fearful old days so fresh," wrote the veteran, but it also left him full of a survivor's awe and pride. The visit to the slopes where he had endured the battle of Chancellorsville was the "most glorious time," he reported, marred only by the regret that he did not get to see the "old long breastwork" at Spotsylvania. Partly as tourists, partly as icons of a refurbished martial ideal, partly just as old men searching for their more active and noble youth, and partly as "symbols of changelessness" in a rapidly industrializing age, veterans like Brewster discovered a heroic nostalgia in these reunions.[39] The former soldier who had so fervently sought a sense of community in the army could now truly belong in a society building monuments—and rapidly forgetting the reality of combat and the deep racial and ideological roots of the war.

Brewster died in October 1893 aboard the clipper ship *Great Admiral* in New York harbor, where his twenty-two-year-old daughter Mary Katherine was about to embark on an around-the-world voyage. Brewster had been the guest of the ship's captain, James Rowell, himself a Civil War veteran. The grief-stricken Mary Kate decided to stay on the voyage as planned. Secure in her possession, and prominent in her plans for work at sea, were her father's original war letters, which she intended to transcribe for publication. A young woman with literary ambitions and considerable skill, Mary Kate cherished her father's letters, which had all been written to her grandmother and aunts. To the end Brewster had an adoring female audience for his letters and his "war stories."[40]

As we imagine Mary Kate Brewster aboard ship somewhere in the Indian Ocean on her way to Australia, vicariously reliving her father's war experiences, we can also imagine American society distancing itself from and sentimentalizing the horror and the causes of the Civil War. By the 1890s the next generation—daughters and sons—were following their parents' lead in constructing an idealized national memory of the war, rooted in a celebration of veterans' valor that rarely included Brewster's horrifying image of the screaming soldier in the trench at Spotsylvania and preferred instead his descriptions of moonlit campgrounds and sun-drenched mornings on the march. Brewster had cursed and embraced war, hated and worshiped violence, condemned slavery and practiced racism. His interior struggle with his own values and with war itself was not the one best fitted to the emerging social memory of the Civil War nor the imagination of a young Victorian woman. But today, Brewster's experiences serve as another reminder of the recurring power of war to attract and destroy individuals, and to draw and repel the human imagination.

NOTES

This is a slightly modified version of the introductory essay for the book *When This Cruel War Is Over: The Civil War Letters of Charles Harvey Brewster* (Amherst: University of Massachusetts Press, 1992). Attempting a contribution to the social and gender history of the common soldier in the Civil War, the piece was reprinted, with the same title as used here, in *Divided Houses: Gender and the Civil War,* ed. Catherine Clinton and Nina Silber (New York: Oxford University, Press, 1993).

1. Paul Fussell, *The Great War in Modern Memory* (New York: Oxford University Press, 1975), 6.

2. Bell I. Wiley, *The Life of Billy Yank: The Common Soldier of the Union* (Baton Rouge: Louisiana State University Press, 1952), 15; Bell I. Wiley, *The Life of Johnny Reb: The Common Soldier in the Confederacy* (1943; reprint, Baton Rouge: Louisiana State University Press, 1978). For the growing literature on the social history of the common soldier and the Civil War era, see Maris A. Vinovskis, "Have Social Historians Lost the Civil War? Some Preliminary Demographic Speculations," *Journal of American History* (June 1989): 34–58; *Toward a Social History of the American Civil War: Exploratory Essays,* ed. Maris A. Vinovskis (New York: Cambridge University Press, 1990); Joseph T. Glatthaar, *The March to the Sea and Beyond: Sherman's Troops in the Savannah and Carolinas Campaigns* (New York: New York University Press, 1985); Joseph T. Glatthaar, *Forged in Battle: The Civil War Alliance of Black Soldiers and White Officers* (New York: Free Press, 1990); Reid Mitchell, *Civil War Soldiers: Their Expectations and Their Experiences* (New York: Viking, 1988); Phillip Shaw Paludan, *"A People's Contest": The Union and Civil War, 1861–1865* (New York: Harper and Row, 1988), 316–38; Randall G. Jimerson, *The Private Civil War: Popular Thought during the Sectional Conflict* (Baton Rouge: Louisiana State University Press, 1988); James I. Robertson Jr., *Soldiers Blue and Gray* (Columbia: University of South Carolina Press, 1988); Michael Fellman, *Inside*

War: The Guerrilla Conflict in Missouri during the American Civil War (New York: Oxford University Press, 1989); Warren Wilkinson, *Mother, May You Never See the Sights I Have Seen: The Fifty-Seventh Massachusetts Veteran Volunteers* (New York: Harper and Row, 1990); Michael Barton, *Goodmen: The Character of Civil War Soldiers* (University Park: Pennsylvania State University Press, 1981); Earl J. Hess, *Liberty, Virtue, and Progress: Northerners and Their War for the Union* (New York: New York University Press, 1985); and Marvin R. Cain, "A 'Face of Battle' Needed: An Assessment of Motives and Men in Civil War Historiography," *Civil War History* 28 (March 1982): 5–27.

3. *Hampshire Gazette and Courier* (Northampton, Mass.), April 23, 30, May 7, 14, June 11, 1861, Forbes Library, Northampton; Alfred S. Roe, *The Tenth Regiment Massachusetts Volunteer Infantry, 1861–1864* (Springfield, Mass.: Tenth Regiment Veterans Association, 1909), 378–84.

4. Roe, *Tenth Regiment,* 18–28.

5. *All for the Union: The Civil War Diary and Letters of Elisha Hunt Rhodes,* ed. Robert Hunt Rhodes (New York: Orion Books, 1991); Geoffrey C. Ward, with Ric Burns and Ken Burns, *The Civil War: An Illustrated History* (New York: Knopf, 1990). For the creation of the brigade in which the Tenth served, see Frank J. Welcher, *The Union Army, 1861–1865: Organization and Operations,* vol. 1, *The Eastern Theater* (Bloomington: Indiana University Press, 1989), 8. On March 13, 1862, Brewster's brigade became part of the Fourth Corps of the Army of the Potomac, and from September 1862 until the end of their service in June 1864 they were part of the Sixth Corps. Roe, *Tenth Regiment,* 318–19.

6. Roe, *Tenth Regiment,* 295. When Brewster's regiment returned to Springfield in June 1864, only 220 of the original nearly 1,000 men remained on active duty.

7. *The Brewster Genealogy, 1566–1907: A Record of the Descendants of William Brewster of the* Mayflower, *Ruling Elder of the Pilgrim Church Which Founded Plymouth Colony in 1620,* comp. and ed. Emma C. Brewster Jones (New York: Grafton Press, 1908), 2:868–69. On the ordinary soldier escaping from ordinary life, see Philip Caputo, *A Rumor of War* (New York: Holt, Rinehart Winston, 1977).

8. Brewster letters, June 15, July 12, and June 21, 1862, Charles Harvey Brewster Collection, Northampton Historical Society, Northampton, Mass.; hereafter cited as CHB letters, date. Some 210 Brewster letters survive, 193 as originals, and 17 as transcribed into journals by Mary Kate Brewster in 1893. The originals and the journals (where some letters contain erasures and embellishments) are housed at the Northampton Historical Society. This essay is based exclusively on original letters. On the importance of letters and connections to "home," see Reid Mitchell, "The Northern Soldier and His Community," in *Toward a Social History,* ed. Vinovskis, 78–92.

9. CHB letters, July 9, 1863.

10. Ibid., November 24, 10, 1861, September 22, November 6, 17, and December 14, 1861. See also November 21, 1861, where he describes himself as "cursed with ill luck all my life."

11. Ibid., January 9, 1862. Brewster was promoted to first lieutenant Septem-

ber 29, 1862, and as adjutant of the regiment December 1862. He was technically a staff officer, not a field officer.

12. Ibid., January 15, 1862.

13. Henry W. Parsons to Aunt Julia, September [?] 1861, Parsons Family Papers, Northampton Historical Society.

14. CHB letters, November 25, 1862, February 23, November 21, 1863. On the social distance between civilians and soldiers, see Mitchell, "The Northern Soldier," in *Toward a Social History*, ed. Vinovskis, 89; and Eric J. Leed, *No Man's Land: Combat and Identity in World War I* (New York: Cambridge University Press, 1979), 213.

15. CHB letters, April 3, 1864.

16. Ibid., June 15, 1864. For the cycles of selective memory among veterans, see Gerald Linderman, *Embattled Courage: The Experience of Combat in the Civil War* (New York: Free Press, 1987), 266–97. Brewster's wartime letters presaged what Linderman aptly calls the "militarization of thought and the purification of memory" (284). See also Leed, *No Man's Land*, 12–33.

17. Linderman, *Embattled Courage*, 7–110.

18. William Manchester, *Goodbye, Darkness: A Memoir of the Pacific War* (Boston: Little, Brown, 1979), 46–47. A growing literature exists on the questions of manhood, male tradition, and war-making. Helpful to me have been Linderman, *Embattled Courage;* E. Anthony Rotundo, "Body and Soul: Changing Ideals of American Middle-Class Manhood, 1770–1920," *Journal of Social History* (spring 1983): 23–38; Kim Townsend, "Francis Parkman and the Male Tradition," *American Quarterly* (spring 1986): 97–112; Peter G. Filene, *Him/Her/Self: Sex Roles in Modern America,* 69–112; and Edward O. Wilson, *On Human Nature* (Cambridge: Harvard University Press, 1978), 99–120. An important critique of Fussell's *Great War in Modern Memory* and useful to understanding what may be peculiarly male about the experience of and writing about war is Lynne Hanley, *Writing War: Fiction, Gender, and Memory* (Amherst: University of Massachusetts Press, 1991), 18–37.

19. CHB letters, May 24, 25, 27, 28, 29, 31, and July 27, 1862.

20. Stephen Crane, *The Red Badge of Courage* (New York: Avon, 1979), 39–40; CHB letters, December 15, 23, 1862.

21. CHB letters, April 30, May 26, 1864. From May 5 to 12, the Army of the Potomac suffered 32,000 casualties, killed, wounded, or missing. During the first seven weeks of Grant's campaign against Lee in Virginia northern casualties reached the appalling figure of 65,000, a daily cost in life and limb that Brewster's letters help document. These seven weeks also constitute almost exactly the final days of the enlistment of the Tenth Massachusetts, which was mustered out on June 22. These casualty figures were horrifying to northerners not only because they brought devastation to so many families in towns like Northampton but also because they offered no clear sign of an end to the war; Lee's lines in Virginia had not been broken as the siege of Petersburg began, though his casualties had been proportionately as high as Grant's. See James McPherson, *The Battle Cry of Freedom* (New York: Oxford University Press, 1988), 732, 741–42.

22. CHB letters, April 23, May 7, 1862. Aitken quoted in Fussell, *Great War,* 174.

23. CHB letters, June 2, 5, 12, 15, 21, and May 10, 1862. Some researchers may wish to follow the theme of Brewster's many physical maladies and the variety of medical treatments and drugs he endured.

24. John Keegan, *The Face of Battle: A Study of Agincourt, Waterloo, and the Somme* (New York: Viking, 1976), 35–45, 320–43.

25. CHB letters, July 30, 1863, May 11, 13, 15, 1864. Many of Bierce's stories would serve as comparisons, but see, for example, "A Horseman in the Sky" and "The Mocking-Bird" in *The Civil War Short Stories of Ambrose Bierce,* comp. Ernest J. Hopkins (Lincoln: University of Nebraska Press, 1970), 97–108.

26. CHB letters, October 23, September 25, 1861, May 21, 1862, and May 23, 26, 1864. Obituary, "The Death of Charles H. Brewster," *Daily Hampshire Gazette* (Northampton, Mass.), October 9, 1893. After the war, Brewster became the first successful professional florist in the upper Connecticut River Valley. One can only imagine how much the old soldier reflected on his deep memories of life and death in the fields of Virginia as he nurtured the perennials in his greenhouses during the 1880s.

27. See Wiley, *Life of Billy Yank,* 109–15; Glatthaar, *Forged in Battle,* 11–12.

28. See Dudley T. Cornish, *The Sable Arm: Black Troops in the Union Army, 1861–1865* (Lawrence: University Press of Kansas, 1956), 24–25; *Freedom: A Documentary History of Emancipation, 1861–1867,* series 2, *The Black Military Experience,* ed. Ira Berlin (New York: Cambridge University Press, 1982), 1–7. In August 1861 Lincoln countermanded the order of Gen. John C. Frémont that would have emancipated all slaves in Missouri. Sensitive about the disposition of the four border states remaining delicately in the Union and mindful of northern racism, the president resisted converting the war into an abolition crusade until 1862, when emancipation as policy and reality transformed the war's purpose.

29. CHB letters, November 17, 24, 1861.

30. Ibid., December 4, 1861.

31. Ibid., January 2, 15, 1862.

32. Ibid., March 4, 5, 8, 12, 1862.

33. Ibid., January 15, 23, February 9, 1862; Ralph Ellison, "What America Would Be Like without Blacks," in *Going to the Territory* (New York: Random House, 1986), 109; Mark Twain, *The Adventures of Huckleberry Finn* (1884; reprint, New York: Penguin, 1966), 282–83; and Abraham Lincoln, "Annual Message to Congress," December 1, 1862, in *The Collected Works of Abraham Lincoln,* ed. Roy P. Basler, 9 vols. (New Brunswick: Rutgers University Press, 1953–55), 5:537.

34. CHB letters, August 20, October 12, 1864. On recruiting black troops, see Glatthaar, *Forged in Battle,* 61–80; *Freedom,* ed. Berlin, 6–15. Brewster's appointment as a recruiter, signed by Gov. John A. Andrew, July 23, 1864, is in Brewster Family Papers, Sophia Smith Collection, Smith College, Northampton, Mass. Brewster was appointed assistant adjutant general on the staff of Col. J. B. Parsons.

35. CHB letters, September 16, August 30, 1864.

36. Ibid., August 4, October 5, 12, 1864. One of the murders Brewster described is that of a "colored barber," who, while jailed with three white sailors, was thrown to his death from a third-story window. A year earlier, in July 1863, as a

newly organized company of the U.S. Colored Troops marched through the streets of Norfolk, Virginia, led by their lieutenant, Anson L. Sanborn, Sanborn was assassinated by a prominent physician and secessionist. The physician was later executed, but the incident and others like it diminished recruiting efforts in the area for many months to come. On the Sanborn incident, see Glatthaar, *Forged in Battle*, 69. As Brewster described these "occasional murders" that relatively no one paid attention to, he concluded that "it is just the difference between a state of war and a state of peace" (CHB letters, October 12, 1864).

37. CHB letters, October 27, 1864. The two examples from a freedman's letter quoted here were not written by Brewster; they come from the Norfolk recruiting area in 1864. See letters by black soldier Rufus Wright, February 2, May 25, 1864, in *Freedom*, ed. Berlin, 661–63. Wright used the phrase "give my love to" eight times in these two short letters, forming the very kind of example that Brewster found so memorable and educative. Abraham Lincoln, "Second Inaugural Address," in *Collected Works*, ed. Basler, 8:333.

38. Brewster obituary, *Daily Hampshire Gazette*, October 9, 1893; Aunt Mary to Mary Kate Brewster, November 9, 1893, Brewster Family Papers, Sophia Smith Collection, Smith College. Brewster's real and personal estate was valued at approximately fifteen thousand dollars at his death in 1893, Administrator's Estate Inventory, filed October 26, 1893, Probate Court, Hampshire County, Northampton, Mass. Brewster's more than twenty land transactions are recorded in Register of Deeds, Hampshire County, Northampton, Mass.

39. CHB letters, to My Dear Children, October 7, 10, 11, 1886. Linderman, *Embattled Courage*, 299. On the GAR see also Stuart McConnell, "Who Joined the Grand Army? Three Case Studies in the Construction of Union Veteranhood, 1866–1900," in *Toward a Social History*, ed. Vinovskis, 139–70.

40. Mary Katherine Brewster, Log Book [diary], 1893–94, 3–7, 19, 21 26–27; Mary Kate Brewster to Gertrude, January 9, 1894, Sydney, Australia, Brewster Family Papers, Sophia Smith Collection, Smith College; Brewster obituary, Mary K. Brewster obituary, *Daily Hampshire Gazette*, October 9, 1898, January 7 1951. Mary Kate Brewster wrote articles for local Massachusetts newspapers while at sea and later in life became a playwright, theater critic, and local Northampton author. For the full texture and significance of Brewster's letters, see Brewster, *When This Cruel War Is Over: The Civil War Letters of Charles Harvey Brewster*, ed. David W. Blight (Amherst: University of Massachusetts Press, 1992).

Abraham Lincoln and Frederick Douglass

A Relationship in Language, Politics, and Memory

In 1937 a former slave, Cornelius Garner, was interviewed at the age of ninety-one. Asked if he had fought in the Civil War, Garner replied to his black interviewer: "Did I fight in de war? Well if I hadn' you wouldn' be sittin' dere writin' today." He described the corner in his native Norfolk, Virginia, where slave auctions used to be conducted on New Year's Day. "Dat day, New Yeah's Day," said Garner, "should be kept by all de colored people. Dat is de day o' freedom. An' day ought to 'member Frederick Douglass too. Frederick Douglass tol' Abe Lincun, 'Give de black man guns an' let him fight.' Abe Lincun say, 'Ef I give him gun, when he come to battle, he run.' Frederick Douglass say, 'Try him an' you'll win de war.' Abe said, 'Alright, I try him.'"[1] Garner's story begins to guide us to the relationship between Abraham Lincoln and Frederick Douglass, in both history and memory.

In addressing the relationship between Abraham Lincoln and Frederick Douglass, we confront two towering personalities of American history—both, indeed, have become mythic figures in the deepest sense of that word, historical actors who because of circumstances and as craftsmen of language have transcended their own time, again and again, to serve various kinds of felt needs in our own time. Both have gone in and out of favor, of historical consciousness, serving as lodestars for current causes in one era, and then vilified or ignored in another.[2] Both have been asked to measure up to every kind of contemporary imperative. What would Lincoln do now? Where are the Lincolns in our time? Did Lincoln really want to free the slaves? Was his racism an impediment to real reform, or was he the master of timing and content in the American emancipation? What would Douglass do today? What would Douglass think of affirmative action? Would he support "reparations" for slavery? Did Douglass's integrationism make him a prophet of the late twentieth century's revolutions in race relations and civil rights? Or was he merely an American patriot, who fell out of touch with his own people, who enjoyed creating his own symbolic and heroic persona in autobiography after autobiography? To which Lincoln do people turn or to which Douglass when they feel the need for the power of transcendent, mythic leadership? In which places in their magnificent rhetoric do we find our own inspirations for what it means to be an American at the beginning of the twenty-first century? Where do we turn, especially, for guidance in our ongoing racial predicament? What did these two have in common and how did they differ during the crisis of the Civil War era? Did they make history together or at odds? How did the lives and ideas of the former slave who dreamed and wrote his way to freedom and the poor farmer's son who dreamed and wrote his way to the presidency converge?

Comparative biography is a risky business, but often irresistible. Both Lincoln and Douglass grew up in genuine poverty, albeit Douglass as human chattel and Lincoln amid the desperation of poor farmers and a kind of wage slavery on the prairie frontier. Both received strokes of good fortune in their rise from obscurity, and both possessed great gifts of intellect, ambition, and a love of books and the music of words. In 1830, when Douglass was twelve years old, he discovered Caleb Bingham's *Columbian Orator,* an elocution manual and a reader for schoolchildren consisting of prose, verse, plays, and especially political speeches from classical antiquity and the Enlightenment era. This "rich treasure" of a book, with its obvious antislavery tone, was crucial in the young slave's dreams of liberation, both physically and through language.[3] Just a year later, in his first winter in New Salem on the Illinois prairie (1831–32), the twenty-one-year-old Lincoln studied the same readings in the *Columbian Orator*—it was among the first books that Lincoln collected and cherished. The two men were destined to develop different temperaments: the former slave would become a radical abolitionist who would have to learn a begrudging pragmatism about the prospects of his people in slaveholding America; the self-taught lawyer-politician who would see the world in pragmatic, legal terms would have to learn to convert his instinctive gradualism about social change and his racial prejudices into the courage to use his power as president to free slaves in the midst of total war in order to save the nation he loved.

One of the most fascinating aspects of each man was his capacity for intellectual growth and change, how each could convert contradiction into hope. On February 12, 1959, in his famous speech eulogizing Lincoln at a joint session of Congress (the Lincoln sesquicentennial), Carl Sandburg rhapsodized about Lincoln in interesting terms. "Not often in the story of mankind," said the poet, "does a man arrive on earth who is both steel and velvet, who is as hard as rock and soft as drifting fog, who holds in his heart and mind the paradox of terrible storm and peace unspeakable." Similarly, W. E. B. Du Bois in 1922 reflected in unforgettable terms on Lincoln's capacity to grow. "I love him," wrote Du Bois, "not because he was perfect, but because he was not and yet triumphed. . . . The world is full of folk whose taste was educated in the gutter. The world is full of people born hating and despising their fellows. To these I love to say: See this man. He was one of you and yet became Abraham Lincoln." Like Sandburg, albeit in different tones, Du Bois was drawn to Lincoln's embodiment of paradox. "There was something left," he said of Lincoln, "so that at the crisis he was big enough to be inconsistent—cruel, merciful, peace-loving, a fighter, despising Negroes and letting them fight and vote, protecting slavery, and freeing slaves. He was a man—a big, inconsistent, brave man."[4] How Lincoln and Douglass, these two men of paradox, found each other during the country's crisis is an important American story not yet fully told. In Douglass's case he didn't so much *embody* paradox as much as he *symbolized* it. His life stands across the nineteenth century as an emblem of the worst and the best in the American spirit. We return to Douglass's story because it has so much to teach us about that journey from slavery to freedom, a soul nearly lost and then found.

On March 4, 1865, Frederick Douglass attended President Abraham Lincoln's second inauguration. Standing in the crowd, Douglass heard Lincoln declare slavery the "cause" and emancipation the "result" of the Civil War. Over the crisp air he heard Lincoln's determination that to win the war "every drop of blood drawn with the lash shall be paid by another drawn with sword."[5] Four years earlier, and many times in between, Douglass had dreamed of writing that speech for Lincoln. That the president himself wrote it in those tragic days of spring 1865 is a testament to the power of events, to Lincoln's own moral fiber, and to the political and rhetorical bond he shared with Douglass.

Douglass attended the inaugural reception that evening at the Executive Mansion. At first denied entrance by two policemen, Douglass was admitted only when the president himself was notified. Weary of a lifetime of such racial rejections, Douglass was immediately set at ease by Lincoln's cordial greeting: "Here comes my friend Douglass," said the president. Lincoln asked Douglass what he thought of the day's speech. Douglass demurred, urging the president to attend to his host of visitors. But Lincoln insisted, telling his black guest: "There is no man in the country whose opinion I value more than yours." "Mr. Lincoln," replied the former slave, "that was a sacred effort."[6] We can only guess at the thrill in Douglass's heart, knowing that the cause he had so long pleaded—a sanctioned war to destroy slavery and potentially to reinvent the American republic around the principle of racial equality—might now come to fruition. He could fairly entertain the belief that he and Lincoln, the slaves and the nation, were walking that night into a new history.

But nothing during the early months of Reconstruction came easily, especially in the wake of Lincoln's assassination at the dawn of peace. In her grief, and with the assistance of her personal aide, Elizabeth Keckley, Mary Todd Lincoln sent mementos to special people. Among the recipients of some of the president's canes were the black abolitionist Henry Highland Garnet and a White House servant, William Slade. But to Douglass Mrs. Lincoln sent the president's "favorite walking staff" (on display today at Cedar Hill, Douglass's home in Washington, D.C.). In his remarkable letter of reply Douglass assured the First Lady that he would forever possess the cane as an "object of sacred interest," not only for himself but also because of Mr. Lincoln's "humane interest in the welfare of my whole race."[7] In this expression of gratitude, Douglass evoked the enduring symbolic bond between the sixteenth president and African Americans, a relationship with a complicated and important history, the latest chapter of which is now represented by an ongoing scholarly and pedagogical debate over who and what really freed the slaves in the Civil War.

Douglass's relationship with Lincoln had not always been so warm. Indeed, Douglass's attitude toward Lincoln moved from cautious support in 1860 to outrage in 1861–62 and eventually to respect and admiration in 1863–65. At the outset of the war Douglass wanted precisely what Lincoln did not want: a "remorseless revolutionary struggle" that would make black freedom indispensable to saving the

Union. In 1861–62 Douglass attacked the administration's policy of returning fugitive slaves to their owners. At one point he referred to Lincoln as "the most dangerous advocate of slave-hunting and slave-catching in the land." In September 1861 Douglass denounced Lincoln's revocation of Gen. John C. Frémont's unauthorized emancipation order in Missouri. In 1862–63 he was offended by the administration's plans for colonization of the freedpeople. Indeed, nothing disappointed Douglass as much as the president's August 1862 meeting with a black delegation at the White House, at which Lincoln told his guests that "we [the two races] should be separated" and that the only hope for equality rested in their emigration to a new land. Douglass reprinted Lincoln's remarks in his newspaper and penned his harshest criticism ever of the president, calling him an "itinerant colonization lecturer" and a "genuine representative of American prejudice and Negro hatred."[8]

But much changed in Douglass's estimate of Lincoln with the advent of the Emancipation Proclamation and the policy of recruiting black soldiers in 1863. As the war expanded in scale and purpose, Lincoln and Douglass began to move toward more of a shared ideological vision of its meaning. On August 10, 1863, Douglass visited Washington, D.C., for the first time and met with Lincoln for a frank discussion of discriminations practiced against black troops. Lincoln said he understood the anguish over unequal pay for black men but considered it a "necessary concession" in order to achieve the larger aim of getting blacks into uniform. Although they did not agree on all issues, Douglass came away from this meeting impressed with Lincoln's forthrightness and respectful of the president's political skills. Douglass relished opportunities to tell of his first meeting with Lincoln. "I felt big there," he told a lecture audience, describing how secretaries admitted him to Lincoln's office ahead of a long line of office-seekers. Disarmed, even awed, by Lincoln's directness, Douglass remembered that the president looked him in the eye and said: "Remember this . . . remember that Milliken's Bend, Port Hudson, and Fort Wagner are recent events; and . . . were necessary to prepare the way for this very proclamation of mine." (All were battles in which blacks had distinguished themselves.) For the first time, Douglass expressed a personal identification with Lincoln. The "rebirth" of the nation about which Lincoln spoke so famously at Gettysburg in November 1863 had long been Douglass's favorite metaphor as well. Lincoln had wished for a shorter war, one that did not necessitate the full conquest of the South—a "result," as he put it in the second inaugural address, "less fundamental and astounding."[9] He would rather have left emancipation to the gradual work of history and statesmanship. But the reality of the war, of the wave of black freedom surging in front of and behind Union armies, made Lincoln the emancipator in the timing and manner that was eventually his own choice. Was Lincoln a reluctant or a willing emancipator? The best answer is, both.

By the end of 1863 Lincoln and Douglass spoke from virtually the same script, one of them with the elegance and restraint of a statesman; the other, the fiery tones of a prophet. One spoke with an eye on legality and public opinion, the other as though he were the national evangelist. In his annual message of December 8, 1863, Lincoln declared that "the policy of emancipation . . . gave to the future a new aspect." The nation was engaged in a "new reckoning" in which it might become "the home of freedom disenthralled, regenerated, enlarged." Lincoln's language makes a striking comparison to a speech Douglass delivered many times across the North in the winter of 1863–64. In "The Mission of the War," Douglass declared that however long the "shadow of death" cast over the land, Americans should not forget the moral "grandeur" of the struggle. "It is the manifest destiny of this war," he announced, "to unify and reorganize the institutions of the country," and thereby give the scale of death its "sacred significance." "The mission of this war," Douglass concluded, "is National regeneration."[10] Together, Lincoln and Douglass had provided the subjunctive and declarative voices of the second American Revolution—and by the last year of the war, they were nearly one and the same. Both had come to interpret the war as the nation's apocalyptic *regeneration*.

In the summer of 1864, with the war at a bloody stalemate in Virginia, Lincoln's reelection was in jeopardy and Douglass's support of him temporarily waned. He briefly considered supporting John C. Frémont's candidacy to unseat Lincoln in the Republican party. But in August, Lincoln invited Douglass to the White House for their extraordinary second meeting. The president was under heavy pressure from all sides: Copperheads condemned him for pursuing an abolitionist war, while abolitionists sought to replace him with the more radical Fremont. Lincoln was worried that the war might end without complete victory and the end of slavery, so he sought Douglass's advice. Lincoln had drafted a letter, denying that he was standing in the way of peace and declaring that he could not sustain a war to destroy slavery if Congress did not will it. Douglass urged Lincoln not to publish the letter and ultimately, because of events and perhaps Douglass's advice, he never did.[11]

Even more important, Lincoln asked Douglass to lead a scheme reminiscent of John Brown and Harpers Ferry. Concerned that if he were not reelected and the Democrats pursued a negotiated, proslavery peace, Lincoln, according to Douglass, wanted "to get more of the slaves within our lines." Douglass went North and organized some twenty-five agents who were willing to work at the front. In a letter to Lincoln on August 29, 1864, Douglass outlined his plan for a "band of scouts" channeling slaves northward. Douglass was not convinced that this plan was fully "practicable," but he was ready to serve. Because military fortunes had shifted dramatically with the fall of Atlanta, this government-sponsored Underground Railroad never materialized. But how remarkable this episode must have been to both Douglass and Lincoln as they realized they were working together now to accomplish the very "revolution" that had separated them ideologically in 1861. Garry Wills has argued that Lincoln performed a "verbal coup" that "revolutionized the revolution" at Gettysburg.[12] By 1864 that performance reflected a shared vision of the meaning of the war. Ideologically, Douglass had become Lincoln's alter ego, his stalking horse and minister of propaganda, the intellectual godfather of the Gettysburg address and the second inaugural address.

With time Douglass would contribute mightily to the creation of some of the Lincoln mythology. Douglass understood as well as anyone how necessary Lincoln's image was to sustaining the freedom and fledgling equality of his people forged in the war and early years of Reconstruction. He was fond of pointing (as Du Bois would later) to Lincoln's example in speaking of the educative nature of the war. "If he did not control events," Douglass said of Lincoln in a December 1865 speech, "he had the wisdom to be instructed by them. When he no longer could withstand the current, he swam with it." The idealist in Douglass saw this educative feature of the war as the bridge from wartime emancipation and black enlistment to peacetime racial democracy, but the realist in him knew that this final goal could only be reached through power politics, against a resurgent racism, an instinctive American constitutional conservatism, embittered war memories on both sides, and on behalf of a needy and largely illiterate population of former slaves. And all this would happen, of course, after Lincoln was gone. But Lincoln's symbol was extraordinarily useful to blacks, and no one understood this better than Douglass. Indeed, Douglass would demonstrate, and black communities would follow his lead through the decades, that for no other group was it more useful or important to "get right with Lincoln" than African Americans.[13]

Douglass spent much of his postwar life (he lived until 1895) trying to preserve an emancipationist-abolitionist memory of the Civil War. In a speech delivered in the wake of the assassination (probably in June 1865), Douglass said that "no class of people . . . have a better reason for lamenting the death of Abraham Lincoln, and for desiring to . . . perpetuate his memory, than have the Colored people." Douglass complained that at some of the funeral parades blacks had been excluded from public mourning. In this emotional and transformative moment just after the war's end, the former slave paid a moving tribute to Lincoln. "What was Abraham Lincoln to the Colored people, and they to him," he asked. "As compared to the long line of his predecessors, many of whom were merely the . . . servile instruments of the Slave Power, Abraham Lincoln, while unsurpassed in his devotion to the welfare of the white race, was in a sense hitherto without example, emphatically, the black man's President: the first to show any respect to their rights as men." On any Lincoln monument, said Douglass, blacks demanded their part in expressing "love and gratitude."[14]

What did Douglass mean here in 1865? Well, he meant what he said. But the context is crucial. In this postassassination speech—before Reconstruction policies had taken shape, and in the national confrontation with martyrdom—Douglass was flushed with hope. In describing the results of the war, Douglass saw a whole new national inheritance. "Henceforth," he declared, "we have a new date, a new era for our great Republic. Henceforth, a new account is opened between the government and the people of the United States. Henceforth, this is to be a . . . common country of all for all." As he had so often done in the previous four years, Douglass saw the war in apocalyptic and rejuvenating terms, and he converted Lincoln's death into his own kind of ode to joy. "The storm cloud has burst," he announced, "and sent down its bolt, and has left the blue sky above, calm and bright as when the morning stars sang together for joy!" Douglass went on in this remarkable speech to proclaim the "inevitability" of the war and all its suffering as the necessary historical means by which a new American republic would be conceived. It was within this millennial conception of history that Douglass found Lincoln's appointed place. He honored the president not only as a real individual but also as a historical actor performing within the logic of history. Douglass employed the refrain "under his rule" to declare a litany of ways Lincoln expanded freedom and saved the Union. "Under his rule," shouted Douglass, blacks "saw millions of their brethren proclaimed free and invested with the right to defend their freedom. Under his rule, they saw the Confederate states—that boldest of all conspiracies against the just rights of human nature, broken to pieces." To Douglass, epochal events were "the great teachers of mankind."[15] Lincoln was thus an emancipator of black people, but so were the tides of history itself in which Lincoln had found himself swept along. Douglass understood that blacks would need Lincoln dearly if they were to hold on to the revolution of 1863. A martyred Lincoln would be even more trusted than the living one; dead, he could never disappoint the cause of black equality.

In no other speech did Douglass address Lincoln's place in Civil War and African American memory so poignantly as at the unveiling of the Freedmen's Memorial Monument in Washington, D.C.'s, Lincoln Park in April 1876. The Freedmen's Memorial speech is too easily dismissed as merely eulogistic or particularly negative. Attended by President Grant, his cabinet, the Supreme Court justices, and many members of the House and Senate, the ceremony was as impressive as the bright spring day, which was declared a holiday by a joint session of Congress. After a reading of the Emancipation Proclamation and the unveiling of the statue (which Douglass later admitted he did not like because "it showed the Negro on his knees"), Douglass took the podium as orator of the day. Here again, context is nearly all: in 1876, the centennial year of American independence, most of the former Confederate states were back under white Democratic control; the civil and political rights of blacks were in great jeopardy; and a new legacy of terror and violence hung over a decade of embittered Reconstruction. That apocalyptic ode to joy he had sung to the martyred Lincoln in 1865 hardly fit the scene of 1876.[16]

No black speaker had ever had an audience quite like this. The government itself was listening to the black orator instruct them on the meaning of Lincoln to African Americans. His address included strong doses of the rail-splitter Lincoln image, the "plebeian" who rose through honesty, common sense, and the hand of God to become the "great liberator." But Douglass spoke with blunt honesty for such a ceremonial occasion, and in words that have rung down through time and been put to many uses. "Abraham Lincoln was not . . . either our man or our model," declared Douglass. "In his interests . . . in his habits of thought, and in his prejudices, he was a white man." Douglass did not make everyone comfortable in the sentiment of a monument unveiling. "He was preeminently the white man's president, entirely devoted to the welfare of white men." Douglass admitted that in the first year of the war, Lincoln would have sacrificed black freedom to save the Union. And in famous phrases, he spoke directly to his distinguished white audience: "You are the children of Abraham Lincoln. We are at best only his step-children; children by adoption, children by forces of circumstances and necessity."[17]

But it was Lincoln's growth to the moment of truth that most occupied Douglass in this remarkable address. He also understood that the occasion was a moment to forge national memory and practice civil religion. Through most of the speech, Douglass spoke to and for blacks (the monument had been commissioned and paid for almost entirely by blacks). But the monument was not only to Lincoln but also to the *fact* of emancipation. The occasion honored Lincoln, but Douglass equally stressed the events that transpired "under his rule and in due time." Most important, in contributing to the Lincoln myth and in commemorating emancipation, Douglass was staking a claim to nationhood and citizenship for blacks at this sensitive, even desperate, moment of the spring of 1876. "We stand today at the national center," he announced, "to perform something like a national act." Douglass struck clear notes of civil religion as he described the "stately pillars and majestic dome of the Capitol" as "our church" and rejoiced that "for the first time in the history of our people, and in the history of the whole American people, we join in this high worship." Douglass was trying to make Lincoln mythic and therefore useful to the cause of black equality, but the primary significance of the Freedmen's Memorial speech lies in its concerted attempt to forge a place for blacks in national memory. "When now it shall be said that the colored man is soulless . . . ," Douglass concluded, "when the foul reproach of ingratitude is hurled at us, and it is attempted to scourge us beyond the range of human brotherhood, we may calmly point to the monument we have this day erected to the memory of Abraham Lincoln."[18] What Lincoln himself had called the "mystic chords of memory" as a source of devotion to the Union, Douglass now claimed as the rightful inheritance of blacks as well. He did so through language, the only secure means he possessed, and the one thing he had most in common with Lincoln.

Although Douglass served up his share of Lincoln legend over time, he never spoke publicly about the sixteenth president without a political purpose that served the cause of black freedom and civil rights. At age seventy-five, on February 13, 1893, at a Lincoln birthday celebration in Brooklyn, New York, before an audience of three hundred prominent Republicans, Douglass delivered a speech called "Abraham Lincoln: The Great Man of Our Century." With a "fine oil painting of the martyred President" hanging in the front of the dining hall, Douglass offered up a "reminiscence" of Lincoln designed to please his fellow Republicans. In this atmosphere of mystic hero worship, Douglass called Lincoln "godlike" and the greatest American who "ever stood or walked upon the continent." Douglass placed Lincoln in the line of classic heroes, those who had been tested by travail and led nations through their "darkest hours." "The time to see a great captain is not when the wind is fair and the sea is smooth," said Douglass, "and the man in the cross-trees . . . can safely sing out, 'all is well.'" Because he had taken the country through its worst storm, Lincoln was "such a captain" and a "hero worthy of your highest worship."[19]

This image of the savior Lincoln was a common theme in Lincoln oratory. But Douglass put it to his own ends. "I had the good fortune to know Abraham Lincoln personally and peculiarly," Douglass proclaimed. The "peculiar" part, of course, was as the black man welcomed at the White House without racist pretension. Douglass rehearsed his two official meetings with the president and even hinted that he had been "invited to tea" at the Soldiers' Home, the Lincoln family's summer retreat in Washington, on another occasion. This was Douglass's way of bringing attention to his own prominence and pride of place in history, but it was also a commentary on the racism so deep in human relationships all over American society. Douglass was fond of using Lincoln's ability to "make me at ease" as a metaphor for what race relations among equals could be in a society that might one day transcend its racial theories and habits. In this remembrance of Lincoln, Douglass further declared that he had never really witnessed the famed humorous side of Lincoln. He met only the sad and "earnest" visage. Almost anticipating Sandburg and other artists to follow, Douglass remembered Lincoln with a poet's sensibility: "The dimmed light in his eye, and the deep lines in his strong American face, told plainly the story of the heavy burden of care that weighed upon his spirit. I could as easily dance at a funeral as to jest in the presence of such a man." All this prepared his audience for a strong dose of martyrdom as the speech neared its conclusion. Douglass remembered walking in the mud of Pennsylvania Avenue behind Lincoln's carriage on the day of his second inauguration, a deep "foreboding" in his mind about plots to murder the president. And then, in a deft stroke, he acknowledged all the forms of criticism Lincoln withstood as a transition to quoting the strongest antislavery lines from the second inaugural address ("If God wills that it [the war] continue until all the wealth piled by the bondman's two hundred and fifty years of toil shall be sunk, and until every drop of blood drawn by the lash shall be paid by another drawn by the sword . . . the judgments of the Lord are true and righteous altogether."). Such inspiration of spirit and language, Douglass claimed, he had never before witnessed. "There seemed at the time to be in the man's soul," declared Douglass, "the united souls of all Hebrew prophets."[20]

Douglass loved the opportunity to match Old Testament wits with his dead friend and symbol. As both friend and symbol, and eventual antislavery prophet, Lincoln had grown immeasurably with time in Douglass's own imagination, and in that of much of American society. Douglass never missed a chance to make Lincoln mythic and useful; he also relished moments to declare his genuine admiration for a man with whom he shared so much historically, ideologically, even spiritually. At the end of the 1893 speech, Douglass contended that Lincoln's assassination was the "natural outcome of a war for slavery." And this Lincoln the liberator was precisely the national memory Douglass used to remind his stalwart Republican audience that in their own day the United States government would exercise "no power . . . to protect the lives and liberties of American citizens in any of our own Southern states from barbarous, inhuman, and lawless violence."[21] Ever the embittered ironist, and even as an after-dinner speaker in the club of his friends, Douglass enlisted Lincoln in the fight against lynching.

During the final decade of Douglass's life, he lived in a large house called Cedar Hill in Washington, D.C. As one entered the front door of Cedar Hill, in the public parlor to the right, immediately visible on the opposite wall, hung a portrait of Lincoln. It was the first symbolic object any visitor saw in a home filled with remembrances of the antislavery struggle and the Civil War era, and it still hangs there today. Douglass's Lincoln on the wall was more than an obligatory icon to impress guests. It was perhaps Douglass's statement that if Abraham Lincoln had not freed the slaves (which of course Douglass knew better than anyone was a complicated proposition), then the United States had not done so either. And if the nation had not forged emancipation out of civil war, then African Americans would have had no future in America. In Lincoln's image on the wall, Douglass could claim, the nation might continue to find a new narrative of its history and its destiny. On almost any occasion Douglass could both honor and appropriate Lincoln. The Lincoln that Douglass fashioned into his lifelong rhetorical, and even visual, companion was an endless storehouse of memory and a legacy to be used as a weapon against the forces of darkness.

When news of Lincoln's assassination reached Rochester on April 13, 1865, Douglass had just returned from a lecture tour and witnessing great joy in several cities at the war's ending. He shared the shock of fellow northerners as a springtime of relief turned overnight into horror and mourning. A throng of Rochester citizens gathered at city hall, as Douglass remembered, "not knowing what to do in the agony of the hour." Called upon to speak, Douglass described himself as "stunned and overwhelmed." "I had . . . made many speeches there [Rochester] which had . . . touched the hearts of my hearers," he recalled, "but never to this day was I brought into such close accord with them. We shared in common a terrible calamity, and this 'touch of nature made us' more than countrymen, it made us Kin."[22]

Douglass would continue to write brilliantly and honestly about the necessity and the struggle of African Americans to sustain their sense of kinship with white Americans and with Abraham Lincoln. But history, with Douglass and Lincoln indispensably bound, had forged the possibility of such a national kinship—a brave dream we are still trying to achieve.

NOTES

This essay was first delivered at the Abraham Lincoln Institute of the Mid-Atlantic, Fourth Annual Symposium, Saturday, March 24, 2001, Smithsonian Museum of American History. This expanded verison was delivered as the tenth annual Frank Klement lecture at Marquette University, October 8, 2001, and published as a pamphlet on that occasion by Marquette University Press.

1. Cornelius Garner, interviewed May 18, 1937, in *Weevils in the Wheat: Interviews with Virginia Ex-Slaves*, ed. Charles L. Perdue Jr., Thomas E. Barden, and Robert K. Phillips (Bloomington: Indiana University Press, 1976), 102–4.

2. On Lincoln and American memory, see Merrill D. Peterson, *Lincoln in American Memory* (New York: Oxford University Press, 1994); and Barry Schwartz, *Abra-*

ham *Lincoln and the Forge of National Memory* (Chicago: University of Chicago Press, 2000). On Douglass and memory, see Waldo E. Martin Jr., "Images of Frederick Douglass in the Afro-American Mind: The Recent Black Freedom Struggle," in *Frederick Douglass: New Literary and Historical Essays,* ed. Eric J. Sundquist (Cambridge, Eng.: Cambridge University Press, 1990).

3. See *The Columbian Orator,* comp. Caleb Bingham, ed. David W. Blight, bicentennial ed. (New York: New York University Press, 1998), introduction. For a comparative treatment of Douglass and Lincoln, see Christopher Breiseth, "Lincoln and Frederick Douglass: Another Debate," *Illinois State Historical Society Journal* 68 (1975): 9–26. For a very critical approach to Lincoln's views on race and slavery, see Lerone Bennett Jr., *Forced into Glory: Abraham Lincoln's White Dream* (Chicago: Johnson Publishing, 2000). For a more favorable approach to Lincoln's role as an emancipator and as commander in chief, see the essays in James M. McPherson, *Abraham Lincoln and the Second American Revolution* (New York: Oxford University Press, 1991).

4. Sandburg quoted in Peterson, *Lincoln in American Memory,* 371; Du Bois, "Abraham Lincoln," *Crisis,* May 1922, and "Lincoln Again," *Crisis,* September 1922, both in *W. E. B. Du Bois: Writings* (New York: Library of America, 1986), 1196, 1198.

5. *The Collected Works of Abraham Lincoln,* ed. Roy P. Basler, 9 vols. (New Brunswick: Rutgers University Press, 1953–55), 7:332–33.

6. Frederick Douglass, *The Life and Times of Frederick Douglass, Written by Himself* (1881; reprint, New York: Collier Books, 1962), 365–66.

7. See Benjamin Quarles, *Lincoln and the Negro* (New York: Oxford University Press, 1962), 247–48; and Benjamin Quarles, *Frederick Douglass* (New York: Atheneum, 1968), 220. The letter is from Frederick Douglass to Mrs. Abraham Lincoln, Rochester, N.Y., August 17, 1865, Gilder Lehrman Collection, Pierpont Morgan Library, New York.

8. "The Inaugural Address," *Douglass Monthly,* April 1861, in *The Life and Writings of Frederick Douglass,* ed. Philip S. Foner, 5 vols. (New York: International Publishers, 1952), 3:76; Lincoln, "Address on Colonization to a Deputation of Negroes," in *Collected Works,* ed. Basler, 5:370–75; "The President and His Speeches," *Douglass Monthly,* September 1862, in *Life and Writings of Frederick Douglass,* ed. Foner, 3:267–70. On Douglass and the colonization issue see David W. Blight, *Frederick Douglass' Civil War: Keeping Faith in Jubilee* (Baton Rouge: Louisiana State University Press, 1989), 122–47.

9. Douglass to George Luther Stearns, August 12, 1863, Abraham Barker Papers, Historical Society of Pennsylvania, Philadelphia; Douglass, *Life and Times,* 346–50; Douglass, "Our Work Is Not Done," speech delivered at the annual meeting of the American Anti-Slavery Society, Philadelphia, December 3–4, 1863, in *Life and Writings of Frederick Douglass,* ed. Foner, 3:383; Lincoln, "Second Inaugural Address," in *Collected Works,* ed. Basler, 7:333.

10. Lincoln, "Annual Message to Congress," December 8, 1863, in *Collected Works,* ed. Basler, 7:49–51, 53; Douglass, "The Mission of the War," delivered in late 1863 and throughout 1864, in *Life and Writings of Frederick Douglass,* ed. Foner, 3:401.

11. See Blight, *Frederick Douglass' Civil War,* 183–84.

12. Douglass to Lincoln, August 29, 1864, in *Life and Writings of Frederick Douglass,* ed. Foner, 3:405–6. The best record of this meeting is Douglass to Theodore Tilton, October 15, 1864, in ibid., 3:422–24. Garry Wills, *Lincoln at Gettysburg: The Words That Remade America* (New York: Simon and Schuster, 1992), 38, 40.

13. Douglass, "Abraham Lincoln—A Speech," December 1865, in Frederick Douglass Papers, Library of Congress (LC), reel 14; David Donald, "Getting Right with Lincoln," in *Lincoln Reconsidered: Essays on the Civil War Era* (1947; reprint, New York: Vintage Books, 1956), 3–18.

14. Speech on Abraham Lincoln (on some pages, titled "On Death of A. Lincoln"), probably June 1865, Washington, D.C., Douglass Papers, LC, reel 14.

15. Ibid.

16. See Blight, *Frederick Douglass' Civil War,* 227–28.

17. "Oration in Memory of Abraham Lincoln," delivered at the unveiling of the Freedmen's Memorial, Lincoln Park, Washington, D.C., April 14, 1876, in *Life and Writings of Frederick Douglass,* ed. Foner, 4:310–12.

18. Ibid., 4:314, 317–19.

19. "Abraham Lincoln: The Great Man of Our Century," address delivered in Brooklyn, N.Y., February 13, 1893, in *The Frederick Douglass Papers,* ed. John W. Blassingame and John R. McKivigan (New Haven: Yale University Press, 1992), 5:535–37.

20. Ibid., 536, 538–43.

21. Ibid., 545.

22. Douglass, *Life and Times,* 371–72.

Problems
in Civil War
Memory

"For Something beyond the Battlefield"
Frederick Douglass and the Struggle for the Memory of the Civil War

Fellow citizens: I am not indifferent to the claims of a generous forgetfulness, but whatever else I may forget, I shall never forget the difference between those who fought for liberty and those who fought for slavery; between those who fought to save the Republic and those who fought to destroy it.

    —Frederick Douglass, "Decoration Day"

We fell under the leadership of those who would compromise with truth in the past in order make peace in the present and guide policy in the future.

    —W. E. B. Du Bois, Black Reconstruction

What you have as heritage,
Take now as task;
For thus you will make it your own.

    —Goethe, Faust

In the first week of January 1883, on the twentieth anniversary of the Emancipation Proclamation, a distinguished group of black men held a banquet in Washington, D.C., to honor the nineteenth-century's most prominent African American leader, Frederick Douglass. The banquet was an act of veneration for Douglass, an acknowledgment of the aging abolitionist's indispensable role in the Civil War era, a ritual of collective celebration, and an opportunity to forge historical memory and transmit it across generations. The nearly fifty guests comprised a who's who of black leadership in the middle and late nineteenth century. For the moment, rivalries and ideological disputes were suppressed. Senator Blanche K. Bruce chaired the event. Robert Smalls, Edward Blyden, the Reverend Benjamin T. Tanner, Professor Richard T. Greener, the young historian George Washington Williams, and the journalist T. Thomas Fortune were just a few of the notables who took part. The celebrants included men from many backgrounds: college professors, congressmen, state politicians, bishops, journalists, and businessmen. Virtually every southern state and six northern states were represented. After a sumptuous dinner, numerous toasts were offered to Douglass, and to nearly every major aspect of black life: to "the colored man as a legislator"; to "the Negro press"; to "the Negro author"; to "the Republican party"; and so forth. Douglass himself finally ended the joyous round of toasts by offering one of his own: to "the spirit of the young men" by whom he was surrounded. Many of the most distinguished guests had come of age only since the Civil War. For them slavery, abolitionism, and even the war itself were the history beyond memory. Douglass had captured an essential meaning of the occasion: the young had gathered in tribute to the old. As they met to celebrate and to understand the pivotal event in their history—emancipation—the meaning of that event was being passed to a new generation of black leaders.[1]

In his formal remarks at the banquet, Douglas demonstrated that during the last third of his life (he lived from 1818 until 1895), a distinguishing feature of his leadership was his quest to preserve the memory of the Civil War as he believed blacks and the nation should remember it. Douglass viewed emancipation as the central reference point of black history. Likewise the nation, in his judgment, had no greater turning point, nor a better demonstration of national purpose. On the twentieth anniversary, Douglass sought to infuse emancipation and the war with the sacred and mythic qualities that he had always attributed to them. "This high festival," Douglass declared, "is coupled with a day which we do well to hold in sacred and everlasting honor, a day memorable alike in the history of the nation and in the life of an emancipated people." Emancipation day, he believed, ought to be a national celebration in which all blacks, the low and the mighty, could claim a new and secure social identity. But it was also an "epoch" full of lessons about the meaning of historical memory. "Reflection upon it [emancipation] opens to us a vast wilderness of thought and feeling," Douglass asserted. "Man is said to be an animal looking before and after. To him alone is given the prophetic vision, enabling him to discern the outline of his future through the mists of the past." Douglass challenged his fellow black leaders to remember the Civil War with awe. "The day we celebrate," he said, "affords us an eminence from which we may in a measure survey both the past and the future. It is one of those days which may well count for a thousand years." This was more than mere banquet rhetoric. It was Douglass's attempt to inspire his colleagues with the idea Robert Penn Warren would later express when he wrote that "the Civil War is our only felt history—history lived in the national imagination."[2]

Douglass's effort to forge memory into action that could somehow save the legacy of the Civil War for blacks—freedom, citizenship, suffrage, and dignity—came at a time when the nation appeared indifferent or hostile to that legacy. The richly symbolic emancipation day banquet of 1883 occurred only months before the U.S. Supreme Court struck down the Civil Rights Act of 1875, "sacrificing" the Civil War amendments, as the dissenting Justice John Marshall Harlan put it, and opening the door for the eventual triumph of Jim Crow laws across the South. The ruling in *United States v. Stanley,* better known as the 1883 Civil Rights Cases, declared that the equal protection clause of the Fourteenth Amendment applied only to states; a person wronged by racial discrimination, therefore, could look for redress only from state laws and courts. In effect, the decision would also mean that the discriminatory acts of private persons were beyond the safeguards of the Fourteenth Amendment. At a mass meeting in Washington, D.C., immediately after the decision, Douglass tried to capture the sense of outrage felt by his people. "We have been, as a class, grievously wounded, wounded in the house of our friends," Douglass proclaimed. In the Supreme Court's decision, Douglass saw "a studied purpose to degrade and stamp out the liberties of a race. It is the old spirit of slavery, and nothing else."[3]

Douglass interpreted the Civil Rights Cases as a failure of historical memory and national commitment. Reflecting on the Supreme Court decision in his final autobiography, Douglass contended that "the future historian will turn to the year 1883 to find the most flagrant example of this national deterioration." White racism, among individuals and in national policy, he remarked, seemed to increase in proportion to the "increasing distance from the time of the war." Douglass blamed not only the "fading and defacing effects of time," but more important, the spirit of reconciliation between North and South. Justice and liberty for blacks, he maintained, had lost ground from "the hour that the loyal North began to shake hands over the bloody chasm."[4] Thus Douglass saw the Supreme Court decision as part of a disturbing pattern of historical change. Historical memory, he had come to realize, was not merely an entity altered by the passage of time; it was the prize in a struggle between rival versions of the past, a question of will, of power, of persuasion. The historical memory of any transforming or controversial event emerges from cultural and political competition, from the choice to confront the past and to debate and manipulate its meaning.

Ever since the war Douglass had exhibited an increasingly keen sense of history. "I am this summer endeavoring to make myself a little more familiar with history," Douglass wrote to Gerrit Smith in 1868. "My ignorance of the past has long been a trouble to me." From the early days of Reconstruction, but especially by the 1870s, Douglass seemed acutely aware that the postwar era might ultimately be controlled by those who could best shape interpretations of the war itself. Winning the peace would be not only a matter of power but also a struggle of moral will and historical consciousness. In the successful rise of the Democratic party, Douglass saw evidence that the South was beginning to win that struggle. In 1870 he complained that the American people were "destitute of political memory." But as he tried to reach out to both black and white readers with his newspaper, Douglass demanded that they not allow the country to "bury dead issues," as the Democrats wished. "The people cannot and will not forget the issues of the rebellion," Douglass admonished. "The Democratic party must continue to face the music of the past as well as of the present."[5]

Some of Douglass's critics accused him of living in the past. American politics, declared a Liberal Republican newspaper in 1872, would "leave Mr. Douglass behind vociferating the old platitudes as though the world had stopped eight years ago." To such criticisms Douglass always had a ready answer: he would not forgive the South and he would never forget the meaning of the war. At the Tomb of the Unknown Soldier in Arlington National Cemetery in 1871, on one of the first observances of Memorial Day, Douglass declared where he stood. "We are sometimes asked in the name of patriotism to forget the merits of this fearful struggle, and to remember with equal admiration those who struck at the nation's life, and those who struck to save it; those who fought for slavery and those who fought for liberty and justice. I am no minister of malice, I would not repel the repentant, but may my tongue cleave to the roof of my mouth if I forget the difference between the parties to that bloody conflict. I may say if this war is to be forgotten, I ask in the name of all things sacred what shall men remember?"[6] Douglass often referred to the preservation of the Union in glowing, nationalistic tones. But in the last third of his life, he demonstrated that the Civil War had also left many bitter elements of memory. Around the pledge to "never forget," Douglass organized his entire postwar effort to shape and preserve the legacy of the Civil War.

By intellectual predilection and by experience, Douglass was deeply conscious that history mattered. As the author of three autobiographies by the 1880s, he had cultivated deep furrows into his own memory. In a real sense, the Frederick Douglass who endures as an unending subject of literary and historical inquiry—because of the autobiographies—is and was the creature of memory. Moreover, Douglass deeply understood that people and nations are shaped and defined by history. He knew that history was a primary source of identity, meaning, and motivation. He seemed acutely aware that history was both burden and inspiration, something to be cherished and overcome. Douglass also understood that winning battles over policy or justice in the present often required an effective use of the past. He came to a realization that in late nineteenth-century America, blacks had a special need for a usable past. "It is not well to forget the past," Douglass warned in an 1884 speech. "Memory was given to man for some wise purpose. The past is the mirror in which we may discern the dim outlines of the future and by which we may make them more symmetrical."[7]

To all who look to history for meaning, those premises may seem obvious. But in the 1880s, according to Douglass, blacks occupied a special place in America's historical memory, as participants and as custodians. He understood his people's psychological need not to dwell on the horrors of slavery. But the slave experience was so immediate and unforgettable, Douglass believed, because it was a history that could "be traced like that of a wounded man through a crowd by the blood." Douglass urged his fellow blacks to keep *their* history before the consciousness of American society; if necessary, they should serve as a national conscience. "Well the nation may forget," Douglass said in 1888; "it may shut its eyes to the past, and frown upon any who may do otherwise, but the colored people of this country are bound to keep the past in lively memory till justice shall be done them." But as Douglass learned, such historical consciousness was as out of date in Gilded Age America as the racial justice he demanded.[8]

In his retrospective thought about the Civil War, Douglass's intention was to forge enduring historical myths that could help win battles in the present. The deepest cultural myths—ideas and stories drawn from history that, through symbolic power, transcend generations—are the mechanisms of historical memory. Such myths are born of divergent experiences and provide the cultural weapons with which rival memories contest for hegemony. Douglass hoped that Union victory, black emancipation, and the Civil War constitutional amendments would be so deeply rooted in recent American experience, so central to any conception of national regeneration, so necessary to the postwar society that they would become sacred values, ritualized in memory. Douglass dearly wanted black freedom and equality—the gift from the Union dead who were memorialized every Decoration Day—to become (as Richard Slotkin put it) one of those "usable values from history beyond the reach of critical demystification."[9] Douglass's hope that emancipation could attain such indelible mythic quality was rooted in his enduring faith in the doctrine of progress and in his moral determinism, a belief that in a society of egalitarian laws good will outweigh evil in the collective action of human beings. Repeatedly, Douglass criticized the claim that emancipation came only by "military necessity" during the war. "The war for the Union came only to execute the moral and humane judgment of the nation," he asserted in 1883. "It was an instrument of a higher power than itself." What drew northerners to Memorial Day observances, Douglass maintained in 1878, was the "moral character of the war, the far-reaching, eternal principles in dispute, and for which our sons and brothers encountered danger and death."[10] By continuing to stress that sacred and ideological legacy of the war, Douglass exposed both his deeper sense of the meaning of the conflict and his fear that such meaning would not successfully compete with rival memories (in both North and South) and could, therefore, be lost.

Douglass's pledge to "never forget" the meaning of the Civil War stemmed from at least five sources in his thought and experience: his belief that the war had been an ideological struggle and not merely the test of a generation's loyalty and valor; his sense of refurbished nationalism made possible by emancipation, Union victory, and radical Reconstruction; his confrontation with the resurgent racism and Lost Cause mythology of the postwar period; his critique of America's peculiar dilemma of historical amnesia; and his personal psychological stake in preserving an African American and an abolitionist memory of the war. Douglass never softened his claim that the Civil War had been an ideological conflict with deeply moral consequences. He abhorred the non-ideological interpretation of the war that was gaining popularity by the 1880s. The spirit of sectional reunion had fostered a celebration of martial heroism, of strenuousness and courage, perhaps best expressed by Oliver Wendell Holmes Jr. and later popularized by Theodore Roosevelt. Holmes experienced and therefore loathed the horror of combat. But to him, the legacy of the Civil War rested not in any moral cause on either side, but in the passion, devotion, and sacrifice of the generation whose "hearts were touched with fire." To Holmes, the true hero— the deepest memory—of the Civil War was the soldier on either side, thoughtless of ideology, who faced the "experience of battle in those indecisive contests." War almost always forces people to ask the existential question *why?* Massive organized killing compels the question, but it seldom reveals satisfying answers. Indeed, the very face of battle, suffering, and death can blunt or deny ideology altogether. Teleological conceptions of war are rarely the luxury of individual soldiers; the veteran's memory rarely focuses on the grand design. Ideology, though always at the root of war, is left to the interpreters, those who will compete to define the meaning and legacy of the wartime experience. "In the midst of doubt, in the collapse of creeds," said Holmes, "there is one thing I do not doubt, and that is that the faith is true and adorable which sends a soldier to throw away his life in obedience to a blindly accepted duty, in a cause which he little understands, in a plan of campaign of which he has no notion, under tactics of which he does not see the use." By the 1880s Holmes's memory of the war became deeply rooted in American culture. What mattered most was not the content of the cause on either side but the acts of commitment to either cause, not ideas but the experience born of conflict over those ideas. Whoever was honest in his devotion was *right*.[11]

Douglass resisted such an outlook and demanded a teleological memory of the war. His Memorial Day addresses were full of tributes to martial heroism, albeit only on the Union side; but more important, they were testaments to the abolitionist conception of the war. The conflict, Douglas insisted in 1878, "was a war of ideas, a battle of principles a war between the old and new, slavery and freedom, barbarism and civilization." After Reconstruction Douglass was one of a small band of old abolitionists and reformers who struggled to sustain an ideological interpretation of the Civil War. His speeches were strikingly similar to the writings of the novelist and former carpetbagger Albion Tourgee. Satirically, Tourgee attempted to answer the Holmesian version of an ideology-free veterans' memory. "We have nothing to do with the struggle that followed" the outbreak of war, wrote Tourgee in 1884. "History hath already recorded it with more or less exactitude. It was long and fierce because two brave peoples fought with the desperation of convictions. It was a wonderful conflict." What people should remember of the war, Tourgee contended, was "*not* the courage, the suffering, the blood, *but only the causes that underlay the struggle and the results that followed from it.*" Like Douglass, Tourgee considered emancipation the great result of the war. He also rejected a core concept of the national reunion: that the South's war effort was honest and, therefore, just as heroic as the Union cause. "Because an opponent is honest," Tourgee asserted, "it does not follow that he is right, nor is it certain that because he was overthrown he was in the wrong." Thinkers like Douglass and Tourgee were not merely trying to "keep alive conflict over issues time was ruthlessly discarding," as Paul H. Buck wrote in 1937.[12] Belligerence was not the only motive of those who argued for an ideological memory of the Civil War. Theirs was a persuasion under duress by the 1880s, a collective voice nearly drowned out by the chorus of reconciliation. They understood the need for healing in the recently divided nation; they could acknowledge the validity of veterans' mutual respect. But they distrusted the sentimentalism of both North and South, and they especially feared Holmes's notion of the "collapse of creeds." Most of all, those northerners who stressed ideas in the debate over the memory of the war saw America avoiding—whether benignly or aggressively—the deep significance of race in the verdict of Appomattox.

Douglass's voice was crucial to the late nineteenth-century debate over the legacy of the Civil War. As Edmund Wilson wrote in analyzing the significance of "detached" American writers of the Civil War era: "They also serve who only stand and watch. The men of action make history, but the spectators make most of the histories, and these histories may influence the action." Douglass had acted in history, but now his principal aim was to help shape the histories. Unlike Holmes and many others, Douglass had not served on the battlefield. But he had served in slavery, he had served on the abolitionist platform, and he had served with his pen and voice as few other black leaders had during the war. Douglass's war was an intellectual and spiritual existence; his action had been more of an inner struggle than a physical test. Perhaps his remoteness from the carnage enabled him to sustain an ideological conception of the war throughout his life. Answering the appeal of the veterans' memory, Douglass maintained that the war "was not a fight between rapacious birds and ferocious beasts, a mere display of brute courage and endurance, but it was a war between men of thought, as well as of action, and in dead earnest for something beyond the battlefield."[13]

The second source of Douglass's quest to preserve the memory of the Civil War was his refurbished nationalism. At stake for the former fugitive slave was the sense of American nationhood, the secure social identity that he hoped emancipation and equality would one day offer every black in America. Douglass expressed this connection between nationalism and memory in his famous speech at the unveiling of the Freedmen's Memorial monument to Abraham Lincoln in Washington, D.C., in April 1876. The Freedmen's Memorial speech is too easily interpreted as merely eulogistic, as simply Douglass's contribution to the myth of Lincoln as Great Emancipator. Attended by President Ulysses S. Grant, his cabinet, Supreme Court Justices, and numerous senators, the ceremony was as impressive as the bright spring day, which had been declared a holiday by joint resolution of Congress. After a reading of the Emancipation Proclamation and the unveiling of the statue (which Douglass later admitted he disliked because "it showed the Negro on his knees"), Douglass took the podium as the orator of the day. His address included strong doses of the rail-splitter Lincoln image, the "plebeian" who rose through honesty, common sense, and the mysterious hand of God to become the "great liberator." But Douglass understood the significance of the occasion; he knew it was a moment to forge national memory and to practice civil religion. Through most of the speech he spoke to and for blacks; the monument had been commissioned and paid for almost entirely by blacks. But the monument was not only to Lincoln; rather, it was to the *fact* of emancipation. The occasion honored Lincoln, but Douglass equally stressed the *events* that transpired "under his rule, and in due time." Most important, Douglass staked out a claim to nationhood for blacks. "We stand today at the national center," he said, "to perform something like a national act." Douglass struck clear notes of civil religion as he described the "stately pillars and majestic domes of the Capitol" as "our church" and rejoiced that "for the first time in the history of our people, and in the history of the whole American people, we join in this high worship." Douglass was, indeed, trying to make Lincoln mythic and, therefore, useful to the cause of black equality. But the primary significance of Douglass's Freedmen's Memorial address lies in its concerted attempt to forge a mythic place for blacks in the national memory, to assert their citizenship and nationhood. "When now it shall be said that the colored man is soulless," Douglass concluded, "when the foul reproach of ingratitude is hurled at us, and it is attempted to scourge us beyond the range of human brotherhood, we may calmly point to the monument we have this day erected to the memory of Abraham Lincoln." Douglass thus made his claims of black equality in the language of national inheritance and a new founding mythology forged by the Civil War.[14]

The third cause of Douglass's concern over the memory of the Civil War was the resurgent racism throughout the country and the rise of the Lost Cause as a cultural movement. Since its origins as a literary and political device immediately after the war, the Lost Cause has been an enigmatic phrase in American history. Historians have defined the Lost Cause in at least three different ways: as a public memory, shaped by a web of organizations, institutions, and rituals; as a dimension of southern and American civil religion, rooted in churches and sacred rhetoric as well as secular institutions and thought; and as a literary phenomenon, shaped by journalists and fiction writers from the die-hard Confederate apologists of the immediate postwar years through the gentle romanticism of the "local color" writers of the 1880s to the legion of more mature novelists of the 1890s and early twentieth century who appealed to a national audience eager for reconciliation.[15] Dividing the movement into the "inner" and "national" memories is also useful in making sense of the Lost Cause. The inner Lost Cause, argued Thomas L. Connelly and Barbara L. Bellows, represents the die-hard generation that fought the war and experienced defeat and dishonor. Led by Jefferson Davis, and especially by the prototypical unreconstructed rebel Gen. Jubal Early, these former Confederate leaders created veterans organizations, wrote partisan Confederate histories, built monuments, made Robert E. Lee into a romantic icon, and desperately sought justification for their cause and explanations for their defeat. The Confederacy, argued the diehards, was never defeated; rather, it was overwhelmed by numbers and betrayed by certain generals at pivotal battles (namely, James Longstreet at Gettysburg). The activities of the initial Lost Cause advocates have been compared to the Ghost Dance of the Plains Indians of the late nineteenth century. As mystics, they remained "captivated by a dream," wrote Gaines Fosters, "a dream of a return to an undefeated Confederacy." The inner Lost Cause was not, however, merely a band of bitter, aging, mystical soldiers. During the 1870s and 1880s they forged an organized movement in print, oratory, and granite, and their influence persisted at least until World War I.[16]

The national Lost Cause took hold during the 1880s primarily as a literary phenomenon propagated by mass-market magazines and welcomed by a burgeoning northern readership. Avoiding the defensive tone and self-pity of earlier Lost Cause writers, successful local colorist John Esten Cooke found a vast and vulnerable audience for his stories of the genteel and romantic heritage of old Virginia. Cooke and other writers such as Thomas Nelson Page and Sara Pryor did not write about a defeated South or the Confederate cause. They wrote about the Old South, about the chivalry and romance of antebellum plantation life, about black "servants" and a happy, loyal slave culture, remembered as a source of laughter, music, and contentment. They wrote about colonial Virginia—the Old Dominion—as the source of revolutionary heritage and the birthplace of several American presidents. Northern readers were treated to an exotic South, a premodern, preindustrial model of grace. These writers sought to capture Yankee readers as much as to vindicate the Confederacy. Northern readers were not asked to reconcile Jefferson's Virginia with the rebel yell at the unveiling of a Confederate monument. They were only asked to recognize the South's place in national heritage and to enjoy sentimental journeys into a nostalgic past of happy race relations, often narrated in the dialect of a faithful slave.[17]

The conditioning of the northern mind in popular literature had its counterpart in veterans' reunions, which in the 1880s and 1890s became increasingly intersectional. Celebration of manly valor on both sides and the mutual respect of Union and Confederate soldiers fostered a kind of veterans' culture that gave the Lost Cause a place in national memory. The war became essentially a conflict between white men; both sides fought well, Americans against Americans, and there was glory enough to go around. Celebrating the soldiers' experience buttressed the nonideological memory of the war. The great issues of the conflict—slavery, secession, emancipation, black equality, even disloyalty and treason—faded from national consciousness as the nation celebrated reunion and ultimately confronted war with Spain in 1898. Many southerners became pragmatic about the memory of the war; they wanted to remember what was best in their past, but most important, they embraced the reunionism implicit in the concept of a New South and demanded respect from northerners. To most southerners, the Lost Cause came to represent this crucial double meaning: reunion and respect. Late in life Frederick Douglass rarely found it possible to concede the South both aspects of the national Lost Cause sentiment; at times he could acknowledge neither reunion nor respect on the terms that popular consciousness demanded. Douglass clung to a "victorious cause" of his own, resisting and wishing away Jim Crow, lynching, and the ongoing betrayal of his people. And Douglass often took his version of the victorious cause to the public forum, demanding justice in the present, the arena of competing and rival memories.[18]

There were ghosts to be called up on all sides. White southerners were finding a balm for defeat and bereavement, autonomy in their own region, and a new place in the Union. Southern memory of the war had begun the long process of achieving resolution; southern ghosts could be purged. For blacks, however, many ghosts were not purged in the late nineteenth century and, indeed, they remain unpurged even today. Some twentieth-century black writers portray the burden of memory much as Douglass did. In August Wilson's play *Joe Turner's Come and Gone,* the hero, Herald Loomis, a former sharecropper who has come north to Pittsburgh in 1911, is haunted by the memory of his seven years' unjust imprisonment on a chain gang. Loomis was kidnapped by a turn-of-the-century slave catcher (Joe Turner) who believed that emancipation was the worst thing that ever happened to the South. As Loomis searches for his wife and a new start in life, he is tormented not only by the memory of chains but also by visions of white bones rising out of the ocean, a clear and powerful image of the slave trade. In the dramatization of Herald Loomis's struggle to reemerge from a second slavery, we can find echoes of Douglass's challenge to America to "never forget" its responsibilities to the freedpeople. Wilson's use of history on stage transmits black cultural memory as a weapon, a source of spirit that enables people to grapple with their historical ghosts in an ever-sovereign present. Similarly, in Toni Morrison's novel *Beloved,* Sethe, a freedwoman living in Ohio during Reconstruction, confronts the return of the living ghost of her daughter, a child she had killed in infancy rather than permit her imminent return to slavery. The ghost, Beloved, is a metaphor for all the haunting horror of slavery that the freed people have carried with them into their new lives. Beloved is memory itself, all-consuming, overwhelming, forcing Sethe to face each "day's serious work of beating back the past." At the end of the book Morrison suggests that to the characters in this wrenching story "remembering seemed unwise." But she also reminds us as readers—as a people—to beware of the path left by Beloved as she vanished: "Down by the stream in back of 124 [Sethe's house] her [Beloved's] footprints come and go, come and go. They are so familiar. Should a child, an adult place his feet in them, they will fit. Take them out and they disappear again as though nobody ever walked there."[19] Collective historical memory, like the deepest personal memories, can overwhelm and control us as do the ghosts in the work of Wilson and Morrison. But historical memory is also a matter of choice, a question of will. As a culture, we choose which footprints from the past will best help us walk in the present.

In the midst of Reconstruction, Douglass began to realize the potential power of the Lost Cause sentiment. Indignant at the universal amnesty afforded former Confederates and appalled by the national veneration of Robert E. Lee, Douglass attacked the emerging Lost Cause. "The spirit of secession is stronger today than ever," Douglass warned in 1871. "It is now a deeply rooted, devoutly cherished sentiment, inseparably identified with the 'lost cause,' which the half measures of the Government towards the traitors have helped to cultivate and strengthen." He was disgusted by the outpouring of admiration for Lee in the wake of the general's death in 1870. "Is it not about time that this bombastic laudation of the rebel chief should cease?" Douglass wrote. "We can scarcely take up a newspaper that is not filled with *nauseating* flatteries of the late Robert E. Lee." At this early stage in the debate over the memory of the war, Douglass had no interest in honoring the former enemy. "It would seem from this," he asserted, "that the soldier who kills the most men in battle, even in a bad cause, is the greatest Christian, and entitled to the highest place in heaven." Douglass's harsh reactions to the veneration of Lee are a revealing measure of his enduring attitudes toward the South, as well as his conception of the meaning of the war. He seemed to relish the opportunity to lecture his readers about their former enemies. "The South has a past not to be contemplated with pleasure, but with a shudder," Douglass cautioned in 1870. "She has been selling agony, trading in blood and in the souls of men. If her past has any lesson, it is one of repentance and thorough reformation."[20]

As for proposed monuments to Lee, Douglass considered them an insult to his people and to the Union. He feared that such monument building would only "reawaken the confederacy." Moreover, in a remark that would prove more ironic with time, Douglass declared in 1870 that "monuments to the Lost Cause will prove monuments of folly." As the

Lost Cause myth sank deeper into southern and national consciousness, Douglass would find that he was losing ground in the battle for the memory of the Civil War.[21]

Douglass never precisely clarified just how much southern "repentance" or "reformation" he deemed necessary before he could personally extend forgiveness. He merely demanded "justice," based on adherence to the Civil War amendments and to the civil rights acts. Given the strength of his nationalism and his own southern roots, Douglass's vindictiveness toward the South probably would have softened more with time had not the resurgent racism of the 1880s and 1890s fueled the spirit of sectional reunion. "A spirit of evil has been revived," Douglass declared in a eulogy to William Lloyd Garrison in 1879; "doctrines are proclaimed which were, as we thought, all extinguished by the iron logic of cannon balls." In the political victories of the southern Democrats and in the increasing oppression of the freedmen, Douglass saw a "conflict between the semibarbarous past and the higher civilization which has logically and legally taken its place." He lamented the passing of so many of the old abolitionists like Garrison whose services would be needed in what Douglass called "this second battle for liberty and nation."[22]

From his position as a stalwart Republican, Douglass's condemnations of resurgent racism often seemed in stark contradiction to his support of the party that increasingly abandoned blacks. His allegiance to and criticism of the Republican party could emerge in bewildering extremes. Campaigning for Alonzo B. Cornell, Republican candidate for governor of New York in 1879, Douglass charged that too many Republicans had caved in to the charms of sectional reunion. The issues of the current election, he asserted, were "precisely those old questions which gave rise to our late civil war." Such rhetoric did not square with the realities of American politics during the Hayes administration. Like an angry revivalist wishing for a reawakening among his fellow party members, Douglass chastised "this tender forbearance, this amazing mercy, and generous oblivion to the past." Yet in an 1880 speech commemorating emancipation, Douglass declared: "Of the Republican party it is the same as during and before the war; the same enlightened, loyal, liberal and progressive party that it was. It is the party of Lincoln, Grant, Wade, Seward, and Sumner; the party to which today we are indebted for the salvation of the country, and today it is well represented in its character and composition by James A. Garfield and Chester A. Arthur."

Over the course of the 1880s his rhetoric shifted to harsher and more realistic assessments as Douglass faced the bitter truth about his party. In an 1888 speech he accused the Republicans of treating the freedmen as "a deserted, a defrauded, a swindled outcast; in law, free; in fact, a slave; in law, a citizen; in fact, an alien; in law, a voter; in fact, a disfranchised man." Douglass pleaded with Republicans not to rest on their laurels and demanded that they convert their original values into a creative force for the new era. "I am a Republican, I believe in the Republican party," he asserted. "But I dare to tell that party the truth. In my judgment, it can no longer repose on the history of its grand and magnificent achievements. It must not only stand abreast with the times, but must create the times."[23]

Douglass's ambivalence toward the Republicans late in life stemmed from more than two decades of loyalty to the party. The party had been the primary vehicle through which he pursued his political ambitions, developed his political consciousness, and exercised some influence in the federal government. Beginning in 1877, when President Rutherford B. Hayes appointed him marshal for the District of Columbia, and through subsequent appointments as recorder of deeds for the District of Columbia (1881–86) and minister to Haiti (1889–91), Douglass achieved a place, albeit largely emblematic, in Washington officialdom. But aside from personal ambition, he had always imbued the Republican party with deeper, historical meanings. He saw it as the vessel of progress and as the institutional custodian of the Civil War's legacy. During the Grant years (1869–77), he had stumped for the Republicans with an almost desperate zeal, as if only through the party could emancipation and the triumphs of radical Reconstruction be preserved. An element of wish fulfillment no doubt both sustained his support of the Republicans and inspired his later attacks on the party. But Douglass's Republican loyalty is best understood as part of his quest to realize a secure, abolitionist memory of the war. He continued to use the Republican party to demand that the nation confront its recent history, not run from it. What Douglass most wanted was not national reunion; he wanted racial justice, promised in law, demonstrated in practice, and preserved in memory.[24]

Whatever he thought of the Republican party, though, the aging Douglass never wavered in his critique of racism. "The tide of popular prejudice" against blacks, Douglass said in 1884, had "swollen by a thousand streams" since the war. Everywhere, he lamented, blacks were "stamped" with racist expectations. Douglass expressed the pain of being black in America: whenever a black man aspired to a profession, "the presumption of incompetence confronts him, and he must either run, fight, or fall before it." The alleged rapes by black men of white women were to Douglass manifestations of the South's invention of a new "crime" to replace their old fear of "insurrection." Lynching, therefore, represented a white, southern invention of new means to exercise racial power and oppression. In a speech in 1884 commemorating the rescue of fugitive slaves in the 1850s, Douglass chastised his Syracuse audience for preferring sectional peace over racial justice. "It is weak and foolish to cry PEACE when there is no peace," he cried. "In America, as elsewhere, injustice must cease before peace can prevail."[25]

The fourth source of Douglass's arguments in the debate over the memory of the Civil War was his conviction that the country had been seduced into "national forgetfulness," a peculiar American condition of historical amnesia. In his numerous retrospective speeches in the 1880s, Douglass discussed the limitations of memory. He knew that memory was fickle and that people must embrace an "ever-changing present." Even his own "slave life," he admitted, had "lost much of its horror, and sleeps in memory like the dim outlines of a half-forgotten dream." But Douglass's greater concern was with collective memory, not merely with personal recollection. Douglass was rowing upstream against a strong current in American thought. As a people, Americans had always tended to reject the past and embrace newness. The overweening force of individualism in an expanding country had ever made Americans a future-oriented people, a culture unburdened with memory and tradition. Douglass was learning to appreciate one of Alexis de Tocqueville's great observations about American society: in America, each generation is a new people, and "no one cares for what occurred before his time." The discovery Tocqueville made in 1831 would ring even truer in the climate of laissez-faire government and social Darwinism of the Gilded Age. American individualism, wrote Tocqueville, makes "every man forget his ancestors . . . hides his descendants and separates his contemporaries from him; it throws him back forever upon himself alone and threatens in the end to confine him entirely within the solitude of his own heart."[26] To Douglass, the individualism that bred indifference and the racism that bred oppression were the twin enemies undercutting efforts to preserve an abolitionist memory of the Civil War.

One of the ambiguities in Douglass's postwar thought is that while attacking the surging individualistic indifference of northerners who wished to forget the war issues, to forgive former Confederates, and to abandon the freedpeople, he was also an outspoken proponent of laissez-faire individualism, a celebrator of "self-made men."[27] There was perhaps no other solution for a black leader who had to preach self-reliance to his people while demanding national commitments from the government and from society at large. Moreover, Douglass was one of Tocqueville's Americans, trapped between the country's historic racism and his own embrace of individualism.

Most assuredly, though, Douglass was not one of those Americans who rejected the past. His laments about historical amnesia often echoed Tocqueville's prescience. He believed that individualism could coexist with social justice, that getting on in the world released no one from the weight of history. "Well it may be said that Americans have no memories," Douglass said in 1888. "We look over the House of Representatives and see the Solid South enthroned there; we listen with calmness to eulogies of the South and of traitors and forget Andersonville. We see colored citizens shot down and driven from the ballot box, and forget the services rendered by the colored troops in the late war for the Union." More revealing still was Douglass's contempt for the northern sympathy with the Lost Cause. He believed northern forgiveness toward the South shamed the memory of the war. "Rebel graves are decked with loyal flowers," Douglass declared, "though no loyal grave is ever adorned by rebel hands. Loyal men are building homes for rebel soldiers; but where is the home for Union veterans, builded by rebel hands?" Douglass had never really wanted a Carthaginian peace. But he felt left out of the nation's happy reunion; the deep grievances of his people—both historic and current—were no longer to be heard. At the very least, Douglass demanded that the power to forgive should be reserved for those most wronged.[28]

The debate over the meaning of the war was not merely a question of remembering or forgetting. Douglass worried about historical amnesia because his version of the war, his memory, faltered next to the rival memories that resonated more deeply with the white majority in both North and South. Douglass may never have fully appreciated the complexity of the experience of the Civil War and Reconstruction for whites. The overwhelming number of white northerners who voted against black suffrage shared a bond of white supremacy with southerners who rejected the racial egalitarianism of radical Reconstruction. The thou-

sands of white Union veterans who remembered the war as a transforming personal experience, but not as the crucible of emancipation
for four million slaves, had much in common with white Georgians who
had found themselves in the path of Gen. William T. Sherman's conquest of Atlanta or the march to the sea. There were many rival memories of the war and its aftermath, and there was much need for forgetting and healing. As Friedrich Nietzsche suggested, personal happiness
often requires a degree of forgetting the past. "Forgetting is essential to
action of any kind," wrote Nietzsche. "Thus: it is possible to live almost
without memory . . . but it is altogether impossible to live at all without
forgetting. . . . [T]here is a degree of the historical sense which is harm-
ful and ultimately fatal to the living thing, whether this living thing be a
man or a people or a culture." Nietzsche captured elements of both
truth and danger in human nature. Douglass focused his efforts on the
dangers of collective forgetting, not on its personal or cultural necessity.
Douglass knew that his people, confined to minority status and living at
the margins of society, could rarely afford the luxury of forgetting. Although he may not have thoroughly discriminated between the rival
memories he confronted, he became fully aware of their power and
their threat. Thus with ever few sympathetic listeners by the late 1880s,
Douglass was left with his lament that "slavery has always had a better
memory than freedom, and was always a better hater."[29]

Those were not merely words of nostalgic yearning for a vanished
past uttered by a man out of touch with changing times. In a sense,
Douglass was living in the past during the last part of his life; for him, the
Civil War and Reconstruction were the reference points for the black
experience in the nineteenth century. All questions of meaning, of a
sense of place, of a sense of future for blacks in America drew upon the
era of emancipation. Hence, the fifth source of Douglass's pledge to
"never forget": a tremendous emotional and psychological investment
in his own conception of the legacy of the conflict. As an intellectual,
Douglass had grown up with the abolition movement, the war, and its
historical transformations. His career and his very personality had been
shaped by those events. So, quite literally, Douglass's effort to preserve
the memory of the Civil War was a quest to save the freedom of his
people and the meaning of his own life.

Douglass embraced his role in preserving an abolitionist memory of
the war with a sense of moral duty. In an 1883 speech in his old hometown of Rochester, New York, he was emphatic on that point. "You will

already have perceived that I am not of that school of thinkers which teaches us to let bygones be bygones; to let the dead past bury its dead. In my view there are no bygones in the world, and the past is not dead and cannot die. The evil as well as the good that men do lives after them. The duty of keeping in memory the great deeds of the past, and of transmitting the same from generation to generation is implied in the mental and moral constitution of man."[30] But what of a society that did not widely share the same sense of history and preferred a different version of the past? Douglass's answer was to resist the Lost Cause by arguing for an opposite and, he hoped, deeper cultural myth—the abolitionist conception of the Civil War, black emancipation as the source of national regeneration.

In trying to forge an alternative to the Lost Cause, Douglass drew on America's reform tradition and constantly appealed to the Constitution and to the rule of law. Moreover, reversing a central tenet of the Lost Cause—the memory of defeat—Douglas emphasized the memory of victory, the sacrifices of the Union dead, and the historical progress he believed inherent in emancipation. This is what Douglass meant in an 1878 Memorial Day speech in Madison Square in New York, when he declared that "there was a right side and a wrong side in the late war which no sentiment ought to cause us to forget."[31]

In some of his postwar rhetoric Douglass undoubtedly contributed to what Robert Penn Warren has called the myth of the "treasury of virtue." He did sometimes imbue Union victory with an air of righteousness that skewed the facts. His insistence on the "moral" character of the war often neglected the complex, reluctant manner in which emancipation became the goal of the Union war effort. In structuring historical memory, Douglass could be as selective as his Lost Cause adversaries. His persistent defense of the Republican party after Reconstruction caused him to walk a thin line of hypocrisy. Indeed, Douglass's millennialist interpretation of the war forever caused him to see the conflict as a cleansing tragedy, wherein the nation had been redeemed of its evil by lasting grace.[32] Douglass knew that black freedom had emerged from history more than from policy deliberately created by human agents. Moreover, he knew that emancipation had resulted largely from slaves' own massive self-liberation. But winning the battle over the legacy of the Civil War, Douglass knew, demanded deep cultural myths that would resonate widely in society. He knew that the struggle over memory was always, in part, a debate over the present. In his view, emancipation and black equality under law were the great results of the war. Hence, while urging old abolitionists not to give up their labors in 1875, Douglass contended that "every effort should now be made to save the result of this stupendous moral and physical contest." Moreover, nine years later Douglass warned that unless an abolitionist conception of the war were steadfastly preserved, America would "thus lose to after coming generations a vast motive power and inspiration to high and virtuous endeavor." Douglass labored to shape the memory of the Civil War, then, as a skilled propagandist, as a black leader confident of the virtue of his cause, and as an individual determined to protect his own identity.[33]

In his book *The Unwritten War: American Writers and the Civil War,* Daniel Aaron observed that very few writers in the late nineteenth century "appreciated the Negro's literal or symbolic role in the war." Black invisibility in the massive Civil War fictional literature, except largely in caricature, is yet another striking illustration that emancipation and the challenge of racial equality overwhelmed the American imagination in the postwar decades. Slavery, the war's deepest cause, and black freedom, the war's most fundamental result, remain the most conspicuous missing elements in the American literature inspired by the Civil War. Black invisibility in America's cultural memory is precisely what Douglass struggled against during the last two decades of his life. Late in life, Douglass was no novelist himself and was not about to write the great Civil War book. But memories and understanding of great events, especially apocalyptic wars, live in our consciousness like monuments in the mind. The aging Douglass's rhetoric was an eloquent attempt to forge a place on that monument for those he deemed the principal characters in the drama of emancipation: the abolitionist, the black soldier, and the freed people. Perhaps the best reason the Civil War remained in Aaron's words "vivid but ungraspable" to literary imagination was that most American writers avoided, or were confounded by, slavery and race, the deepest moral issues in the conflict.[34]

The late nineteenth century was an age when white supremacy flourished amid vast industrial and social change. The nation increasingly embraced sectional reunion, sanctioned Jim Crow, dreamed about technology, and defined itself by the assumptions of commerce. Near the end of his monumental work *Black Reconstruction,* W. E. B. Du Bois declared himself "aghast" at the way historians had suppressed the significance of slavery and the black quest for freedom in the literature on the Civil War and Reconstruction era. "One is astonished in the study of his-

tory," wrote Du Bois, "at the recurrence of the ideas that evil must be for- ✔
gotten, distorted, skimmed over. The difficulty, of course, with this philosophy is that history loses its value as an incentive and example; it
paints perfect men and noble nations, but it does not tell the truth." As
Du Bois acknowledged, it was just such a use of history as "incentive and .
example" for which Douglass had labored.[35]

Although his jeremiads against Lost Cause mythology and his efforts
to preserve an abolitionist memory of the conflict took on a strained
quality, Douglass never lost hope in the regenerative meaning of the
Civil War. It was such a great divide, such a compelling reference point,
that he believed the nation would, in time, have to face its meaning and
consequences. In an 1884 speech Douglass drew hope from a biblical
metaphor of death and rebirth—the story of Jesus' raising Lazarus from
the dead. "The assumption that the cause of the Negro is a dead issue,"
Douglass declared, "is an utter delusion. For the moment he may be
buried under the dust and rubbish of endless discussion concerning
civil service, tariff and free trade, labor and capital, but our Lazarus is
not dead. He only sleeps."[36]

Douglass's use of such a metaphor was perhaps a recognition of tem-
porary defeat in the struggle for the memory of the Civil War. But it also
represented his belief that, though the struggle would outlast his own
life, it could still be won. Douglass gave a Memorial Day address in 1883
at Mount Hope Cemetery in Rochester, where he would himself be
buried some twelve years later. The sixty-five-year-old orator angrily dis-
avowed the sectional reconciliation that had swept the country. He
feared that Decoration Day would become an event merely of "anachro-
nisms, empty forms and superstitions." One wonders if the largely white
audience in Rochester on that pleasant spring afternoon thought of
Douglass himself as somewhat of an anachronism. In a country reeling
from labor unrest, worried about Gilded Age corruption, the farmers'
revolt, and the disorder of growing cities, Douglass's listeners (even in
his old hometown) may not have looked beyond the symbolic trappings
of the occasion. One wonders how willing they were to cultivate their
twenty-year-old memory of the war and all its sacrifice, to face the deeper
meanings Douglass demanded. The aging Douglass could still soar to
oratorical heights on such occasions. He asked his audience to reflect
with him about their "common memory." "I seem even now to hear and
feel the effects of the sights and the sounds of that dreadful period,"
Douglass said. "I see the flags from the windows and the housetops flut-

tering in the breeze. I see and hear the steady tramp of armed men in blue uniforms. I see the recruiting sergeant with drum and fife calling for men, young men and strong, to go to the front and fill up the gaps made by rebel powder and pestilence. I hear the piercing sound of trumpets." These were more than Whitmanesque pictures of bygone peril and glory. In a nation soon to acquiesce in the frequent lynching of his people and shattering their hopes with disfranchisement and segregation, Douglass appealed to history, to what for him was authentic experience, to the recognition scenes that formed personal and national identity. On an ideological level, where Douglass did his best work, he was still fighting the war; he was as harsh as ever in his refusal to concede the Confederate dead an equal place in Memorial Day celebrations. "Death has no power to change moral qualities," he argued. "What was bad before the war, and during the war, has not been made good since the war." A tone of desperation entered Douglass's language toward the end of his speech. Again and again he pleaded with his audience not to believe the arguments of the Lost Cause advocates, however alluring their "disguises" might seem. He insisted that slavery had caused the war, that Americans should never forget that the South fought "to bind with chains millions of the human race."[37]

No amount of nationalism, individualism, or compassion could ever change Douglass's conception of the memory and meaning of the Civil War. His pledge to "never forget" was both a personal and a partisan act. It was an assertion of the power of memory to inform, to inspire, and to compel action. Douglass was one of those nineteenth-century thinkers who by education, by temperament, and especially by experience believed that history was something living and useful. Even in the twilight of his life, there was no greater voice for the old shibboleth that the Civil War had been a struggle for union *and* liberty. "Whatever else I may forget," Douglass told those assembled at Mount Hope Cemetery, "I shall never forget the difference between those who fought for liberty and those who fought for slavery; between those who fought to save the Republic and those who fought to destroy it." The jubilee of black freedom in America had been achieved by heroic action, through forces in history, through a tragic war, and by faith. Among Douglass's final public acts, therefore, was his fight—using the power of language and historical imagination—to preserve that jubilee in memory and in reality. In a Rochester cemetery, he stood with the Union dead, waved the last bloody shirts of a former slave, a black leader, a Yankee partisan, and anticipated the dulling effects of time and the poet Robert Lowell's vision of "the stone statues of the abstract Union soldier" adorning New England town greens, where "they doze over muskets and muse through their sideburns."[38]

NOTES

This essay first appeared in a special roundtable on memory in the *Journal of American History*, spring 1989. It is reprinted here with minor revisions.

1. *People's Advocate*, January 6, 1883, Leon Gardiner Collection, Historical Society of Pennsylvania, Philadelphia. The banquet was organized by Prof. J. M. Gregory of Howard University.

2. Ibid.; Robert Penn Warren, *The Legacy of the Civil War* (1961; reprint, Cambridge: Harvard University Press, 1983), 4. Douglass's image here reflects his apocalyptic view of history. On his apocalyptic conception of the Civil War, see David W. Blight, "Frederick Douglass and the American Apocalypse," *Civil War History* 31 (December 1985): 309–28.

3. Rayford W. Logan, *The Betrayal of the Negro: From Rutherford B. Hayes to Woodrow Wilson* (New York: Collier, 1965), 114–18; Frederick Douglass, "The Civil Rights Case: Speech at the Civil Rights Mass-Meeting held at Lincoln Hall, October 22, 1883," in *The Life and Writings of Frederick Douglass*, ed. Philip S. Foner, 5 vols. (New York: International Publishers, 1950), 4:393, 402.

4. Frederick Douglass, *The Life and Times of Frederick Douglass: His Early Years as a Slave, His Escape from Bondage, and His Complete History* (1892; reprint, New York: Collier, 1962), 539.

5. Frederick Douglass to Gerrit Smith, August 24, 1868, in *Life and Writings of Frederick Douglass*, ed. Foner, 4:210; *New National Era*, November 24, 1870.

6. *Golden Age*, quoted in *New National Era*, August 8, 1872; Frederick Douglass, "Address at the Grave of the Unknown Dead," May 30, 1871, reel 14, Frederick Douglass Papers, Manuscript Division, Library of Congress; hereafter FD Papers, LC.

7. Frederick Douglass, "Speech at the Thirty-third Anniversary of the Jerry Rescue," 1884, reel 16, FD Papers, LC. On the nature and importance of historical memory, see Hayden White, *Tropics of Discourse: Essays in Cultural Criticism* (Baltimore: Johns Hopkins University Press, 1978), 26–50; *The Invention of Tradition*, ed. Eric Hobsbawm and Terence Ranger (New York: Cambridge University Press, 1983); Jaroslav Pelikan, *The Vindication of Tradition* (New Haven: Yale University Press, 1984); Michael Kammen, *A Season of Youth: The American Revolution and the Historical Imagination* (New York: Knopf, 1978); *Memory Observed: Remembering in Natural Contexts*, ed. Ulric Neisser (San Francisco: W. H. Freeman, 1982); and David Lowenthal, *The Past Is a Foreign Country* (New York: Cambridge University Press, 1985). On the Civil War in the northern memory, see Daniel Aaron, *The Unwritten War: American Writers and the Civil War* (New York: Knopf, 1973); Oscar Handlin, "The Civil War as Symbol and as Actuality," *Massachusetts Review* 3 (autumn 1961): 133–43; Kammen, *Season of Youth*, 256–59; Paul H. Buck, *The Road to Reunion, 1865–1900* (Boston: Little, Brown, 1937), 228–309; and James M.

McPherson, *The Abolitionist Legacy: From Reconstruction to the NAACP* (Princeton: Princeton University Press, 1975), 95–139, 333–38.

8. Douglass, "Speech at the Thirty-third Anniversary of the Jerry Rescue"; Frederick Douglass, "Address Delivered on the Twenty-sixth Anniversary of Abolition in the District of Columbia," April 16, 1888, reel 16, FD Papers, LC.

9. Richard Slotkin, *The Fatal Environment: The Myth of the Frontier in the Age of Industrialization, 1800–1890* (New York: Atheneum, 1985), 19. My understanding of the structure of cultural myth, and its uses and misuses by historians, is derived from ibid., 3–32; Bruce Kuklick, "Myth and Symbol in American Studies," *American Quarterly* 24 (October 1972): 435–50; Sacvan Bercovitch, *The American Jeremiad* (Madison: University of Wisconsin Press, 1978), xi–xii, 132–220; Clifford Geertz, *The Interpretation of Cultures: Selected Essays by Clifford Geertz* (New York: Basic Books, 1973), 28–30, 33–141, 213–20; Kammen, *Season of Youth,* 3–32, 221–58; and Warren I. Susman, *Culture as History: The Transformation of American Society in the Twentieth Century* (New York: Pantheon, 1984), 3–26.

10. Frederick Douglass, "Speech on Emancipation Day," September 1883, reel 15, FD Papers, LC. For Douglass's attacks on the idea of "military necessity," see also "The Black Man's Progress on This Continent," *New National Era,* July 27, 1871. Frederick Douglass, "Speech in Madison Square," Decoration Day, 1878, reel 15, FD Papers, LC.

11. Oliver Wendell Holmes, *Occasional Speeches,* comp. Mark De Wolfe Howe (Cambridge: Belknap Press, Harvard University Press, 1962), 4–5, 76. Excellent discussions of Holmes are found in George M. Fredrickson, *The Inner Civil War: Northern Intellectuals and the Crisis of the Union* (New York: Harper and Row, 1965), 218–21; Cruce Stark, "Brothers At/In War: One Phase of Post–Civil War Reconciliation," *Canadian Review of American Studies* 6 (fall 1975): 174–81; and Aaron, *Unwritten War,* 161–62.

12. Albion W. Tourgee, *An Appeal to Caesar* (New York: Fords, Howard, and Hulbert, 1884), 37, 44; Buck, *Road to Reunion,* 242. On Tourgee, see Otto H. Olsen, *Carpetbagger's Crusade: The Life of Albion Winegar Tourgee* (Baltimore: Johns Hopkins University Press, 1965); Richard Nelson Current, *Those Terrible Carpetbaggers: A Reinterpretation* (New York: Oxford University Press, 1988), 367–82, 401–6; and Aaron, *Unwritten War,* 193–205.

13. Edmund Wilson, *Patriotic Gore: Studies in the Literature of the American Civil War* (Boston: Northeastern University Press, 1984), 669; Douglass, "Speech in Madison Square." On the conflict between ideological and nonideological conceptions of the war, see Fredrickson, *Inner Civil War,* 196–98, 217–38.

14. On the Freedmen's Memorial speech, see Benjamin Quarles, *Frederick Douglass* (Englewood Cliffs, N.J.: Prentice Hall, 1968), 276–78. Quarles maintains that the speech was "distinctly not one of [Douglass's] best." See also Nathan Irvin Huggins, *Slave and Citizen: The Life of Frederick Douglass* (Boston: Little, Brown, 1980), 102–3. Frederick Douglass, "Oration in Memory of Abraham Lincoln," April 14, 1876, in *Life and Writings of Frederick Douglas,* ed. Foner, 4:317–19, 314, 310–11. For the "mystic chords" quotation, see Abraham Lincoln, "First Inaugural Address," March 4, 1861, in *The Collected Works of Abraham Lincoln,* ed. Roy P.

Basler, 9 vols. (New Brunswick: Rutgers University Press, 1953–55), 4:271. On black attitudes toward Lincoln during the war, see Benjamin Quarles, *Lincoln and the Negro* (New York: Oxford University Press, 1962).

15. Gaines M. Foster, *Ghosts of the Confederacy: Defeat, the Lost Cause, and the Emergence of the New South, 1865–1913* (New York: Oxford University Press, 1986), 4–5, 36–46, 104–14; Charles Reagan Wilson, *Baptized in Blood: The Religion of the Lost Cause, 1865–1920* (Athens: University of Georgia Press, 1980), 12–14, 37–78; Thomas L. Connelly and Barbara L. Bellows, *God and General Longstreet: The Lost Cause and the Southern Mind* (Baton Rouge: Louisiana State University Press, 1982), 39–72. See also C. Vann Woodward, *The Origins of the New South, 1877–1913* (Baton Rouge: Louisiana State University Press, 1951), 154–58.

16. Connelly and Bellows, *God and General Longstreet*, 2–38; Foster, *Ghosts of the Confederacy*, 47, 60.

17. See Connelly and Bellows, *God and General Longstreet*, 39–72.

18. Foster, *Ghosts of the Confederacy*, 66–75. On the New South, see Woodward, *Origins*, especially 142–74. On the generational impact of the war in southern memory and on generational change in general, see David Herbert Donald, "A Generation of Defeat," in *From the Old South to the New: Essays on the Transitional South*, ed. Walter J. Fraser Jr. and Winfred B. Moore Jr. (Westport, Conn.: Greenwood Press, 1981), 3–20; and Werner Sollors, *Beyond Ethnicity: Consent and Descent in American Culture* (New York: Oxford University Press, 1986), 208–36.

19. August Wilson, *Joe Turner's Come and Gone* (New York: New American Library, 1988), 54–56. The play had its world premier at the Yale Repertory Theater, May 2, 1986. I saw it in May 1988 in New York City. Toni Morrison, *Beloved* (New York: Knopf, 1987), 274–75. Another excellent example from the recent Afro-African literary tradition showing the power of historical memory over life in the present is David Bradley, *The Chaneysville Incident* (New York: Harper and Row, 1981). On Bradley and black novelists' use of history, see Klaus Ensslen, "Fictionalizing History: David Bradley's 'The Chaneysville Incident,' *Callaloo* 11 (spring 1988): 280–95.

20. Douglass, "Wasted Magnanimity," *New National Era*, August 10, 1871; Douglass, "Bombast," ibid., November 10, 1870.

21. Douglass, "The Survivor's Meeting: A Soldier's Tribute to a Soldier," *New National Era*, December 1, 1870; "Monuments of Folly," ibid. Douglass was also outraged by southerners' attempts to write the Lost Cause outlook into American history textbooks. "They have taken to making rebel schoolbooks and teaching secession and disloyalty in their primary schools," Douglass reported. See "Still Firing the Southern Heart," ibid., February 23, 1871.

22. Frederick Douglass, "Speech on the Death of William Lloyd Garrison," June 2, 1879, reel 15, FD Papers, LC. The emergence of the New South in the 1880s caused great uncertainty among old abolitionists. They shared some of the optimism of the new era, but they also lamented the demise of Reconstruction and feared the control an autonomous South could wield over race relations. See McPherson, *Abolitionist Legacy*, 107–20; and Woodward, *Origins*, 107–74.

23. Frederick Douglass, "Campaign Speech on Behalf of Alonzo B. Cornell,"

1879, reel 15, FD Papers, LC; Frederick Douglass, "Emancipation," August 4, 1880, ibid.; Frederick Douglass, "Address Delivered on the Twenty-sixth Anniversary of the Abolition of Slavery in the District of Columbia," April 16, 1888, reel 16, ibid.

24. See Quarles, *Frederick Douglass,* 252–82; and Waldo E. Martin, *The Mind of Frederick Douglass* (Chapel Hill: University of North Carolina Press, 1984), 79–91.

25. Douglass, "Speech at the Thirty-third Anniversary of the Jerry Rescue."

26. Frederick Douglass, "Thoughts and Recollections of the Antislavery Conflict," undated speech, reel 19, FD Papers, LC; Alexis de Tocqueville, *Democracy in America,* ed. Thomas Bender (New York: Modern Library, 1981), 115, 397. On the significance of Tocqueville in understanding American individualism and the rejection of the past, see Robert Bellah et al., *Habits of the Heart: Individualism and Commitment in American Life* (Berkeley: University of California Press, 1985), 27–51, 255–307.

27. Frederick Douglass, "Self-Made Men," reel 18, FD Papers, LC. Beginning in 1874 or earlier, Douglass delivered this speech during numerous lecture tours. On Douglass's conception of self-made men, see Martin, *Mind of Frederick Douglass,* 253–78.

28. Douglass, "Address Delivered on the Twenty-sixth Anniversary of Abolition in the District of Columbia." On Confederate veterans homes funded by the Grand Army of the Republic, see Foster, *Ghosts of the Confederacy,* 94.

29. Friedrich Nietzsche, "On the Uses and Disadvantages of History for Life," in *Untimely Meditations,* trans. R. J. Hollingdale (New York: Cambridge University Press, 1983), 62; Douglass, "Thoughts and Recollections of the Antislavery Conflict." On the concept of historical forgetting, see Lowenthal, *The Past Is a Foreign Country,* 204–6. On northerners and black suffrage, see C. Vann Woodward, *American Counterpoint: Slavery and Racism in the North-South Dialogue* (Boston: Little, Brown, 1964), 173–83.

30. Douglass, "Speech on Emancipation Day."

31. Douglass, "Speech in Madison Square."

32. Warren, *Legacy of the Civil War,* 59–76. Warren illuminates the ambiguities and contradictions in the dual development of the Lost Cause and the "treasury of virtue." For Douglass's discussion of the National Lincoln Monument Association, see *New National Era,* October 27, 1870. This monument, never constructed as planned, was to be seventy feet high and contain many statues of Civil War military and political personalities and allegorical figures. In his editorial, Douglass seemed flushed with excitement. He saw the monument as "an eternal sentinel guarding the era of emancipation; an immortal herald proclaiming to all the races of men the nation's great civil and moral reforms. In a word, a splendid bronze and granite portraiture of the final triumph of liberty and equality on American soil," *New National Era,* October 27, 1870. On later efforts for a monument to black soldiers (also unsuccessful), see John Hope Franklin, *George Washington Williams: A Biography* (Chicago: University of Chicago Press, 1987), 171–74.

33. Frederick Douglass, "Address at the Centennial Celebration of the Aboli-

tion Society of Pennsylvania," reel 15, FD Papers, LC; Douglass, "Speech at the Thirty-third Anniversary of the Jerry Rescue."

34. Aaron, *Unwritten War,* 332–33, xviii, 340. On fiction and the Civil War, see also Robert A. Lively, *Fiction Fights the Civil War: An Unfinished Chapter in the Literary History of the American People* (Chapel Hill: University of North Carolina Press, 1957); and Joyce Appleby, "Reconciliation and the Northern Novelist, 1865–1880," *Civil War History* 10 (June 1964): 117–29. On black literary activity and memory in the nineteenth and twentieth centuries, see Arlene A. Elder, *The "Hindered Hand": Cultural Implications of Early African-American Fiction* (Westport, Conn.: Greenwood Press, 1978). For the power of war over the imagination, especially in literary forms, see Paul Fussell, *The Great War and Modern Memory* (New York: Oxford University Press, 1975), 310–35.

35. W. E. B. Du Bois, *Black Reconstruction in America, 1860–1880* (New York: Atheneum, 1935), 725, 722, 715.

36. Douglass, "Speech at the Thirty-third Anniversary of the Jerry Rescue."

37. Douglass, "Decoration Day," May 1883, reel 17, FD Papers, LC.

38. Ibid.; Robert Lowell, "For the Union Dead," in *Norton Anthology of American Literature: Shorter Edition,* ed. Ronald Gottesman et al. (New York: Norton, 1980), 1842.

A Quarrel Forgotten or a Revolution Remembered?
Reunion and Race in the Memory of the Civil War, 1875–1913

It's gonna hurt now; anything dead coming back to life hurts.
    —*Toni Morrison,* Beloved
*I believe that the struggle for life is the order of the world. . . .
[I]f it is our business to fight, the book for the army is a war-song,
not a hospital sketch.*
    —*Oliver Wendell Holmes Jr., "A Soldier's Faith"*
*Americans . . . have the most remarkable ability to alchemize all
bitter truths into an innocuous but piquant confection and to
transform their moral contradictions, or public discussion of
such contradictions into a proud decoration, such as are given
for heroism on the field of battle.*
    —*James Baldwin, "Many Thousands Gone"*

The historical memory of a people, a nation, or any aggregate evolves over time in relation to present needs and ever-changing contexts. Societies and the groups within them remember and use history as a source of coherence and identity, as a means of contending for power or place, and as a means of controlling access to whatever becomes normative in society. For better and worse, social memories—ceaselessly constructed versions of a group past—are the roots of identity formation. In spite of all we would like to think we have learned about how *culture* is invented and how *heritage* is a social construct that ultimately defies fixed definition, people jealously seek to own their pasts. The post-1989 world has demonstrated this dilemma with tragic consequences. As historian John Gillis has aptly put it, "identities and memories are not things we think *about,* but things we think *with*."[1] As such, the historical, in the form of social memory, becomes political.

The study of historical memory might be defined, therefore, as the study of cultural struggle, of contested truths, interpretations, moments, events, epochs, rituals, or even texts in history that thresh out rival versions of the past that are in turn put to the service of the present. As events in world politics, curriculum debates, national and international commemorations and anniversaries have shown, historical memories can be severely controlled, can undergo explosive liberation or redefinition from one generation or even one year to the next. The social, political, and psychological stakes of historical memory can be high. The "public" that consumes history is vast, and the marketplace turbulent. Like it or not, we live in an era where the impulse to teach the young to have an open sense of history is not enough; that sensibility will be challenged. The pragmatic, questioning sense of history will encounter social memory—in the classroom, at the international negotiating table, at the movies, and in the streets. This dilemma desperately needs trained historians seeking evidence, demanding verification, offering reasoned explanations of events. But the truth is that historians and their cousins in related disciplines are only playing one part in this drama. As Natalie Zemon Davis and Randolph Starn, among others, have cautioned, "whenever memory is invoked we should be asking: by whom, where, in which context, against what ?"[2]

As Ken Burns's 1990 PBS film series *The Civil War* demonstrated once again, one of the most vexing questions in the formation of American historical memory has been to understand the meaning and memory of the Civil War. The Civil War itself has long been the object of widespread nostalgia and the subject of durable myth-making in both North and South. In the final episode of the film series scant attention is paid to the complicated story of Reconstruction. The consequences of this American *Iliad* are only briefly assessed as viewers (likely quite taken by an artistically brilliant and haunting film) are ushered from the surrender at Appomattox, through some fleeting discussion of Reconstruction politics, past Ulysses S. Grant's final prophecy of an "era of great harmony," to Joseph E. Johnston's bareheaded encounter with pneumonia and quick death after attending the funeral in 1891 of his former battlefield rival William Tecumseh Sherman, and finally to that irresistible footage of the old veterans at the 1913 and 1938 Gettysburg Blue-Gray reunions. Along the way, the narrative is punctuated by the Mississippi writer Shelby Foote informing us that the war "made *us* an *is*" (a reference to how "the United States is" rather than "are" became a common expression) and historian Barbara Fields reminding us of William Faulkner's claim that history is "not a *was* but an *is*." The film does leave one with a sense that the Civil War was an event with lasting significance for the entire world, that the past and the present inform, even flow into one another, and that legacies have power over us. But it is a point made as much with feeling, with music and sentiment, as it is with historical analysis. The Blue and the Gray—men out of a distant past, who were once such familiar images at American train stations and on town greens—became television images for the first time. They charmed millions of late twentieth-century viewers, their very presence at those picaresque reunions declaring that the nation had survived all the carnage in the previous episodes. They looked at us reassuringly as narrator David McCullough announced: "the war was over."[3]

The Civil War is epic history converted into superb television. The series moves and instructs its varied audiences; it leaves indelible sounds and images in the hearts and minds of viewers; and it teaches that the Civil War was a terrible passage through which Americans were forever changed. Among the broad populace of history enthusiasts, and in American and international classrooms, that film series is now a principal source of popular memory about the Civil War. I have used this film series with many American students, as well as with German students at the University of Munich in 1993. The reactions of German students were especially interesting. They typically asked questions like, why are there so many sunsets and moonrises in this film? Why is it so "sentimental"? Some actually brought in their own personal collections of Civil War ballad music or Negro spirituals. One student said "The Battle Hymn of the Republic" had always been one of his favorite songs along with those of Elvis Presley and Jimi Hendrix. But another German student asked me whether Americans had ever considered comparing the devastation and sense of loss in their Civil War with the Thirty Years War in Europe. To this question, a stretched analogy, I had to answer that most Americans have never heard of the Thirty Years War. Sometimes, perspective is all. Burns touched many heartstrings, and left some puzzlement as well, among European viewers of his film.

Some questions asked by students go to the heart of another problem: the American tendency toward claims of exceptionalism and consensus in our historical consciousness. On one level the ending of Burns's remarkable film series offers a vivid reminder of just how much interpretations of the Civil War provide an index of our political culture, of how much the central issues of the war—union and slavery, reunion and racial equality, diversity as the definition of America or as the source of its unraveling—remain a challenge for each succeeding generation of Americans. However, on another level, the ending of the film offers many Americans the legacy they find most appealing: the rapid transition from the veteran just returned to his farm, standing on a corn wagon in 1865 (almost an image of a horn of plenty), to the 1913 Gettysburg reunion is the stuff of earnest nostalgia, and it makes good fast-forward history. As Richard Slotkin wrote, "Burns evokes as well as anyone the paradoxical and complex emotion of Civil War nostalgia, in which one recognizes the awful tragedy of the war, yet somehow *misses* it." In American collective memory, sectional reconciliation virtually required that some of the deeper tragedies of that conflict be "missed." Such an ending (as in Burns's film) becomes transhistorical in American social memory: the time between the real battle of Gettysburg and its fiftieth anniversary reunion is at once a great distance and no distance at all. Time itself can be transcended, and in those mystical exchanges between gracious old veterans on what seem ancient battlefields, one can entertain the notion that American history endures all traumas in its troubled but inexorable path of progress, and that the day may arrive when there will no longer be any need to think historically about long-term consequences. Abraham Lincoln's haunting passage about the "mystic chords of memory, stretching from every battlefield and patriot grave" had, indeed, swelled "the chorus of the Union" and conquered time itself. The pleading poetry in Lincoln's first inaugural address in 1861 (from which Burns takes his title for the final episode, "The Better Angels of Our Nature") was delivered, of course, in the midst of crisis and on the brink of war. But the deeper conflicts and contradictions buried in the new "patriot graves" (after the Civil War) could be finely displaced, comfortably forgotten, and truly "mystic" as Joshua Lawrence Chamberlain, the hero of Little Round Top at the battle of Gettysburg (and one of Burns's principal "characters"), describes the 1913 reunion as a "transcendental experience" and a "radiant fellowship of the fallen." American history had "progressed" through Reconstruction, the Gilded Age, the myriad crises of the 1890s, vicious racial violence, unprecedented labor strife, a short foreign war with Spain, through massive urbanization and industrialization, to become a society divided by a racial apartheid and seething with ethnic pluralism on the eve of World War I. Rarely was there a more confirming context for William Dean Howells's turn-of-the-century assertion that "what the American public always wants is a tragedy with a happy ending."[4]

Explanations of the meaning and memory of the Civil War—whether expressed in fiction, monuments, historiography, movies, politics, journalism, public schooling, veterans' organizations, the strongly gendered attractions of war-gaming, tourism, or reenactments—have, intentionally or not, provided a means of assessing the illusive question of national self-definition in America. Such constructions of the memory of our most divisive event have also reflected the persistent dilemma of race in public policy, as well as our ongoing challenge to build one political structure that can encompass the interests of the many. By and large, the legions of Americans who transmit a fascination for the Civil War across generations still prefer the drama of the immediate event to discussions of causes and consequences; they continue to be enthralled with the fight as much, if not more, than its meanings. This is partly a measure of human nature, of audiences, and of public tastes for history generally. Burns effectively mixed the broad military struggle with the voices of ordinary people and the perspectives of local communities. The influence of the new social history is altogether apparent in the film. We learn that the Civil War was a ruthless and all-encompassing experience in places like Clarksville, Tennessee, and Deer Isle, Maine. We hear the common soldier's syntax, and the war's meaning interpreted from the diaries of ordinary women. Burns put slavery and emancipation at the center of the wartime story; Frederick Douglass's compelling voice commands attention at several turning points in the narrative. Emancipated slaves are real people, and they too help to tell the story. But in the end, the film series is still a narrative about the making and consequences of war (and the horror and destruction are unmistakable), told from headquarters and the perspectives of larger than life individuals. The legends of such figures as Robert E. Lee, Stonewall Jackson, Nathan Bedford Forrest, William Tecumseh Sherman, and Lincoln himself are well preserved in Burns's self-conscious attempt at documentary epic. As a filmmaker-historian, all these were, of course, artistic as well as historical choices for Burns; at times he simply created what works best on film, with a clear artifice in mind.[5]

For Americans broadly, the Civil War has been a defining event upon which we have often imposed unity and continuity; as a culture, we have preferred its music and pathos to its enduring challenges, the theme of reconciled conflict to resurgent, unresolved legacies. We have displaced complicated consequences by endlessly focusing on the contest itself. We have sometimes lifted ourselves out of historical time, above the details, and rendered the war safe in a kind of Passover offering as we watch the Blue and the Gray veterans shake hands across the little stone walls at Gettysburg. Like stone monuments, monumental films, as well as some monumental books, are sometimes as much about forgetting as they are about remembering. Deeply embedded in American mythology of mission, and serving as a mother lode of nostalgia for antimodernists and military history buffs, the Civil War remains very difficult to shuck from its shell of sentimentalism. Historian Nina Silber has demonstrated how "a sentimental rubric took hold of the reunion process" during the three decades after the war. Indeed, Silber showed how gender (conceptions of manliness and femininity, and the popular literary ritual of intersectional marriage) provided a principal source of metaphor and imagery through which sectional reconciliation was achieved.[6]

Through scholarship and schooling, much has changed in recent decades regarding the place of the black experience in the era of the Civil War. But in the half century after the conflict, as the sections reconciled, the races increasingly divided. The intersectional wedding that became such a staple of popular culture, had no interracial counterpart in the popular imagination. Quite the opposite was the case. So deeply at the root of the war's causes and consequences, and so powerful a source of division in American social psychology, "race"—and its myriad manipulations in American culture—served as the antithesis of a culture of reconciliation. The memory of slavery, emancipation, and the Fifteenth Amendment never fit well into a culture in which the Old and New South were romanticized and welcomed back to a new nationalism. Persistent discussion of the "race problem" (or the "Negro question") across the political and ideological spectrum at the turn of the century meant that American society could not also remember a "Civil War problem" or a "Blue-Gray problem." Interpretations of the Civil War in the broad American culture continue to illustrate what Daniel Aaron meant when he said that, among American writers, the conflict "has not been so much unfelt, as it is unfaced." And if W. E. B. Du Bois was at all correct with his famous 1903 declaration that "the problem of the twentieth century is the problem of the color line," then we can begin to see how the problem of "reunion" and the problem of "race" were trapped in a tragic, mutual dependence.[7]

This essay seeks to suggest in the broadest terms how American culture processed the meaning and memory of the Civil War and

Reconstruction down to World War I, with special emphasis on these overlapping themes of reunion and race. Through selected examples, we can observe how black and white voices spoke both to, as well as completely around, each other in this process. In the introduction to the 1991 edition of *Imagined Communities,* Benedict Anderson warned us about the delusion of "shedding" ourselves of the problem of nationalism in the modern world. "The 'end of an era of nationalism,' so long prophesied," wrote Anderson, "is not remotely in sight. Indeed, nationness is the most universally legitimate value in the political life of our time." Moreover, in his discussion of the function of "memory and forgetting" in the shaping of nationalism, Anderson left this telling comment about the American Civil War: "A vast pedagogical industry works ceaselessly to oblige young Americans to remember/forget the hostilities of 1861–65 as a great 'civil' war between 'brothers' rather than between—as they briefly were—two sovereign nation-states. (We can be sure, however, that if the Confederacy had succeeded in maintaining its independence, this 'civil war' would have been replaced in memory by something quite unbrotherly.)" There may never be an end to nationalism as we know it, just as there is no end to history. But there are manifest breaks in the process of history, events and commemorations of those events that expose how we use history.[8]

In "The New Negro," philosopher Alain Locke believed he discerned one of those turning points, both in black self-consciousness and in the nation's race "problem." And the change had everything to do with memory and forgetting. "While the minds of most of us, black and white, have thus burrowed in the *trenches* of the Civil War and Reconstruction," wrote Locke, "the actual march of development has simply *flanked* these positions, necessitating a sudden reorientation of view. We have not been watching in the right direction; set North and South on a sectional axis, we have not noticed the East till the sun has us blinking." Preoccupied in remembering/forgetting the war as a North-South fight, mired in the increasingly nostalgic details of a heroic war in a lost past, American culture had lost sight of what the fight had been all about. Time would tell whether Locke's optimism about a new generation of blacks' "spiritual coming of age" would be a solution to or an evasion of these problems in American historical memory, whether the blinking of a new era would turn to collective insight.[9] For more than two decades before Locke wrote, the reform fervor of the Progressive era, with its quests for order, honesty, and efficiency, and its impulse against monopolism, compelled Americans to look inward and forward, but they did so in a culture full of sentimentalized remembrance. Moreover, for at least the same twenty years black thinkers had been fashioning definitions of the "new Negro" for the new century. But what would be the place of "new Negroes" at Blue-Gray reunions in the land of Jim Crow? In a society inexorably looking ahead, the culture of sectional reconciliation would force millions, consciously or not, to divert their eyes.

The chronological reach of this essay is long and therefore risks oversimplification. Large aspects of the topic will have to be left outside the purview of a single essay, notably the impact of popular literature (the plantation school) on northern readers and editors in the late nineteenth century, the post-Reconstruction generation of black and white writers who wrote directly and indirectly about the legacies of the Civil War and emancipation, the myriad ways sectional politics and the emergence of Jim Crow (in law and life) melded into an uneasy national consensus from the 1880s to World War I, and the cultural nostalgia rooted in the alienation born of rapid industrialization.[10] Instead, I have selected two ways to demonstrate the dialectic between race and reunion as the memory of the Civil War evolved in American culture: first, an encounter between two major African American leaders, Alexander Crummell and Frederick Douglass, over how blacks should best remember slavery and the Civil War; and second, the fiftieth anniversary Gettysburg Blue-Gray reunion as a ritual of national reconciliation, an event in which race, black participation in the war, the very idea of slavery as cause and emancipation as result of the war might be said to be thunderously conspicuous by their absence.

In 1875, as the march away from radicalism and protection of African American rights threatened to become a full retreat, Frederick Douglass gave a Fourth of July speech in Washington, D.C., entitled "The Color Question." Events, both personal and national, had cast a pall over the normally sanguine Douglass, forcing him to reflect in racialized terms on the American centennial that was to be celebrated the following year. The nation, Douglass feared, would "lift to the sky its million voices in one grand Centennial hosanna of peace and good will to all the white race . . . from gulf to lakes and from sea to sea." As a black citizen, he dreaded the day when "this great white race has renewed its vows of patriotism and flowed back into its accustomed channels." Douglass looked back upon fifteen years of unparalleled change for his people, worried about the hold of white supremacy on America's historical consciousness, and asked the core question in the nation's struggle over the memory of the Civil War: "If war among the whites brought peace and liberty to the blacks, *what will peace among the whites bring*?"[11] For more than a century, through cycles of great advancement and periods of cynical reaction in American race relations, Douglass's question in various forms has echoed through our political culture. Answers to Douglass's question have depended, of course, on context—on time, place, one's positioning along the color line, the available sources for scholars, access to power, the medium through which the history is transmitted, and differing revisionist questions and agendas. But always, the answers have emerged from the contentious struggle over the content, meaning, and uses of the past. John Hope Franklin recognized this in a 1979 essay on what he described as the "enormous influence" of the combination of Thomas Dixon's novel *The Clansman* (1903), D. W. Griffith's 1915 film *Birth of a Nation,* and Claude Bowers's popular history *The Tragic Era* (1928), all produced within the first three decades of the twentieth century. Franklin's analysis of how history can be used as "propaganda" in the shaping of a nation's memory of itself echoed Ralph Ellison's poignant comment during the same year. Nothing in our past, said Ellison, like the question of race in the story of the Civil War and Reconstruction, had ever caused Americans to be so "notoriously selective in the exercise of historical memory."[12] All practice of historical memory formation is, of course, selective. How some selections become or remain dominant, taking on mythic dimensions, and others do not, is the tale to be told.

The 1880s were a pivotal decade in the development of traditions and social memories of the Civil War. The Lost Cause in the South, as well as a growing willingness to embrace sectional reconciliation among northerners, underwent cultural transformation. The situation among black intellectuals was similar; an index of their struggle over how and if to remember slavery and the Civil War era can be found in a debate between Alexander Crummell and Frederick Douglass. Then as now, no single persuasion controlled African American thought; black social memory was often as diverse as were debates within the Grand Army of the Republic (GAR) or among advocates of the Lost Cause tradition. As editors, ministers, community leaders, or writers, black intellectuals in the late nineteenth century were as compelled as anyone else to engage in what became an intraracial debate over the meaning and best uses of the age of emancipation. The contours of such debates were established well before Booker T. Washington and W. E. B. Du Bois came to embody the classic division in black thought over historical consciousness and political strategies.[13]

At Storer College, in Harpers Ferry, West Virginia, on May 30, 1885 (Memorial Day), Alexander Crummell, one of the most accomplished and well-traveled black intellectuals of the nineteenth century, gave a commencement address to the graduates of that black college, which had been founded for freedmen at the end of the Civil War. Crummell, an Episcopal priest, educated at the abolitionist Oneida Institute in upstate New York and at Cambridge University in England in the 1840s, had spent nearly twenty years as a missionary and an advocate of African nationalism in Liberia (1853–71). Crummell later considered the Storer address, entitled "The Need of New Ideas and New Aims for a New Era," to be the most important he ever gave. Although Crummell could not resist acknowledging that Harpers Ferry was a setting "full of the most thrilling memories in the history of our race" (because of John Brown's raid), his aim was to turn the new generation of blacks, most of whom would have been born during the Civil War, away from dwelling "morbidly and absorbingly upon the servile past" and instead to embrace the urgent economic and moral "needs of the present." As a minister and theologian, and as a social conservative, Crummell's concerns were not only racial uplift—his ultimate themes were family, labor, industrial education, and moral values—but the unburdening of black folks from what he believed was the debilitating, painful memory of slavery. Crummell made a careful distinction between memory and recollection. Memory, he contended, was a passive, unavoidable, often essential part of group consciousness; recollection, on the other hand, was active, a matter of choice and selection, and dangerous in excess. "What I would fain have you guard against," he told the graduates, "is not the memory of slavery, but the constant *recollection* of it." Such recollection, Crummell maintained, would only degrade racial progress in the Gilded Age; for him, unmistakably, "duty lies in the future."[14]

Prominent in the audience that day at Harpers Ferry (probably in the front row or on the stage) was Frederick Douglass, whom Crummell described as his "neighbor" from Washington, D.C. According to Crummell's own account, his call to reorient African American consciousness from the past to the future met with Douglass's "emphatic and most earnest protest." Douglass rose to the occasion, as he did so many times in the 1880s on one anniversary or Memorial Day after another, to assert an African American–abolitionist memory of the Civil War era, which almost always included an abiding reminder of the nature and significance of slavery.[15] No verbatim account of what Douglass said at Harpers Ferry survives, but several other speeches from the 1880s offer a clear picture of what the former abolitionist may have said. Douglass and Crummell shared a sense of the dangers and limitations of social memory, especially for a group that had experienced centuries of slavery. A healthy level of forgetting, said Douglass, was "Nature's plan of relief." But in season and out, Douglass insisted that whatever the psychological need for avoiding the woeful legacy of slavery, it would resist all human effort to suppress it. The history of black Americans, he said many times in the 1880s, could "be traced like that of a wounded man through a crowd by the blood." Better to confront such a history, he believed, than to wait for its resurgence.[16]

Douglass's many postwar speeches about the memory of the conflict typically began with acknowledgment of the need for healing and getting on with life. But then he would forcefully call his audiences to remembrance of the origins and consequences, as well as the sacrifices, of the Civil War. He would often admit that his own personal memory of slavery was best kept sleeping like a "half-forgotten dream." But he despised the politics of forgetting that American culture seemed to necessitate in the 1880s. "We are not here to visit upon the children the sins of the fathers," Douglass told a Memorial Day audience in Rochester, New York, in 1883, "but we are here to remember the causes, the incidents, and the results of the late rebellion." Most of all Douglass objected to the white supremacist historical construction that portrayed emancipation as a great national "failure" or "blunder." The entire racist theory that slavery had protected and nurtured blacks, and that freedom had gradually sent him "falling into a state of barbarism" forced Douglass to argue for an aggressive use of memory. The problem was not merely the rise of the Lost Cause myth of southern virtue and victimization. The problem was "not confined to the South," declared Douglass in 1888. "It [the theory of black degeneration coupled with historical misrepresentations of emancipation and Reconstruction] has gone forth to the North. It has crossed the ocean. It has gone to Europe, and it has gone as far as the wings of the press, and the power of speech can carry it. There is no measuring the injury inflicted upon the negro by it."[17] Such, Douglass understood, were the stakes of conflicts over rival versions of the past, when combined with sociobiological theories of racial inferiority and put to the service of the present. Douglass died the year before the *Plessy v. Ferguson* Supreme Court decision. But he had lived long enough to peer across the horizon and see the society America was becoming in the age of Jim Crow. In all discussion of the "race question" in America, Douglass had long understood, the historical was always political.

Even before the most violent outbreaks of lynching and an increasingly radical racism took hold in the South, there was good reason to be worried about uses of the theory of black degeneration. The theory would eventually be spread widely in popular literature, emerge full-blown in minstrelsy, film, and cartoons, and most tellingly, gain many spokesmen in academic high places. Produced by historians, statisticians in the service of insurance companies, and scientists of all manner, a hereditarian and social Darwinist theory of black capacity fueled racial policies of evasion and repression. By the turn of the century, the Negrophobia practiced in daily conversations among many ordinary whites was now buttressed by highly developed, academic notions of blacks as a "vanishing race," destined to lose the struggle of natural selection.[18]

In 1900 Paul B. Barringer, chairman of the medical faculty at the University of Virginia, gave the keynote address at a major symposium (on heredity and the southern "Negro problem") of the Tri-State Medical Society, in Charleston, South Carolina. Barringer began with a discussion of dog species and habits, and the dangers of "indiscriminate breeding." He then found his central theme, the "habits of a race." Barringer's clinical analysis of his topic demonstrated the structure of thought Douglass and others had good reason to fear. "Let us apply this biological axiom to the human race, taking as our example . . . the Southern Negro," declared the doctor. "I will show from the study of his racial history (phylogeny) that his late tendency to return to barbarism is as natural as the return of the sow that is washed to her wallowing in the mire. I will show that the degradation under which he was formed and the fifty centuries of historically recorded savagery with which he came to us cannot be permanently influenced by one or two centuries of enforced correction if the correcting force be withdrawn. . . . [W]hen the correcting force of discipline was removed he, like the released planet, began to fall . . . a motion as certain in its results as the law of gravitation. Fortunately for us experience (history) shows that these savage traits can be held down, and we have seen that if held down long enough, they will be bred out. In this one fact lies the hope of the South." With these words and more, Barringer demonstrated that for the sheer virulence of white supremacy and racial demagoguery, some academics took no back seat to politicians. Throughout his speech he mixed social with biological prescriptions. He predicted the worst: "unless a brake is placed upon the natural ontogeny of this savage, the South will be uninhabitable for the white." But Barringer preferred to place his hope in "education of trade or industrial type" for blacks. "Then and not till then," he concluded, "will the franchise become for him [blacks] a reality and the Jim Crow car a memory."[19]

Although black intellectuals were by no means immune to notions of "race" as the source of group characteristics and traits—such a conception was pervasive in turn-of-the-century Western thought—they would, as a whole, denounce the Barringers and their ideas. Against such racism, whether in this vicious, biological form or in a calmer, paternalistic mode, older memories of emancipation had to contend with newer memories of segregation and lynch mobs in black communities. Indeed, what African American historical memory faced in the new century was not just a pedagogical and historiographical consensus about the "failure" of Reconstruction, which seemed to render further discussion of the Fourteenth and Fifteenth Amendments mute. Most bluntly, what the racial egalitarian legacy of the Civil War faced was, as George Fredrickson has shown, the sense of permanence and determinism in white supremacist theory and practice. "Race" theory, whether held passively or advanced aggressively, had everything to do with the way white Americans chose to remember emancipation, or whether they chose to remember it at all. From such spokesmen as Barringer, Douglass's question—"what will peace among the whites bring?"—received some loud and terrible answers.[20]

Although Douglass and Crummell had great respect for each other, they spoke during their Storer confrontation with different agendas, informed by different experiences, and representing different traditions. Crummell had never been a slave; he achieved a classical education, was a missionary of evangelical Christianity, a thinker of conservative instincts, and had spent almost the entire Civil War era in West Africa. He returned to the United States twice during the war to recruit black Americans for possible emigration to Liberia, while Douglass worked aggressively as a war propagandist of the Union cause, demanded emancipation, and recruited approximately one hundred members of the Fifty-fourth Massachusetts black regiment (two of whom were his sons Charles and Lewis). Crummell represented a brand of black nationalism that has survived through Marcus Garvey and beyond: a combination of Western, European Christian civilizationism, and race pride and purity. Crummell contended that the principal problems faced by American blacks were moral weakness, self-hatred, and industrial primitiveness. In the 1870s Crummell became the founding pastor of Saint Luke's Episcopal church in Washington, D.C., while Douglass became a regular speaker at the middle-class Metropolitan A.M.E. church in the same city.[21]

Douglass, the former slave, had established his fame by writing and speaking about the meaning of slavery; his life's work and his very identity were inextricably linked to the transformations of the Civil War. The past made and inspired Douglass; there was no meaning for him without memory, whatever the consequences of "recollection." He believed he had remade himself from slavery to freedom, and he believed that blacks generally had been regenerated in the second American Revolution of emancipation and the Civil War. The past had also made Crummell, but his connection to many of the benchmarks of African American social memory had been largely distant, and informed by African nationalism and Christian mission. For Douglass, emancipation and the Civil War were truly *felt* history, a moral and legal foundation upon which to demand citizenship and equality. For Crummell, they were the potentially paralyzing memories to be resisted; they were not the epic to be retold, merely the source of future needs. Crummell sought to redeem Africa and to inspire moral values in the freedpeople by the example of an elite black leadership. Douglass was devoted to the same values and essentially the same model of leadership; he sought, preeminently, however, to redeem the civil and political rights promised by the verdicts of Fort Wagner and Appomattox. Both men believed that the talented had to uplift the ordinary, although they, certainly in Douglass's case, had fallen out of touch with much of the material plight of southern freedmen. Crummell had tried to be a founding father of Liberia; Douglass dearly wished to see himself as a founding father of a reinvented American republic. Both were from the same generation, had traveled far, seen great changes, and at Storer College, were speaking to the postfreedom generation. For different reasons and with different aims, Crummell and Douglass sought to teach this new generation how to understand and use the legacy of slavery and the Civil War era, how to preserve and destroy the past.

This contrast could be overdrawn in the pursuit of dualities in African American thought. But such a comparison is suggestive of the recurring dilemma of black intellectuals in American history. Is the black experience in America a racial memory, or is it thoroughly intertwined with collective, national memory? Is the core image of the black experience in America represented by black institutions, cultural forms, and aesthetics that have flourished by rejecting American nationalism or European cultural forms, or by the black Civil War soldier and the Fourteenth Amendment? By Booker T. Washington's image of the "hand and the fingers," or Thurgood Marshall standing on the steps of the Supreme Court after winning *Brown v. Board of Education?* In a Garvey-UNIA parade, or in the Selma march? In Malcolm X at a Harlem street rally, or Martin Luther King at the Lincoln Memorial? Can there be a single, core image at all? When does it matter how benchmark African American memories are directly linked to the changing master narratives of American history, and when does it not? Are there not multiple core images of African American historical memory, jagged, diverse, regional, rural, and urban? These kinds of questions are, in part, what keeps African American history at the center of research agendas in the new histories. Dichotomies have sometimes blurred more truth than they have revealed. All such comparisons—among scholars or in larger public uses of memory and history—must, of course, be historicized. However politicized, romanticized, regionalized, or class based these questions have become in each succeeding generation, the answers have always been contested and complex. Rival memories among black thinkers should be treated as equally dynamic as similar struggles in the larger culture.[22]

As America underwent vast social changes in the late nineteenth century, and fought a foreign war in 1898, so too the memory of the Civil War transformed as it was transmitted to new generations. This is a complex story, but one of the principal features of the increasingly sentimentalized road to reunion was the celebration of the veteran, especially at Blue-Gray reunions, which became important aspects of popular culture in an age that loved pageantry, became obsessed with building monuments, and experienced a widespread revival of the martial ideal.[23] A brief focus on the fiftieth anniversary reunion at Gettysburg in 1913 may help illuminate the relationship of race and reunion in Civil War memory. As early as 1909 the State of Pennsylvania established a commission and began planning for the 1913 celebration. In the end, the states appropriated some $1,750,000 to provide free transportation to veterans from every corner of the country. Pennsylvania alone spent at least $450,000, and the federal government, through Congress and the War Department, appropriated approximately $450,000 to build the "Great Camp" for the "Great Reunion" as it became known. More than 53,000 veterans attended the reunion, and again as many spectators were estimated to have descended upon the small town of Gettysburg for the July 1–4 festival of reconciliation.[24]

The railroad transportation of any Civil War veteran living anywhere in the United States was paid by public monies. Some 100 veterans arrived in Gettysburg from California, 10 of them Confederates. Vermont sent 669 men, 4 of them listed as Confederates. Nevada and Wyoming were the only states not accounted for at the reunion, although New Mexico sent only one lone Union veteran. The whole event was an organizational, logistical, and financial triumph. A small army of souvenir salesmen flooded the streets of the town of Gettysburg, and no fewer than 47 railroad companies operating in or through Pennsylvania alone were paid a total of $142,282 for the transportation of veterans. The event was covered by 155 reporters from the national and international press, which provided headlines (along with stunning photographs) in most newspapers during the week of the reunion. Once the old men had arrived in their uniforms, decked out in ribbons and graced with silver beards, the tent city on the old battlefield became one of the most photogenic spectacles Americans had ever seen. For most observers, the veterans were men out of another time, images from the history beyond memory, icons that stimulated deep feelings, a sense of pride, history, and idle amusement all at once. They were an irresistible medium through which Americans could see their inheritance and be deflected from it at the same time.[25]

Many reunions had been held and a vast array of monuments constructed at Gettysburg long before 1913. But if social memory on the broadest scale is best forged and transmitted by performed, ritual commemorations, as many anthropologists have argued, then the memory of the Civil War as it stood in the general American culture in the early twentieth century never saw a more fully orchestrated nor more highly organized expression than in Gettysburg at the battle's semicentennial. The Great Camp, covering 280 acres, serving 688,000 "cooked meals," prepared by 2,170 cooks, laborers, and bakers using 130,048 pounds of flour must have warmed the heart of even the most compulsive advocates of Taylorism. Frederick W. Taylor's *Principles of Scientific Management* had just been published in 1911, and the Taylor Society had been founded in the same year, as the Civil War semicentennial began. The 47 miles of "avenues" on the battlefield, lit by 500 electric arc lights provided a perfect model of military mobilization and mass production. Those 32 automatic "bubbling ice water fountains" throughout the veterans' quarters offered a delightful, if hardly conscious, experience with "incorporation." Taylorite advocates of efficiency warmly approved the extraordinary "preparedness" of the Red Cross and the army medical corps in its efforts to provide first-class hospital care for the veterans during the encampment. The average age of a veteran at the event was 74, and the Pennsylvania Commission's report celebrated the fact that only 9 of the old fellows died during the reunion, a statistic many times lower than the national average for such an age group. Moreover, efficiency enthusiasts could marvel at the 90 elaborate, modern latrines (men's and women's) constructed all over the encampment. The commission's report was careful to include notes on the successful functioning of all latrine mechanisms, cleaning procedures, and estimates of tonnage of waste material. The press was full of celebration of such efficiency. The *Philadelphia Inquirer* marveled that "more painstaking care, more scientific preparation and a better discipline than has ever before been known [occurred] on such an occasion." The camp was "policed in a way," observed the *Inquirer,* "that made it the healthiest place on earth. . . . [T]here never was anything better done in our history."[26]

As one would expect, the theme of the reunion from the earliest days of its conception was nationalism, patriotism, and harmony—the great "Peace Jubilee," as the planning commission had announced as early as 1910. Fifty years after Pickett's Charge (and the Emancipation Proclamation, which was utterly ignored during the week's ceremonies), Douglass's question received a full-throated answer. There are only isolated references to the attendance of black veterans at the 1913 reunion. In a book by Walter H. Blake, a New Jersey veteran who compiled a narrative of anecdotes and personal reminiscences of his journey to the event, one finds the claim that "there were colored men on both sides of the lines." The Pennsylvania Commission "had made arrangements only for negroes from the Union side," lamented the New Jersey veteran, "forgetful of the fact that there were many faithful slaves who fought against their own interests in their intense loyalty to their Southern masters." Numerous black men worked as camp laborers, building the tent city and distributing mess kits and blankets (they appear in photographs published by the commission and elsewhere). Nowhere in its detailed, 281-page published report does the Pennsylvania Commission indicate how many black veterans attended the reunion. The commission was explicitly concerned that *"only"* those determined to be a "known veteran of the Civil War" by their documented honorable discharges were to receive free transportation. Presumably this included black GAR members; if so, further research may reveal how many, if any attended, as well as how black veterans may have responded to the reunion's tone and purpose. One of Walter Blake's anecdotes of the reunion is what he calls a "very pretty little incident" where "a giant of an old negro, Samuel Thompson," was resting under a shade tree. Some Confederate veterans came up to shake hands with "the old darky" and exchange greetings. It is not made clear whether Thompson was a veteran or not. Blake declares this incident another triumph for kindness and concludes without the slightest sense of irony: "no color line here."[27]

The reunion was to be a source of lessons transmitted between generations, as several hundred Boy Scouts of America served the old veterans as aides-de-camp, causing scenes much celebrated in the press. Like any event fraught with so much symbolism, the reunion also became a "site" for contentious politics. Suffragists lobbied the veterans' camp, asking that they shout "votes for women" rather than the refurbished "rebel yell," a scene much derided by some of the press. Most of all, the reunion was a grand opportunity for America's political officialdom, as well as purveyors of popular opinion, to declare the meaning and memory of the Civil War in the present. One does have to wonder if there had ever been an assembly quite like this in the history of the modern world: can we imagine another event commemorated by so many actual participants in so grand a manner, involving such imagery of past, present, and future? Lafayette's tour of America in 1827, the U.S. centennial in 1876, and the Columbian Exposition in Chicago in 1893, as well as other world's fairs, come to mind as possible comparisons. But for the transmission of a public, social memory of an epoch, such a platform had rarely existed as that given the state governors and the president of the United States on July 3 and 4, 1913.[28]

On the third day of the reunion the governors of the various states spoke. All, understandably, asserted the themes of sectional harmony ✓ and national cohesion. As one would expect, soldiers' valor was the central idea of such reunion rhetoric. Perhaps William Hodges Mann, governor of Virginia, struck the most meaningful chord of memory on that occasion. "We are not here to discuss the Genesis of the war," said Mann, "but men who have tried each other in the storm and smoke of battle are here to discuss this great fight, which if it didn't establish a new standard of manhood came up to the highest standard that was ever set. We came here, I say, *not to discuss what caused the war of 1861–65,* but to talk over the events of the battle here as man to man." The following day, July 4, in the great finale of the reunion staged in a giant tent erected in the middle of the field where Pickett's Charge had occurred, the Blue and the Gray gathered to hear what turned out to be a short address by Woodrow Wilson, just recently inaugurated, the first southern president elected since the Civil War. "We are debtors to those fifty crowded years," announced Wilson; "they have made us all heirs to a mighty heritage." What have the fifty years meant, Wilson asked. The answer struck that mystic chord of memory that most white Americans, North and South, probably desired to hear: "They have meant peace and union and vigor, and the maturity and might of a great nation. How wholesome and healing the peace has been. We have found one another again as brothers and comrades, in arms, enemies no longer generous friends rather, our battles long past, the *quarrel forgotten*—except that we shall not forget the splendid valor, the manly devotion of the men then arrayed against one another, now grasping hands and smiling into each other's eyes. How complete the Union has become and how dear to all of us, how unquestioned, how benign and majestic as state after state has been added to this, our great family of free men!"[29]

That great "hosanna" that Douglass had anticipated forty years before had certainly come to fruition. "Thank God for Gettysburg, Hosanna!" declared the *Louisville Courier-Journal.* "God bless us everyone, alike the Blue and the Gray, the Gray and the Blue! The world ne're witnessed such a sight as this. Beholding, can we say 'happy is the nation that hath no history'?" In Ernest Renan's famous essay in 1882, "What Is a Nation?" he aptly described a nation as "a large-scale solidarity . . . a daily plebiscite" constantly negotiated between "memories" and "present-day consent," and requiring a great deal of "forgetting." In varieties of irony, the United States in 1913 fit Renan's definition.[30]

The deep causes and consequences of the Civil War—the role of slavery and the challenge of racial equality—in those fifty "crowded years" had been actively suppressed and subtly displaced by the celebration of what Oliver Wendell Holmes Jr. had termed a "soldier's faith," the celebration of the veterans' manly valor and devotion. Oh, what a glorious fight they had come to commemorate, and in the end, everyone was right, no one was wrong, and something so transforming as the Civil War had been rendered a mutual victory of the Blue and the Gray by what Governor Mann called the "splendid movement of reconciliation." And Wilson's great gift for mixing idealism with ambiguity was in perfect form. He gave his own, preacherly, restrained endorsement of the valor of the past. Then, putting on his Progressive's hat, he spoke to the present. "The day of our country's life has but broadened into morning," he declared. "Do not put uniforms by. Put the harness of the present on." Wilson's speech offers a poignant illustration of the significance of presidential rhetoric in the creation of American nationalism and historical memory.[31]

If, as Garry Wills has argued, Abraham Lincoln in the brevity of the Gettysburg address in 1863 "revolutionized the revolution" and offered the nation a "refounding" in the principle of *equality* forged out of the crucible of the war, then Woodrow Wilson, in his Gettysburg address fifty years later offered a subtle and strikingly less revolutionary response. According to Wills, Lincoln had suggested a new constitution at Gettysburg, "giving people a new past to live with that would change their future indefinitely." So did Wilson in 1913. But the new past was one in which all sectional strife was gone and in which all racial strife was ignored or covered over in claims for Wilson's own brand of Progressivism. He appealed to a social and moral equivalent of war directed not at the old veterans but at the younger generations who "must contend, not with armies, but with principalities and powers and wickedness in high places." He came with "orders," not for the old men in Blue and Gray, but for the "host" of the American people, "the great and the small, without class or difference of race or origin . . . our constitutions are their articles of enlistment. The orders of the day are the laws upon our statute books." Lincoln's "rebirth of freedom" had become in fifty years Wilson's forward-looking "righteous peace" (Wilson's New Freedom program in the 1912 election campaign). The potential in the second American Revolution had become the "quarrel forgotten" on the statute books of Jim Crow America. Wilson, of course, did not believe he was speaking for or about the ravages of segregation, or other aspects of racial division in America, on his day at Gettysburg. He was acutely aware of his presence at the reunion as a southerner and no doubt still negotiating the uneasy terrain of a minority president, elected by only 42 percent of the popular vote in the turbulent four-way election of 1912. Wilson's Progressivism was antimonopolist, antitariff, and concerned with banking reform and other largely middle-class causes. Although racial issues only rarely occupied him while president, he was instinctively a states' righter.[32] Educated by events, and rising beyond his own constraints, Lincoln had soared above the "honored dead" to try to imagine a new future in America. Wilson soared above the honored veterans and described a present and a future where white patriotism and nationalism flourished, where society seemed threatened by disorder, and where the principle of equality might be said, by neglect and action, to have been living a social death.

The ceremonies at Gettysburg in 1913 represented a public avowal of the deeply laid mythology (some scholars prefer the term "tradition") of the Civil War that had captured popular consciousness by the early twentieth century.[33] The war was remembered as primarily a tragedy that led to greater unity and national cohesion, and as a soldier's call to sacrifice in order to save a troubled, but essentially good union, not as the crisis of a nation deeply divided over slavery, race, competing definitions of labor, liberty, political economy, and the future of the West (issues, some of which were hardly resolved by 1913).

Press reports and editorials demonstrate just how much this version of Civil War history had become what some theorists have called "structural amnesia" or social "habit memory."[34] The issues of slavery and secession, rejoiced the conservative *Washington Post,* were "no longer discussed argumentatively. They are scarcely mentioned at all, except in connection with the great war to which they led, and by which they were *disposed of for all time.*" To the extent slavery involved a "moral principle," said the *Post,* "no particular part of the people was responsible unless, indeed, the burden of responsibility should be shouldered *by the North for its introduction.*" Echoing many of the governors (North and South) who spoke at the reunion, the "greater victory," declared the *Post,* was that won by the national crusade to reunite the veterans and not that of the Army of the Potomac in 1863. The *New York Times* hired Helen D. Longstreet (widow of the Confederate general James Longstreet, who had been much maligned by Lost Cause devotees for his caution at Gettysburg and his Republicanism after the war) to write daily columns about the reunion. She entertained the *Times*'s readers with her dialogues with southern veterans about the value of Confederate defeat and the beauty of "Old Glory." She also challenged readers to remember the sufferings of women during the Civil War and to consider an intersectional tribute to them as the theme of the next reunion. The nation's historical memory, concluded the *Times,* had become so "balanced" that it could never again be "disturbed" by sectional conflict. The editors of the liberal magazine the *Outlook* were overwhelmed by the spirit of nationalism at the reunion and declared it a reconciliation of "two conceptions of human right and human freedom." The war, said the *Outlook,* had been fought over differing notions of "idealism": "sovereignty of the state" or "sovereignty of the nation." Demonstrating just how much slavery had vanished from understandings of Civil War causation in serious intellectual circles, the *Outlook* announced that "it was slavery that raised the question of State sovereignty; but it was not on behalf of slavery, but on behalf of State sovereignty and all that it implied, that these men fought." So normative was this viewpoint—not to be replaced with a new historiographical consensus for several decades—that the *Outlook*'s special correspondent at the reunion, Herbert Francis Sherwood, could conclude that the veterans' "fraternity . . . showed that no longer need men preach a reunited land, for there were no separated people." Such was the state of historical consciousness in Jim Crow America. In the larger culture, slavery (and the whole black experience) was read out of the formulas by which Americans found meanings in the Civil War. As in all deep ironies, the *Outlook* was both accurate and oblivious in its interpretation of the reunion; thus could it conclude without blinking that "both sides" had fought for "the same ideal—the ideal of civil liberty."[35]

The Gettysburg reunion was an event so full of symbolic meaning, and perhaps so photogenic, that it compelled editorial comment from far and wide. The *Times* (London) correspondent reported back to England that the reunion had sent a "great and memorable lesson . . . eradicating forever the scars of the civil war in a way that no amount of preaching or political maneuvering could have done." Reporters from every section of the country registered their sense of awe and wonderment at the Gettysburg celebration. "The Reunion fifty years after stands alone in the annals of the world," said the *Cincinnati Enquirer,* "for no similar event has ever taken place." The *San Francisco Examiner,* in an editorial that modeled Lincoln's Gettysburg address in form, declared the "jubilee" to be the "supreme justification of war and battle." Now "we know that the great war had to be fought, that it is well that it was fought," announced the *Examiner,* "a necessary, useful, splendid sacrifice whereby the whole race of men has been unified." Such martial spirit and claims of ritual purging were answered (albeit a minority voice) by the *Charleston (S.C.) News and Courier.* The newspaper in the city where secession began urged readers not to glorify the "battle itself," for it was "a frightful and abominable thing." If war "thrills us," declared the *News and Courier,* "we lose a vitally important part of the lesson." But the *Brooklyn Daily Eagle* kept the discussion on a higher scale and a theme that allowed, all at once, for a recognition of northern victory, southern respect, and faith in American providential destiny. "Two civilizations met at Gettysburg," proclaimed the *Daily Eagle,* "and fought out the issue between them under the broad, blue sky, in noble, honorable battle. . . . In one, as historians have pointed out, the family was the social unit—the family in the old Roman sense, possibly inclusive of hundreds of slaves. In the other, the individual was the only social unit. Within half a century those two civilizations have become one. Individualism has triumphed. Yet has that triumph been tempered with a fuller recognition than ever before the war, of the charm and dignity and cultivation of what has yielded to the hand of Fate. . . . The ways of Providence are inscrutable." The Brooklyn editor had neatly wrapped the whole package in nostalgia for the masses. He offered mystic honor to the Lost Cause of patriarchal "family" structure, combined with an uneasy celebration of the triumph of individualism in the age of industrialization, all justified by God's design.[36]

Such homilies about nationalism and peace, though often well meaning in their context, masked as much as they revealed. One should not diminish the genuine sentiment of the veterans in 1913; the Civil War had left ghastly scars to be healed in the psyches of individual men, and in the collective memories of Americans in both sections. The war's impact on the social psychology of Americans of both sections and both races had been enormous. Monuments and reunions had always, understandably, combined remembrance with healing and, therefore, with forgetting. But it is not stretching the evidence to suggest that white supremacy was a silent master of ceremonies at the Gettysburg reunion. No overt conspiracy need be implied, but commemorative rituals are not merely benign performances; their content and motivation must be explored along with their form. The reunion was a national ritual where the ghost of slavery might, once and for all, be exorcized, and where a conflict among whites might be transmogrified into national mythology.

Black newspapers of the era were, understandably, wary and resentful of the celebration of the great "Peace Jubilee." At a time when lynching had developed into a social ritual of its own horrifying kind in the South and when the American apartheid had become almost fully entrenched, black opinion leaders found the sectional love-feast at Gettysburg to be more irony than they could bear. "We are wondering," declared the *Baltimore Afro-American Ledger,* "whether Mr. Lincoln had the slightest idea in his mind that the time would ever come when the people of this country would come to the conclusion that by the 'People' he meant only white people." Black memory of the Civil War seemed at variance with what had happened at the reunion. The *Afro-American* captured the stakes and the potential results of this test of America's social memory. "Today the South is in the saddle, and with the single exception of slavery, everything it fought for during the days of the Civil War, it has gained by repression of the Negro within its borders. And the North has quietly allowed it to have its own way." The *Afro-American* asserted the loyalty of black soldiers during the war and of citizens since, and pointed to President Wilson's recent forced segregation of federal government workers. The "blood" of black soldiers and lynched citizens was "crying from the ground" in the South, unheard and strangely unknown at the Blue-Gray reunion. When the assembled at Gettysburg paused to hear Lincoln's lines about that "government of the people," suggested the *Afro-American,* it ought to "recall the fact that at least part of the people of this country are Negroes and at the same time human beings, and civilized human beings at that; struggling towards the light, as God has given them to see the light."[37]

These reactions in the black press are especially telling given one of the most striking ironies of all during that summer of 1913: the Wilson administration's increasingly aggressive program of racial segregation in federal government agencies, which were major employers of black Americans. On the day after Decoration Day the official segregation of black clerks in the Post Office Department began. And on July 12, only a week after Wilson spoke at Gettysburg, orders were issued to create separate lavatories for blacks and whites working at the Treasury Department. These and other segregation policies, stemming in part from many new white southerners who had come to Washington with the Wilson administration (some racial radicals and some moderates), caused deep resentment and protest among blacks, led largely by the National Association for the Advancement of Colored People (NAACP). Such policies, and the sense of betrayal they caused among blacks, prompted

Booker T. Washington, no friend of the NAACP, to declare that he had "never seen the colored people so discouraged and bitter" as they were in the summer of 1913. That summer the NAACP launched a sometimes successful campaign against segregation practices in the federal government.[38]

The *Washington (D.C.) Bee* was even more forthright than other papers in its criticism of the planned reunion at Gettysburg. "The occasion is to be called a Reunion! A Reunion of whom? Only the men who fought for the preservation of the Union and the extinction of human slavery? Is it to be an assemblage of those who fought to destroy the Union and perpetuate slavery, and who are now employing every artifice and argument known to deceit and sophistry to propagate a national sentiment in favor of their nefarious contention that emancipation, reconstruction and enfranchisement are a dismal failure." The *Bee*'s editor, W. Calvin Chase, asserted that the Blue-Gray ritual was not a "reunion" at all, but a "Reception" thrown by the victors for the vanquished. But most important, he argued that the event was a national declaration of a version of history and a conception of the legacy of the Civil War. The message of the reunion, wrote Chase, was "an insane and servile acknowledgement that the most precious results of the war are a prodigious, unmitigated failure."[39] Commemorative rituals can inspire decidedly different interpretations; sometimes it depends simply on whether one is on the creating or the receiving end of battles over historical memory. Sometimes it depends on whether a construction of social memory is to be used to sustain or dislodge part of the social order.

As with the earlier generation in the 1880s, when Douglass and Crummell conducted their debate, the stakes of social memory in 1913 were roughly the same. An interpretation of national history had become wedded to racial theory. The sections had reconciled; nationalism flourished; some social wounds had healed; and Paul Buck could later confidently write, in his Pulitzer Prize–winning *Road to Reunion* (still the only major synthetic work written on this subject), of the "leaven of forgiveness" that grew in a generation into the "miracle" of reconciliation, and of a "revolution in sentiment" whereby "all people within the country felt the electrifying thrill of a common purpose." Such a reunion had been possible, Buck argued, because Americans had collectively admitted that the "race problem" was "basically insoluble," and had "taken the first step in learning how to live with it." Gone with the wind, indeed. Peace between North and South, Buck wrote, unwittingly answering

Douglass's question, had given the South, and therefore the nation, a "stability of race relations" upon which the "new patriotism" and "new nationalism" could be built. A segregated society required a segregated historical memory and a national mythology that could blunt or contain the conflict at the root of that segregation. Buck sidestepped, or perhaps simply missed, the irony in favor of an unblinking celebration of the path to reunion. Just such a celebration is what one finds in the *Atlanta Constitution*'s coverage of the Gettysburg reunion in 1913. With mystic hyperbole and what may seem to us strange logic, the *Constitution* declared that "as never before in its history the nation is united in demanding that justice and equal rights be given all of its citizens." No doubt these sentiments reflected genuinely held beliefs among some white southerners that Jim Crow meant "progress." The *Constitution* gushed about the "drama" and "scale" of the symbolism at the Gettysburg reunion, even its "poetry and its fragrance." But most important was "the thing for which it stands—the world's mightiest republic purged of hate and unworthiness, *seared clean of dross* by the most fiery ordeal in any nation's history." Such were the fruits of America's segregated mind and its segregated historical consciousness.[40]

Theorists and historians have long argued that myth as history often best serves the ends of social stability and conservatism. That is certainly the case with the development of Civil War mythology in America. But we also know that mythic conceptions or presentations of the past can be innovative as well as conservative, liberating instead of destructive, or the result of sheer romance. Whether we like it or not, history is used this way generation after generation. "Only a horizon ringed with myths," warned Friedrich Nietzsche in 1874,"can unify a culture." We would do well to keep in mind C. Vann Woodward's warning that "the twilight zone that lies between living memory and written history is one of the favorite breeding places of mythology." But great myths have their "resilience, not completely controllable," as Michael Kammen reminded us. This reality is precisely the one W. E. B. Du Bois recognized in the final chapter of his *Black Reconstruction in America*, published just two years before Buck's *Road to Reunion*. Du Bois insisted that history should be an "art using the results of science" and not merely a means of "inflating our national ego." But by focusing on the subject of the Civil War and Reconstruction in the 1930s, he offered a tragic awareness, as well as a trenchant argument, that written history cannot be completely disengaged from social memory. Du Bois echoed the *Atlanta*

Constitution editor, admitting that there had been a "searing of the memory" in America, but one of a very different kind. The "searing" Du Bois had in mind was not that of the Civil War itself, but that of a white supremacist historiography and a popular memory of the period that had "obliterated" the black experience and the meaning of emancipation by "libel, innuendo, and silence."[41] The stakes in the development of America's historical memory of the Civil War have never been benign. The answers to Douglass's question have never been benign either. "Peace among the whites" brought segregation and the necessity of later reckonings. The Civil War has not yet been disengaged from a mythological social memory, and perhaps it never will be. Likewise, the American reunion cannot be disengaged from black experience and interpretations, nor from the question of race in the collective American memory.

Like other major touchstones of American history, the Civil War will continue to be used for ends that serve the present. There are many reasons for this, but one of the most compelling is perhaps the fact that emancipation in America (contrary to every other country in the century of emancipations) came as a result of total war and social revolution. Revolutions sometimes go backward, as well as revive in new, reconstructed forms from one generation to the next. All such historical problems, of course, must be contextualized and particularized. But the Civil War and emancipation may remain in the mythic realm precisely because, in the popular imagination anyway, they represent reconciled discord, a crucible of tragedy and massive change survived in a society that still demands a providential conception of its history. Facing the deepest causes and consequences of the Civil War has always forced us to face the kind of logic Nathan Huggins insisted upon in his final work. "The challenge of the paradox [of race in American history]," wrote Huggins, "is that there can be no white history or black history, nor can there be an integrated history that does not begin to comprehend that slavery and freedom, white and black, are joined at the hip."[42]

NOTES

This essay evolved from a conference paper and was published in a book I coedited with Brooks D. Simpson in honor of our mentor Richard H. Sewell, *Union and Emancipation: Essays on Politics and Race in the Civil War Era* (Kent, Ohio: Kent State University Press, 1997). It is published here in slightly revised form.

1. John R. Gillis, "Memory and Identity: The History of a Relationship," in *Commemorations: The Politics of National Identity,* ed. John R. Gillis (Princeton: Princeton University Press, 1994), 5.

2. Natalie Zemon Davis and Randolph Starn, introduction to special issue on memory and countermemory, *Representations* (spring 1989): 2. There are many theoretical works that discuss social memory as a matter of cultural conflict. Some places to start are Maurice Halbwachs, *The Collective Memory,* trans. Francis J. Ditter Jr. and Vida Yazdi Ditter (1950; reprint, New York: Harper and Row, 1980), 22–49; *Memory in American History,* ed. David Thelen (Bloomington: Indiana University Press, 1991); Michael Kammen, *Mystic Chords of Memory: The Transformation of Tradition in American Culture* (New York: Knopf, 1991), 3–14; Friedrich Nietzsche, "The Use and Abuse of History," in *The Use and Abuse of History,* trans. Adrian Collins, introd. Julius Kraft (New York: Liberal Arts Press, 1949); Peter Burke, "History as Social Memory," in *Memory: History, Culture, and the Mind,* ed. Thomas Butler (London: Blackwell, 1989), 97–113; Pierre Nora, "Between Memory and History: Les Lieux de Memoire," *Representations,* no. 26 (spring 1989): 7–25; Barry Schwartz, "The Social Context of Commemoration: A Study in Collective Memory, *Social Forces* (December 2, 1982): 374–402; *The Invention of Tradition,* ed. Eric Hobsbawm and Terrence Ranger (Cambridge, Eng.: Cambridge University Press, 1983); David Lowenthal, *The Past Is a Foreign Country* (New York: Cambridge University Press, 1985), pts. 2 and 3; Charles S. Maier, *The Unmasterable Past: History, Holocaust, and German National Identity* (Cambridge: Harvard University Press, 1988); Benedict Anderson, *Imagined Communities: Reflections on the Origin and Spread of Nationalism* (New York: Verso), 187–206; and the many rich essays in *Commemorations: The Politics of National Identity,* ed. Gillis.

3. *The Civil War,* episode 9, "The Better Angels of Our Nature," produced and directed by Ken Burns, WETA television, Washington, D.C. Fields is quoting from Faulkner's *Absalom, Absalom!*

4. Richard Slotkin, "'What Shall Men Remember?': Recent Work on the Civil War," *American Literary History* (spring 1991): 13; Chamberlain is quoted in *The Civil War,* episode 9; Howells is quoted in Allan Gurganus, *The Oldest Living Confederate Widow Tells All* (New York, Knopf, 1984), epigraph. For a trenchant critique of the "master narrative" of American history rooted in the idea of "automatic progress," see Nathan Irvin Huggins, "The Deforming Mirror of Truth," introduction to *Black Odyssey: The African-American Ordeal in Slavery* (New York: Vintage, 1990).

5. For a similar critique of the PBS film series, one that argues effectively that Burns employed an American "family" metaphor as the overall framework, see Bill Farrell, "All in the Family: Ken Burns's *The Civil War* and Black America," *Transition: An International Review* 58 (1993): 169–73.

6. Nina Silber, *The Romance of Reunion: Northerners and the South, 1865–1900* (Chapel Hill: University of North Carolina Press, 1993), 3. See also David W. Blight, *Race and Reunion: The Civil War in American Memory* (Cambridge: Belknap Press, Harvard University Press, 2001), chap. 7.

7. Daniel Aaron, *The Unwritten War: American Writers and the Civil War* (New

York: Knopf, 1973), 328; W. E. B. Du Bois, *The Souls of Black Folk* (1903; reprint, New York: Signet, 1969), 54, 78.

8. Anderson, *Imagined Communities*, 3, 201.

9. Alain Locke, "The New Negro," in *The New Negro*, ed. Alain Locke (1925; reprint, New York: Atheneum, 1968), 4, 16, emphasis added.

10. On nostalgia as a psychological and social phenomenon, see Jean Starobinski, "Nostalgia," *Diogenes* (summer 1966): 80–103; and Renato Rosaldo, "Imperialist Nostalgia," *Representations* (spring 1989): 107–22. See Blight, *Race and Reunion*.

11. Frederick Douglass, "The Color Question," July 5, 1875, reel 15, Frederick Douglass Papers, Library of Congress, emphasis added. On this stage of Reconstruction, see William Gillette, *The Retreat from Reconstruction, 1869–1879* (Baton Rouge: Louisiana State University Press, 1979).

12. John Hope Franklin, "The Birth of a Nation: Propaganda as History," in *Race and History: Selected Essays, 1938–1988* (Baton Rouge: Louisiana State University Press, 1989), 10–23 (reprinted from *Massachusetts Review [1979]);* Ralph Ellison, "Going to the Territory," address given at Brown University, September 20, 1979, reprinted in Ralph Ellison, *Going to the Territory* (New York: Random House, 1986), 124. On Dixon's significance, see Joel Williamson, *The Crucible of Race: Black-White Relations in the American South since Emancipation* (New York: Oxford University Press, 1984), 140–76.

13. On the turn in American cultural attitudes in the 1880s, see Gerald Linderman, *Embattled Courage: The Experience of Combat in the Civil War* (New York: Free Press, 1987), 266–97; Gaines M. Foster, *Ghosts of the Confederacy: Defeat, the Lost Cause, and the Emergence of the New South* (New York: Oxford University Press, 1987), 63–162; Paul M. Gaston, *The New South Creed: A Study in Southern Myth-Making* (New York: Knopf, 1970); Silber, *Romance of Reunion*, 93–123; and Kammen, *Mystic Chords*, 91–116. On the dynamics of black thought, see August Meier, *Negro Thought in America, 1880–1915: Racial Ideologies in the Age of Booker T. Washington* (Ann Arbor: University of Michigan Press, 1970), 3–82.

14. Alexander Crummell, *Africa and America: Addresses and Discourses* (1891; reprint, New York: Negro Universities Press, 1969), iii, 14, 18, 13. I am indebted to Robert Gooding-Williams for bringing Crummell's speech to my attention. On Crummell, see Wilson J. Moses, *Alexander Crummell: A Study of Civilization and Discontent* (New York: Oxford University Press, 1990); and Alfred A. Moss Jr., *The American Negro Academy: Voice of the Talented Tenth* (Baton Rouge: Louisiana State University Press, 1981), 19–34, 53–62. Crummell was the founder of the American Negro Academy.

15. See David W. Blight, "For Something beyond the Battlefield: Frederick Douglass and the Memory of the Civil War," *Journal of American History* (spring 1989): 1156–78; and John David Smith, *An Old Creed for the New South: Proslavery Ideology and Historiography, 1865–1918* (Westport, Conn.: Greenwood Press, 1985), 287–88.

16. Frederick Douglass, "Speech at the Thirty-third Anniversary of the Jerry Rescue," 1884, reel 16, Frederick Douglass Papers, Library of Congress.

17. Frederick Douglass, "Thoughts and Recollections of the Antislavery Conflict," speech undated, but it is at least early 1880s; "Decoration Day," speech at Mount Hope Cemetery, Rochester, New York, May 1883; and "Address Delivered on the Twenty-sixth Anniversary of Abolition in the District of Columbia," April 16, 1888, Washington, D.C., all in reel 15, Frederick Douglass Papers, Library of Congress.

18. On white racial thought, see George M. Fredrickson, *The Black Image in the White Mind: The Debate on Afro-American Character and Destiny, 1817–1914* (New York: Harper and Row, 1971), 228–82; and Williamson, *The Crucible of Race,* 111–223.

19. Paul B. Barringer, "The American Negro, His Past and Future," address delivered February 20, 1900, Charleston, S.C., copy in Widener Library, Harvard University. On Barringer, see Williamson, *Crucible of Race,* 177; Fredrickson, *Black Image in the White Mind,* 252–53; and Smith, *Old Creed for the New South,* 286. Barringer was a leader of the University of Virginia faculty from 1896 to 1903 and later a founder of Virginia Polytechnic Institute.

20. Fredrickson, *Black Image in the White Mind,* 320–22. On the role of white supremacy in the development of a historiographical consensus, see Smith, *Old Creed for a New South,* 103–96, 239–77.

21. See Moses, *Crummell,* 226–28; William S. McFeely, *Frederick Douglass* (New York: Norton, 1991), 238–304; and David W. Blight, *Frederick Douglass' Civil War: Keeping Faith in Jubilee* (Baton Rouge: Louisiana State University Press, 1989), 189–245.

22. Other such comparisons of black intellectuals and competing conceptions of memory might be Booker T. Washington and his various critics, historian George Washington Williams and activist Ida B. Wells-Barnett, A.M.E. Church bishop Henry McNeal Turner, and historian-activist Archibald Grimke. The list could be much longer. On W. E. B. Du Bois in this regard, see David W. Blight, "W. E. B. Du Bois and the Struggle for American Historical Memory," in *History and Memory in African American Culture,* Geneviéve Fabre and Robert O'Meally (New York: Oxford University Press, 1994), 45–71.

23. See David Glassberg, *American Historical Pageantry: The Uses of Tradition in the Early Twentieth Century* (Chapel Hill: University of North Carolina Press, 1990); T. J. Jackson Lears, *No Place of Grace: Antimodernism and the Transformation of American Culture, 1880–1920* (New York: Pantheon, 1981), 97–138; Wallace E. Davies, *Patriotism on Parade: The Story of Veterans' and Hereditary Organizations in America, 1783–1900* (Cambridge: Harvard University Press, 1955); and Kammen, *Mystic Chords of Memory.* On the development of patriotism and nationalism, see John Bodnar, *Public Memory, Commemoration, and Patriotism in the Twentieth Century* (Princeton: Princeton University Press, 1992).

24. *Fiftieth Anniversary of the Battle of Gettysburg: Report of the Pennsylvania Commission,* December 31, 1913 (Harrisburg: W. S. Ray, state printer, 1915), 39–41. The exact count of veterans at the reunion was 53,407. Not every state participated in providing funds for veterans' transportation, especially some of the southern and southwestern states. On commemoration at Gettysburg over the

years, see also Edward Tabor Linenthal, *Sacred Ground: Americans and Their Battle-fields* (Urbana: University of Illinois Press, 1991), 89–126; John S. Patterson, "A Patriotic Landscape: Gettysburg, 1863–1913," *Prospects* (1982): 315–33.

25. *Fiftieth Anniversary of the Battle of Gettysburg*, 31, 36–37. The Pennsylvania Commission's report contained dozens of photographs, with one compelling scene after another of the spirit of reconciliation as well as the generational transmission of national memory. In a few of those photographs one sees black laborers and camp workers constructing the tents, serving as bakers, or passing out blankets and mess kits. Nowhere is there any photograph of a black veteran.

26. Ibid., 6, 39–41, 49–51, 53, 57–58. Paul Connerton, *How Societies Remember* (New York: Cambridge University Press, 1989); and Alan Trachtenberg, *The Incorporation of America: Culture and Society in the Gilded Age* (New York: Hill and Wang, 1982); *Philadelphia Inquirer,* July 6, 1913. An essay might be written on the "scientific management" and efficiency aspects of the Gettysburg reunion alone. For understanding the Gettysburg community's extraordinary preparation for the reunion, I have relied in part on the *Gettysburg Compiler,* March–July 1913, microfilm copy at the Gettysburg National Military Park.

27. *Fiftieth Anniversary of the Battle of Gettysburg*, 6, 25; Walter H. Blake, *Hand Grips: The Story of the Great Gettysburg Reunion of 1913* (Vineland, N.J.: G. E. Smith, 1913), 66–67.

28. For the Boy Scouts and the suffragists at the reunion, see *Washington Post,* June 28, 30, 1913; *New York Times,* July 1, 1913; and *Fiftieth Anniversary of the Battle of Gettysburg*, 49–51. On the notion of "sites" of memory, see Nora, "Between Memory and History."

29. The Mann speech is reprinted in *Fiftieth Anniversary of the Battle of Gettysburg*, 144, 174–76, emphasis added; Wilson's speech, in *The Papers of Woodrow Wilson,* ed. Arthur Link (Princeton: Princeton University Press, 1978), 28:23, emphasis added.

30. *Louisville Courier-Journal,* July 4, 1913; Ernest Renan, "What Is a Nation?" in *Nation and Narration,* ed. Homi K. Bhabha, trans. Martin Thom (London: Routledge, 1990), 11, 19.

31. Oliver Wendell Holmes, "A Soldier's Faith," an address delivered on Memorial Day, May 30, 1895, at a meeting called by the graduating class of Harvard University, in *Speeches of Oliver Wendell Holmes, Jr.* (Boston: Little, Brown, 1934), 56–66; *Fiftieth Anniversary of the Battle of Gettysburg*, 176. On the role of language in the creation of nationalisms, see Anderson, *Imagined Communities,* 154.

32. Garry Wills, *Lincoln at Gettysburg: The Words That Remade America* (New York: Simon and Schuster, 1992), 38, 40; *Papers of Woodrow Wilson,* ed. Link, 28:24–25. On the Wilson administration and racial segregation, see Henry Blumenthal, "Woodrow Wilson and the Race Question," *Journal of Negro History* 48 (January 1963): 1–21; and Williamson, *Crucible of Race,* 358–95. On the 1912 election and Wilson's Progressivism in relation to race, see Nell Irvin Painter, *Standing at Armageddon: The United States, 1877–1919* (New York: Norton, 1987), 268–72.

33. See Foster, *Ghosts of the Confederacy,* 7–8. Foster avoids the term "myth" in favor of "tradition." See also Alan T. Nolan, *Lee Considered: General Robert E. Lee and*

Civil War History (Chapel Hill: University of North Carolina Press, 1991). Nolan comfortably uses the term "myth." Distinctions between these slippery terms are important, but myth seems to be an appropriate terminology in this instance. On the idea of myth for historians, there are many good sources, but see Richard Slotkin, *The Fatal Environment: The Myth of the Frontier in the Age of Industrialization, 1800–1890* (New York: Atheneum, 1985), 1–48; Warren I. Susman, *Culture as History: The Transformation of American Society in the Twentieth Century* (New York: Pantheon, 1973), 7–26; and Kammen, *Mystic Chords of Memory*, esp. 431–71.

34. Burke, "History as Social Memory," 106; Connerton, *How Societies Remember*, 22–25, 28–31. Connerton's anthropological analysis of commemorative rituals is provocative and useful, but the content and the form, the meaning and the performance must be examined with equal vigor. On commemorations, see also Schwartz, "The Social Context of Commemoration," and the many essays in Gillis, *Commemorations.*

35. *Washington Post,* June 30, 1913, emphasis added. The *Post* also took direct aim at Progressive reformers in the context of the nationalism expressed at Gettysburg. *New York Times,* July 1–4, 1913; *Outlook* 104 (July 12, 1993): 541, 554–55, 610–12.

36. *Times* (London), July 4, 1913; *Cincinnati Enquirer,* July 6, 1913; *San Francisco Examiner,* July 4, 1913; *Charleston (S.C.) News and Courier,* July 1, 1913; *Brooklyn Daily Eagle,* July 2, 1913.

37. *Baltimore Afro-American Ledger,* July 5, 1913.

38. See Williamson, *Crucible of Race,* 364–95. Booker T. Washington, *New York Times,* August 18, 1893, quoted in Blumenthal, "Woodrow Wilson and the Race Question," 8. An especially interesting counterattack on the Wilson administration segregation policies in 1913 is Oswald Garrison Villard, "Segregation in Baltimore and Washington," address delivered to the Baltimore branch of the National Association for the Advancement of Colored People, October 20, 1913, copy in Widener Library, Harvard University. Villard had been a friend and supporter of Wilson's and was then national chairman of the NAACP. The central figure in the NAACP's often successful resistance to the Wilson administration segregation schemes was Archibald Grimke, the NAACP branch director for Washington, D.C. On Grimke's role in the 1913 disputes, see Dickson D. Bruce Jr., *Archibald Grimke: Portrait of a Black Independent* (Baton Rouge: Louisiana State University Press, 1993), 184–200. It is also interesting to note that in the NAACP's monthly *Crisis,* editor W. E. B. Du Bois made no mention whatsoever of the Gettysburg reunion. Instead, he wrote a celebration of the Fifty-fourth Massachusetts black regiment, including a full-page photograph of the Shaw/Fifty-fourth Memorial in Boston. See *Crisis,* July 1913, vols. 5–8, 122–26.

39. *Washington (D.C.) Bee,* May 24, June 7, 1913.

40. Paul H. Buck, *The Road to Reunion, 1865–1900* (Boston: Little, Brown, 1937), 126, 319, 308–9. The term "miracle" was frequently used in reviews of Buck's book as a means of referring to the triumph of sectional reconciliation. Arthur Schlesinger Sr. also used the term on the jacket of the original edition. Among the many letters Buck received about his book was one from Margaret

Mitchell, author of *Gone With the Wind,* which had just won the Pulitzer Prize for literature the year before. "I am sure your wonderful book, 'The Road to Reunion,'" wrote Mitchell, "has never had as interested a reader as I. I am especially sure that no reader took greater pleasure in the Pulitzer award than I. My sincere congratulations to you," Margaret Mitchell (Mrs. John R.) Marsh to Paul Buck, May 10, 1938, in Buck's "scrapbook" collection of reviews commemorating his Pulitzer Prize, Paul Buck Papers, Harvard University Archives. *Atlanta Constitution,* July 2, 1913, emphasis added.

41. Friedrich Nietzsche, *The Birth of Tragedy* (1874; reprint, Garden City, N.Y.: Doubleday, 1956), 136; C. Vann Woodward, *The Strange Career of Jim Crow* (New York: Oxford University Press, 1955), viii; Kammen, *Mystic Chords,* 37; W. E. B. Du Bois, *Black Reconstruction in America, 1860–1880* (New York: Atheneum, 1935), 714, 717, 723, 725. It is worth pointing out here that 1913 was also the fiftieth anniversary of emancipation, an event much commemorated in black communities, popular culture, pageants, poetry, song, and literature. The U.S. Congress held hearings in order to plan an official recognition of emancipation. Du Bois testified before a Senate committee on February 2, 1912. See hearings, "Semicentennial Anniversary of Act of Emancipation," Senate Report no. 31, 62d Congress, 2d session. Du Bois wrote and helped produce, under the auspices of the NAACP, "The Star of Ethiopia," a pageant that was performed in 1913, 1915, and 1916. See Glassberg, *American Historical Pageantry,* 132–35; and William H. Wiggins Jr., *O Freedom!: Afro-American Emancipation Celebrations* (Knoxville: University of Tennessee Press, 1987), 49–78. See also Blight, "W. E. B. Du Bois and the Struggle for American Historical Memory."

42. Huggins, "Deforming Mirror of Truth," *Black Odyssey,* xliv.

The Shaw Memorial
in the Landscape of
Civil War Memory

What, was it all for naught, those awful years
That drenched a groaning land with blood and tears?
Was it to leave this sly convenient hell,
That brother fighting his own brother fell?
　　　—Paul Laurence Dunbar, "To the South, on Its New Slavery"

Like every generation of Americans since 1865, we live in a time of tension and change regarding the meaning and memory of the Civil War and the age of emancipation. What John Hope Franklin once called "the verdict of Appomattox" is still not, nor perhaps will it ever be, a completely settled subject.[1] This essay suggests ways of understanding the place of the Shaw Memorial and the Fifty-fourth Massachusetts regiment that it depicts in the broad landscape of Civil War remembrance, to outline the context of the 1890s in which it was unveiled, and to reflect upon the meaning and memory of the memorial a century later.

We live in a time when public struggles over the content and meaning of the past—between history and heritage—have important political stakes. Scholars, teachers, and public historians should embrace this enthusiasm for the past in all its forms, harness it in the interest of learning and understanding in every way possible. But this should be done with no illusions; the marketplace for history is vast and turbulent, and often those in the academy are only playing small parts in a cast of thousands.

For many reasons, the late 1990s represent a telling historical moment in which to reflect on the Shaw Memorial and the story it embodies. The unsuccessful call of Gov. David Beasley of South Carolina in late 1996 for removal of the Confederate battle flag flying over the state capitol seems to have indicated that a politician's fate in some southern states may hinge on his or her position on the viability of

Confederate heritage. Beasley was defeated in his November 1998 bid for reelection. In Virginia, Gov. George Allen Jr. declared April 1997 Confederate History Month for the third year running amid considerable controversy, racial division, and an NAACP protest. In April 1998 Virginia's new governor, James S. Gilmore III, issued a similar proclamation, honoring the sacrifice of Confederate soldiers but including this time a declaration that "slavery was a practice that deprived African Americans of their God-given inalienable rights [and] which degraded the human spirit." The inclusion of the statement about slavery prompted R. Wayne Byrd Sr., president of Virginia's Heritage Preservation Association, to call a news conference at the Richmond capitol to denounce Gilmore's portrayal of slavery as an "insult." "Southern life on a plantation," said Byrd, was more properly remembered as a time when "master and slave loved and cared for each other and had a genuine family concern."[2] Academic historians are well advised to remember that paradigms may change fundamentally in their interpretive discipline, but in the larger realm of public history and memory, great myths have durability beyond their control. We need to engage those myths, argue with them, and fold as much history into their discussion as possible. Heritage has to be met with good history in the civic arena.

Augustus Saint-Gaudens's masterpiece, with its images of twenty-three black United States soldiers, their individuality and collective purpose captured almost miraculously in that relief, has special resonance again today. While a movement grows in the popular culture, led by the Sons of Confederate Veterans organization, to claim that thousands of "black Confederates" served the southern cause, we need to keep Saint-Gaudens's vision of the men of the Fifty-fourth regiment marching, in the words of art historian Vincent Scully, as "all one will moving forward," clear in our minds.[3] We should always be open to new interpretations, but we also have to be ready to declare how much historical claims by anyone have to do with evidence. Moreover, we need to understand how much such claims have to do with the racial politics of our own time, how much they have to do with ways the present sometimes determines the past, with the manner in which some Americans are always seeking to give new legitimacy to the Confederacy, and thereby to current political motives.

In curriculums, roundtables, book clubs, film, tourism, and among collectors and reenactors, the Civil War may be as popular in historical interest as it has ever been. In the 1890s when the Shaw Memorial was unveiled, the South's Lost Cause mythology had achieved a remarkably wide appeal; it had captured a broad segment of the American historical imagination, and the "loss" in war by the South had become for many (including northerners) a "victory" over the experiment of racial equality during Reconstruction. As a public memory, a web of organizations, public rituals, and monument building, the Lost Cause became a civil religion, a heritage community formed out of the chaos of defeat in the Reconstruction South. As a version of history, the Lost Cause allowed white southerners in the post-Reconstruction era to form a collective identity as victims and survivors. As the story went, the Confederacy had only been defeated by superior numbers and resources; its heroism on the battlefield represented the true continuity of state sovereignty from the founding fathers, and its principal legacy in the New South era was the white supremacy necessary to control the children of Reconstruction (black and white).

Lost Cause mythology had many opponents who kept alive a victorious, emancipationist, Unionist legacy of the war, especially Frederick Douglass, the carpetbagger and novelist Albion Tourgee, a variety of reformist newspapers, black churches and intellectuals, as well as some fringe elements of the Republican party. But those voices had lost ground steadily in civic life, in public commemorations, and in history textbooks down through the 1890s. Douglass vehemently had warned of this trend as early as 1870 when he reacted to the first wave of Confederate monument building and the growing secular sainthood of Robert E. Lee. "The spirit of secession is stronger today than ever," Douglass complained. "It is now a deeply rooted, devoutly cherished sentiment, inseparably identified with the 'lost cause,' which the half measures of the government towards the traitors has helped to cultivate and strengthen." And by 1884 Tourgee worried that the national history already had been perverted by the spirit of sectional reconciliation. The North, Tourgee complained, was "too busy in coining golden moments into golden dollars to remember a past that is full of the glory of noble purposes." "The South," he said, "surrendered at Appomattox; the North has been surrendering ever since."[4]

In the 1990s, that older Lost Cause may have transfigured once again (it has had many lives) into yet another revival of the eternal fascination in our culture with the Confederacy, its "rebellion," its heroes and causes, and its cult of fallen soldiers. As legacy and symbol, the Confederacy has also played a major role in the ways Americans confront or evade the dilemma of race. In a wonderfully wry voice, the southern novelist Allan Gurganus wrote: "Trust me. The South is no place for beginners. Its power of denial can turn a lost war into a vibrant, necessary form of national chic." Gurganus is among the many white southerners resisting the Confederate revival. Ruefully, he chided his fellow southerners to give up on the Confederate battle flag, as well as other symbols and lore, especially what he called the South's "secret power: our habit of anticipating defeat while never accepting it." In our own time, we can see that the Shaw Memorial may have at least another century of useful work to do—by its very presence as a work of art, and as a public declaration of specific and enduring meanings of the Civil War. As Booker T. Washington said in his dedication speech at the unveiling, "the full measure of the fruit of Fort Wagner, and all that this monument stands for," would never be realized until blacks and whites had achieved genuine forms of equality of economic opportunity and had learned to fully embrace each other's humanity. Similarly, writing in the 1920s, the critic Thomas Beer may have been quite prescient when he said that though the American Civil War "ceased physically in 1865, its political end may be reasonably expected about the year 3000."[5]

If the landscape of Civil War memory is so scarred yet ever replenished, so cluttered with monuments rooted in artistic formula and social forgetting, but monuments that also move us emotionally, why is this memorial unique? Where does it fit in the competing narratives of what some of us would still call America's national history? The Shaw Memorial and the events it commemorates compel us to acknowledge that wars have meanings that we are obliged to discern, that nations still have histories, and once had (and may still have) a need for a sense of mission. Issues and questions such as these force us to confront others that are central to African American history. Why did it take total war on such a scale to begin to make black people free in America? How did a struggle between white northerners and southerners over conflicting conceptions of the future of their societies become, for nineteenth-century blacks, a struggle over whether they had any future in America at all? Or a question many younger students bring to this matter: why did black men in the middle of the nineteenth century have to die in battle or of disease, by the thousands, in order to be recognized as men, much less as citizens?

Answers to these questions lie deep in our political and cultural history, and deep in the nature of racism itself. The answers do not lie in a kind of teeter-totter approach to history, considering the contribution of one group, and then another group, and then another in isolation. Pursuing these questions might reveal a narrative of authentic *tragedy* at the heart of the Civil War, and therefore at the center of American history. Americans rarely have been fond of seeing their history as tragic; a forward-looking, expanding republic with great resources and a providential sense of its destiny has had little room for treating the darker, fated collisions and bitter contradictions in our past. Victory narratives—of conquest, social and economic progress—have always sold best in the American marketplace; they have been good for commerce, good for foreign policy, and good tools of immigrant assimilation. It may be only human and the product of modern sensibilities to seek one's identity in a victory narrative out of the past. But we also have to be ready to explore how this use of the past for the formation of personal and national identity may be peculiarly American. "Americans love a tragedy," as William Dean Howells wrote, "as long as it has a happy ending." And no one ever captured the tragic sense one can attain in gazing at Saint-Gaudens's monument as well as W. E. B. Du Bois in *Black Reconstruction,* where he wrote: "How extraordinary, and what a tribute to ignorance and religious hypocrisy, is the fact that in the minds of most people, even those of liberals, only murder makes men. The slave pleaded; he was humble; he protected the women of the South, and the world ignored him. The slave killed white men; and behold, he was a man!"[6]

The tyranny of slavery brought America to the bloodletting of 1861; the tyranny of racism, and the necessity to resist it, brought the men of the Fifty-fourth to Camp Meigs, near Boston in 1863, and to that magnificent march down Beacon Street, captured for all time on the Shaw Memorial. The tyranny of war, and the inexorable demands that the men of the Fifty-fourth display their manhood, sent them charging against the parapet at Battery Wagner. If America is about new beginnings for fundamental ideas, if the Civil War was a second founding of the American republic and a "new birth" of freedom, then the story of the Fifty-fourth regiment and the Shaw Memorial is not about a *contribution* to the story. It is about our national promises and betrayals, about the civic ideology at the heart of our society, and about the *transcendence* that makes all tragedy meaningful. The men of the Fifty-fourth Massachusetts, as well as many other black regiments, embodied a whole cluster of meanings; they carried the highest aims of the Union cause and inevitably became the perfect target for what the Confederate cause sought to preserve. Probably only war could have wrought such a moment of truth in the nineteenth century, and hence the fate of the Fifty-fourth.

Their heroism was not merely the exhibition of physical courage in battle; it was their audacious faith to join up, salute, train, suffer, and give their lives for the chance to establish their own human dignity and their claims of belonging in their own land. Their deaths gave a new name to, and started a new narrative of, the idea of racial equality. If one looks very carefully at the faces on the monument, one can feel their determination, their lonely courage, their diversity of ages and back-grounds, in short, their humanity, as they move forward toward death. There is no hesitation in their step; they seem to represent an idea we are not at all comfortable with today—the notion that people can be asked, indeed, that it might be fated and necessary that they die for ideas.

The twentieth century, the most violent in modern history, has left us weak and sometimes wordless in the face of the violence we have com-mitted as a species. Sometimes, our own culture in the United States, as well as those in other nations, has simply abdicated facing that history, and sometimes we have stood up to it responsibly. In the case of the Civil War, understanding it requires a narrative told *through* the full story of emancipation, not around it, hovering above it, or packaged in feel-good notions of how America was simply living out its destiny of pro-gressive freedom. That narrative cannot be served up with moral clarity; it has to accommodate evil and good, fierce hatred and deep compas-sion, great attainments and great loss. It has to be a narrative of tragedy, one that takes seriously the mystery of human suffering and accounts for the knowledge and change born from that suffering.

This tragic sensibility has to be something Saint-Gaudens understood in giving us the monument. After observing the unveiling in May 1897, particularly after watching the survivors of the Fifty-fourth march to the monument, Saint-Gaudens recorded his thoughts with rapture: "There stood before the relief 65 of these veterans. . . . [T]he Negro troops . . . came in their time-worn frock coats. . . . Many of them were bent and crippled, many with white heads, some with bouquets. The impression of those old soldiers, passing the spot where they left for the war so many years before, thrills me even as I write these words. They faced and saluted the relief, with the music playing 'John Brown's Body.' . . . They seemed as if returning from the war, the troops of bronze marching in the opposite direction . . . and the young men in bronze showing these veterans the vigor and hope of youth. It was a consecration."[7] To those who look closely, and who know some history, the Shaw Memorial still has these elements of the sacred, of true *consecration*, of a kind of transubstantiation—not of the bread into wine, but of the past into the present. The eternal fascination and nostalgia for Civil War history is often rooted, ironically, in a transgenerational yearning for a time when Americans were so alive with hatreds and passions, when they killed each other and overturned their society in epic proportions. The Shaw Memorial gives us at the very least an object through which to contemplate our own positions in that yearning.

In 1878, fifteen years after the charge on Battery Wagner, Frederick Douglass delivered a Memorial Day speech in New York's Madison Square. Douglass appealed to military pathos and to the notion of heroic soldiers' sacrifice. But more than that, he demanded that his audience remember that the Civil War had been a struggle of ideologies on both sides. The conflict had been "a war of ideas," Douglass declared, "a battle of principles . . . a war between the old and the new, slavery and freedom, barbarism and civilization." It "was not a fight," he insisted, "between rapacious birds and ferocious beasts, a mere display of brute courage and endurance, but it was a war between men of thought, as well as of action, and in dead earnest for something beyond the battlefield." Although no single white southern mind existed in the wake of the war, many former Confederates, ironically, agreed with Douglass (albeit from entirely different perspectives). In 1867, in his book *The Lost Cause*, Edward A. Pollard, wartime editor of the *Richmond Examiner*, concluded his long work with a warning to all who would ever try to shape the memory of the war. "All that is left the South," said Pollard, "is the war of ideas." The war may have decided the "restoration of the union and the excision of slavery," declared Pollard, "but the war did not decide Negro equality." Thus as the memory of the war became so deeply contested, the Shaw Memorial was necessary in 1897 and remains necessary today and for generations to come.[8]

This focus on ideology illustrates one of the oldest and most important questions in Civil War remembrance: do we remember the *meaning* of the war or just the *fight*? Would we rather feel—or see—the spectacle of battle, or face the unending challenge of its moral and political consequences? Are we ennobled by Saint-Gaudens's relief or deflected by it? When we look at the memorial does our eye follow Shaw on his eternal ride into military glory, as Robert Lowell put it in his great poem, with "wren-like vigilance, a greyhound's gentle tautness" leading "his black soldiers to death, he cannot bend his back"? Or do we see those black soldiers' faces arched forward and, with William James in his 1897 dedication speech, "almost hear the bronze Negroes breathe"? To which kind of meaning does our gaze lead? Which kind of details do we see or evade? Which kind of memory, to borrow again from Lowell, "sticks . . . in the city's throat": the meaning or the fight?[9]

Douglass anticipated this kind of separation in popular memory in his greatest wartime speech, "The Mission of the War," delivered many times across the North in 1863–64. "A great battle lost or won is easily described, understood, and appreciated," said Douglass, "but the moral growth of a great nation requires reflection, as well as observation, to appreciate it." In that passage, it was as if Douglass had somehow already anticipated the thousands of regimental histories, battle memoirs, and veterans' reunion rituals of the late nineteenth century, not to mention the industry of Civil War nostalgia in our own time. His argument would echo again and again in African American memory of the war. At the height of the 1868 presidential campaign, Benjamin Tanner, editor of the A.M.E. church's *Christian Recorder*, issued a robust reminder to the Civil War generation and those to follow. "The Abolition of Slavery, the Civil Rights Bill, and the Enfranchisement of colored men of the South," declared Tanner, "are measures which, in the future pages of history, will outshine the lustre of Gettysburg, of Vicksburg, of Sherman's march, and of Appomattox Court House. Indeed without those great acts of legislation, these victories would be almost unmeaning. Feats of arms are glorious only as they make way for the advance of great principles."[10] What we need today are more movies, books, and journalism suggested by Douglass's and Tanner's nineteenth-century historical priorities, and fewer five-hour epics on the battle of Gettysburg, more public history interpretation that speaks to the political and racial meanings of the Civil War, rather than to the endless mantra of soldiers' sacrifice and reconciliation.

When this monument was unveiled in 1897, it took its place almost alone, thematically, in the landscape of Civil War memory. By that time the sectional reunion was virtually complete, founded on a racial apartheid that was becoming the law and practice of the land. Hundreds of small regimental monuments dotted the landscape on dozens of former battlefields, as well as in countless cemeteries, and brought an abstract calm to busy town squares. Several giant equestrian statues of Civil War generals already stood on the avenues and in front of the court-houses of major cities. Most southern governors, and many congress-men and senators, were Confederate veterans. Here and there in the South, a lone black politician was still elected to office, one even to the U.S. Congress (in North Carolina in 1896). But the slow wave of explicit disfranchisement laws, followed by an ever more specific series of segre-gation laws, had begun to roll over southern political life. By 1897 the farmers' revolt and the Populist movement, which had threatened to re-align American politics on class and racial lines, had run its course in almost every southern state as the country faced yet another cycle of economic depression. The *Plessy v. Ferguson* Supreme Court decision, authorizing the "separate but equal" doctrine, was but a year old when Boston turned out to honor the survivors of the Fifty-fourth.

In spite of the cunning practices of Jim Crow's visible and invisible structures in the 1890s, blacks made great strides in education, property ownership, the growth of churches in several denominations, and in the flowering of intellectual life among a new generation educated in both southern and northern schools. But in the great sectional reunion that swept over American cultural and political life, there were no "truth and reconciliation" commissions, no national forums or teach-ins of racial healing to balance the endless rituals of sectional healing—apart from those that offered accommodation to the new regime of racial separa-tion or could simply build small worlds behind it. The Blue and the Gray long since had been "clasping hands across the bloody chasm" of mu-tual, soldiers' valor. But as Du Bois said in *The Souls of Black Folk*, "no man clasped the hands" of another, and equally important, set of veterans—former slaves and former masters, and the children of both who, ac-cording to Du Bois, lived in a condition of "hatred" at the beginning of the twentieth century.[11]

By the mid-1890s it was only the rare northern Memorial Day speech that did not pay equal honor to the Confederate and Union veterans, as a means of continuing the spirit of sectional reconciliation, as well as commercial growth. On the night before the unveiling of Saint-Gaudens's monument in Boston, Henry Lee Higginson, Civil War vet-eran, entrepreneur, friend of Col. Robert Gould Shaw, and frequent cer-emonial speaker, delivered the official oration in Sanders Theater at Harvard University. He paid a moving tribute to Shaw and the black sol-diers who had "atoned," he said, "for the sin of slavery." Higginson could only lay such a burden of atonement on the men of the Fifty-fourth because in the beginning of the speech he had absolved white southerners of any specific responsibility. Higginson intended nothing "harsh to our brothers of the South," he said; "the sin of slavery was national, and caused the sin of disunion."[12] This viewpoint, the idea that somehow the Civil War had come by acts of natural law and inanimate forces, had helped to pave the road to reunion. The doctrine of original sin, especially when applied to nations, has a way of implicating everybody and absolving everybody all at once. No one had been truly wrong; heroism and devotion had rendered everyone right, North and South. In a war where no one was deemed wrong, and where the defeated side had gained one political victory after another for twenty years, we can begin to see the unique position the Shaw Memorial occupied in 1897. In a popular culture infused with white supremacy and the spirit of sectional comity, and in a legal system now governed only by a "thin disguise" that would promote racial hatred and discrimination, as Justice John Marshall Harlan put it in his famous dissent in *Plessy*, Saint-Gaudens's monument took its place as an inspiring exception.

At the beginning of the 1890s, many black writers, editors, and orators, as well as their white allies, resisted this American reunion forged out of the betrayal of the Civil War constitutional amendments and a deepening racial inequality. All who would resist the new regime of race relations knew they faced a hardened version of recent history. The young journalist and civil rights activist Ida B. Wells knew it in her writings about the "threadbare lie" at the heart of white southerners' excuse for lynching. The young African American educator Joseph Price (who founded Livingstone College in Salisbury, N.C., and died too young) may have captured the legacy of Reconstruction best in 1890 when he declared, "the South was more conquered than convinced; it was overpowered rather than fully persuaded. The Confederacy surrendered its sword at Appomattox, but did not there surrender its *convictions*." At the end of the decade, Charles Chesnutt, in his novel, *The Marrow of Tradition* (based directly on the Wilmington, North Carolina, riot and massacre against that city's black community in 1898), offered a trenchant summation of America's twisted and violent racial condition. The "weed" of slavery had been cut down, Chesnutt wrote, but "its roots remained, deeply imbedded in the soil, to spring up and trouble a new generation." As lynchings grew in frightful numbers, those "weeds" seemed to sprout all over the American landscape, and not only in the South. Only four days after the unveiling of the Shaw Memorial, a large mob in Urbana, Ohio, a town some forty miles from Columbus, broke into a jail housing a black man named Charles Mitchell, who had been accused and convicted in a trial of a "few minutes," of assaulting a white woman. Although two in the mob were killed, a detachment of the local militia could not stop the fury. Mitchell was hung from a tree on the courthouse grounds in the town square on June 4, 1897. This horrible act occurred virtually beneath the shadow of a large monument of a standing Union cavalry officer in the square. Most poignantly, however, several members of the Fifty-fourth and Fifty-fifth Massachusetts regiments had been recruited from Champaign County, surrounding Urbana, and some of them were buried in the local cemetery as honored Union dead.[13]

As we think of the Shaw Memorial's appearance on the landscape of Civil War memory in 1897, we need to account for the distance between the honor paid to Sgt. William H. Carney—first black winner of the Congressional Medal of Honor—and his comrades, and the inhumanity and death inflicted on Charles Mitchell in Ohio. Hard as it is to tell, they are parts of the same narrative, and they have to be connected. As we imagine the scenes in Urbana, Ohio, we can reflect with Lowell, in "For the Union Dead," on those ubiquitous soldiers' monuments, "the stone statues of the abstract Union soldier" adorning town squares, where "they doze over their muskets and muse through their sideburns." In some locales they even silently witnessed lynchings.[14]

The context of the unveiling in 1897 might be brought into even sharper focus by looking at other, equally important, distances in the interplay of Civil War memories. In late 1895, in Fort Mill, South Carolina, a hundred miles or so inland from Battery Wagner (where originally a plan had existed to build a memorial to Shaw), a monument to the "faith and loyalty" of the southern slave in the war was erected. According to the *Charleston (S.C.) News and Courier,* the granite shaft stood in the town square of Fort Mill, next to monuments to the Confederate soldier and one to Confederate women, as "the most significant and unique" of southern war memorials. Honor paid to "faithful slaves" became a standard element at Confederate reunions, in popular lore, and at community festivals; several "loyal slave" monuments dotted the southern landscape by the early twentieth century. Indeed, the image of the "loyal slave" and the "old time plantation Negro"—fashioned endlessly in the popular fiction of Thomas Nelson Page, in regular newspaper articles, and in stories in the *Confederate Veteran* magazine—had become a mythic icon of American culture by the time the Shaw Memorial appeared. The United Daughters of the Confederacy lobbied Congress for many years to build a "National Mammy Monument" in the District of Columbia. An appropriation for such a monument passed the U.S. Senate in 1922 but failed in the House of Representatives. The model for the mammy memorial, designed by artist George Julian Zolnay, consisted of an elaborate fountain, a sitting figure of mammy, and three children assembled about her. Originally planned for a site on Massachusetts Avenue at Sheridan Circle, such a mammy memorial narrowly missed becoming part of America's permanent remembrance of slavery.[15]

Moreover, in February 1896 the White House of the Confederacy was reopened and dedicated as a museum in Richmond, Virginia. Created by the Ladies Memorial Society and the United Daughters of the Confederacy, the former mansion occupied by Jefferson Davis during the war became the repository of sacred relics and the ideology of the Lost Cause. At the dedication, Virginia governor Charles O'Ferrall paid tribute to the steadfastness of southern womanhood and delivered a kind of New South appeal for preserving a heritage and facing the future. A longer oration followed by the former Confederate general Bradley T. Johnson. Johnson served up a combination of unreconstructed white supremacy and Confederate triumphalism that would have baffled or offended much of the audience at the unveiling in Boston a year later. To him, nothing was "lost" about the South's cause. "The world is surely coming to the conclusion," announced Johnson, "that the cause of the Confederacy was right." White southerners had merely "resisted invasion" and had never fought for slavery, he contended. With a historical logic that came to dominate both scholarly and popular understandings of the meaning of the war and its aftermath, Johnson declared slavery "only the incident" of the conflict, never its cause. And as that logic goes, he could therefore conclude that it was the North that had forced a contest of "race domination" on the South. Johnson summed up the legacy of the Civil War in a declaration in which many Americans had come to at least benignly acquiesce. "The great crime of the century," he said, "was the emancipation of the Negroes."[16]

Within three weeks of the unveiling of the Shaw Memorial in Boston, the United Confederate Veterans organization held its seventh annual convention in Nashville, Tennessee, June 22–24, 1897. Several thousand veterans and their families gathered for a festival, not so much dedicated to the Lost Cause as to honor a noble legacy of heroism and to celebrate a flourishing remembrance of a righteous cause. In that same year the *Confederate Veteran* magazine, published out of Nashville, claimed a circulation to 161,332 homes across the South and elsewhere in the nation. The keynote speaker at the 1897 reunion was Gov. John H. Reagan of Texas, a former member of Jefferson Davis's cabinet in the Confederacy. He took as his primary theme the causes of the Civil War. Reagan delivered a long survey of how "African slavery" did cause the war, but only as an "inheritance" entailed upon the South by Europe. The agony and agitation the nation suffered over slavery had been caused by antislavery northerners. Then Reagan caught his second wind: "You must understand that I do not make this recital for the purpose of renewing the prejudices and passions of the past, but only for the purpose of showing to our children and to the world that the ex-Confederates were *not responsible* for the existence of African slavery in this country and were *not responsible* for the existence of the great war which resulted from the agitation of that question, and that they were neither traitors nor rebels."[17] Within the same month Saint-Gaudens could weep with joy and transcendence as he watched the black veterans march in front of his monument, and a former Confederate official could announce ceremoniously and sincerely that the South was absolved of any responsibility for the war and any responsibility for the slavery the men of the Fifty-fourth had died to destroy. The meaning of Battery Wagner had been captured in bronze forever in Boston, but its meaning would remain a battleground, likely forever as well, in other times and places.

The conflicts and distances between historical memories are ultimately why such memories matter. The Shaw Memorial, therefore, is not merely a monument we can pass by as yet another emblem of our ancestors' vague or forgotten deeds. As we think about why the memorial is different, we need to remember that whatever the motives of the committee that sponsored it (through fourteen years), whatever Saint-Gaudens's deepest intentions, however we react to Shaw's preeminence on horseback, the memorial entered a debate, a landscape of remembrance where armies of memory and forgetting still contended for high stakes. The monument is different; the regiment fought for ideals that seem higher than the mere abstractions we see through our own eyes in all the thousands of other Civil War monuments we pass by in our towns and cities. The Fifty-fourth's memorial is different because it helps tell the narrative of emancipation. It takes Oliver Wendell Holmes's idea of a "soldiers' faith" and converts it into a moral purpose larger than the late nineteenth century's craving for the manly, strenuous life. It allows us to take the risk of seeing soldiering as a testing of ideas, instead of merely notions of masculinity. It gives us a picture through which to see the human aims in that war, as well as its beastliness. As we reflect on that memorial's uniqueness, we might also exercise some caution. At the time of the war, of course, black soldiers carried the burden of the expectations of their alleged "difference." They were the "experiment" in whether black men could fight, learn discipline, lead, face danger, and so forth. Their "traits" were under constant scrutiny. In a piece in *Century Magazine* in conjunction with the unveiling of the Shaw Memorial, Thomas Wentworth Higginson, who had commanded the First South Carolina Volunteers during the war, related the story of Gen. Rufus Saxton receiving a long list of questions about the behavior of his black Union troops in South Carolina. Saxton ordered his secretary to cross out all the interrogatories and at the bottom of the page simply write, "They are intensely human."[18]

At the century mark in the life of a great memorial, and well into the second century of the story the Shaw Memorial commemorates, hope rests on the historian's ability to reach broad publics with education and acts of remembrance. Greater appreciation and hope might also be drawn out of all the poetry and writing inspired by the Fifty-fourth's story and by the sculpture commemorating it. We might draw our own challenge from the tattered hope that no poet will ever again be moved to write, as Paul Laurence Dunbar did in 1900 in his poem "Robert Gould Shaw":

Why was it that the thunder voice of Fate
   Should call thee, studious, from the classic groves . . . ,
Far better the slow blaze of Learning's light,
The cool and quiet of her dearer fane,
Than this hot terror of a hopeless fight,
This cold endurance of the final pain,—
Since thou and those who with thee died for right
Have died, the Present teaches, but in vain![19]

NOTES

This essay was originally delivered in 1997 as a lecture at a conference in Boston. The conference was sponsored by the National Park Service to mark the one-hundredth anniversary of the unveiling of Augustus Saint-Gaudens's Shaw Memorial on Boston Common. Previously published in *Hope and Glory: Essays on the Legacy of the Fifty-fourth Massachusetts Regiment,* ed. Martin H. Blatt, Thomas J. Brown, and Donald Yacovone (Amherst: University of Massachusetts Press, 2001), it is revised here to include new material on the Urbana, Ohio, lynching and to update the chronology of other events.

1. John Hope Franklin, "A Century of Civil War Observances," *Journal of Negro History* 47 (April 1962): 98.

2. On Gov. David Beasley's efforts to remove the Confederate battle flag from official use, see Allan Gurganus, "At Last the South Loses Well," *New York Times,* December 8, 1996; Jack Hitt, "Confederate Semiotics," *Nation,* April 28, 1997. For information on Gov. George Allen's proclamation in the state of Virginia, I have relied on conversations with John Coski, librarian and director, the Museum of the Confederacy, Richmond, Virginia. On James Gilmore's proclamation, see "Slavery 'Abhorred,' Gilmore Says," *Washington Post,* April 10, 1998. I thank James Horton for providing me information on Gilmore and the Virginia controversy, and I thank Tom Brown for clarifying my understanding of Beasley's efforts in South Carolina. On the neo-Confederate movement in the South today, see "Rebels with a Cause," *Intelligence Report,* no. 99, Southern Poverty Law Center, summer 2000, in Intelligence Report Archives http://www.splcenter.org/intelligenceproject/ip-4.html.

3. Vincent Scully, art historian emeritus, Yale University, quoted from an address delivered at the unveiling of a restored casting of the Shaw Memorial, Saint Gaudens National Historic site, Cornish, N.H., July 13, 1998, author's notes. On "black Confederates," see "Forgotten Confederates: An Anthology about Black Southerners," ed. Charles Kelley Barrow, J. H. Segars, and R. B. Rosenberg, *Journal of Confederate History Series* vol. 14; "Black Southerners in Gray: Essays on Afro-Americans in Confederate Armies," ed. Richard Rollins, *Journal of Confederate History Series* vol. 11; and Ervin L. Jordan Jr., *Black Confederates and Afro-Yankees in Civil War Virginia* (Charlottesville: University Press of Virginia, 1995). Also see the Web site for the Sons of Confederate Veterans, "Black History Month: Black Confederate Heritage," February 1997 (http://www.scv.org/scvblkhm.htm); and Dan Hoover, "Civil War Controversy: Blacks in Rebel Gray," *Greenville (S.C.) News,* March 2, 1997 (clipping provided by John Coski).

4. Frederick Douglass, "Wasted Magnanimity," *New National Era,* August 10, 1871; Albion Tourgee, *Continent* 5 (April 2, 1884): 444; and *Continent* 6 (July 30, 1884): 156.

5. Gurganus, *New York Times,* December 8, 1996; Booker T. Washington, "A Speech at the Unveiling of the Robert Gould Shaw Monument," Boston, May 31, 1897, in *The Booker T. Washington Papers,* ed. Louis Harlan (Urbana: University of Illinois Press, 1975), 4:287; Thomas Beer quoted in Daniel Aaron, *The Unwritten War: American Writers and the Civil War* (New York: Knopf, 1973), xiii. An excellent essay on the contexts in which the Shaw Memorial emerged is Stephen J. Whitfield, "'Sacred in History and in Art': The Shaw Memorial," *New England Quarterly* 60 (March 1987): 3–27.

6. Howells is quoted in Allan Gurganus, *Oldest Confederate Widow Tells All* (New York: Ivy Books, 1984), epigraph; W. E. B. Du Bois, *Black Reconstruction in America, 1860–1880* (New York: Atheneum, 1935), 110.

7. Saint-Gaudens quoted in Sidney Kaplan, "The Sculptural World of Augustus Saint-Gaudens," *Massachusetts Review* (spring 1989): 36. On Saint-Gaudens, see Whitfield, "'Sacred in History and in Art,'" 8–10; Robert Hughes, "American Renaissance Man," *Time,* January 13, 1986; Burke Wilkinson, *Uncommon Clay: The Life and Works of Augustus Saint-Gaudens* (San Diego: Harcourt, Brace, Jovanovich, 1985); Kathryn Greenthal, *Augustus Saint-Gaudens: Master Sculptor* (Boston: G. K. Hall, 1985); and Theodore J. Karamanski, "Memory's Landscape," *Chicago History* 26 (summer 1997): 54–72.

8. Frederick Douglass, "Speech in Madison Square," Decoration Day, May 30, 1878, reel 15, Frederick Douglass Papers, Library of Congress; Edward A. Pollard, *The Lost Cause: A New Southern History of the War of the Confederates* (New York: E. B. Treat, 1867), 750, 752.

9. Robert Lowell, "For the Union Dead," in *Norton Anthology of American Literature* (New York: Norton, 1980), 1:842; William James, "Robert Gould Shaw," speech delivered in Boston, May 31, 1897, in *Memories and Studies by William James* (New York: Longman's, Green, 1911), 40.

10. Frederick Douglass, "The Mission of the War," delivered in New York City, February 13, 1864, in *The Life and Writings of Frederick Douglass,* ed. Philip S. Foner (New York: International Publishers, 1952), 3:401; Benjamin T. Tanner, "The Issues before the People," *Christian Recorder,* September 19, 1868.

11. W. E. B. Du Bois, *The Souls of Black Folk* (1903; reprint, Boston, Bedford Books, 1997), 54–55.

12. Henry Lee Higginson, "Robert Gould Shaw," an address delivered in Sanders Theater, May 30, 1897, in *Four Addresses by Henry Lee Higginson* (Boston: Merrymount Press, 1902), 72–73, 102.

13. Ida B. Wells, *Southern Horrors: Lynch Law in All Its Phases,* in *Selected Works of Ida B. Wells-Barnett,* comp. Trudier Harris (New York: Oxford, 1991), 17; Joseph C. Price, "The Race Problem Stated," in *Negro Orators and Their Orations,* ed. Carter G. Woodson (New York: Russell and Russell, 1940), 490, emphasis added; Charles Chesnutt, *The Marrow of Tradition* (Ann Arbor: University of Michigan Press, 1969), 269–70; *Boston Evening Transcript,* June 4, 1897. On the Urbana lynching and the burial of members of the Fifty-fourth in that town, see David T. Thackery, *A Light and Uncertain Hold: A History of the Sixty-sixth Ohio Volunteer Infantry* (Kent: Kent State University Press, 1999), 235–36.

14. Lowell, "For the Union Dead," 842.

15. "A Monument to the Southern Slave," from *Charleston (S.C.) News and Courier,* cited in *Baltimore Afro-American,* August 3, 1895. Six or seven "loyal slave" memorials of various kinds have been identified across the South. I am indebted to James Loewen for sharing his information on such monuments. On the Fort Mill monument, see Kirk Savage, *Standing Soldiers, Kneeling Slaves: Race, War, and Monument in Nineteenth-Century America* (Princeton: Princeton University Press, 1997), 155–61. "Faithful slave" stories and reminiscences became a regular

feature in the *Confederate Veteran,* which began publication in 1893. For some examples, see *Confederate Veteran,* May, December 1899; March 1903; March, September, July 1905; March 1906; August, October 1909; October, December 1914. On the national "Mammy Monument," see *Goldsboro (N.C.) Argus,* July 8, 1923, *Amsterdam News* (New York City), August 22, 1923, and *Southwestern Christian Advocate* (New Orleans), October 4, 1923.

16. Speeches by O'Ferrall and Johnson, in *In Memoriam Sempiternam,* pamphlet from dedication ceremonies, Confederate Museum, Richmond, 1896, copy in library, the Museum of the Confederacy, Richmond, Va., 44, 47, 50.

17. *Confederate Veteran,* July 1897, emphasis added.

18. Thomas Wentworth Higginson, "Colored Troops Under Fire," *Century Magazine* 54 (June 1897): 199.

19. Paul Laurence Dunbar, "Robert Gould Shaw," in *The Paul Laurence Dunbar Reader,* ed. Jay Martin and Gossie H. Hudson (New York: Dodd, Mead, 1975), 320.

Healing and History
Battlefields and the Problem
of Civil War Memory

Those of us gathered here today in Ford's Theater, the place where the Civil War's culminating tragedy took place, probably all share a set of passions.[1] We all love or appreciate the past. Sometimes we just have that passion for the pastness of the past; we love things that are old and speak to us from another age. Sometimes it is a passion for detail, for the wonderful stuff of research, the joy of discovery, the relationships of real people, real events, and real documents. Sometimes it is a passion for the truth. Perhaps we share a passion for language as well, for the story, for the beauty and music of words. The other passion that we may share is the one that brings us here today. It is probably our least holy and least sexy passion—our quest to understand *context*. It is hard to make context sound exciting, but without it we take the risk of having no history at all. Without context, we can end up with only objects to examine; we risk simple, single, causal explanations of the past. If we do not pursue context we may allow our students and our audiences to abandon explanation or interpretation altogether in favor of what they believe or wish to be accurate about the past. Although a tendency may exist in all of us to make the past what it needs to be in order to serve our present, we must challenge ourselves to broaden contextual interpretations—including those of the Civil War at the sacred sites where the conflict was fought. One way to do this is to consider how battlefields became sites of "healing" in American history.

By looking at the history of how some battlefields became important commemorative sites, we may better understand how they have been used as places of reconciliation and healing, sometimes at the expense of other kinds of learning. Frederick Douglass left us many challenges that might serve as clarion calls for our collective enterprise. On Memorial Day 1878, Douglass gave a speech in Madison Square in New York City. It was one year after the political compromise of 1877 that had settled the sectional dispute over the presidential election of 1876. The "end" of Reconstruction, politically, had taken place, and the nation seemed to be reconciling all over American culture. Douglass was deeply worried about the future of black civil rights, the freedpeople's liberties—the very meaning for which, in his view, the Civil War had been fought. He was worried that too many Americans were losing an understanding of the deepest context of the war and its consequences. The conflict of 1861–65, said Douglass, had been "a war of ideas, a battle of principles . . . a war between the old and the new, slavery and freedom, barbarism and civilization." It "was not a fight," he insisted, "between rapacious birds and ferocious beasts, a mere display of brute courage and endurance, but it was a war between men of thought, as well as of action, and in dead earnest for something beyond the battlefield."[2]

In 1961 the southern poet and novelist Robert Penn Warren, in his *Legacy of the Civil War,* offered a similar challenge. "The Civil War is our *felt* history—history lived in the national imagination," said Warren. "Somewhere in their bones," he declared, most Americans have a storehouse of "lessons" drawn from the Civil War. Exactly what those lessons should be, and who should determine them, has been the most contested question in American historical memory, at least since 1863. Among those lessons, wrote Warren, is the realization that "slavery looms up mountainously" in the story, "and cannot be talked away." But Warren acknowledged another lesson of equal importance for Americans of all persuasions: "When one is happy in forgetfulness, facts get forgotten."[3]

Americans faced an overwhelming task after the Civil War and emancipation: how to understand the tangled relationship between two profound ideas—*healing* and *justice.* On some level, both had to occur, but given the potency of white supremacy in nineteenth-century America, these two aims never developed in historical balance. One might conclude that this imbalance between the outcomes of sectional healing and racial justice was simply America's inevitable historical condition, and thus celebrate the remarkable swiftness of the reunion. But theories of inevitability—of irrepressible conflicts or irrepressible reconciliations—are rarely satisfying. Human reconciliations—when tragically divided people can unify again around aspirations, ideas, and the positive bonds of nationalism—are to be cherished. But sometimes reconciliations come with terrible costs, both intentional and unseen. The sectional reunion after so horrible a civil war was a political triumph by the late nineteenth century, but it could not have been achieved without the resubjugation of many of those people the war had freed from centuries of bondage. This is the tragedy lingering on the margins and infesting the heart of American history from Appomattox to World War I.

For many whites, especially veterans and their family members, healing from the war was simply not the same proposition as doing justice to the four million emancipated slaves and their descendants. On the other hand, a simple justice, a fair chance to exercise their basic rights and secure access to land and livelihood were all most blacks ever demanded of Reconstruction and beyond. The rub, of course, was that there were so many warring definitions of healing in the South, and the nation's collective memory had never been so shattered.

In the wake of the Civil War, there were no "truth and reconciliation" commissions through which to process memories of either slavery for blacks or the experience of total war for southern whites. Defeated white southerners and black former slaves faced each other on the ground, seeing and knowing the awful chasm between their experiences, unaware that any path would lead to *their* reconciliation. Yankee and Confederate soldiers would eventually find a smoother path to bonds of fraternalism and mutual glory. As is always the case in any society trying to master the most conflicted elements of its past, healing and justice had to happen *in history* and *through politics*. Americans have had to work through the meaning of their Civil War in the only place it could happen—in the politics of memory. As long as we have a politics of race in America, we will have a politics of Civil War memory, and likely a politics of how we forge that memory at our battlefields.

For Americans broadly, the Civil War has been a defining event upon which we have often imposed unity and continuity. As a culture we have often preferred its music and pathos to its enduring challenges, the theme of reconciled conflict to resurgent, unresolved legacies. The greatest enthusiasts for Civil War history and memory often displace complicated consequences by endlessly focusing on the contest itself. Over time, Americans have needed deflections from the deeper meanings of the

Civil War. It haunts us still; we *feel* it, to borrow from Warren, but often do not *face* it.

In the half century after the war, as the sections reconciled, by and large, the races divided. *Race* was so deeply at the root of the war's causes and consequences, and so powerful a source of division in American social psychology, that it served as the antithesis of a culture of reconciliation. The memory of slavery, emancipation, and the Fourteenth and Fifteenth Amendments never fit well into a developing narrative in which the Old and New South were romanticized and welcomed back to a new nationalism, and in which devotion alone made everyone right, and no one truly wrong in the remembered Civil War. Persistent discussion of the "race problem" across the political and ideological spectrum throughout the late nineteenth century meant that American society could not easily remember its "Civil War problem" or a "Blue-Gray problem." Battlefields served particularly well as the places where this separation in memory became most explicit; no "race problem" was allowed to invade the increasingly mystical reconciliation of the Blue and the Gray on the landscapes that the aging veterans had rendered sacred.

In a popular novel, *Cease Firing*, the southern writer Mary Johnston, a Virginian imbued with Lost Cause tradition and a determination to represent its complexity, imagined a telling dialogue that may have captured the memory most Americans, then and even now, want to embrace about the Civil War. On the last page of the book, Robert E. Lee's Army of Northern Virginia is retreating west toward its final collapse and surrender at Appomattox in the last week of the war. The April breezes are not yet warm and the rivers to be forded still run cold. One Confederate soldier asks another what he thinks it all means. "I think that we were both right and both wrong," says the veteran of many battles, "and that, in the beginning, each side might have been more patient and much wiser. Life and history, and right and wrong and minds of men look out of more windows than we used to think! Did you never hear of the shield that had two sides and both were precious metal?"[4]

There was, of course, no lack of honor on either side in that fateful surrender at Appomattox in 1865. And Johnston captured an honest soldier's sentiment that had reverberated down through veterans' memory for decades. But outside of this pathos and the endearing mutuality of sacrifice among soldiers that came to dominate national memory, another process was at work—the denigration of black humanity and dignity, and the attempted erasure of emancipation from the national narrative of what the war had been about. That other process led the black scholar and editor W. E. B. Du Bois to conclude in the same year as Johnston's novel that "this country has had its appetite for facts on the Negro problem spoiled by sweets."[5] Deflections and evasions, careful remembering and necessary forgetting, and embittered and irreconcilable versions of experience are all the stuff of historical memory.

Over time, in a variety of ways, Civil War battlefields have become sites of healing and reconciliation in our national culture. But at first they were places of death and destruction, graveyards and sites of haunted memory, for both the victors and the vanquished. In the immediate wake of the war, the battlefields, in combination with devastated southern cities, made America for the first time, a land with *ruins*. Unlike the haunting, destroyed abbeys of the English civil war of the seventeenth century or Rome's ancient, majestic city of ruins, America's destruction was brand new—new, but instantaneously historic, and at many battlefields and burial grounds, therefore, *sacred*. Americans were now a people with so much bloody history that they would forever live in a modern society, burdened by a historic landscape—full of sites they would have to memorialize, romanticize, and even explain.

No one understood this better than defeated white southerners, but their ruins inspired different reactions, depending on time and perspective. In October 1865, just after release from a five-month imprisonment in Boston, former Confederate vice president Alexander H. Stephens rode a slow train southward. In northern Virginia, he found that "the desolation of the country from Alexandria to near Charlottesville was horrible to behold." When Stephens reached northern Georgia, his native state, he was again shocked: "War has left a terrible impression on the whole country to Atlanta. The desolation is heartsickening. Fences gone, fields all a-waste, houses burnt." As time passed during Reconstruction, other southerners, such as Father Abram Ryan, known as the Poet Priest of the Lost Cause, found inspiration and spiritual renewal in the South's ruins. "A land without ruins is a land without memories," said Ryan. Through its battlefield landscapes, he imagined, the South would achieve its "consecrated cornet of sorrow" and with time win "the sympathy of the heart and of history." From such landscapes and from such sentiments, the defeated Confederacy did attain a kind of exotic and romantic niche in American popular imagination, an idea Tony Horwitz uncovered and may have immortalized in *Confederates in the Attic*.[6]

In the wake of the war, thousands of northern readers learned of the condition of the defeated South, its material and political condition, as well as it famous battlefields, from northern travel writers. In *The South: A Tour of Its Battlefields and Ruined Cities,* the novelist and poet John T. Trowbridge wrote the longest and most lyrical of such accounts. Trowbridge was one of the first battlefield tourists; he began his journeys in late August 1865, at Gettysburg. Guided by the local civilian hero of the battle, John Burns, Trowbridge began his tour on Cemetery Hill. The supreme "stillness" of the summer day was broken only by the "perpetual click-click" sound of stonecutters preparing headstones in the soldiers' cemetery. The scene moved Trowbridge deeply; it was already "the time-hallowed place of the dead." He felt an "overpowering sense of the horror and wickedness of war" as he watched workmen still digging trenches and laying foundations for gravestones. He watched a veritable production line making stones lettered Unknown, and felt compelled to contemplate the meaning of it all. Trowbridge could have been speaking for thousands of tourists in our own time who visit this most famous of American battlefields. "Grown accustomed to the waste of life through years of war," he wrote, "we learn to think too lightly of such sacrifices. 'So many killed,'—with that brief sentence we glide over the unimaginably fearful, and pass on to other details." Trowbridge demanded meaning from what he observed, not merely a feeling of the grandeur of the massive fight. But the meaning remained to him "vague and uncertain. It lies before us like one of those unidentified heroes," he said, "hidden from sight, deep-buried, mysterious, its headstones lettered 'Unknown.'"[7]

Cemetery Hill at Gettysburg moved Trowbridge to ponder warily the nation's rebirth in that first summer after the war. "Will it ever rise?" he asked. The "uncounted thousands" of dead soldiers, he wrote, had "confronted, for their country's sake, that awful uncertainty." Strolling reflectively among the cemetery workmen, Trowbridge "looked into one of the trenches . . . and saw the ends of the coffins protruding. It was silent and dark down there." It was as though the elusive meaning of the war was in that trench; the coffin captured the observer as no abstract monument ever could. "I chose out one coffin from among the rest," remembered Trowbridge, "and thought of him whose dust it contained,—your brother and mine, although we never knew him." The author tried to think of the man's childhood, his parents and home life. But he could only conclude: "I could not know; in this world, none will ever know." Trowbridge altered his gaze, resumed his tour, and moved on to "other details" further south.[8]

In Richmond and other places in Virginia, Trowbridge interviewed a number of former slaveholders and former slaves, and he began to "know" more and think more clearly about the meaning of the war. But so often at Civil War battlefields, Americans are still walking in Trowbridge's footsteps, observing and moved, but not knowing why so many men died on those beautiful landscapes. We cannot see the coffins protruding from the ground anymore, nor hear the stonecutter's hammer; we need help in bridging the gap between the graves and their meanings. The most important forms of healing are probably those that come from a combination of emotion and knowledge that instructs and even surprises us, rather from that which confirms what we already want to believe.

Another remarkable series of travel accounts was the result of a three-month tour in 1869 by Russell Conwell, a twenty-six-year-old Union veteran, writing for the *Boston Daily Evening Traveler.* Many of Conwell's twenty-five extensive letters were reflections on the battlefield sites or cemeteries he visited. Stunned at how "shattered and ruined" much of Virginia's countryside still appeared, he remarked that the war had "transformed the 'Garden of the South' into the 'Graveyard of America.'" He talked to farmers whose plows kept disturbing the remains of dead soldiers. Conwell entertained his readers with a combination of the sacred and the humorous. Who could have resisted his story of attending the wedding of a crippled Union veteran from New Hampshire and a young Virginia girl who, during the Peninsula Campaign, along with an old black woman, had nursed the badly wounded soldier to health while he was stranded in the woods. The rural wedding scene included a black fiddler providing music for this particular reconciliation among common folk. Conwell observed half-buried ruins and earthworks everywhere. Around old battlefields he encountered a steady stream of lead and bone hunters who sold their scrap findings to eke out a living. At Cold Harbor battlefield, he met "several Negroes with large sacks, collecting the bones of dead horses which they sold to the bone-grinders of Richmond."[9]

When Conwell reached Charleston, South Carolina, he visited the remains of Fort Wagner on Morris Island. There he met an older black man who claimed to have been a member of the Fifty-fourth Massachusetts and wounded in its famous charge of July 1863. The black veteran and his family lived in a "bomb-proof" nearby and made a living "digging for old iron in the sand." "The products of his industry," remarked Conwell, "reminded us of the stacks in a New England hay field. He sells it by the ton." In this image of the Reconstruction South in 1869, we are reminded that old battlefields can have deep and unexpected contexts. Before leaving the beach by the remains of Fort Wagner, Conwell described "old haversacks, belts, bayonet scabbards, and shoes" still strewn on the sand. At his feet, human skulls and bones rolled up in the surf. The skulls "lay grinning," he said, "and filled us with sad sensations, which still haunt our dreams. The sad and the beautiful, how strangely combined!" Conwell's Yankee partisanship flowed through as he departed. The whole scene, he believed, was a living memorial to "the cause of human freedom."[10]

Visitors to today's battlefields will meet no veterans as bone-collectors; no skulls will wash up in the surf at their feet. We will not encounter actual haversacks from battle strewn on the ground. In the interpretation of battle sites, we may not be confronted with images or information about a black veteran scraping out a life in an old bomb-proof, collecting mounds of metal—we may never know what followed from those battles in the aftermath of the war, among whites and blacks, on the ground in the South. The sad and the beautiful, strangely combined: Conwell put it aptly—it was always one of my own first reactions when I visited battlefields as a child and as a young adult. But from the metaphors Trowbridge and Conwell provide—gazing at skulls, talking to black bone-collectors, and pondering the meanings of coffins at the Gettysburg cemetery—we ought to be able to imagine new ways to enrich the story, to broaden the historical meanings we take from these sacred sites.

During the first decade or so after the war, Civil War veterans on both sides tried to forge new lives. Veterans' organizations and reunions lagged until the late 1870s; women, South and North, tended to lead memorial activity. But especially in the 1880s, battlefields increasingly became sites of regimental reunions, a growing industry of monument building, the object of detailed mapping (such as John Bachelder's life-long work at Gettysburg), and eventually a growing array of Blue-Gray reunions. Bitterness between Yankee and Confederate veterans could still emerge, especially over such issues as the possible return of battle flags and the long-standing reluctance of most former Confederates to return to Gettysburg at all.[11]

But aging soldiers shared much in the Gilded Age; a kind of "culture of character" emerged as a core ideology that knit them together. Old soldiers tended to measure each other as preservers of an older, more wholesome society, uncorrupted by materialism and rooted in individual honor. They came to see their war experience as a special shared possession, and the battlefields where they reassembled twenty or thirty years after the fact, as their own sites of healing. Upon his return to Gettysburg in 1884, Samuel Armstrong, a Union veteran and founder of the black college Hampton Institute, recollected the agony of his battle experience. "Those days were full of horrible sights," he said. "Yet in all these sickening scenes there was, I think, no hatred; the malice and rascality engendered by war is at the rear. There is a certain mutual respect among those who accept the wager of battle." Armstrong may have underestimated the "hatreds" men felt at the moment of truth in battle. He had not read Edward Porter Alexander's memoir in which the former Confederate general wrote honestly about his joy in killing Yankees and seeing them dead on the ground.[12] But in the mutuality of sacrifice, in the shared claim to a special realm of experience and manliness, in their obsessions for detail in preserving and mapping battlefields, veterans themselves became America's first Civil War "buffs." They began to transform those battlefields into places of sectional healing, though rarely if ever places of racial healing.

In 1888 George Kilmer, a member of the Abraham Lincoln post of the GAR in New York, published in *Century Magazine* a list of some twenty-four Blue-Gray reunions of one kind or another between 1881 and 1887, and then updated the list with three or four more he discovered from the 1870s. Kilmer believed that these gatherings reflected a shared "faith" among soldiers and that increased "business relations" and intersectional migration had helped foment these events. Some meetings consisted of southern and northern veterans' groups touring the other section's cities and being ceremonially received by their former foes. Some occurred in the aftermath of the assassination of President James Garfield in 1881. Some occurred at historical anniversaries such as the Bunker Hill centennial in Boston in 1875. But increasingly these reunions met at battlefields, often on anniversaries, such as at Fredericksburg, Chancellorsville, and the Wilderness in Virginia in October 1887, and at Kennesaw Mountain in Georgia that same month.[13]

At Gettysburg the early history of Blue-Gray fraternalism was mixed. A first attempt in 1874 was abandoned when it became clear that it was simply too early for soldiers to mingle at the scene of such sensitive memories. Reconstruction politics also delayed such fraternalism; as long as the "bloody shirt" was so useful on both sides in the struggles over the meaning of the war, Blue-Gray reunions were not easy to organize. Confederates were also deeply divided among themselves between Virginians and North Carolinians over responsibility for defeat at Gettysburg. But by 1887, on the twenty-fourth anniversary of the battle, some five hundred members of the Philadelphia Brigade veterans' organization met with some two hundred survivors of Pickett's Division. They met in an elaborate ceremony in the town square to shake hands, and then after speeches acknowledging mutual valor, they gathered out at the "high water mark" where they had met in 1863 in some of the most celebrated combat of the war. They pitched tents and spent the night, exchanging stories, hats, and mementos, including for a few, locks of hair. One reporter remarked that it was hard to tell who was from North or South.[14]

All was not sweetness in Blue-Gray relations, however, especially when the Democratic president, Grover Cleveland, not a veteran, suggested the return of battle flags. An 1888 attempt at a larger reunion on the twenty-fifth anniversary was a disappointment. Some Union veterans were not yet ready to share the Gettysburg landscape with Confederates. "No God-knows-who-was-right bosh must be tolerated at Gettysburg," wrote the editor of a veterans' journal. "The men who won the victory there were eternally right, and the men who were defeated were eternally wrong."[15] With time, though, an "everyone-was-right bosh" did overtake the practice of Blue-Gray fraternalism.

Sometimes reunions were explicitly organized for intersectional political and business dealings. On Memorial Day weekend in 1895, a huge Blue-Gray affair met in Chicago to unveil a large monument in Oakwood Cemetery to the 6,229 Confederate soldiers who had died during the war at the Camp Douglas prison compound. The event was the brainchild of John C. Underwood, a Kentucky Confederate veteran and business entrepreneur. Underwood's earlier efforts at such gatherings in Philadelphia in 1885 and Columbus, Ohio, in 1889 had largely failed. But in 1890 he moved his "headquarters" to Chicago and helped found the "Ex-Confederate Association of Chicago." Many surviving former Confederate generals were honored in receptions at the Palmer

House hotel, including James Longstreet, Fitzhugh Lee, Wade Hampton (the latter two former governors of their states by then), and Stephen D. Lee of Mississippi. A crowd estimated at 100,000 participated in the parade and unveiling ceremonies, and Wade Hampton was the keynote speaker. Chicago papers gushed with admiration for the event. Even the progressive *Inter-Ocean* marveled that "yesterday it mattered not who wore the blue or wore the gray."[16]

Such spectacles were emotionally irresistible to most people. But other motives animated participants as well. The leader of the Chicago Citizens' Committee welcomed the Confederate soldiers in the interest of "closer commercial relations and business union . . . a larger degree of investment of capital [by the North] in the vast resources of the Southern states." Responding for the Confederate veterans, Stephen Lee said: "We invite you again to invade us, not with your bayonets this time, but with your business. We want to hear in our land the voices of your industry." But other themes had to be put to rest first. When Underwood himself spoke at the banquet, he declared the purpose of the reunion to be "harmonious forgetfulness." "It is not now profitable," he announced, "to discuss the right or wrong of the past. . . . [N]either should the question be raised as to the morals of Massachusetts selling her slaves and South Carolina holding hers, nor as to the profit of merchandising the negro on the block in New York or for the sugarcane fields of the Mississippi coasts."[17] In this vision of Blue-Gray fraternalism, slavery was everyone's and no one's responsibility. America's bloody racial history was to be banished from consciousness; the only notions of equality were soldiers' heroism and the exchange of the business deal.

Later in 1895, one of the most spectacular reunions of the decade occurred at the dedication of the Chickamauga and Chattanooga National Military Park, September 18–20. An estimated 50,000 people attended, including the vice president of the United States, Adlai Stevenson, numerous governors, and many surviving generals from both sides. Among the many speakers was Gen. Lew Wallace, author of *Ben Hur* and the former governor of New Mexico. Capturing the tone of the reunion, Wallace asked "Remembrance! Remembrance of what? Not the cause, but the heroism it invoked." And Alabama governor W. C. Oates, a Confederate veteran, told his southern comrades to stand "proud," for "they fought for a just cause, which though lost, was partially won." Oates actually addressed slavery, though he acknowledged it was the "pandora's box of American politics." He painted a picture of benevolent masters fated to their lot. Cruelty existed in slavery, Oates admitted, but "the negroes simply passed through the fiery furnace of slavery to reach civilization, which was the only road by which they could have obtained it." Some veterans were thus willing to speak of the war's causes, contexts, and meanings at battlefields. But often only in ways that fit neatly into the imperatives of an emerging white supremacist society. One context for the Chickamauga reunion is that on the very same day, in Atlanta, Booker T. Washington was delivering his "Atlanta compromise" speech, urging black and white southerners to "cast down their buckets where they are."[18] Washington electrified the nation's press and thousands of readers with perhaps the most important sectional reconciliation speech ever delivered, rooted of course in the futile dream that racial reconciliation could be forged in mutual economic progress.

One further example of the uses of battlefields for national reconciliation is in order. As it stood in the general American culture in the early twentieth century, Civil War memory never saw a more fully orchestrated expression than that at Gettysburg on the battle's fiftieth anniversary in July 1913. With their railway tickets paid for by the government, more than 53,000 veterans, Blue and Gray, came to Gettysburg. Veterans came from every state except two. The states and the federal government appropriated well over two million dollars to put on this remarkable festival of harmony and reconciliation.[19] The reunion came off as a kind of public avowal of a glorious fight that led to greater national unity.

All the governors, as well as many surviving officers, spoke during the four days of the reunion. Gov. William Hodges Mann of Virginia, himself a Confederate veteran, struck the keynote of the reunion. "We are not here to discuss the Genesis of the war," he declared, "but men who have tried each other in the storm and smoke of battle are here to discuss the great fight. . . . We came here, I say, not to discuss what caused the war of 1861–65, but to talk over the events of the battle as man to man." No time or space was allowed at the four-day spectacle for discussion of causes and consequences. There was no rhetoric about emancipation or the unresolved history of Reconstruction. Nor was there any consideration of the war's second great outcome by 1913—the nation's disastrous abandonment of racial reconciliation. The "Peace Jubilee," as the reunion was called, was a Jim Crow reunion. There is no evidence that any black veterans attended or were welcome in spite of what is shown in episode 11 of Ken Burns's television series on the Civil War. The only blacks in attendance were laborers who helped build the tent city, who constructed and cleaned the latrines and dispensed blankets to the white veterans. This stunning and photogenic gathering of old veterans, which was covered by the national and international press for several days, featured an enfeebled reenactment by actual participants of part of Pickett's Charge and the familiar handshakes across the stone walls on Cemetery Ridge. There had never been such a spectacle of resolution and patriotism on this scale in America. "Thank God for Gettysburg, Hosanna!" proclaimed the *Louisville Courier-Journal.* "God bless us everyone, alike the Blue and the Gray. . . . The world ne'er witnessed such a site as this. Beholding, can we say 'happy is the nation that hath no history'?"[20]

At a time when lynching had developed into a social ritual of its own horrifying kind (the NAACP counted seventy in 1913) and when American apartheid had become fully entrenched, many black leaders and editors found the sectional love feast at Gettysburg more than they could bear. "A Reunion of whom?" asked the *Washington (D.C.) Bee.* Only those who "fought for the preservation of the Union and the extinction of slavery" or also those who "fought to destroy the Union and perpetuate slavery, and who are now employing every artifice . . . known to deceit . . . to propagate a national sentiment in favor of their nefarious contention that emancipation, reconstruction and enfranchisement are a dismal failure?"[21] Black responses to such reunions as that at Gettysburg in 1913 and a host of other similar events demonstrated how fundamentally at odds black memories were by then from the spirit and character of the national reunion. In that contradiction lay an American tragedy not yet fully told by 1913 and considered out of place at Blue-Gray reunions.

African American responses to the 1913 Gettysburg reunion were especially telling in the context of the Wilson administration's efforts that very summer to aggressively resegregate federal agencies in Washington, D.C., Woodrow Wilson, elected president in 1912 and inaugurated that spring of 1913, came to the Pennsylvania town on July 4, the last day of the reunion, to give his Gettysburg address. Wilson did not really want to come; he wanted no part of this festival of sectional peace, and as the first southerner elected president since the Civil War, he wished not to have to test the politics of such an event. Up until about four days before the reunion he planned not to attend. But one of his aides said to him in effect: You don't get it; you don't quite understand what is going on up at Gettysburg. You need to be there.[22]

President Wilson rode into Gettysburg by train, was quickly put into an open car and whisked out to the battlefield where a huge tent awaited him filled with some 12,000 of the veterans. He walked into the tent accompanied on either side by a Union veteran and a Confederate veteran, each holding their respective flags. In his brief speech, Wilson declared it "an impertinence to discourse upon how the battle went, how it ended," or even "what it signified." Wilson's charge, he claimed, was to comprehend what the fifty years since the battle had meant. His answer struck the mystic chord that most Americans were prepared to hear: "They have meant peace and union and vigor, and the maturity and might of a great nation. How wholesome and healing the peace has been! We have found one another again as brothers and comrades, in arms, enemies no longer, generous friends rather, our battles long past, the *quarrel forgotten*—except that we shall not forget the splendid valor, the manly devotion of the men then arrayed against one another, now grasping hands and smiling into each other's eyes."[23] Wilson's great gift for ambiguity was in perfect form. The Civil War had thus become the quarrel forgotten on the statute books of Jim Crow America. A nation can have too much memory, but a nation can also forget too much.

I close with a reflection on Memorial Day, with a consideration of the origins of this tradition and an attempt to broaden our very definition of a battlefield. Go with me to Charleston, South Carolina, in 1865 at the very end of the war. Charleston, of course, was the place where the war began, a city of enormous symbolic and strategic importance. During approximately the last eight months of the war the city was bombarded by Union artillery from around the harbor and from gunboats. For many blocks up from Battery Park, some of those magnificent mansions that make that city one of the most beautiful in North America were all but destroyed. The city was evacuated on February 18, 1865, as most of the white population fled to the interior. Among the first troops to enter the town and march up Meeting Street, the main thoroughfare of Charleston, was the Twenty-first U.S. Colored Infantry. Their commander, Lt. Col. A. G. Bennett, accepted the formal surrender of the city from the mayor.[24]

Black Charlestonians were the bulk of the population remaining in the city in those final weeks of the war. They had witnessed death all around them for many months, and they began to plan their own rituals of mourning and celebration. On March 3 a large crowd gathered in Francis Marion Square in the heart of Charleston. Thirteen black women elegantly dressed in the finest clothes they could find and representing, they said, the thirteen original states, presented Gen. Quincy A. Gillmore, the Union commander, with a U.S. flag, a bouquet of flowers, and a fan for Mrs. Lincoln in Washington. On March 29 African Americans in Charleston organized an elaborate parade of some four thousand people. The march, celebrating black freedom, included two wagons (floats). The first wagon rolled along carrying an auction block and an auctioneer selling two black women and their children. The second wagon contained a coffin labeled on its side: Death of Slavery—Sumter Dug His Grave on the 13th of April, 1861.[25] In this mock slave auction and victory parade the freedpeople of Charleston declared the meaning of the war. They drew a line of demarcation between past and present. These were days of awe and wonderment, of sorrow and gaiety. The freedpeople of Charleston had converted Confederate ruin into their own festival of freedom.

On April 14 a celebration took place out at the mouth of the harbor in Fort Sumter itself. Four years to the day after the surrender of the fort, Gen. Robert Anderson returned to Charleston with many northern dignitaries to raise the flag he had lowered in 1861. Three thousand African Americans crammed on to the island fortress for the ceremony. In attendance were abolitionist William Lloyd Garrison and President Lincoln's secretary John G. Nicolay. Also among the throng were former abolitionist and writer, and now major in the Union army, Martin Delany, as was the son of Denmark Vesey, the leader of a slave rebellion who was executed in Charleston in 1822. The former slave and boat pilot Robert Smalls was nearby Fort Sumter aboard the *Planter* (which was filled with a contingent of freedpeople), the steamer he had commandeered and sailed out of Charleston to freedom during the war. The Reverend Henry Ward Beecher was orator of the day. The audience heard Beecher condemn South Carolina's secessionists to eternal damnation. Many in that special audience hoped for more guidance from Beecher about the confused and delicate questions of Reconstruction, but on that count they heard little in what unfolded as primarily a festival of victory, thanksgiving, and celebration. When hearing a regimental band play "John Brown's Body," Garrison, who two decades earlier had a price put on his life by the State of South Carolina, broke down and wept. Flowers were blooming everywhere amid the ruins of

Charleston; for so many, remembrance at this early date was but a fragrance full of warring emotions. As the flag reached its height on the staff in the fort, guns all around Charleston harbor opened up in a salute. The grand day ended that evening at a banquet in the city as Anderson, among others, offered many toasts, some of which were to President Lincoln, who was that very night assassinated in Ford's Theater in Washington. Thus the day that had begun with such jubilation ended with tragedy.[26]

During the next two weeks in Charleston, as elsewhere, mourning over Lincoln's death swept through the community of blacks and their Unionist and white abolitionist allies. Death required attention all over the land. "The dead, the dead, the dead," as Walt Whitman lamented in one of his poems—if we really want to understand the deepest roots of reconciliation from the Civil War, it is somehow rooted in dealing with all the dead at the end of the bloody struggle. A Union quartermaster general's report shortly after Appomattox noted that only about one-third of the Union dead in the war were interred in identifiable graves. The federal government instituted an elaborate program of locating and burying the Union dead all over the South in newly created national cemeteries, and by 1870, some 300,000 northern soldiers were reinterred in 73 national cemeteries, with 58 percent identified. Retrieval and recognition of the Confederate dead took much longer because of inadequate resources. Early Reconstruction policies had not extended the federal program of reinterment to Confederates.[27] All this death on the battlefield, as well as the deaths of thousands of soldiers in prisons, and hundreds of nameless freedpeople in contraband camps, presented an overwhelming psychological, spiritual, and logistical challenge of memorialization.

Charleston had more than its share of this burden. During the final year of the war, the Confederate command in the city had converted the planters' race course (horse racing track) into a prison. Union soldiers were kept in terrible conditions in the interior of the track, without tents or other coverings. At least 257 died from exposure and disease, and were hastily buried without coffins in unmarked graves behind the judges' stand of the race course. After the fall of the city, Charleston's blacks, many of whom had witnessed the suffering at the horse track prison, insisted on a proper burial of the Union dead. The symbolic power of the planters' race course was not lost on the freedpeople, and in conjunction with James Redpath and the missionaries and teachers among three freedmen's relief associations at work in Charleston, they planned a May Day ceremony that a *New York Tribune* correspondent called "a procession of friends and mourners [such] as South Carolina and the United States never saw before."[28]

The first Decoration Day, as this event came to be recognized in some circles in the North, involved an estimated 10,000 people, most of them former slaves. During April twenty-eight black men from one of the local churches built a suitable enclosure for the burial ground at the race course. In some ten days' labor, they constructed a fence ten feet high, enclosing the burial ground, and landscaped the graves into neat rows. The wooden fence was whitewashed and an archway was built over the gate to the enclosure. On the arch, painted in black letters, the workmen inscribed Martyrs of the Race Course. At nine o'clock in the morning on May 1 the procession to this special cemetery began as 3,000 black schoolchildren (newly enrolled in freedmen's schools) marched around the race course, each with an armload of roses and singing "John Brown's Body." The children were followed by 300 black women representing the Patriotic Association, a group organized to distribute clothing and other goods among the freedpeople. The women carried baskets of flowers, wreaths, and crosses to the burial ground. The Mutual Aid Society, a benevolent association of black men, next marched in cadence around the track and into the cemetery, followed by a procession of white and black citizens. All dropped their spring blossoms on the graves in a scene recorded by a newspaper correspondent: "When all had left, the holy mounds—the tops, the sides, and the spaces between them—were one mass of flowers, not a speck of earth could be seen; and as the breeze wafted the sweet perfumes from them, outside and beyond . . . there were few eyes among those who knew the meaning of the ceremony that were not dim with tears of joy." While the adults marched around the graves, the children were gathered in a nearby grove, where they sang "America," "We'll Rally around the Flag," and "The Star-Spangled Banner."[29]

The official dedication ceremony was conducted by the ministers of all the black churches in Charleston. With prayers, the reading of biblical passages, and the singing of spirituals, black Charlestonians gave birth to an American tradition. In so doing, they declared the meaning of the war in the most public way possible—by their labor, their words, their songs, and their solemn parade of roses and lilacs and marching feet on the old planters' race course. One can only guess at which passages of scripture were read at the graveside on this first Memorial Day. But among the burial rites the spirit of Leviticus 25:12–13 was surely there: "For it is the jubilee; it shall be holy unto you. . . . In the year of this jubilee ye shall return every man unto his possession."

After the dedication, the crowds gathered at the race course grandstand to hear speeches by Union officers, local black ministers, and abolitionist missionaries, all chaired by James Redpath, the director of freedmen's education in the coastal region. Picnics ensued around the grounds, and in the afternoon, a full brigade of Union infantry, including the 54th Massachusetts and the 35th and 104th U.S. Colored Troops, marched in double column around the martyrs' graves and held a drill on the infield of the race course. The war was over, and Memorial Day had been founded by African Americans in a ritual of remembrance and consecration. They had created for themselves, and for us, the Independence Day of the second American Revolution.

According to a reminiscence written long after the fact, "several slight disturbances" occurred during the ceremonies on this first Decoration Day, as well as "much harsh talk about the event locally afterward." But a measure of how white Charlestonians suppressed the memory of this founding in favor of their own creation of the practice a year later came fifty-one years afterward, when the president of the Ladies Memorial Association of Charleston received an inquiry for information about the May 1, 1865. parade. A United Daughters of the Confederacy official wanted to know if it was true that blacks and their white abolitionist friends had engaged in such a burial rite. Mrs. S. C. Beckwith responded tersely: "I regret that I was unable to gather any official information in answer to this."[30] In southern and national memory, the first Decoration Day was nearly lost in a grand evasion.

The oval of the old race course is still there in Hampton Park, adjacent to the Citadel. There are many other towns that have claimed pride of place for founding Memorial Day. The good people of Columbus, Mississippi, of Petersburg, Virginia, of Waterloo, New York, and other towns are all well intentioned in their claims for the spring of 1866. But a year earlier, African Americans did as much to create this tradition as anyone else, and they did it first. A monument to this first Decoration Day should be erected in Charleston.

I will end as I began. Frederick Douglass gave us the charge for this conference, for the very ideal we meet about today, in a speech during the war. "The Mission of the War," an address Frederick Douglass gave all over the North in 1863–64, was laced with the same essential argument about the Civil War being a reinvention of the American republic as that found in Lincoln's Gettysburg address. "A great battle lost or won," declared Douglass, "is easily described, understood, and appreciated. But the moral growth of a great nation requires reflection as well as observation to appreciate it." It was, after all, the "rebirth" of that nation that Abraham Lincoln had in mind when he spoke those words at Gettysburg about the "last full measure of devotion."[31]

NOTES

In its original form, this essay was delivered as a lecture at Ford's Theater in Washington, D.C., May 8, 2000, at a conference entitled "Rally on the High Ground: Symposium on Strengthening Interpretation of the Civil War Era" sponsored by the National Park Service. It was published in *Rally on the High Ground: The National Park Service Symposium on the Civil War*, ed. Robert K. Sutton (Washington, D.C.: Eastern National, 2001). The piece was slightly revised here for republication.

1. See *Rally on the High Ground: The National Park Service Symposium on the Civil War*, ed. Robert K. Sutton (Washington, D.C.: Eastern National, 2001), 23–35.

2. Frederick Douglass, "Speech in Madison Square," Decoration Day, 1878, reel 15, Frederick Douglass Papers, Library of Congress

3. Robert Penn Warren, *The Legacy of the Civil War* (1961; reprint, Cambridge: Harvard University Press, 1983), 4, 7, 60.

4. Mary Johnston, *Cease Firing* (1912; reprint, Baltimore: Johns Hopkins University Press, 1996), 457.

5. W. E. B. Du Bois, editorial in *Crisis*, April 1912.

6. Alexander H. Stephens, *Recollections of Alexander H. Stephens: His Diary Kept When a Prisoner at Fort Warren, Boston Harbor, 1865*, ed. Myrta Locket Avary (New York: Doubleday, 1910), 537–39; Abram J. Ryan, "The South," a lecture given in Nashville, Tenn., 1878, quoted in Charles Reagan Wilson, *Baptized in Blood: The Religion of the Lost Cause, 1865–1920* (Athens: University of Georgia Press, 1980), 59. See Tony Horwitz, *Confederates in the Attic: Dispatches from the Unfinished Civil War* (New York: Pantheon, 1998).

7. John T. Trowbridge, *The South: A Tour of Its Battlefields and Ruined Cities* (1866; reprint, New York: Arno Press, 1969), 18–20.

8. Ibid., 23.

9. Conwell's letters are published in Russell H. Conwell, *Magnolia Journey: A Union Veteran Revisits the Former Confederate States*, arranged by Joseph C. Carter (University: University of Alabama Press, 1974), 59–60, 22–23.

10. Ibid., 77–78.

11. See *The Bachelder Papers: Gettysburg in Their Own Words*, ed. David L. Ladd and Audrey J. Ladd, 3 vols. (Dayton, Ohio: Morningside House, 1994); Carol Reardon, *Pickett's Charge in History and Memory* (Chapel Hill: University of North

Carolina Press, 1997), 69–72. On Blue-Gray fraternalism, see David W. Blight, *Race and Reunion: The Civil War in American Memory* (Cambridge: Harvard University Press, 2001), chaps. 5–6.

12. Samuel C. Armstrong to John Bachelder, Hampton, Va., February 6, 1884, in *Bachelder Papers*, 2:1002–3; Alexander quoted in William McWillie Notebooks, Mississippi Department of Archives and History, Jackson, Miss., in Gary W. Gallagher, *The Confederate War: How Popular Will, Nationalism, and Military Strategy Could Not Stave Off Defeat* (Cambridge: Harvard University Press, 1997), 105. On the "culture of character," see Stuart McConnell, *Glorious Contentment: The Grand Army of the Republic, 1865–1900* (Chapel Hill: University of North Carolina Press, 1992), 106.

13. George L. Kilmer, "A Note of Peace: Reunions of the Blue and the Gray, " *Century* 36 (July 1888): 440–42; Kilmer, "Fraternization—The Blue and the Gray," *Century* 38 (May 1889): 157. See also Blight, *Race and Reunion*, 201–2.

14. Reardon, *Pickett's Charge in History and Memory*, 84–107.

15. *National Tribune* (Washington, D.C.), June 14, 1888, in Reardon, *Pickett's Charge in History and Memory*, 110.

16. *Chicago Inter-Ocean*, May 31, 1895. On the Chicago reunion, see John C. Underwood, *Report of Proceedings Incidental to the Erection and Dedication of the Confederate Monument; Reception and Entertainment of Renowned Southern Generals and Other Distinguished Personages, at Chicago, Illinois . . . May 29–June 1, 1895*, souvenir edition (Chicago: William Johnston Printing, 1896), copy in Newberry Library, Chicago.

17. Underwood, *Report of the Proceedings*, 35, 118.

18. *Dedication of the Chickamauga and Chattanooga National Military Park, September 18–20, 1895*, comp. H. V. Boynton (Washington, D.C.: Government Printing Office, 1896), 179–81, 187; Booker T. Washington, "Atlanta Exposition Address," Atlanta, Ga., September 18, 1895, in *Booker T. Washington Papers*, ed. Louis R. Harlan (Urbana: University of Illinois Press, 1974), 3:584.

19. *Fiftieth Anniversary of the Battle of Gettysburg: Report of the Pennsylvania Commission, December 31, 1913* (Harrisburg: W. S. Ray, state printer, 1915), 31, 36–41.

20. Mann speech reprinted in ibid., 144; *Louisville Courier-Journal*, July 4, 1913.

21. *Washington (D.C.) Bee*, May 24, June 7, 1913.

22. See Joel Williamson, *Crucible of Race: Black-White Relations in the American South since Emancipation* (New York: Oxford University Press, 1984), 364–95.

23. Wilson's speech in *The Papers of Woodrow Wilson*, ed. Arthur Link (Princeton: Princeton University Press, 1978), 28:23, emphasis added.

24. Charles N. Rosen, *Confederate Charleston: An Illustrated History of the City and the People during the Civil War* (Columbia: University of South Carolina Press, 1994), 98–147.

25. Ibid., 150–53.

26. Justus Clement French, *The Trip of the Steamer Oceanus to Fort Sumter and Charleston, S.C.* (Brooklyn: "The Union" Steam Printing House, 1865), 119, 65–69; Willie Lee Rose, *Rehearsal for Reconstruction: The Port Royal Experiment* (New

York: Oxford University Press, 1964), 341–45; Rosen, *Confederate Charleston*, 150–53.

27. Drew Gilpin Faust, *"A Riddle of Death": Mortality and Meaning in the American Civil War* (Gettysburg: Gettysburg College, 1995), 10–18.

28. *New York Tribune*, April 8, May 13, 1865.

29. Ibid.; *Charleston (S.C.) Daily Courier,* May 2, 1865. I first encountered evidence of this Memorial Day observance in a document, "First Decoration Day," Military Order of the Loyal Legion Collection, Houghton Library, Harvard University, boxes unnumbered. Other mentions of the May 1, 1865, event at the Charleston race course include Paul H. Buck, *The Road to Reunion, 1865–1900* (New York: Knopf, 1937), 120–21. Buck misdates the event as May 30, 1865, does not mention the race course, gives James Redpath full credit for creating the event, and relegates the ex-slaves' role to "black hands [strewing flowers] which knew only that the dead they were honoring had raised them from a condition of servitude." See also Whitelaw Reid, *After the War: A Tour of the Southern States, 1865–1866* (1866; reprint, New York: Harper and Row, 1965), 69. James Redpath claimed much of the credit for the founding of Memorial Day because of his role in the creation of the race course cemetery. Redpath did lead a group of ministers and missionaries who first visited the grounds and resolved to repair the site. See Charles F. Horner, *The Life of James Redpath and the Development of the Modern Lyceum* (New York: Barse and Hopkins, 1926), 111–18.

30. Earl Marble, "Origin of Memorial Day," *New England Magazine* 32 (June 1905): 467–70; "Report of the President of the Ladies Memorial Association, Charleston, S.C., June 5, 1916," 3, Ladies Memorial Association Papers, South Carolina Historical Society, Charleston.

31. Frederick Douglass, "The Mission of the War," delivered many times from late fall 1863 through 1864, in *The Life and Writings of Frederick Douglass,* ed. Philip S. Foner (New York: International Publishers, 1952), 4:401; Abraham Lincoln, "Address Delivered at the Dedication of the Cemetery at Gettysburg," in *The Collected Works of Abraham Lincoln,* ed. Roy P. Basler, 9 vols. (New Brunswick: Rutgers University Press, 1953–55), 7:23.

Fifty Years of Freedom

The Memory of Emancipation at the Civil War Semicentennial, 1911–1915

*But the men composing the same group in two successive periods
are like two tree stumps that touch at their extremities but do not
form one plant because they are not otherwise connected.*
    —*Maurice Halbwachs*, The Collective Memory
*This country has had its appetite for facts on the Negro problem
spoiled by sweets.*
    —*W. E. B. Du Bois*, Crisis

Everyone who studies the relationship between his-
tory and memory these days in a serious, critical way, does so, I suspect,
because of the *politics* of memory. Social history, it might also be said, has
led us to social memory. But we are also drawn, perhaps, because the
study of memory allows us a new kind of access to that old problem of
"presentism" (to revive one of David Hackett Fischer's "fallacies"). Suppress it as we will, somebody's "present" hovers over every problem in
the study of memory. How cultures and groups use, construct, or try to
own the past in order to win power or place in the present is why the
broad topic of memory matters. The process by which societies decide
how and when to remember and forget is "always dangerous," as
Friedrich Nietzsche reminded us in "The Use and Abuse of History."
"The same life that needs forgetfulness," wrote Nietzsche, "needs sometimes its destruction; for should the injustice of something ever become
obvious . . . the thing deserves to fall. Its past is critically examined, the
knife put to its roots, and all the 'pieties' are grimly trodden under
foot."[1] What Nietzsche described is the inherently political character of
conflicts over the uses of the past, whether they result from the critical,
interpretive work of historians or public controversies in museums. Serious confrontations with the past—facing down the pieties—is "always
dangerous." Precisely because of this political danger, we need studies

of memory that are rooted in good research, sensitive to deep contexts and to the varieties of memory at play in any given situation. We need studies that search for the ways collective memories have evolved into the forms they take in any context. Fiftieth anniversaries of major events (as we have learned in our own time with commemorations of World War II and the Holocaust) provide good laboratories for investigation.

The process of how societies or nations remember collectively itself has a history. Popular versions of the past that truly take hold as deep myths or, as Eric Hobsbawm has effectively termed them, "invented traditions," exist in all societies. The most lasting and tenacious of those traditions, as Hobsbawm has argued, tend to become ritualized practices and interpretations "which clearly meet a felt—not necessarily a clearly understood—need among particular bodies of people." Invented traditions are eminently manipulable from one context to another. "They have to be discovered before being exploited and shaped," argued Hobsbawm. "It is the historian's business to discover them retrospectively—but also to try to understand why, in terms of changing societies in changing historical situations, such needs came to be felt."[2]

In America, in eastern and western Europe, in much of Africa and elsewhere, we seem to be living through a time when public struggles over the content and meaning of the past have important political stakes. It is as though we are living, once again, through one of those eras when old certainties have dissolved and many of the institutions, empires, or ideologies that had defined much of the geopolitics of the world have collapsed into a new order/disorder, the outlines of which we only dimly see or control. The growing American pluralism (which we have renamed multiculturalism to make it fit all manner of meanings) inspires many of us, and frightens others into retreats or attacks. At the beginning of the twenty-first century, the question of what stories are welcome in the national narrative is a deeply contested one, as is the question of whether there is a national, master narrative any more at all. Melancholia and anxiety are, and perhaps always have been, the underside of great and exciting change. The end of the Cold War and all that has flowed from this epochal shift has tended to take our mass culture on what seems a rudderless journey into nostalgia, a search for lost crises, lost civic unity, lost causes, lost heroes, lost apologies, cultural introspection and retrospection. In the United States in the late 1990s we debated whether the president should "apologize" to African Americans for slavery, as if in this age of instant communication and internet knowledge we can set the past right by a heartfelt announcement of national contrition. Well meaning in many quarters, the discussion of the apology for slavery has tended to be facile retrospection without having to engage any real history. The same may be true of the debate over the likelihood and form of "reparations" to African Americans for the experience and legacies of slavery. That sensitive debate needs more discussion of policy initiatives in our own time, more direct confrontation of historical knowledge, than of damage and guilt.[3]

The discussions of both these issues—an apology or reparations—are full of "felt needs," to use Hobsbawm's term, but the only invented tradition that may emerge from this particular public process may be the old American tendency to deny or avoid serious confrontations with the past. Many Americans, frankly, would simply like to see an end to the discussion of slavery and its legacies. But in scholarship and especially in the realm of public history, we cannot let our society take a holiday from understanding the deep imprint slavery, the Civil War, Reconstruction, and the era of lynching and Jim Crow left on generations of Americans. A look back to a prior era's confrontations with these struggles over memory may inform us in our own time on how best to act, to educate, and to debate these issues. Understanding the *history* of memory is one careful way to know how to confront that memory when it disturbs our present.

This essay is an exploratory look at the semicentennial of the Civil War and emancipation in the period 1911–15. It has three primary aims: one, to suggest the varieties of memory of the Civil War and emancipation at play in the fiftieth anniversary period among whites and blacks; two, to demonstrate how the American reunion was by 1913 the result of a segregated American memory, how the two commemorations—the war and emancipation—overlapped and did not overlap, how they were happening in the same time, but did not fit the same spaces; and three, to show how slavery, the Civil War, and emancipation were by 1913, and perhaps still are, America's unmastered past.

In 1961 John Hope Franklin delivered an address to the Association for the Study of Negro Life and History on the varieties of Civil War commemorations. Disturbed by the racism practiced in the national centennial just underway—what he called a "national circus"—Franklin reflected on the persistent American tendency to dissolve the conflict at the root of the Civil War and to constantly drum it into a "common unifying experience." Franklin analyzed the fiftieth anniversary as a time when the nation collectively found it "convenient to remember that slavery had been abolished and to forget that the doctrine of the superiority of the white race was as virulent as ever." Franklin observed the irony that a magazine editor in 1911 could rejoice that President Taft and Robert Lincoln (the president's son) could play a round of golf at Augusta, Georgia, without any hostility in the heart of the old Confederacy, yet express not the slightest concern for how black Georgians were treated by white Georgians in that same commemorative year.[4] Such irony, silence, studied disregard, and aggressive disavowal of the meaning of black freedom abounded in white America during the semicentennial—and are still present today. Such perceptions need to be uncovered and explained.

As Americans took stock of who they were in relation to their Civil War at its fiftieth anniversary, they were playing out the important retrospective chapter in Jim Crow's "strange career." The stark distance between the ways blacks and whites tended to remember the Civil War and emancipation by the turn of the century is reflected in two speeches delivered in Augusta, Georgia, the one by a Confederate veteran in 1903 and the other by a black minister in 1909. Together they illuminate the problem of the color line in historical memory. At a United Confederate Veterans reunion on Memorial Day 1903, Maj. J. C. C. Black spoke to a large gathering of his comrades who stood on the tops of chairs and tables, waved hats and canes, "shouting . . . in delirium." "We did not fight to perpetuate African slavery," declared Black, "but we fought to preserve and perpetuate for our posterity the God-given right of the freedom of the white man." A journalist covering the occasion picked up the same theme in his account. "It was indeed for the freedom of the white man that the people of the South went to war a third of a century ago," reported the *Atlanta News,* and it was "for the supremacy of the white man that the war of moral suasion, the campaign of enlightened discussion is going on today." In a statement of a dominant, white southern point of view, the reporter described the "bondage" of the South to northern interests and the cause which the old veterans now embodied as that of "Anglo-Saxon emancipation."[5]

On Emancipation Day, January 1, 1909, also in Augusta, Georgia, a black Baptist minister, Silas X. Floyd, delivered an address entitled "Abraham Lincoln: Sent of God" to a large celebration sponsored by black churches, fraternal orders, and the local Lincoln League. Floyd admonished those blacks who believed that they should forget that "our race was once enslaved in this country." "Did you ever see . . . a Confederate veteran who desired to forget that he once wore the gray," asked Floyd, "or who was unwilling to teach his children that he once proudly marched in battle behind Lee and Gordon, Jackson and Johnston? Did you ever see a Union soldier who was ashamed of the part which he took in the Great War?" Floyd waxed biblical and reminded his people that they too had a great story to tell and preserve: "And don't you remember that, when the children of Israel under the . . . leadership of Moses were on the march from Egypt . . . to Canaan . . . don't you remember that, after they had safely crossed the Red Sea, the Lord commanded them to set up memorial stones by which the event should be remembered? And yet some old Negroes wish to forget all about slavery—all about the past—and stoutly maintain that we have no right to be celebrating each year the day that brought freedom to our race. . . . May God forget my people when they forget this day."[6] Floyd's speech reflects many dilemmas that southern blacks faced. He was young and charismatic, a member of the postfreedom generation challenging the slavery generation. He raised the central question blacks faced in contemplating their past in America: the meaning of more than two centuries of slavery and the meaning of emancipation in the Civil War. How to look back, and then forward, with pride and inspiration? Indeed, how to understand and declare their history in the Jim Crow South?

A quick and poignant way to begin to see the varieties of Civil War memory at play in the semicentennial is provided in a scene of James Weldon Johnson's classic *Autobiography of an Ex-Colored Man,* published anonymously in 1912. The protagonist has just left Fisk University in Nashville, Tennessee, where he has heard the Fisk Jubilee Singers perform, and is riding the train to Macon, Georgia. Since he is passing, he is in a Pullman car. A robust conversation ensues between four characters: a northern, "Jewish-looking man," who is a cigar manufacturer experimenting with Havana tobacco in Florida; a "slender bespectacled young man" from Ohio, who teaches at a state college in Alabama; a "white-mustached, well-dressed" man, an old Union soldier who "fought through the Civil War" and has numerous investments to attend to in the South; and a loud, "tall, raw-boned, red-faced man" who is a Texas cotton planter. The discussion moves from mundane matters of the present—the weather, crops, and business—to politics, and then rather quickly to the "Negro question." The Jew is portrayed as the diplomat, taking all sides at once and opposing no one. The young northern professor had believed in black rights and opportunity, but a year in the Deep South had given him a version of compassion fatigue; he now confessed that he thought the race question should be left to white southerners to handle as they wished. A contentious debate ensued, however, between the veteran of the Grand Army of the Republic and the Texas planter. The debate is one between generations, sections, and very different conceptions of the meaning of the Civil War. The young Texan argues that the "Civil War was a criminal mistake on the part of the North and that the humiliation which the South had suffered during Reconstruction could never be forgotten." The old Union soldier retorts that the "South was responsible for the war and that the spirit of unforgetfulness on its part was the greatest cause of present friction." At issue was the meaning of black freedom. The Texan assures the audience of listeners that the Anglo-Saxon race will always rule the world, while the noble veteran gives a liberal, neoabolitionist commentary on the "moral responsibility" to help uplift blacks socially and guarantee their "essential rights of men." The Union veteran bests the New South planter in education and eloquence. After a long exchange about the meaning of what a "race" is and the requisite query from the Texan to the old Yankee of whether he would allow his daughter to "marry a nigger," this discussion among white men ends in laughter, with almost everyone taking a drink from the Texan's flask. Johnson's protagonist watches with a "chill . . . sick at heart" over what he heard from the planter, but admits to an odd sense of admiration for the steadfastness with which southerners "defend everything belonging to" them.[7]

Johnson captured many elements of Civil War memory in this single scene: worn-out Yankee liberalism, noble neoabolitionism on the part of an old soldier, white ethnic indifference to southern and racial issues, and of course, white southern hostility to any element of the emancipationist legacy of the Civil War. All of them are busy making money, except the gaunt Ohio professor, and he did not drink from the flask either. That Johnson's passing protagonist, black but not black, observes this conversation is a fitting metaphor for one of the ways many African Americans would have to watch the semicentennial of *their* Civil War—deeply interested and implicated, but segregated and invisible.

Other ways of understanding the variety of Civil War memory would include adopting Joel Williamson's three-part analysis of white southern mentalities on race relations—liberal, conservative, and radical. Southern "liberals," according to Williamson, were the smallest group by the turn of the century, but they carried over a conspicuous, articulate faith in black capacities and the progress of race relations from the experience of Reconstruction. "Conservatives," the core of the southern white mind, never relinquished the cardinal belief in Negro inferiority and sought in myriad ways to fix the subordinate place of black folk in American life, North as well as South. And the "radicals," led in the early twentieth century by the Ben Tillmans, James Vardamans, and Thomas Dixons, advanced a racial vision of America where blacks had no place in society, where they would vanish, of their own accord or by force. According to Williamson, all three of these mentalities, though changing over time and with radical racism increasingly influential by the semicentennial, "evoked the past to meet the present" with agility and everpliant northern as well as southern audiences.[8]

There are many representative examples one can observe to understand the range of white southern attitudes toward the past, but a single illustration from a 1914 congressional debate may suffice. Several states and the federal government either funded, or contemplated funding, celebrations and expositions for the fiftieth anniversary of emancipation. Du Bois in the *Crisis*, as well as other black newspapers, charted and debated these expositions with great interest. In the summer of 1914, a Giles B. Jackson of Richmond, Virginia, whom Du Bois accused of engaging in "very disreputable" business practices, requested $55,000 from the U.S. Congress for an emancipation celebration in the former Confederate capital. Sen. Thomas Martin of Virginia represented a liberal outlook of a sort, declaring himself a close observer of southern blacks and arguing that they had "made a progress that is almost astounding, considering the opportunities which they have had." He was all for a celebration of "fifty years of their freedom." Vardaman of Mississippi held firm to the white supremacist banner. Whites had "assisted" blacks in every way, said Vardaman, but making "citizens and voters of them" ought "never be done." Hence, he opposed any such appropriation to celebrate emancipation. A third senator, Frank White of Alabama, held up a version of the conservative racialist tradition, reaching deep into the Lost Cause mythology. White supported the appropriation as a way of honoring the "loyalty" of former slaves during the war, "more," he said, "for what they did for us during the struggle in which their freedom was the issue than for what they did for us in other times." White said southern blacks deserved white gratitude because they "camped with us . . . marched with us . . . supplied our every want . . .

guarded our homes and protected our women and children . . . [and] carried their dead masters back to their wives."[9] In this romantic familial imagery, blacks were made into Confederate veterans of a sort; they were to be allowed their celebration as gratitude for wartime service. An emancipation commemoration on such terms as these would not in the least transgress the Jim Crow social and political structure that these very senators had helped to construct by 1914.

Moreover, such discussions on the floor of Congress may demonstrate the ways in which white southern attitudes about race and reunion had all but overwhelmed northern neoabolitionist thought. Or as Williamson put it, "Conservatives had opened the beachheads that allowed the Radicals to land. Both were shock troops in this latter-day battle of Gettysburg in which the northern line was broken and the North invaded. The fruit of the racial campaign was not so much to conquer the North, as it was to free the South." When Du Bois reported this congressional debate about emancipation celebrations in the *Crisis*, he did so with disgust and irony, and he placed it right before a verbatim recording of the rules of the recently enacted North Carolina white primary.[10]

That "beachhead" among northern whites was not gained, of course, without resistance. For nearly two decades by the time of the semicentennial, neoabolitionists and reformers of various kinds had trumpeted the "progress" and accomplishments of blacks in all walks of life. This stemmed from many sources: it was the natural subject of black middle-class intellectual and social circles; it countered the increasingly racist public culture of the country at large; it was a central function of the primarily white founders of the NAACP in its formative years; and it became a major part of the increasingly bitter struggle between the leadership of Booker T. Washington and that of W. E. B. Du Bois in black America. All discussions of black progress since emancipation were, at least tacitly, commentaries on the meaning and memory of the Civil War as the great divide in African American history.

The fiftieth anniversary season brought this entire idea of black *progress* to a crescendo, coming as it did in the wake of the 1910 and 1912 elections, when the terms "progressivism" and "progressive movement" had become part of public, political language. Oswald Garrison Villard, grandson of William Lloyd Garrison, may have spoken for two generations of white neoabolitionists in 1913 when, in a fiftieth anniversary article about black economic progress, he declared the rise in property ownership "an astounding showing which by itself gives the lie to those who declare that the negro cannot be compared in efficiency with the white man." Three years after "scientific management" (Taylorism) had gone public, and trumpeting the third of Daniel Rodgers's helpful categories of progressive "social languages"—the quest for efficiency—Villard and others countered theories of black retrogression, as well as the claims of permanency for Jim Crow, with article after article about social scientific progress.[11]

Many magazines and journals ran special issues commemorating emancipation and the progress of the race. In September 1913 *The Annals of the American Academy of Political and Social Science* published a special issue devoted entirely to "the Negro's progress in fifty years." Twenty-four essays, by eleven blacks and six northern and seven southern whites, including social scientists, writers, and educators, covered subjects such as business and labor conditions, population growth, sharecropping, public health, statistics on criminality and debt, urban migration, the growth of literacy, and so forth. The collection ended with pieces by Booker T. Washington on industrial education and the public schools, and Du Bois on the Negro in literature and art. This collection is an example of what Daniel Rodgers calls the "new breed" sociology and the "antiphilosophical scientism" of the late Progressive era. Many of these works accentuate the role of the social scientific expert, as well as celebrate achievement through the compilation of "facts." Du Bois was clearly not comfortable appearing in this volume; his own piece was a token nod to the arts and not his best work. He admired pieces by Kelly Miller, R. R. Wright, Monroe Work, and other black contributors, as well as articles by some whites, such as J. P. Lichtenberger, the editor, which cast the growth of black literacy as a "phenomenal race achievement." But a segregationist, white supremacist purpose motivated several pieces in the volume, such as Howard Odum's on the need for separate Negro schools; Ray Stannard Baker's on confidence in the white South when it came to black voting rights; and Thomas Edwards's rosy picture of tenant farming.[12] Each essay, however cast in data, was a marker about the relationship of past and present; some were social science in the service of an optimistic, interracial memory of emancipation, and others justified the segregated society forged by national reunion. The volume can be read as a microcosm of the nation's dilemma with how to remember emancipation and its legacies.

White neoabolitionist memory took many forms. A strong dose of nostalgia characterized much neoabolitionist consciousness. Worried that they had lost the long battle over black rights—that they had lost the struggle over the memory of the Civil War—former abolitionists, or their sons and daughters, seized the occasion of the semicentennial to remember the glory days and make demands on the present. In February 1913 Fanny Garrison Villard (daughter of William Lloyd Garrison) wrote a remarkable recollection of Emancipation Day, January 1, 1863, in Boston, where she had stood by her father's side at the Music Hall and Tremont Temple celebrations. Waxing mystic, she described the "Watch Night," waiting for the news of Lincoln's signing of the proclamation, as "indescribably thrilling." Her recollection conforms in some ways to Frederick Douglass's description of the same scenes in his *Life and Times* (1881). She remembers singing "Blow Ye the Trumpet, Blow," hearing an orchestra play Handel, Mendelssohn, and Beethoven, and Ralph Waldo Emerson deliver his "Boston Hymn." She remembered a gathering the following evening, surrounded by Emerson, George Luther Stearns, Franklin Sanborn, Wendell Phillips, Julia Ward Howe, and her father where a bust of John Brown was unveiled. Fanny Villard declared herself fortunate to have such an "antislavery heritage," and then in the final paragraph of this nostalgic tour de force, she returned to the reality of the present, declaring that what "concerns us today is . . . whether our duty to the liberated bondmen has been fulfilled. The answer is alas! No." Whether neoabolitionist expressions of nostalgia—on a personal or public level—may fit what Michael Kammen has called the "creative" or the "destructive" function of nostalgia requires more research.[13] But it is, I think, a fruitful path to take in uncovering the Progressive era's preoccupation with the backward glance.

The varieties of black memory of emancipation and the war are as diverse as region, education, generation, experience, and political and social outlook would, of course, shape them. One is reminded here of Du Bois's frequent lament that "the Negro" was so commonly referred to as a single entity and that blacks were "southerners" too.[14] Space allows only the development of a few examples. In 1910 Mary White Ovington, a white social worker and already an important operative with the NAACP, recorded the recollections of several ex-slaves in southern Alabama. Anticipating the WPA narratives to follow in the thirties, these reminiscences provide an interesting picture of ordinary freed people in old age, given their opportunity to reflect on their past at the semicentennial. Ovington found an interesting range of old folks who told of personal pain, hardship, family breakups, labor conditions, progress toward property ownership, and insights, as well as tall tales about the war and the coming of freedom.

Perhaps a woman identified only as Granny left a story with the most scope and impact. Very old, with features of "an African," Granny told of being sold away from her four children in North Carolina, sent in the domestic slave trade westward to Alabama, forced to give birth to a fifth child fathered by her new, cruel master. She remembered crying when the master's son died in the Confederate army, because he was a "kind chile." She related tales of being whipped, of her desperate fears of running away, and of how she survived only on her faith in "Master Jesus." As Ovington was about to leave, she asked Granny about the photograph of Lincoln on the mantel in her cabin. "I love dat face, Miss," Granny answered. "I love it so dat der lady down here, she done gib me der picture. Dose eyes, dey follow me, dey's so kind. I don' know how ter tell you how much I lub dat man dat made us free—*an' all der oders, too dat helped.*" Granny and Ovington are both reminded of a lyric from a plantation song as they "looked out on the fields where men guided the mules in the plowing," and the ex-slave concludes: "I's seen a heap o' sorrow an' trouble, but it's ober for me. I t'ank de Lord dat I's free; dat us all, chillen, an' women, an' men, is free." Is this a collaborative work of nostalgia in the reminiscence industry or a revealing window into freedmen's memory? Is it neoabolitionist pathos or the place to start in any consideration of black social memory in the fiftieth anniversary season? It is probably a mixture of all these elements, and a continuation of the kind of writing Du Bois had begun in *The Souls of Black Folk,* especially the chapter called "Of the Black Belt," works that sought to counter the tremendous growth industry of the plantation school of popular literature (spread most widely by Thomas Nelson Page) that fashioned an enduring picture of the Old South and slavery full of contented and loyal black folk.[15] There were no happy darkies in Du Bois's Black Belt of 1903, and the only element of comedy in Ovington's recording of Granny in 1910 is deeply embedded in the old woman's tragic sensibility.

A rough categorization of black memory might include black antiquarianism; the genuinely patriotic mode, characterized by a fierce claim that the black experience ought to be at the center of America's national memory; a progressive-celebratory mode that manifested in numerous emancipation expositions, in pageantry, and sometimes in public and educational avoidance of the slave past; a conservative-assimilationist form of black nationalism that asserted self-improvement more than, or in place of, historical consciousness; a combination of pan-Africanism and -Ethiopianism, the concern among a variety of writers and religious leaders that black destiny included the creation of an exemplary civilization, perhaps in Africa or elsewhere (seeing the American emancipation as only a part of a long continuity of Christian development); and finally, what we might call a black jeremiadic memory, the use of commemorative moments as occasions for bitter appeals against injustice, past and present. Virtually all these categories overlap and flow into one another in African American thought.[16]

Numerous local emancipation commemorations may fit the category of antiquarian through their collecting of objects and their exhibitions of crafts and wares. Most certainly the Frederick Douglass Shoe Company of Lynn, Massachusetts, did. The company sold a Fred Douglass brand for men and a Phillis Wheatley brand for women by mail order. The National Afro-Art Company of Washington, D.C., offered 11-inch busts of Richard Allen, Douglass, and Booker T. Washington for $1.25 each. The *New York Age* offered 20-by-24-inch photogravures of several black historical figures for $3.00 each.[17] Such collecting, as well as the consumer appeal now attached to black history, fits its age of mass-market culture. But it may also have represented for many black families a form of empowerment, class aspirations, and a way of declaring and exhibiting a heroic past. These objects may also have been icons through which the dialectic of double consciousness (being black and American) played out in a segregated society.

The Tuskegee Institute president Booker T. Washington, the most influential black leader in America, labored both quietly and publicly to gain congressional approval for emancipation exhibitions. But a Bookerite memory of slavery, emancipation, and the war emerged full-blown, especially in Washington's speeches, as well as those of his legions of followers. In a typical address at Auburn, New York, in June 1914, dedicating a memorial to the recently deceased Harriet Tubman, Washington eulogized the liberator of fugitive slaves as an example of the "law-abiding negro" who "brought the two races nearer together and made it possible for the white race to know the black race." The Wizard of Tuskegee turned his tribute to this underground revolutionary into an exaltation about the "progress" of fifty years. He declared Tubman's work "not in vain" after ticking off the acreage of black land ownership and the numbers of black-owned grocery stores, dry goods stores, shoe stores, drugstores, and banks. Business enterprise was the legacy of the Underground Railroad in the age of capital. He ended the speech, as he did most of his commemorative-progressive orations, with the argument that the "antislavery heroes" had freed two races in the South, the white and the black.[18]

The patriotic mode may be best illustrated by a James Weldon Johnson poem. "Fifty Years," published January 1, 1913, in the *New York Times,* reprinted in black newspapers, and delivered as a reading at some commemorations to follow, offers an interesting case of the patriotic mode of memory. Anticipating Langston Hughes and Woody Guthrie, Johnson's poem is a striking statement about African American birthright. Some seven verses into the poem, Johnson strikes his central theme:

Then let us here erect a stone,
  To mark the place, to mark the time;
A witness to God's mercies shown,
  A pledge to hold this day sublime.
And let that stone an altar be,
  Whereon thanksgivings we may lay,
Where we in deep humility,
  For faith and strength renewed may pray.
With open hearts ask from above
  New zeal, new courage and new pow'rs,
That we may grow more worthy of
  This country and this land of ours.
For never let the thought arise
  That we are here on sufferance bare;
Outcasts, asylumed 'neath these skies,
  And aliens without part or share.
This land is ours by right of birth,
  This land is ours by right of toil;
We helped to turn its virgin earth,
  Our sweat is in its fruitful soil.

Johnson claims the center of America's historical memory by right of immigration and by right of labor. In the poem's middle he claims it by right of soldiering, of "blood" and devotion to the "flag": "We've bought a rightful sonship here, / And we have more than paid the price." As the poem reaches its hopeful ending, Johnson celebrates the abolitionist tradition as America's national destiny.[19]

Such a poetic sensibility provided the tone for the many local meetings and public expositions celebrating emancipation during the semicentennial season. The states of New York, New Jersey, Pennsylvania, and Illinois gave appropriations of varying amounts for expositions ($20,000 in Pennsylvania and approximately $25,000 in New York). Cities as large as Washington, D.C., Chicago, Philadelphia, New Orleans, and Atlanta, and as small as Richmond, Indiana; Savin Rock, Connecticut; Corpus Christi, Texas; and Quincy, Illinois, had their own celebrations. Some expositions, modeled on world's fairs, were elaborate celebrations of black progress on every front; others were essentially speeches, readings, or musical events. Organizations of all kinds, such as the National Baptist Convention, the Freedmen's Relief Committee of Philadelphia, and the National Association of Colored Nurses, held their own celebrations. Research into as many of these local commemorations as possible will reveal regional, and perhaps even class, gender, and political, patterns of remembrance. A clear theme of each was the celebration of black progress and achievement in the professions, business, education, inventions, women's status, and the arts. In New Jersey the organizing committee worked on and off for more than a year, dividing themselves into some thirty-seven "leagues," each devoted to sending out questionnaires and gathering facts and statistics on everything from needlework and dressmaking to real estate and music. Some even did "house-to-house canvasses" to gather such data, leading the editor of the *Topeka (Kan.) Capital* to rejoice in all the commemoration, especially "these cheering statistics."[20]

By far the most elaborate exposition was organized in New York City, by Du Bois and others, and staged at the Twelfth Regiment Armory, Sixty-second Street near Broadway, October 22–31, 1913. It was called the National Emancipation Exposition, and Du Bois declared that he and the other commissioners were "determined to make this . . . a complete picture of Negro progress and attainment in America." Du Bois's own social scientific and Victorian earnestness were in full form. "With detailed charts, models, moving pictures, maps and a few typical exhibits," he said, "a complete picture of present conditions will be presented, while a magnificent pageant . . . with music and costume, will give the historic setting." He promised "no endless repetition and country-fair effect," only "one fine and dignified presentation of *great facts* in simple form, with a frame of beauty and music."[21]

Here we have the progressive-celebratory mode of black remembrance in full flower—the "great facts" about the present put into "historic setting," past and present achievement displayed as arguments about current oppression, and grand appeals to public memory as reform. Beyond the fifteen divisions of Negro life and labor, all represented by booths, photographs, and other displays, and the extraordinary Temple of Beauty in the Great Court of Freedom, complete with Egyptian wall paintings and obelisks, it was "The Star of Ethiopia" pageant, written and directed by Du Bois (with the assistance of Charles Burroughs), that provided the most remarkable element of the New York exposition. By the early twentieth century, pageantry had become a popular form of public history and theater, as well as a mirror of social and community tensions during the Progressive era and beyond."The Star of Ethiopia" consisted of a cast of 350 people, depicting five epochs in six episodes of African and American history from the "gift of iron" in prehistoric African societies, to the "gift of the Nile" from ancient Egyptian civilization, to the "gift" of the "faith of Mohammed," to America where blacks experience slavery and the "gift of Humiliation," complete with the singing of spirituals and a "Dance of Death and Pain," to the age of the "gift of Struggle toward Freedom" led by "brave maroons and valiant Haytians," Crispus Attucks and Nat Turner. The final episode brought the age of emancipation and its aftermath, the "gift of Freedom," with William Lloyd Garrison, John Brown, Abraham Lincoln, David Walker, Frederick Douglass, and Sojourner Truth all represented amid marching black Union soldiers and a chorus of "O Freedom." The pageant was performed four times during the New York celebration, playing to large crowds; a total of some thirty thousand people (almost all black) attended the exhibition.[22]

Du Bois staged "The Star of Ethiopia" two more times, in Washington, D.C., in 1915, and in Philadelphia in 1916. He experienced considerable hostility—outright refusal of support—within the NAACP leadership over his work on the pageant and the exposition, both in 1913 and 1915. "What a task that was!" Du Bois declared, reflecting in December 1915. "I have been through a good many laborious jobs and had to bear on many occasions accusations difficult to rest under, but without doubt the New York Emancipation Exposition was the worst of all my experiences. Such an avalanche of altogether unmerited and absurd attacks it had never been my fortune to experience." Much criticism seems to have been directed at the epic level of pomp and romanticization evident in the pageant. Some upright reformers and aesthetes saw pageantry as a vulgar art form, and no doubt some blacks themselves may have seen a pandering or an uncomfortable backward glance on slavery, as a hundred bondsmen danced their mournful steps on stage. This may also have been an early precursor of some of our current disputes over just how public history and memory should become, of what ought be the substance of historical commemoration, and who ought to have authority to do it. To Du Bois, the pageant in 1913 was "this one new thing in the dead level of uninteresting exhibitions." "We had our ups and downs," he wrote, "it was difficult to get hold of the people . . . more difficult to keep them." But as though he were a participant in the great debate over Disney's Virginia Theme Park, Du Bois concluded: "This is what the people want. . . . [T]his is the gown and paraphernalia in which the message of education and reasonable race pride can deck itself."[23] In those words Du Bois aptly captured the dilemma and the inspiration of the scholar and activist-journalist turned public historian during the fiftieth anniversary season. He mixed the patriotic, progressive-celebratory, and Ethiopian voices with remarkable results.

But those were not the only voices Du Bois and other black leaders used during the semicentennial. Sometimes with angry editorials and sometimes with satire, parable, or poetry Du Bois forged the jeremiadic mode of black memory as well as anyone. Du Bois's poetry and short fiction in these years are replete with images of death and rebirth, of Christ figures and resurrections. In April 1913 he published a poem in the *Crisis* called "Easter-Emancipation, 1863–1913." The "I" of this long, enigmatic poem is the slave woman as Christ figure, who is repeatedly crucified and enveloped in "the folding and unfolding of Almighty wings" (the "wings of Ethiopia"?). Through her many agonies and deaths come life and freedom. These apocalyptic, death-rebirth images were tough medicine for the semicentennial. They were warnings about the evil and sorrow in the past and the persistent betrayals of the present. In his January 1913 editorial on emancipation, Du Bois reminded his readers that the American people had not freed the slaves "deliberately and with lofty purpose" but in a war to "destroy the power of the South." Bringing full civil and political rights to the freedmen was a "task of awful proportions." Facing it, Du Bois said, "the nation faltered, quibbled and finally is trying an actual *volte-face*." Turning away from historical responsibility in such an about-face, Americans had built "barriers to decent human intercourse and understanding between the races that today few white men dare call a Negro friend." In despairing tones, Du Bois declared that too many in the "reactionary South and the acquiescent North" support a program of black subjection and "would greet the death of every black man in the world with a sigh of relief." On the cover of that special emancipation issue of the *Crisis* was an extraordinary drawing by Laura Wheeler of an elderly black man with eyes lowered and head slightly bowed with dignity.[24]

A year earlier, in the January 1912 *Crisis,* Du Bois wrote perhaps his most striking fiftieth-anniversary piece. Modeled on Jonathan Swift's famous story "A Modest Proposal," Du Bois called his satire "A Mild Suggestion." Similar to Johnson's parable in the Pullman car, Du Bois's satire places five characters on the deck of a ship: the Little Old Lady, the Westerner, the Southerner, the New Yorker, and the Colored Man. The Southerner is recovering from severe seasickness, but as the sun comes out all resume a conversation about the Negro problem within hearing of the Colored Man. The usual solutions of education, work, emigration, and so forth are discussed. Finally they ask the black man for his opinion. He sits down and lays out his "perfect solution." He urges rejection of education because it will only lead to "ambition, dissatisfaction and revolt," scorns work because it can only bring job competition and the disruption of social circles, and refuses emigration because it is impractical and inhumane. Instead, the colored man proposes that on January 1, 1913, "for historical reasons," each white American who has a black friend invite him or her to dinner. This, he thought, would encompass "black mammies and faithful old servants of the South." Those blacks without such an invitation would be urged to come to white churches and YMCAs or YWCAs. There they would be seated in a fully integrated manner at dinner. All remaining blacks in the country should be "induced to assemble among themselves at their own churches or at little parties and house warmings." Stragglers and vagrants should also be rounded up and watched. Then, he suggested, at the ringing of a bell, or "singing of the national hymn," blacks at the dinners were to be given cyanide of potassium pills; those at the large meetings were to be dispatched with stilettoes and all others shot with Winchester rifles. With the Southerner staring and forgetting "to pose," the Westerner staring in "admiration," the New Yorker "smiling," and the Little Old Lady in "tears," the Colored Man concludes: "The next morning there would be ten million funerals, and therefore no Negro problem." No celebratory voice here, no cant about progress, and no nostalgia.

Only a riveting satire, a prophetic altar call to a national conscience, the bitterest of appeals against everything from lynching (the NAACP counted more than seventy in 1913) to the meaning of segregation. In a time of celebration, Du Bois would not let black folk think about Emancipation Day, past or present, without a reminder, however bleakly it would be taken, from his Colored Man in this story who, while admitting that his solution "may seem a little cruel," asks whether it is "more cruel than present conditions."[25]

Like James Weldon Johnson and others, Du Bois employed many modes of remembrance in 1913. Writing of black folk in southern towns in a remarkable but little-known essay in 1904, he described how an "awful incubus of the past broods like a writhing sorrow, and when we turn our faces from that past, we turn it not to forget but to remember." Satire has always been a literary or journalistic form that works well in worlds of absurdity; so much of segregated America and the semicentennial of emancipation and the Civil War was just such a world. George Bernard Shaw once claimed that on the satirist depended "the salvation of the world." And Swift himself said in 1728 that satire is motivated not merely by ridicule but by "a public spirit, prompting men of genius and virtue to mend the world so far as they are able."[26]

NOTES

This essay was originally delivered as a paper at a conference on comparative emancipations at the University of Norwich, England, in September 1998. It was subsequently published in a special issue, "After Slavery: Emancipation and Its Discontents," in the journal *Slavery and Abolition*, August 2000.

1. Friedrich Nietzsche, "The Use and Abuse of History," in *The Use and Abuse of History*, trans. Adrian Collins, intro. Julius Kraft (New York: Liberal Arts Press, 1949), 29; David Hackett Fischer, *Historians' Fallacies: Toward a Logic of Historical Thought* (New York: Harper and Row, 1970), 135–42. On the need for studies of memory in their contexts and the overall idea of varieties of memory, see Michael Kammen, review essay, *History and Theory: Studies in the Philosophy of History* 34 (1995): 246–61.

2. Eric Hobsbawm,"Mass-Producing Traditions: Europe, 1870–1914," in *The Invention of Tradition*, ed. Eric Hobsbawm and Terence Ranger (Cambridge, Eng.: Cambridge University Press, 1983), 3–7.

3. For two of the more interesting reflections on the idea of an apology for slavery, see Ira Berlin, "Before We Apologize, We Should Learn What Slavery Means," *Washington Post*, June 29, 1997; and Patricia Williams, "Apologia Qua Amnesia," *Nation*, July 14, 1997. On the role of melancholia in this age of memory-consciousness, see Charles S. Maier, "A Surfeit of Memory? Reflections

on History, Melancholy, and Denial," *History and Memory: Studies in the Representation of the Past* 5 (fall–winter 1993): 136–52. On the reparations debate, see Randall Robinson, *The Debt: What America Owes to Blacks* (New York: Dutton, 2000).

4. John Hope Franklin, "A Century of Civil War Observances," *Journal of Negro History* (April 1962): 98–99, 106. On the Civil War centennial from a black perspective, see also J. A. Rogers, "Civil War Centennial, Myth and Reality," *Freedomways* (winter 1963): 7–18.

5. *Atlanta News,* May 31, 1903.

6. *Atlanta Constitution,* January 2, 1909.

7. James Weldon Johnson, *The Autobiography of an Ex-Colored Man* (1912; reprint, New York, Avon, 1960), 156–66.

8. Joel Williamson, *The Crucible of Race: Black-White Relations in the American South since Emancipation* (New York: Oxford University Press, 1984), 4–7, 36–39.

9. *Congressional Record,* 63d Congress, 2d session, vol. 51, July 8, 1914, 11797–98.

10. Williamson, *Crucible of Race,* 335; *Crisis* 8 (September 1914): 227–28.

11. Oswald Garrison Villard, *New York Evening Post,* January 4, 1913; Daniel T. Rodgers, "In Search of Progressivism," *Reviews in American History* (December 1982): 123, 125–27. For understanding neoabolitionists I rely on James McPherson, *The Abolitionist Legacy: From Reconstruction to the NAACP* (Princeton: Princeton University Press, 1975). On black memory and "progress of the race" publications and rhetoric, see David W. Blight, *Race and Reunion: The Civil War in American Memory* (Cambridge: Belknap Press, Harvard University Press, 2001), chap. 9.

12. "The Negro's Progress in Fifty Years," *The Annals of the American Academy of Political and Social Science* 49 (September 1913): 184. For Du Bois's critique of this issue, see *Crisis* 7 (February 1914): 202.

13. Fanny Garrison Villard, "How Boston Received the Emancipation Proclamation," *American Review of Reviews* 47 (February 1913): 177–78. On nostalgia, see Michael Kammen, *Mystic Chords of Memory: The Transformation of Tradition in American Culture* (New York: Knopf, 1991), 275–92.

14. *Crisis* 3 (February 1912): 153.

15. Mary White Ovington, "Slaves' Reminiscences of Slavery," *Independent,* May 26, 1910, 1131–36; W. E. B. Du Bois, *The Souls of Black Folk* (1903; reprint, New York: Signet, 1969), chap. 7.

16. In *Race and Reunion,* chaps. 9–10, I streamline and develop these categories of black memory more thoroughly.

17. Mail order advertisement, *Crisis* 10 (May 1915): 47; *New York Age,* October 5, 1911.

18. Booker T. Washington, "Extracts from an Address at the Unveiling of the Harriet Tubman Memorial," Auburn, N.Y., June 12, 1914, in *Booker T. Washington Papers,* ed. Louis Harlan (Urbana: University of Illinois Press, 1981), 13:58–61. On Washington's support for emancipation exhibitions, see *Washington (D.C.) Bee,* August 6, 1910.

19. James Weldon Johnson, *Fifty Years and Other Poems* (Boston: Cornhill Company, 1917), 1–5.

20. Du Bois monitored, promoted, and criticized these celebrations. See *Crisis* (February–November 1913); *Crisis* 10 (May 1915): 31–32. On African American celebrations, see William H. Wiggins Jr., *O Freedom!: Afro-American Emancipation Celebrations* (Knoxville: University of Tennessee Press, 1987,) esp. 49–78. For the Atlanta pageant, see *Atlanta Constitution*, July 3, 1913. *Crisis* 6 (October 1913): 297; *Crisis* 6 (August 1913): 183. Du Bois declared that the New Jersey exposition had "many disappointments" in its scope and execution. *Topeka Capital*, August 7, 1910.

21. *Crisis* 6 (August 1913): 183, emphasis added.

22. For photographs of the exhibits as well as the pageant, see *Crisis* 7 (December 1913): centerfold, and 11 (December 1915): 89–93. On the fifteen divisions or categories of exhibits, see *Crisis* 6 (October 1913): 297. The script of the "Star of Ethiopia" is reprinted in *Crisis* 7 (November 1913): 339–41. Attendance figures are in *Crisis* 7 (December 1913): 84. See David Glassberg, *American Historical Pageantry: The Uses of Tradition in the Early Twentieth Century* (Chapel Hill: University of North Carolina Press, 1990), 131–34; and David Glassberg, "History and the Public: Legacies of the Progressive Era," *Journal of American History* 73 (March 1987): 957–80.

23. *Crisis* 11 (December 1915): 89. On the hostility and criticism, see Du Bois's report to the board of directors of the NAACP, "The Pageant," 1915, and Du Bois to Joel Spingarn, November 3, 1915, both in W. E. B. Du Bois Papers, reel 5, University of Massachusetts Library, Amherst, Mass.

24. *Crisis* 15 (January 1913): 128–29.

25. "A Mild Suggestion," *Crisis* 3 (January 1912): 115–16.

26. W. E. B. Du Bois, "The Development of a People," *International Journal of Ethics* 14 (April 1904): 304; Shaw and Swift quoted in Jonathan Swift, *A Modest Proposal and Other Satires,* intro. George R. Levine (Amherst, N.Y.: Prometheus Books, 1955), 14.

Homer with a Camera, Our "Iliad" without the Aftermath
Ken Burns's Dialogue with Historians

The Civil War was our great, epic, Homeric poem of national self-definition.
   —*Ken Burns*

However thickly strewn a tragedy may be with ghosts, portents, witches, or oracles, we know that the tragic hero cannot simply rub a lamp and summon a genie to get him out of his trouble.
   —*Northrop Frye*

Collaborations as well as conflicts between historians and filmmakers have intensified in recent years. The sheer power of the film medium has inevitably attracted historians. The old tension between writers of historical fiction and writers of formal history has almost been replaced by the high stakes tension between sound, verifiable history, and history that can be rendered filmic, between the emotive medium of film and the analytical medium of history. The tension between the history we write and the visual mediums through which it can reach unprecedented mass audiences represents one of the greatest professional challenges of our time. At stake, simply, is the nature and quality of the national or social memory, the vast public's knowledge and understanding of its past.

Good history has always relied on a kind of poetry among its best storytellers; good poetry has always instructed us about the past. As the poet-historian Robert Penn Warren wrote in 1953, "historical sense and poetic sense should not, in the end, be contradictory, for if poetry is the little myth we make, history is the big myth we live, and in our living, constantly remake."[1] Ken Burns, the maker of *The Civil War* and several other distinguished documentary films, understands this mutual dependence of poetry and history. Burns has a deep and infectious sense of history. As a graduate in film studies from Hampshire College in Massachusetts, he took only one history course in his formal education, and that in Russian history. Burns has described himself as a "narrative amateur historian . . . interested in telling stories, anecdotes." "I'm interested in people, biography," he told David Thelen in an interview in the *Journal of American History,* "and I know that these interests and tendencies are the structural building blocks of whatever I'm doing." Acknowledging the influences of the various scholars he has worked with, he nevertheless declared that he approached *The Civil War* series "essentially with my heart, to feel my way to a kind of truth for myself of how this material should be structured and presented." Likening himself to a "painter" who may choose "oil over water colors" and who "might favor certain particular earth tones in the oil paints," Burns justifiably concluded that this "does not mean that I am lazy about how I *attend* to history. . . . [I]t just means that I am primarily an artist."[2] When a filmmaker with such widely recognized talents so eloquently describes himself as an artist working in the materials of history, why should there be any tension between the historians and the artist? In the century and a quarter since history became a professional discipline, haven't historians repeatedly acknowledged their debt to, indeed their envy of, the poets', novelists', and other narrators' abilities to portray the past and to forge the modern historical imagination?

Robert Brent Toplin's collection of nine essays by historians responding to Burns's *Civil War,* and in some cases, responding to each other, offers some answers to the challenges faced in historian-filmmaker collaborations. It also demonstrates the enduring significance of the Civil War in American historical memory. The book contains what *The Civil War* series, given its extensive educational use, has long needed: a serious discussion in print of the merits and flaws of this evocative film. To that end Toplin has provided an important service, and the legions of us who teach with this film can make direct pedagogical use of these essays.[3]

On the one hand, one can feel a certain sympathy for Burns. Nitpicking historians can ultimately blunt the kind of historical imagination most filmmakers deal in; historical accuracy and interpretation of the big questions are simply not the same imperatives in a visual medium as they are in books. Scholarly fine points would hardly have animated those millions of viewers captured and moved by this film for several evenings, many of whom probably hummed "Ashokan Farewell" (the film's theme song) in their morning shower. On the other hand, Burns has always invited, knowingly or not, some of the very criticisms he scorns. Reserving his full rights as an artist, he has also insisted on—and received—the mantle of a historian. As Burns himself might put it, he has been very publicly "brevetted" as a full professor in the historians' guild.[4]

As is his right, Burns has openly attacked what he dislikes about "academic" history. The new social history of the last decades, according to Burns, became a "tyranny" over the past, ruining the public's taste for a history that "began to seem like the reading of the telephone book." In many forums he has compared himself to "Homer, singing the epic verses of his people," part of the movement to "rescue history from the academy, which has done a terrific job in the last hundred years of murdering our history."[5] Burns, of course, has a good point about how and why historians lost some of their audience. Language and form matter, and always will, in how history is imagined and transmitted. But Burns's determination to chastize the historical profession for its widely acknowledged sins grates on many who know that good storytellers never vanished, that good writing never died. The triumph of social history did diminish the significance of the event and of biography. But neither events nor biographies were truly "murdered" in the historiographical revolutions of the past three decades. On this issue Burns has chosen his strawman clumsily. He often seems unaware of just how much the greatest of social historians still model some of the great narrative historians when they sit down to write. Moreover, historians have been in the forefront of defending the integrity of scholarship and clear writing against the worst excesses of postmodernism, cultural studies, and jargon in the academy. Debates about returning to narrative and the necessity of reaching larger "publics" with good history are much older than the phenomenon of Burns's success on PBS. Most important, Burns seems unwilling to acknowledge that embedded in good storytelling are, inherently, interpretations—the very stuff of history. Narrative can still be a form of explanation.

At heart, Burns loves the epic qualities in history; he embraces the heroic, both in individuals and in the sagas of nations. So be it. But this view of history has a name, and such an outlook lends itself to certain kinds of interpretations. As a historian, Burns is a thoroughly American brand of the Whiggish persuasion. He wants to be some combination of our Homer and Macaulay, perhaps our Carl Sandburg with a camera. The stories he tells, therefore, are epic in form: they are going somewhere; they are imbued with the doctrine of progress; and they will reach resolution. The contingencies along the way are dramatic turns— stories that compel their telling—in the sweep of providential development. Or as Burns himself has put it, history is "our story . . . the great pageant of everything that has come before this moment."[6]

In Toplin's own essay in this volume he helped readers place the interpretation at work in *The Civil War* within the contexts of recent American history. He revealed how the film series, given its brilliant craftsmanship with music, authentic voices, and still photographs, appears to many viewers to have no point of view. In short, it appeals to people as great television. Distrustful of the didactic tendencies of historians, and receptive to a moving story, millions of viewers felt that Burns had brought them, personally and emotionally, closer to the real Civil War than they had ever been. The film seems to exude a balanced, objective perspective carried masterfully by the responsible voice of narrator David McCullough, our Walter Cronkite of historians, and the counterpoise of the irresistible, present-tense drawl of Shelby Foote with the moral earnestness of the African American historian Barbara Fields. The numerous and well-known actors used as voices provide an Abraham Lincoln, a Mary Chesnut, or a Ulysses Grant that could quickly become familiar and comfortable in living rooms. As Toplin said, all of this artistry made the series look "like a visual textbook," and herein lies a major reason for its success.[7]

But as Toplin observed, Burns's approach was driven by at least three sets of assumptions and influences: the Vietnam War and its harrowing lessons about the horror of combat and the potential futility of warmaking; the Civil Rights revolution and its lessons about the enduring significance of black liberation and racial equality in American history; and a 1980s brand of new nationalism, a sense of a shared past that blurs the old sectionalism. There are no villains on the Confederate side in Burns's Civil War; a Yankee, George McClellan, is the only character the audience is truly invited to either loathe or enjoy as comic relief. War itself is villainized; the face of battle is rendered real and unforgettable. But something deep inside the horror and transformation in this *civil* war had to be evaded in order to sustain an ultimate story of reconciliation (namely, the history of its aftermath). Toplin, who is otherwise a great admirer and defender of Burns as a filmmaker, did well to show how so beguiling a film was made with "slanted perspectives."[8] One wishes, though, that Toplin (as well as others in this book) had stopped briefly to define and deepen his loose use of the term "tragedy" as applied to the Civil War. Toplin did not follow through on the implications of his own criticisms. We need to know *why* the Civil War was tragic, not merely that it resulted in massive death and destruction. Only then will we understand its Homeric qualities, its deepest connections to questions of fate and destiny, those old and enduring elements of true tragedy.

Few historians have written as much or as well about the relationships between history and artistry, novelists and scholars as C. Vann Woodward. His essays on these issues are always worth rereading when such tensions reemerge. In this volume he provided a fatherly critique of how a group of historians, many his former students, served, and in his view, misserved Burns on this project. His essay is an interesting, if somewhat self-serving, window into the consulting process on this film. According to his account, Woodward had to bring a shrill and didactic pack of scholars into line in order to prevent them from waylaying Burns's artistry in the interest of particular interpretations of the Civil War's meaning.

Ironically, military historian Gary Gallagher levied some of the stiffest criticisms of Burns, but not before offering a sincere defense of popular interest in history, especially that of Civil War "buffs." Burns's greatest achievement, said Gallagher, was his "ability to fire the imaginations of millions of Americans, sending them in large numbers to libraries and bookstores." This said, Gallagher persuasively outlined how Burns's treatment of the military dimensions of the war was "utterly conventional" and betrayed an "ignorance of modern scholarship." Among other points, Gallagher maintained that Burns employed an old-fashioned geographical imbalance between the eastern and western theaters of the war, stressed Gettysburg at the expense of many other neglected turning points, never fully developed the significance of technology in the war, and served up a thoroughly traditional profile of Robert E. Lee as a military genius, never recognizing the vigorous debate over the years about his ideas and generalship. Most telling, Gallagher observed that by giving the Confederacy a "mantle of hopelessness" from the beginning of the film, Burns fed into the Lost Cause mythology, the notion that the South fought a heroic struggle against overwhelming numbers and resources. Those contingencies that made Confederate victory possible at certain junctures did not quite fit into the epic of victory and defeat destined to be reconciled. According to Gallagher, Burns sacrificed too much complexity to Shelby Foote's charm, to simplification and "fetching anecdotes."[9]

Catherine Clinton, too, admired much of the artistry of *The Civil War*, admitting that historians owe Burns a "debt of gratitude" for helping expand the audience for the books they write. Her essay provided some much needed wit in this book. With a sense of humor some will take as perverse, she can declare herself a "fan" of Burns's film, warn her fellow historians not to get too jealous of the filmmaker's "coronation" as "Homer for America's own *Iliad*," and then proceed to blister the artist for his evasions of women in the series. Clinton asked a useful question: in all the emphasis in the film series on human suffering and death in war, where are the widows? Or in her words, "Mrs. Sullivan Ballou, where are you?"[10] Clinton offered her own revisions—a collection of quotations from letters and diaries from white and black women that might have been used in order to more deeply represent what the war meant to women on a daily and lasting basis.

In his essay, Gabor Boritt was certainly a fan of Burns's craftsmanship. He admired how, as filmmakers, Burns's staff had the "eyes and ears of poets." Boritt made the important point that the secret to Burns's success may be his very "fresh-eyed innocence." The ability to imagine how laymen, even children, will comprehend historical material on film is crucial to the filmmaker. It is very much part of Burns's own professional self-understanding. "If I have one gift," he remarked in an interview, "I think it is that I have an ability in the editing room to be my audience's representative, to demand from the film that I am making something that an interested but ignorant member of the audience, an eighth grader perhaps, might need to know to keep them in their chair."[11] Boritt pointed out many mistakes made in the film with photographs, and his candidate for sin of omission is immigrants, who were nearly 20 percent of the Union armies, and might have brought even more flavor to the voices. In his focus on Gettysburg, Boritt effectively criticized the inordinate influence of Michael Shaara's novel *The Killer Angels* on Burns, especially in giving him his most noble character, Joshua Chamberlain. Indeed, the trajectory of Chamberlain's career, his heroic service and battle wounds, made perfect material for the narrative strategy Burns employed.

Eric Foner and Leon Litwack were largely alone in the book in demanding that Burns account for not treating the question of the war's legacies. Foner scrutinized the ninth, and final, episode of the film and found it "profoundly disturbing" that after many hours of attention to battles and leaders of the war itself, only scant attention was given to Reconstruction and the long-term consequences of the conflict. Likewise, Litwack found the treatment of legacies the "most appalling and revealing shortcoming" in the series.[12] These were not merely the nit-pickings of scholars whose work did not influence the film. Foner and Litwack were historian-critics doing their job—illuminating Burns's *interpretation* for all those who care to understand it. When Burns sat in the editing room with his final episode, he chose not only to represent his eighth grader but also to align himself with a hackneyed, sentimental, and appealing theory of American history—that no matter how terrible our conflicts nor how profound our tragedies, Americans solve their problems and reconcile their differences like a troubled family destined for reunion. Burns knows a good deal about the deep myths that unify this society, and he has done much to reconstruct them.

After eight episodes of haunting focus on a nation and a society torn asunder, Burns and his writer, Geoffrey Ward, fast-forwarded through the complexities of Reconstruction to the uplifting accomplishment of reunion fifty years later. The audience is ushered from the surrender at Appomattox through some fleeting discussion of postwar politics, past Grant's final prophecy of an "era of great harmony," to Joseph E. Johnston's bareheaded encounter with pneumonia and quick death after attending the funeral in 1891 of his former rival William Tecumseh Sherman, and finally to that irresistible footage of the old veterans at the 1913 and 1938 Gettysburg Blue-Gray reunions. The film does leave one with the feeling that the past flows into the present and that legacies have power over us. But the point is made with sentiment rather than explanation. The Blue and the Gray—men out of a distant past, who were once familiar images on every American town green—became television images for the first time. They charmed millions; they were beautiful old men representing a reconciled nation. The trouble, as Foner and Litwack made clear, is that the audience never learns how and why that reconciliation came about, at what political and social costs sectional reunion triumphed while racial division only deepened. As Foner said, when faced with this kind of interpretive challenge, Burns "consistently opts for nostalgia." Not only are there no villains in this story, but with former Congressman James Symington's commentary, the audience is allowed to comfortably conclude that all the soldiers had fought a good fight and "shared a common love of liberty." In his thrashing of Burns's approach, Litwack argued that Burns missed an opportunity to explore the meaning of the social revolution of emancipation, and wedded to a "romantic vision" of history, he simply could not make a film about the Civil War that would "afflict the comfortable, the complacent" understanding of this era held by the vast public.[13]

In his essay, scriptwriter Geoffrey Ward pleaded for understanding from his fellow historians about the demands of the medium of film and wished for less "recrimination" in the criticism of this film's interpretation. He described the wide divergences between popular and scholarly criticisms of the film, a point that should temper how all of us respond to history on film. Contingents of the Sons of Confederate Veterans picketed some of Burns's appearances, accusing him of making a film full of Yankee bias, whereas some scholars have unrelentingly demanded a film largely about emancipation. Ward was in a sensitive position; writing scripts under rigid space restraints inevitably relies on formulas and dramatic narrative, not on analytical traditions. But *The Civil War* was an eleven-hour proposition, and some of Ward's responses were simply lame. To the query about the absence of political contexts, Ward countered that "even enlightened PBS viewers have a low tolerance for the subtleties of, say, the Wilmot Proviso." He missed the point. To the demand for more on Reconstruction, Ward relied on the unsustainable claim that there are not enough photographs. Worse, he maintained that "by the logic which dictates that a film about the Civil War must also include the full story of Reconstruction . . . , anyone making a film about the First World War would have to include the Second, anyone trying to cover the Great Society would also have to assess the Reagan Revolution." This odd logic relied on a skewed sense of chronology. Moreover, the rancor in these exchanges might subside if Ward, Burns himself, and his legion of informed admirers would engage the debate by admitting that this was a film driven by a central story, the drama of the war itself and its most appealing individual characters, as well as by a particular vision of the whole of American history, by an artifice emanating from a deep understanding of audience expectation. Ward did, however, score one point in complaining about Litwack's overzealous comparison of *The Civil War* to D. W. Griffith's *Birth of a Nation*.[14]

Finally, we are left with Burns's own essay-defense of his enterprise and his craft. When he wrote about filmmaking, and criticized television itself, Burns was informative and insightful. When he described his own historical imagination and his love for all the "loud, raucous, moving, exquisite collection of noises" that make up the "aggregate . . . music" of the American past, he could be as inspiring as Sandburg was with his prose poem on Lincoln. When he talked about perching on "roof-tops and at battlefields at precisely the time and day and moment the battles took place" in order to "take back a little of the magic of the past," we can all feel the pull to be filmmakers rather than archival scholars. But when he wrote about the substance of history itself, he often fell into a ponderous, hyperbolic style. By trying to write in an oracular manner about the "tyranny" and "stranglehold" of the academy over history, Burns failed to confront specific criticisms of his own work. Most incongruous was the claim that "we, as filmmakers, had no set agenda." Even if this were believable, the next sentence betrayed the point. "We felt slavery was bad," Burns continued, "George McClellan timid, but that the rest of the war, North and South, male and female, black and white, civilian and military, was a vast and complicated family drama, poetic as well as social in dimension . . . , instructive to the heart as well as the head."[15] The "epic" that Burns sought to tell is this "family drama," rooted in a Whiggish scheme of history and an Americanized sense of tragedy that requires not only catharsis but also progress and happy endings. We all have agendas; Homer did, and so does our Homer with a camera.

NOTES

This essay was published in *Reviews in American History* in June 1997 and is reprinted here in a slightly revised form.

1. Robert Penn Warren, from the revised edition of Warren's *Brother to Dragons*, quoted in C. Vann Woodward, "History in Robert Penn Warren's Fiction," in *The Future of the Past* (New York: Oxford University Press, 1989), 234. It is worthy of note that Burns is a great admirer of Warren's work (an admiration this author shares), especially his *Legacy of the Civil War* (Cambridge: Harvard University Press, 1961). I became aware of this in conversations and correspondence with Burns, especially Ken Burns to David Blight, January 31, 1991, in possession of the author. In that same letter Burns makes the filmmaker's apt plea that we must not "forget to filter our new forms through new ways of seeing."

2. "The Movie Maker as Historian: Conversations with Ken Burns," an interview with David Thelen, *Journal of American History* 81 (December 1994): 1034–35.

3. *Ken Burns's* The Civil War: *Historians Respond*, ed. Robert Brent Toplin (New York: Oxford University Press, 1996). A flaw that both the volume editor and Ox-

ford University Press should account for is why the first six essays are footnoted and the final three are not.

4. "The Movie Maker as Historian," 1034. In his interview with Thelen, Burns related the story of C. Vann Woodward saving him from a "rather embarrassing exchange" with historian-consultants. At the break in the hallway, Burns "brevetted C. Vann Woodward a major general in the field." The historical profession, by and large, has returned the honor.

5. *Ken Burns's* The Civil War, ed. Toplin, 161; "The Movie Maker as Historian," 1032.

6. "The Movie Maker as Historian," 1032.

7. *Ken Burns's* The Civil War, ed. Toplin, 21.

8. Ibid., 35.

9. Ibid., 42–43, 58.

10. Ibid., 65, 67; "The Movie Maker as Historian," 1043.

11. *Ken Burns's* The Civil War, ed. Toplin, 84–85.

12. Ibid., 106, 134.

13. Ibid., 112, 138, 140.

14. Ibid., 144, 146.

15. Ibid., 156, 168, 161, 169–70. For a critique of the "family" metaphor in *The Civil War,* see Bill Farrell, "All in the Family: Ken Burns's *The Civil War* and Black America," *Transition: An International Review* 58 (1993): 169–73.

Postludes

W. E. B. Du Bois and the Struggle for American Historical Memory

The greatest enemy of any one of our truths may be the rest of our truths.
   —*William James, "What Pragmatism Means"*
The mystery which haunts American experience . . . is the mystery of how we are many and yet one.
   —*Ralph Ellison, "Going to the Territory"*

On February 23, 1968, the one hundredth anniversary of W. E. B. Du Bois's birth, Martin Luther King Jr. delivered one of the last major addresses of his life at Carnegie Hall in New York. It is interesting and fitting to note how King chose to best honor Du Bois's legacy. Above all Du Bois's other achievements, King stressed his role as historian. Du Bois's "singular greatness," argued King, was his "unique zeal" that "rescued for all of us a heritage whose loss would have profoundly impoverished us." Similarly, David Levering Lewis, in his remarkable biography, convincingly showed how Du Bois's distinctive "signature" endures in his capacity, in several genres, to compress huge pieces of history into single essays, paragraphs, and images. King especially emphasized Du Bois's work on Reconstruction, a period traditional historians had for three generations portrayed as a tragic mistake and a sordid interlude in American race relations. King was no professional historian, but his own prophetic sense of history enabled him to grasp the social implications of historical consciousness. With too much continuity, "the collective mind of America," declared King, "became poisoned with racism and stunted with myths." Traditional historians' treatment of the black experience, argued the Civil Rights leader, "was a conscious and deliberate manipulation of history and the *stakes* were high."[1] The question of the stakes involved in struggles over rival versions of history not only leads us to the political and social meanings of what historians do but also provides an angle of understanding about the confluences of history and memory for intellectuals and for larger societies.

America is currently undergoing a deep cultural shift, an extended attempt to democratize its collective social memory at the same time we struggle to understand new conceptions of a "whole" national history. This epochal curricular and cultural challenge will have no particular end to reach; it is a process, and will likely have only turning points, peaks and valleys, nonsense and wisdom along the path, one can hope, to a sense of strength in multiplicity. It is also important, especially for young people in search of a compass, to know that debates over what we now loosely call "multiculturalism" are not new; the ship of diversity is not sailing in uncharted waters. Moreover, this question of the stakes involved in national and collective memories of all kinds is of profound importance in the larger world we live in—a global marketplace of warring identities and deadly ethnic memories. As any conversation about the United Nations' ability to respond to the bewildering array of conflicts will demonstrate, the parts are overwhelming even the best of efforts to envision a whole, both within nations and in the world. Collectively, the peoples of developed and less developed countries seem to be marching to two discordant tunes. One is the music that tugs us along, searching for moral clarity and lost certainties, and played at an understandable, if endless, array of commemorations, remembrances, and anniversaries. The other music is polyphonic, the fitful songs of groups, new nations or old tribes acting upon their sense of heritage, claiming their place and identities against those who have repressed them during the past generation or for five centuries. We are being taught anew the potential of group identities and narrow nationalisms, combined with economic deprivation, to compel people to kill for memory.[2] We need prior models through which to study this phenomenon; we need seriously to look at pluralistic approaches to history attempted long before our own era, as well as at how historical outsiders have claimed redefinitions of the center without denying a center's existence. This essay explores Du Bois's historical imagination and (selectively) some of his historical works as a means of finding one such model.

Passion and violence often govern cultural conflict over memory. The historical memory of a people, a nation, or any aggregate evolves over time in relation to present emotional and social needs, and everchanging contexts. As theorists and historians like Benedict Anderson and Eric Hobsbawm have demonstrated, the resilience of nationalism as a universal organizing value of political life in the world has served deep human needs, and ceaselessly compelled the construction of official histories wherever modern societies wish to declare themselves a unity.[3] Societies remember and use history as a source of coherence and identity, as a means of contending for power and place, and as a means of controlling whatever becomes normative in society. For better or worse, and in spite of all we have learned about how culture is invented and how heritage is a social construct that defies fixed definition, people jealously seek to own their pasts. The public that consumes history is vast, and the marketplace turbulent. Like it or not, we live in an era where the impulse to teach the young to have an open sense of history is not enough; that understanding will be challenged. The pragmatic, questioning sense of history will encounter multiple social memories—in the classroom, at the international negotiating table, at the movies, and in the streets. This dilemma desperately needs trained historians seeking evidence, demanding verification, offering reasoned explanations of events. But the truth is that historians, and their cousins in related disciplines, are only playing one part in this drama. Collective memories are that which the world's peoples (including multiple America) are prone to think *with* more than *about*.

Although his achievements were sometimes stunted by a legendary arrogance, his work contained some flawed research, and some of his sweeping arguments are surely debatable, Du Bois was, nevertheless, a pioneer in illuminating the phenomenon of "official" and "alternative" histories in America, especially with reference to history and race. He spent much of his career as a scholar and an artist, trying to dislodge American history from its racist moorings. He became, if you will, a kind of self-appointed sounder, not only of America's peculiar "race concept" but also of the full range of tragedy and possibility in American history. Such ambitions necessitated active confrontation with the traditional historiography about slavery and race, with scientific racism (though he himself took a long time to overcome a nineteenth-century conception of "race"), with indifference, and with the mythology of the Lost Cause, which had swept much of American popular culture by the early twentieth century. In his essay "The Propaganda of History," the final chapter of his most significant historical work, *Black Reconstruction in America*, Du Bois declared himself "aghast" at what American historians had done to the fields of Reconstruction and African American history.[4] The

American historical community had not only subordinated the black experience but also rendered it virtually unknown. The state of popular historical misunderstanding in the first third of the twentieth century is what Du Bois sought to overturn. Examples abound of his sheer contentiousness on this matter. For example, in 1908 Charles Francis Adams wrote an article on the Negro problem and the solid South for *Century Magazine*. Du Bois took such exception to the piece that he wrote to Adams: "One of the most unfortunate things about the Negro problem is that persons who do not for a moment profess to be informed on the subject insist on informing others. This, for a person who apparently boasts of advanced scientific knowledge is most deplorable and I trust that before publishing further matter on the race problem, *you will study it. To this end I am sending you some literature.*" Whether directed at his colleagues and coworkers or at fellow scholars in correspondence, "Du Boisian displeasure," as David Lewis aptly put it, "was almost never like an explosion; it was a shard of ice down the back."[5]

In Du Bois's historical writing he was not merely crying foul at racist historians for leaving blacks out of the story of American history. He was surely partisan to the extent that he sought to restore, even exalt, his own people's history. At the same time, he believed such a restoration could only enrich American history. He was very much interested in how multiple parts could make a new whole, how pluralism might be a new conceptual framework for American history. Long before he would actually write *Black Reconstruction,* he appealed for financial support and wider interest in the project. In 1909 he wrote to Richard Watson Gilder, editor of *Century Magazine,* requesting funding for a "careful authentic history of the part which the Negro played in the Reconstruction governments." Du Bois would eventually get some funding for that project, albeit not from *Century.* But he sent Gilder a straightforward statement of his intention. He seemed driven by the imperatives both of scholarship and of the construction of popular social memory. He said he wanted to tell the story from the perspective of the "black voter and office holder." "This history," he reminded Gilder, "so well worth saving, is passing away rapidly as the reconstruction Negroes die and I want especially to gather it and preserve it." Du Bois wanted to create and restore, provoke and explain. "Of course," he concluded his appeal to Gilder, "I should aim ... to write unbiased history and not an apology for my side."[6] Such were the noble aims, and perhaps the impossible restraint, of a black history to be written in segregated America.

Eventually, Du Bois helped to spark a major historiographical turn in the study of Reconstruction and race among American historians. This turn, initiated by Du Bois at least as early as the publication of *The Souls of Black Folk* in 1903, took many years to bear fruit (with major historiographical consequences in the 1960s and 1970s). Du Bois appreciated the political and social stakes of historical debates; he understood the power of historical images and myths in shaping social policy and human interactions. In his historical writings, therefore, a tension developed between art, politics, and the pursuit of scientific truth. As Arnold Rampersad has shown, Du Bois made a gradual but persistent turn away from the scientific empiricism in which he was trained to the poetic sensibilities that characterized so much of his writing after he left Atlanta to edit the *Crisis* in 1910.[7] Du Bois's efforts to forge an alternative historical memory should be understood in the context of this turn in his work from social science toward social criticism and art.

Du Bois came of age and was trained during the era (1880–1900) when history assumed the mantle of a "science." He was by any estimation a skilled social scientist who, at Harvard, studied philosophy with William James, Josiah Royce, and George Santayana, and history with Albert Bushnell Hart. "It was James with his pragmatism and . . . Hart with his research method," Du Bois wrote in his autobiography, "that turned me back from the lovely but sterile land of philosophic speculation, to the social sciences as the field for gathering and interpreting that body of fact which would apply to my program for the Negro." Du Bois understood himself to be an emerging historical sociologist, though Harvard did not yet recognize the field. Although Du Bois's rhetoric can be overwrought and his arguments self-righteous, he would always be, in his own way, committed to the sheer accumulation of the "body of fact" that might be thrust before an ignorant or contentious world. In an autobiographical piece written in 1944 for Rayford Logan's *What the Negro Wants*, Du Bois admitted that he had "rationalized" his personal story into a "coherent unity" that masked some of the "hesitancies" and "graspings" of his life. Indeed, as Lewis has shown, we would do well to use Du Bois's autobiographical writings with caution. In a variety of ways, his complicated family history may have prompted Du Bois, the incessant autobiographer, to write, as Lewis said, with "carefully calibrated amnesia." That can be said of virtually all important autobiographers. But Du Bois's self-assured claim that his early career had a singular aim rings true. "*History* and the other social sciences," he wrote, "were to be my *weapons,* to be sharpened and applied by research and writing."[8] So, always the trained historian in search of verifiable evidence, he also came to use history as a strategy to confront and overcome traditional, often white supremacist, versions of American history.

In his earliest writings one already finds the tensions between scientific truths and art, between data and politics, and between past and present.[9] In his commencement address at Harvard in 1890, "Jefferson Davis as a Representative of Civilization," the twenty-two-year-old Du Bois offered up Davis, the recently deceased former president of the Confederacy, as an American "Teutonic hero." Boldly, he used Davis as a symbol of the "type of civilization" (national and not merely southern) that had advanced itself by "murdering Indians," that had created a culture "whose principle is the rise of one race on the ruins of another," and that was driven by an "overweening sense of the I and a consequent forgetting of the Thou." The veiled implication of Du Bois's speech was that America's quest for sectional reconciliation had led it not only to honor former Confederate leaders but also to fashion a society where might made right, where unbridled individualism reigned, and where racism flourished. The "glamour of history," and therefore the rise of a nation, declared Du Bois, depended on strength and force. "The Anglo-Saxon loves a soldier—" declared Du Bois. "Jefferson Davis was an Anglo-Saxon; Jefferson Davis was a soldier." In his few minutes of commencement glory Du Bois urged his Harvard audience to make way for the rise of the quieter, creative, "submissive" culture of blacks, "the race of whose rights Jefferson Davis had not heard." Implicit in Du Bois's message was the notion (or the hope) that the day of Anglo-Saxon hegemony had passed and the rise of the black race had commenced. Moreover, the speech was an anguished cry for justice, for inclusion, and for a new "standard" by which to judge civilization. While there were elements of nineteenth-century racialist thinking (claims of distinguishable racial characteristics) in the young Du Bois's rhetoric, and he too would one day exalt the soldier, at bottom, the address was a direct challenge to the historical memory and moral imagination of his audience (Harvard and America). "You whose nation was founded on the loftiest ideals," demanded Du Bois, "and who many times forget those ideals with a strange forgetfulness, have more than a sentimental interest, more than a sentimental duty. You owe a debt to humanity for this Ethiopia of Out-stretched Arm, who has made her beauty, patience, and her grandeur law."[10] By addressing his audience so personally as *you,*

Du Bois asserted that history had left a collective responsibility in America. Slavery and racism were everyone's legacy and everyone's problem. The link between Jefferson Davis, "civilization," and "you" was not only a remarkable stroke of irony for such a young orator but also a clear indication that Du Bois had launched his lifelong quest to contend for the nature and meaning of America's historical memory.

Du Bois's early conception of history as contending memories is further illustrated in *The Suppression of the African Slave Trade to the United States, 1638–1870,* his doctoral thesis and the first volume published in the Harvard Historical Monograph Series. Written after his return from two pivotal, even transforming, years at the University of Berlin, where he studied a good deal of economics, *Suppression* was primarily a legalistic analysis of the long effort to abolish the slave trade. But an ethical tone informs the volume and pervades its concluding chapter. Du Bois's moralism was typical of American historiography during the 1890s.[11] Even under the new veneer of scientific analysis, most historians claimed the duty of teaching moral lessons; hence the final section of *Suppression* is entitled "The Lessons for Americans." But something deeper may have motivated Du Bois's language in the final passages of *Suppression.* He was fully aware that by the mid-1890s American society was in the midst of a near crusade of sectional reconciliation, the celebration of the mutual heroism of North and South in the Civil War, and the quest for a present and a future that allowed people to forget slavery and racial conflict, a position now championed by the popular historian James Ford Rhodes. Moreover, as aloof as the young Germanophile could be, Du Bois could hardly have been completely detached from the poverty and oppression he had already witnessed in the South or the racism he had encountered at Harvard when he wrote of the enrichment of the Western world "in just such proportion as Americans stole Negroes and worked them to death" in the eighteenth and nineteenth centuries. His chastisement of the "moral apathy" of antebellum Americans, as one generation after another postponed the slavery problem, was spurred by the moral weaknesses of an era of lynching in the 1890s. As Du Bois's voice turns from description to moralizing in the final pages of *Suppression,* we see not only the Ph.D. candidate's attempt to attach an ethical conclusion to his monograph but also the turn toward art and polemics in Du Bois's work.[12]

In Du Bois's earliest formal work of history one also finds an engagement with the oldest and most enduring conception of the American past: the providential view of America as a chosen nation, a people of progress who ultimately solve their problems, an omniscient society thriving above threat or conflict. Du Bois was one of the earliest historians, therefore, to challenge what many have called the "master narrative" of American history. Whether in the 1890s or the 1990s, the "aggravating persistence" of racism in American society makes "challenging demands on the past," wrote Nathan Huggins, "demands that cannot be comprehended through the sanitized and innocent master narrative." Anticipating much of the historiography of his own generation and of the modern "consensus" school of the 1940s and 1950s, Du Bois challenged his readers to reflect from the heart as well as the head and to acknowledge contradiction and paradox: "No American can study the connection of slavery with United States history, and not devoutly pray that his country may never have a similar social problem to solve, until it shows more capacity for such work than it has shown in the past. It is neither profitable nor in accordance with scientific truth to consider that whatever the constitutional fathers did was right, or that slavery was a plague sent from God and fated to be eliminated in due time. We must face the fact that this problem arose principally from the cupidity and carelessness of our ancestors." Du Bois's tone in this passage reflects his awareness that he lived in a nation still unwilling to believe that the "growing evil" of slavery had opened "the highway that led straight to the Civil War." Americans, he maintained, lacked historical consciousness and, therefore, "moral foresight." They congratulated themselves "more on getting rid of a problem than on solving it."[13] The young Du Bois illuminated America's struggle in the 1890s to contend with the memory of slavery, racism, and the Civil War. He also quietly announced one of the principal aims of all his future historical work: to forge a social memory, through scholarship and popular journalism, that might help solve or transcend the race problem, rather than simply getting rid of it.

From his most scientific studies of black urban and rural life (*The Philadelphia Negro* [1899]; the Atlanta University Studies) to his essays, fiction, and poetry, a sense of history informs nearly everything Du Bois wrote. Du Bois was a student of race, and therefore of conflict, and his very subject matter placed him in an oppositional—and sometimes advantageous—position to comment on the struggle over memory in American society. Du Bois came to see himself as a historical outsider in America, but one who could use his American duality, the famous double consciousness about which he wrote in *Souls of Black Folk,* as a lens through which to observe and interrogate the nation's history. The almost hypnotic hold that Du Bois's construction of "twoness," of "two warring ideals" (the competing identities of being black and American) has had on students of African American culture is now widely critiqued and even dismissed by some as an idea bound by Du Bois's own personal experience and outlook. The double consciousness concept is not, and never has been, a static description of African American identity.[14] The range of claims made on either side of the divide between blackness and Americanness, between racial distinctiveness and universality, are as old as the antebellum generation of black leadership who faced choices of how best to negotiate the miserable reality of American racism. Throughout American history, many black leaders, like other ethnic, immigrant, or labor leaders, just got up in the morning and tried to change the conditions of their people. It is hard to imagine Harriet Tubman musing for long on such existential questions of identity.

Existential crises were reserved, perhaps, for a Hegelian writer like Du Bois, who tried to take the pulse of history and find a new place in it for black people. As he would in various ways in several other works, Du Bois asserted in *Souls* that the black experience stood at the center of national history, at least for those who cared to look at conflict rather than only continuity, at irony rather than pleasing myth. His image of the "swarthy spectre" sitting in its "accustomed seat at the nation's feast" frames his claim that "the nation has not yet found peace from its sins" in the fortieth year since emancipation.[15] Specters haunt, and American memory was haunted, Du Bois seemed to be saying; the country's collective memory awaited new voices, new scholars, and storytellers who might peer into its contradictions and make irony the lifeblood of the story rather than merely the unseen background. At the very least, such an approach might change the seating arrangement at the feast.

The novelist John Edgar Wideman declared that if he were allowed only one book with which to teach post–Civil War American history, it would be *Souls of Black Folk.* Such a comment attests to some of the functions of *Souls* as a work of history. But Wideman also claimed that each time he taught or read the book, when he closed it, "beauty and pain linger." He found himself transported to beautiful memories of the A.M.E. Zion church in which he was raised, a place of hope and sustenance, and he is also left with the message of pain, the "disquieting thought," the fear that "nothing has changed" about race in America through time. In Du Bois's own time many perceptive readers wondered about the somber tone of *Souls of Black Folk*. In 1906 William James wrote to Du Bois questioning the despair of the book. "You must not think I am personally wedded to the minor key," Du Bois answered. "On the contrary I am tuned to the most aggressive and unquenchable hopefulness. I wanted in this case simply to reveal fully the other side to the world." Although tinged with bravado, Du Bois's answer to James reveals his sense of writing about the tragic "other side" of American experience. This endless dialectic between the beauty and the pain, the progress and the regression, black invisibility and centrality in American history is just what Du Bois sought to capture by bringing the black experience to the heart of the story. For many blacks, the penetrating psychological insights of *Souls of Black Folk* were like nothing else they had read. "I am glad, glad you wrote it," Jessie Fauset wrote to her close friend; "we have needed someone to voice the intricacies of the blind maze of thought and action along which the modern, educated colored man and woman struggles."[16] Like Ralph Waldo Emerson, Du Bois's mastery of the essay form revealed the personal meanings in larger historical experience. Like Frederick Douglass, Mark Twain, and Charles Chesnutt before him, he converted duality into an analytical device, rather than merely a burden.

Du Bois probably never gave up believing in an ethical basis for history, even after he embraced a more materialist, economic analysis in the 1930s. But he eloquently warned about the problem of official domination in the construction of historical memory. "With sufficient general agreement among the dominant classes," he declared in 1935, "the truth of history may be utterly distorted and contradicted and changed to any convenient fairy tale that the masters of men wish."[17] Memories rise and fall from dominance, sometimes through the force of armies, and always, it seems, through the use of language. As intellectuals all over eastern Europe, parts of the former Soviet Union, South Africa, or China are demonstrating in our own time, and as black writers have understood in America at least since the first slave narratives, the ownership of language—the liberation of words from debasement and control by the masters of plantations or states—can rescue the human spirit from totalitarian control. Words and, indeed, the images and myths they convey are the stuff of memory. They can be innovative or reactionary, liberating or destructive. Modes of power and persuasion keep any version of social memory dominant, and hence the danger and the inspiration of historical revisionism. "Only a horizon ringed with myths," warned Friedrich Nietzsche in 1874, "can unify a culture."[18] This bitter, resilient truth, for better or worse, abides in Du Bois's work.

In *Time and Narrative* Paul Ricoeur demonstrated how we can only begin to understand and mark time with memory. Social memory becomes embedded through narratives we construct to give it collective meaning and substance. We need stories, the "poetic act of emplotment," argued Ricoeur, to render the bewilderment of time and experience intelligible. Deep understanding is usually derived from the deepest memories, those that have somehow engaged the "soul" and elicited lasting narratives. "It is *in* the soul, hence as an impression," said Ricoeur, "that expectation and memory possess extension." Passionate debates over the actual nature and meaning of the past—often involving claims of collective guilt or responsibility—are concerned, while they remain in the realm of reason at least, not with retribution but with anticipation, with present and future stakes. As Steven Knapp has argued, the "ethical relevance" of the past (any exercise of collective memory) derives from an "agent's imaginative relation to the future consequences of some contemplated action." In other words, we have not only art so that we will not die of reality but also narratives as an authoritative means of negotiating between retribution and forgiveness, between ignorance and knowledge, between lies and enlightenment. In this context, I am reminded of Frederick Douglass's timeless definition of racism as a "diseased imagination."[19]

Certainly Du Bois understood how deeply embedded the problem of racism was in American historical narratives, as well as how much those narratives continued to shape the future. He said as much many times, notably in *The World and Africa* where he charged that it is "the greatest indictment that can be brought against history as a science and against its teachers that we are usually indisposed to refer to history for the settlement of pressing problems." This was not merely another call for a usable history; it was a warning against selective, willfully narrow history, history that resulted from "certain suppressions in the historical record current in our day" and from "the habit, long fostered, of forgetting and detracting from the thought and acts of the people of Africa." Du Bois also had future consequences in mind in his moralizing about national "duty" in the final pages of *Suppression of the African Slave Trade*. Moreover, he had present and future purposes in mind for the image of John Brown he constructed in his biography of the abolitionist in 1909.

Du Bois's short historical synthesis of blacks throughout the African diaspora, *The Negro,* published in 1915, was intended in great part to historicize Africa in a world scrambling to colonize that continent's land and resources. And, finally, as Rampersad has argued, "duty" was itself the hero of Du Bois's essay on the Freedmen's Bureau, "Of the Dawn of Freedom," in *Souls,* a work filled with lessons for a turn-of-the-century world struggling with the problem of the color line.[20]

As for the problem of narratives that reflect deep memory, that engage the "soul," we need only look to the title and content of Du Bois's most famous book. Lewis characterized the publication of *Souls* as "fireworks going off in a cemetery . . . sound and light enlivening the inert and the despairing. It was an electrifying manifesto, mobilizing a people for bitter, prolonged struggle to win a place in history." In the "forethought" of *Souls,* Du Bois addressed the "Gentle Reader" directly and invited him or her to see "buried" treasures, "things which if read with patience may show the meaning of being black" in America. In these essays and one short story, Du Bois used a poetic sensibility to make an offering to the souls of Americans. Du Bois's vexed sometimes mystical attachments to "race" as a source of ideals and gifts, an outlook he expressed most fully at twenty-nine in the essay "The Conservation of Races," also survives full-blown in portions of *Souls.*[21] But the book was like a gift of narratives—across the color line—that might help mediate America's treacherous journey between memory and expectation about race. It probed the past to comprehend what "progress" might mean in the America of the new century. The message was jeremiadic and idealistic, racial and national, personal and collective all at once.

Many scholars have stressed the importance of aesthetic appeal in the art of memory. The emotional power of a historical image or of an individual or collective memory is what renders it lasting. As Frances Yates has shown, unforgettable images that inspired awe and a sense of sacred space were what gave meaning to the memory "wheels," "theaters," and "palaces" of the Italian Renaissance. As Patrick Hutton has contended, even with the modern revolution that the printing press brought to the art of memory, the power of single, poetic images, events, or moments are what still gave substance to cultural memory. Even under the influence of highly individualized modern psychology and the electronic media revolution, whether we believe in the collective unconscious or not, the memory palaces of our own time can be a single image conveyed in a novelist's metaphor, a scene in a movie, a song lyric, a photograph on the front page, or even, we might hope, a historian's persuasive prose. We may be focused, introspectively, on the printed page or more passively at the television screen, instead of listening to the ancient storyteller's voice, but the object is the same: to invoke the emotional threads of memory through aesthetic sensibilities.[22]

According to Rampersad, Du Bois's turn toward art came in 1897 after he first "experienced the goad of southern racism." That year the young scholar-teacher published the original version of "Of Our Spiritual Strivings," which became the first chapter of *Souls*. Throughout the rest of *Souls*, what prompts repeated imagery of "veils" and other metaphoric barriers are those moments when imagined freedom seems almost tangible, but just beyond reach. In the fictional story "The Coming of John" (chapter 13 of *Souls*), "the veil that lay between him and the white world" is first revealed to a young black man as he becomes educated. Moreover, as John, full of zeal, returns to his sleepy southern hometown to help his people, he finds that he no longer speaks their language and that it was "so hard and strange to fit his old surroundings again." Utterly out of step with his fellow blacks and about to be lynched by whites, John's homecoming is a tragic "waste of double aims."[23] For Du Bois, education and bitter experience had revealed the "veil" to such a black southerner as his character John. Through some kind of dissenting imagination, therefore, (in history or fiction) he was searching for ways to peer through such barriers.

Although *Souls* is on the surface a collection of essays, it is also a self-conscious attempt to write a historical epic. Du Bois takes his reader on many journeys to sacred places of memory, similar, at least imaginatively, to what Pierre Nora has called *lieux de memoire*. In his ironic autobiographical tale "Of the Meaning of Progress" (chapter 4 of *Souls*), Du Bois the schoolteacher ushers us "once upon a time" to a remote, segregated hill town in eastern Tennessee, where a bright but poverty-ridden young black woman named Josie dreams of an education. Du Bois tries to engage the reader's senses—on as many emotional levels as possible—as we hear the music thunder from two black churches, enter a makeshift and "sad-colored schoolhouse," and listen to the "dark fatalism" of the freedmen and freedmen's sons and daughters. But this is not merely a romantic tale set amid the humble poor and the blue Appalachians. It is a tragic narrative of human struggle, of crushed hope and death. It is also a historian's challenge to the theory of progress in America, told by a narrator who must ride a Jim Crow car in and out of this "little world" that Du Bois seeks to plant in American memory.[24]

Moreover, in "Of the Black Belt" (chapter 7 of *Souls*), Du Bois takes us, again by Jim Crow car, on a revealing journey to the "crimson soil of Georgia." With vivid imagery, he describes a "monotonous" quality of the landscape of the former Cotton Kingdom, yet he "did not nod, nor weary of the scene; for this is *historic ground.*" Here is Du Bois the artist-scholar combining descriptions of nature with the social history of the legions of sharecroppers. Here is a more believable Georgia than that of Margaret Mitchell. Here is a landscape and a society truly "gone with the wind," where only the "black tenant remains," and the "shadow-hand of the master's grand nephew or cousin or creditor stretches out of the gray distance to collect the rack-rent remorselessly." Remnants of the big houses, the "parks and palaces of the Cotton Kingdom," remain, but that "merry past" now lies in "silence . . . , ashes, and tangled weeds." Here is even the beginning of a challenge to the plantation school's depiction (in literature and history) of the benign world of masters and slaves living in harmonic balance. Du Bois portrays this "Egypt of the Confederacy" as a society built by the blood and toil of generations of blacks, and as a "cause lost long before 1861." On every level, Du Bois's journey through Georgia is an imaginative way to dissent from the traditional image and history of slavery and the South. He frequently invents the voices of freedmen themselves to tell the story. In a scene framed by the "bare ruin of some master's home," an old ex-slave says: "I've seen niggers drop dead in the furrow, but they were kicked aside, and the plow never stopped. Down in the guard house, there's where the blood ran." In "Of the Black Belt" Du Bois combined the beauty and power of nature, the sweep of history in epic proportions, and the painful ruck of the freedmen's daily lives to forge an indelible memory, a memory that countered the romance of the Lost Cause and national reunion. There are no happy darkies in the Black Belt; race relations have not been better off left to the South's own devices. And finally, he described a prison farm (a metaphor for the whole landscape and for the collective despair of black debtors) where the present is so full of the past that the tenses become blurred. "It is a depressing place," wrote Du Bois, "bare, unshaded, with no charm of past association, only a memory of forced toil,—now, then, and before the war. They are not happy, these men whom we meet throughout this region." In effect, slavery has transcended time in Du Bois's imagery. Neoslavery had emerged by the turn of the century, and two generations of black tenants bore their burdens with a combination of hope and gloom.[25] For progressive Americans yearning for alternative conceptions of southern history, for a history that spoke of real conditions and legacies rather than nostalgia for lost simplicity, this was compelling stuff in 1903. Du Bois was trying to demonstrate that historical epic could mix the bitterly tragic with its sweeter drafts. Whatever his success or failure with realism, there are no resolutions or happy endings in his Black Belt.

Examples abound in *Souls* of Du Bois's attempt to revise history, both with evidence and with aesthetic appeal. In his essay on the Freedmen's Bureau, "Of the Dawn of Freedom" (chapter 2), he presents a logical case for viewing the agency in a more positive historical light, rather than as a villain in the tragedy of Reconstruction. Du Bois offers a sympathetic portrayal of the "tremendous undertaking" that the Freedmen's Bureau represented in its all too short life: its charge to provide for refugees, create schools, administer abandoned lands, and extend political rights and justice to the freedpeople. He does not ignore the failings of the bureau, nor of its agents. But this is an essay designed to create a new framework of history in which the plight of the freed people might be more easily understood. At bottom, the essay is a fin de siècle probing for legacies. It begins and ends with the same famous sentence: "The problem of the twentieth century is the problem of the color-line." Du Bois provides ample imagery in which to *see* history anew. First, he urges readers to cast their vision to the rear of the grim parade of history. He suggests three images in the procession of Sherman's march across Georgia: "The Conqueror, the Conquered, and the Negro." "Some see all significance in the grim front of the destroyer," wrote Du Bois, "and some in the bitter sufferers of the Lost Cause. But to me neither soldier nor fugitive speaks with so deep a meaning as that dark human cloud that clung like remorse on the rear of those swift columns. . . . In vain they were ordered back . . . , on they trudged and writhed and surged until they rolled into Savannah a starved and naked horde of tens of thousands."[26] Here is the epic of emancipation with the nameless freedmen, inexorably both liberated and self-liberated in a terrible war, given equal billing in this memory theater with the tragic planters and the awesome William Tecumseh Sherman.

Moreover, in a stunning passage about passion in the South after the war, Du Bois suggested "two figures" that typified the era of Reconstruction and demonstrated the power of its legacy:

the one a gray-haired gentleman, whose fathers had quit themselves like men, whose sons lay in nameless graves; who bowed to the evil of slavery because its abolition threatened untold ill to all; who stood at last, in the evening of life, a . . . ruined form, with hate in his eyes;— and the other a form hovering dark and mother-like, her awful face black with the mists of centuries, had aforetime quailed at that white master's command, had bent in love over the cradles of his sons and daughters, and closed in death the sunken eyes of his wife,—aye, too, at his behest had laid herself low to his lust, and borne a tawny man-child to the world, only to see her dark boy's limbs scattered to the winds by midnight marauders riding after 'damned niggers.' These were the saddest sights of that woeful day; and no man clasped the hands of these passing figures of the present-past; but hating, they went to their long home, and hating their children's children live today.[27]

Past and present met in this imagery with frightful intensity and authentic tragedy. Here were not the "forms" of old soldiers who had met in battle and could now clasp hands in mutual respect. Here were the veterans of an even deeper conflict, and perhaps a deeper tragedy. They were alternative veterans to those now exalted at national Blue-Gray reunions. Here was the image of an old male slaveholder, the broken symbol of power and sexual domination, and an old black woman, representing Mammy, mother, and survivor. The heritage of slavery lived on in these "two passing figures of the present-past."

Or in other words, the problem of slavery lived on in the problem of the freedmen, and the problem of the freedmen lived on in the problem of the color line. But more important still, no racial reconciliation could ever match the vaunted sectional reconciliation without a serious confrontation with the hostility rooted in sexual abuse, lynching, and racism. Du Bois used gender here to render his imagery all the more meaningful. An essay on the Freedmen's Bureau had been converted into an unforgettable statement about the most persistent evils of slavery and racism. Du Bois could have chosen no starker example than white male sexual abuse of black women. As he would later write, Du Bois could forgive the white South almost anything: "its slavery, for slavery is a world-old habit . . . ; its fighting for a well-lost cause, and for remembering that struggle with tender tears." But he would never forgive the "persistent insulting of black womanhood which it [the white South] sought and seeks to prostitute to its lust."[28] Deep memory, Du Bois had exhibited in his writing, was rooted in stark imagery and never easily reconciled. In this imagery, Du Bois illustrated that though the sections, North and South, had reconciled, the races had not. Indeed, the message was that the issues of race and reunion were trapped in a tragic, mutual dependence.

These few examples may suffice to demonstrate some of the historical intentions and devices Du Bois employed in *Souls*. As a text, the book is often used for psychological purposes—for the pedagogical aims of understanding American racial identity formation. The book's historical uses and meanings are not as often or as readily grasped by young readers who may be eager to allow Du Bois to take them on a journey of racial memory, rather than a journey into alternative visions of American histories and futures (circa 1903).

In *Black Reconstruction,* a project that was more than twenty years old when it came out in 1935, Du Bois assumed the posture of an empiricist. But in the preface he acknowledged the dual function of the historian: "to tell and interpret." It is especially interesting that in a one-page preface Du Bois believed it necessary to "say frankly in advance" that his most basic assumption was that blacks were "ordinary human beings," that he sought to refute any theory of Negro inferiority, and that he understood that this might curtail his audience. The weight of traditional interpretations of slavery and the Civil War and Reconstruction inspired and haunted this long book. Du Bois admitted that he would not convert any diehard racists, but that he would no longer allow emancipation and black enfranchisement after the war to be so easily dismissed as "gestures against nature." *Black Reconstruction* would, therefore, be more than what we are accustomed to calling revisionist history, just another point of view or interpretation. It would be an effort to retell what Du Bois considered "the most dramatic episode in American history . . . the sudden move to free four million black slaves in an effort to stop a great civil war, to end forty years of bitter controversy, and to appease the moral sense of civilization." In 1930, in response to a correspondent eager to know how to interpret the Reconstruction era, Du Bois asserted that "the story of Reconstruction from the point of view of the Negro is yet to be written. When it is written, one may read its tragedy and get its truth." In 1932 Du Bois told another correspondent that he intended to "show that instead of Negro freedom and enfranchisement being an isolated matter that can be treated separately from the main current of history, that it is an integral part, and particularly a part of the economic history of the United States from 1860 to 1880." He had just finished reading Charles Beard's *Rise of American Civilization,* he told Harry Laidler, and signaling some of the flawed Marxism that would characterize the book, announced himself determined to demonstrate the primacy of material conditions, economic motivations, and monied oligarchies in the story of Reconstruction. In 1934, in an attempt to obtain some final funding, ironically from the Carnegie Foundation, to complete the manuscript for *Black Reconstruction,* Du Bois wrote an apt description of the long-term value of his own book before it was published. "I think I have a book of unusual importance," he said. "Of course, it will not sell widely; it will not pay, but in the long run, it can never be ignored."[29] These private statements, prior to publication, indicate a good deal about Du Bois's desires to engage big questions, to subvert older interpretations, and to write a narrative about the whole of American history, and not just a peculiarly black part.

The first chapter of *Black Reconstruction,* "The Black Worker," is a meditation on the meaning of slavery in American history. Coupled with the final chapter, "The Propaganda of History," these two essays independently can serve as a primer for the field of African American history as it has developed since the 1930s. Although Du Bois's tone was unquestionably polemical, he did strive for some balanced perspective. He acknowledged that slaveholders were not unremittingly evil people, and even that the institution of slavery was "not usually a deliberately cruel and oppressive system." He allowed that slaves may have been reasonably housed and fed. But looking back upon the historiography of slavery, as well as at popular attitudes toward the Old South as they stood in the 1930s, Du Bois declared inconceivable "the idyllic picture of a patriarchal state with cultured and humane masters under whom slaves were as children, guided and trained in work and play, given each such mental training as was for their good." Instead, he offered a picture of a labor system bent on the "ultimate degradation of man" and the "psychological" disorientation of individuals. Ironically, such a picture anticipated the future work of Stanley Elkins and critiqued the former work of Ulrich B. Phillips at the same time.[30]

To Du Bois the broadest significance of slavery lay in its definition of the limits of American democracy. As long as labor, freedom, and constitutional rights were defined in racial terms, he suggested, America's historical self-definition would always be stunted. Du Bois quoted at length from Frederick Douglass's famous Fourth of July oration in 1852 to underscore the fundamental irony and dishonesty at the core of American history. Du Bois called Douglass the voice of the exploited "black worker," vaguely setting up his subsequent class analysis of Reconstruction. But more important, he appropriated Douglass's scorching phrases to the long-term aim of an alternative history, one not characterized by "deception, impiety, and hypocrisy—a thin veil to cover up crimes." He used the former slave, in some of his angriest rhetoric, to expose that American history where the "ten thousand wrongs of the American slave" were kept in "the strictest silence," and where he who would reveal them was considered an "enemy of the nation" for daring to "make those wrongs the subject of public discourse." The heroes of the slavery era, Du Bois contended, were the fugitive slaves who constantly tested the power of slavery by their escapes and their witness. Indeed, fugitive slaves like Douglass not only provided leadership but also furnished a "text for the abolition idealists." Such texts (the slave narratives) as many historians and critics have argued in recent years, provided the foundation of African American literary and political history. Moreover, if the black worker, as Du Bois contended, was the "founding stone" of the antebellum economic system that tumbled into civil war, then the slave narrative—the entire abolitionist literature—was the "founding stone" of an alternative American history. Here was a use of history to fashion a new vision of the future, both analytical and, in a way, sacred.[31]

Near the end of *Black Reconstruction* Du Bois returned to Douglass as he continued to explore the meaning of slavery. "No one can read that first thin autobiography of Frederick Douglass," Du Bois declared, "and have left many illusions about slavery. And if truth is our object, no amount of flowery romance and personal reminiscences of its protected beneficiaries can keep the world from knowing that slavery was a cruel, dirty, costly, and inexcusable anachronism, which nearly ruined the world's greatest experiment in democracy." Writing at the very time the WPA slave narratives were being collected and well before any serious rediscovery of Douglass or the other antebellum black writers, Du Bois made an important claim about black sources and history, even if he did romanticize it: some of the most important witnesses had never been asked; the very notion of a *source* needed redefinition; and an entire history was yet to be told. In what may have been an ironic reference to Booker T. Washington, Du Bois insisted that black history did not begin with emancipation: "*up from this slavery* gradually climbed the Free Negro with clearer, modern expression and more definite aim long before the emancipation of 1863."[32] Such a conception of black history was not one blacks alone were to possess. Explicitly, Du Bois made it clear that in probing the meaning of slavery, America might better understand the nature of its republican experiment.

Du Bois's "Propaganda of History" (the final chapter) is an indictment of American historiography and an incisive statement of the meaning of race in American historical memory. If the stakes in *Souls of Black Folk* were the spiritual and psychological well-being of blacks in the age of segregation—the creation of an alternative memory to that forged by white popular literature and reinforced by Booker T. Washington—then the stakes in *Black Reconstruction* were collective *national* memory and the struggle over the nature of history itself. According to Du Bois (as of 1935) there were essentially five tragic flaws in American historiography: first, most American historians, consciously or unconsciously, conspired in an avoidance of conflict, especially on the issue of race; second, American historians spurned moral judgment or responsibility for the wrongs of the past; third, slavery, both as an institution and as a cause of the Civil War, had never forthrightly been confronted; fourth, the active role of blacks, as well as abolitionism broadly defined, in the achievement of freedom had been ignored or suppressed; and fifth, the highly developed "hideous mistake" thesis about Reconstruction was rooted in false assumptions, mass production, and popular racism. This wall of historiography and popular culture could not easily be scaled. Its flaws were not sins, wrote Du Bois, of "mere omission and ... emphasis."[33] They had to be engaged with new research, aggressive arguments, and even with counter "propaganda." Du Bois's devastating critique of American historiography provides one of the most acute examples we have of the interdependence of history and society, of how deeply rooted collective historical memories are in social structure, popular beliefs, and professional academic interests. Du Bois's *Black Reconstruction* challenged more than historiography; it challenged the racism and the social theory through which most Americans gained any level of historical consciousness. The work is more important for these interpretive aims than any original research. Indeed, Du Bois made very little use of archival sources in universities and state repositories across the South in the early 1930s. He relied primarily upon government documents, published proceedings of state conventions, and monographs.

Moreover, he largely ignored newspapers. These flaws in the research have always led some to simply dismiss the book. David Lewis pointed to the limitations of such research, but reminded us that, as John Hope Franklin and others bitterly discovered, those southern archives were rigidly segregated in the twenties and thirties, as were the public facilities surrounding them.[34]

Apart from some of the legend that surrounds this book, *Black Reconstruction* should be seen for what Du Bois intended: a forceful reinterpretation, an assault on traditional conceptions of American history that would, in turn, serve the political ends of black people. He meant for this book to awaken historians, move readers, cause trouble; its style was often sermonic, prophetic. Nowhere is Du Bois's penchant for an Old Testament (Lewis calls it "Carlylean") prose style more apparent than in *Black Reconstruction*. Such a style still grates on the ears of many scholars and late twentieth-century readers. A striking example comes at the end of chapter five as Du Bois, writing not for the graduate seminar but as a black Isaiah in the marketplace of white supremacist historiography, describes emancipation: "It was all foolish, bizarre, and tawdry. Gangs of dirty Negroes howling and dancing; poverty-stricken ignorant laborers mistaking war, destruction and revolution for the mystery of the free human soul; and yet to these black folk it was the Apocalypse. The magnificent trumpet tones of Hebrew scripture, transmuted and oddly changed, became a strange new gospel. All that is Beauty, all that was Love, all that was Truth, stood on the top of these mad mornings and sang with the stars. A great human sob shrieked in the wind, and tossed its tears upon the sea—free, free, free."[35] Was this history—such passages that ended with descriptions of a "land fire drunk" and singing Schiller's lyrics to Beethoven's "Ode to Joy"? That is a debate left best to graduate seminars. What is certain is that it is now hard to imagine the great revision Reconstruction history has undergone without these trumpet tones that helped to launch it.

American historiography on race has come so far since the 1930s that the avoidance of conflict no longer seems as pressing a problem as it once did. Likewise, since the turbulent 1960s and 1970s the notion of history as moral discourse may seem to have returned to its proper place on the periphery of historians' concerns. But almost all debates over "new" histories and "old" histories, over events versus social process, over the various ways to return to "narrative," or indeed, over the question of "multiculturalism," have hinged in great part not only on the

proper subject matter of history but on the issues Du Bois identified in
1935: conflict/continuity, scholarly dispassion/moral judgment, and
the inclusion of those still perceived as outsiders. The current challenge
of multicultural studies in the academy, and in public policy, would benefit from the perspective of looking back at such models. Du Bois did not
advocate a personal needs-based history; by and large he resisted the
kind of ahistorical chauvinism that the Reagan era has brought us from
both ends of the ideological spectrum. It is true that after his rather
bloody break with the NAACP in the thirties, Du Bois advocated a kind
of selective, separate institutional development for blacks. Aging, frustrated, and ever more alienated from Jim Crow America, Du Bois, right
or wrong, saw legitimate ends in separate development. But from the
twenties through the forties his work is full of what many would now call
a multicultural vision of American history. In 1924 he declared that the
United States should never see itself as merely a "continuation of English nationality." "America is conglomerate. This is at once her problem and her glory." In 1946, as the Cold War revved up, Du Bois concluded his book *The World and Africa* with the following cosmopolitan
epilogue: "I dream a world of infinite and invaluable variety . . . in a
realm of true freedom . . . in gift, aptitude, and genius—all possible
manner of difference . . . each effort to stop this freedom of being is a
blow at . . . real democracy."[36] These visions all rest in their particular
contexts, but it is clear that Du Bois saw pluralism as the source of a new
American historical narrative, not as its obstacle.

Du Bois's comments on the meaning of conflict and moral responsibility in American history have had many interesting echoes in the
more than half a century since he wrote them. In the conclusion of
Black Reconstruction, looking especially to the Civil War era, he warned
against using history merely "for our pleasure and amusement, for inflating our national ego." A meaningful black history might so contro-
vert white supremacy that it was deemed "neither wise nor patriotic to
speak of all the causes of strife and the terrible results to which sectional differences in the United States had led." There had to be a place
for slavery, massive civil war, and postwar racial violence in the doctrine
of American progress. Avoidance might be the only effective remedy,
then, to sustain a historical memory rooted in the contradiction of
white supremacy and progress. Du Bois chastised "reticent" historians
who blinked or bowed in the face of an issue such as slavery. "Our histories tend to discuss American slavery so impartially," he wrote, "that

in the end nobody seems to have done wrong and everybody was right. Slavery appears to have been thrust upon unwilling helpless America, while the South was blameless in becoming its center. The difference of development, North and South, is explained as a sort of working out of cosmic social and economic law." In this passage Du Bois captured the spirit and substance of much that had been written , inside and out of the academy, about the meaning of slavery and the Civil War in the seventy years since Appomattox. He was trying to advance a new set of *facts* into the historical equation at the same time he insisted that history was inherently a moral discourse. "War and especially civil strife leave terrible wounds," he contended. "It is the duty of humanity to heal them."[37]

One of the facts with which Du Bois was most concerned was the role of slavery in causing the Civil War. This question was, and still is, pivotal in the broad development of American historical memory. Du Bois was incredulous toward interpretations of Civil War causation that ignored the slavery question. He considered it simply self-evident that the Confederacy existed and fought for the perpetuation of slavery. No amount of stress on Unionism, states' rights, or "differences in civilization" could, in his view, ever diminish the centrality of slavery as the moral and political cause of the war. He identified the stakes involved between contending memories when he pointed to a monument in North Carolina that had, in his view, achieved "the impossible by recording of Confederate soldiers: 'they died fighting for liberty!'"[38]

These sentiments toward the Confederate dead and toward the whole conception of the Civil War as a struggle between white men over southern independence or national union are strikingly similar to those Frederick Douglass expressed a generation earlier. Douglass deeply resented monuments to Confederate leaders and soldiers, and he especially resisted the way sectional reconciliation had been forged through the mutual respect of white southern and northern veterans. Du Bois restated these resentments and demonstrated how the values of honor and valor and the concept of the good fight on both sides had helped usher the idea of black emancipation into the background of America's memory of the Civil War. To forget about slavery as a cause of the war was one of the surest ways to forget about the challenges of black freedom and equality during the age of Jim Crow. One could "search current American histories almost in vain," wrote Du Bois, "to find . . . even a faint recognition of" the thousands of black soldiers who fought in the

Civil War, and of the fact that the freedpeople were not "inert recipients of freedom at the hands of philanthropists."[39]

In this historiographical manifesto, Du Bois observed that the greatest obstacle to any development of a new American historical memory regarding race was the "chorus of agreement" about Reconstruction. By the 1930s, in the academy, in popular culture, and in the schools, when Americans reflected upon their past they tended to look to the "tragedy" of Reconstruction for lessons and meaning. The South had been "grievously . . . wounded"; blacks had been "set back" by mistaken radical policies; and the nation as a whole was shamed and retarded in its growth to greatness. "There is scarce a child in the street," wrote Du Bois, "that cannot tell you that the whole effort was a hideous mistake." Du Bois explained why this historiography, both popular and academic, was so "overwhelming." It had been initiated and sustained by two great popularizers, James Ford Rhodes and Claude Bowers. Rhodes, an Ohio businessman, combined the techniques of mass production, an overriding thesis of Negro inferiority, and a conservative's contempt for democracy to "manufacture" (as Du Bois put it) his famous multivolume *History of the United States from the Compromise of 1850* (the first volume published in 1893 and the final of seven volumes in 1906). Rhodes's wide popularity and influence over school textbooks and curriculums was matched in the 1920s by the journalist Bowers's best-selling *Tragic Era,* a work that took the tragic legend of Reconstruction to its fullest development and largest audience yet. Du Bois's characterization of Bowers's work as a "classic example of historical propaganda of the cheaper sort" demonstrates not only his disgust, but his awareness that the popularization of historical memory is, in part, a struggle over power and social domination.[40]

Within the academy, according to Du Bois, the "frontal attack on Reconstruction" was most formidable of all. He surveyed the wide range of Reconstruction historiography produced in the first third of the twentieth century, but centered his critique on John W. Burgess and William A. Dunning. Burgess, a southerner by birth but a former Union soldier who became an Amherst College graduate and a professor of political science at Columbia University, used a frank theory of white supremacy and an overt defense of authority to condemn Reconstruction as an attempt to overthrow the natural order. Readers of Burgess's work would not only witness the political mistakes of Reconstruction, as well as the efforts to push history beyond its evolutionary limits, but also encounter a bold-faced, academic argument that black people had simply not risen above "barbarism," and had never "created any civilization of any kind." At the turn of the century Burgess, of course, voiced the prevailing racial ideology of the age; his perspective was not unique and his work appeared to be scholarly by all existing conventions. History, rooted in such sentiments, had convinced Du Bois that all struggles over historical memory would, therefore, have to be fought on both sides with some degree of "propaganda." Du Bois respected the more careful and scholarly Dunning (also of Columbia) as a "less dogmatic" historian.[41] But in many ways, the "Dunning school" of Reconstruction historiography, with its enormous influence on two generations of scholars, its dozen or more state-by-state monographs, and even with its few exceptions that did acknowledge blacks as part of the story, provided the greatest obstacle of all to an alternative memory. Most of the Dunning school works, however scholarly or scientific, had been written in the service of the tragic legend of Reconstruction and a theory of white supremacy.

What Du Bois illuminated in the final chapter of *Black Reconstruction* is the social organization of remembering and forgetting. Versions of historical memory—their sources and meaning—can be suppressed in the interest of social cohesion or dominance. Following the lead of Carter Woodson and a handful of less visible black and white historians, Du Bois helped to launch the long attempt to rescue black history in America from what many scholars have called a "structural amnesia." The United States during the early twentieth century was not in the strict sense a totalitarian state. There was no official state censor governing scholarship and ideas; no single authority could be said to have had the power of creation or erasure of official memories, as in totalitarian societies (with the exception of the World War I years). But it is not stretching the analogy too far to suggest that the age of Jim Crow, with its depths of scholarly and popular racism, approximated the totalitarian model for the construction of social memory. Geoffrey Hosking has argued that in totalitarian societies authority structures can only be sustained by a powerful guiding mythology—official histories or memories.[42] The case was not altogether different in America. The authority structure of white supremacy had been almost as well served by the historiography on Reconstruction as it had been by Jim Crow laws, official acquiescence in lynching, or "coon songs" and blackface minstrel shows. Such was the aim, said Du Bois, of those Reconstruction historians who ridiculed "the Negro" as the "impossible joke in the whole development." Du Bois sadly described the results of this structural control of historical memory. "We have in fifty years," he wrote, "by libel, innuendo, and silence, so completely misstated and obliterated the history of the Negro in America ... that today it is almost unknown." History had been effectively used, he maintained, to teach Americans to "embrace and worship the color bar as social salvation."[43]

Du Bois's critique of Reconstruction historiography led him, finally, to a meditation on the epistemology of history and on the proper role of the historian. By training and temperament he was interested in how historians create and convey knowledge. Du Bois never stopped referring to history as a "science," and he always remained committed to the ideal of finding historical, if not objective, "truth." By the 1930s he certainly was no longer a hard-boiled empiricist, but he could not easily relinquish the belief in history "either as a science or as an art using the results of science." But Du Bois appreciated and exploited the subjectivity of the historian's craft. In a 1937 memorandum about his proposed *Encyclopedia of the Negro,* he demonstrated that, though he was never indifferent to the pursuit of truth, he knew its limitations. "No scientific work done by living, feeling men and dealing with humanity," wrote Du Bois, "can be wholly impartial. Man must sympathize with misfortune, deplore evil, hope for good, recognize human fellowship. All that social science can do is so to limit natural human feeling by ascertained facts as to approach a fair statement of truth."[44] Du Bois was a relativist, with an evolving, sometimes clear, sometimes ambiguous, but often aggressive conception of right and wrong interpretations.

The restraint apparent in 1937 seemed under great duress two years earlier when Du Bois finished *Black Reconstruction.* Because he wrote in a "field devastated by passion and belief" and because racism so infested the historiography of Reconstruction, Du Bois argued that of "sheer necessity" he had written an "arraignment of American historians and an indictment of their ideals." Although he vowed to "let no searing of the memory by intolerable insult" distract him from a search for facts, he acknowledged that the "one fact" driving his analysis was that most recent historians of Reconstruction "cannot conceive Negroes as men." Reconstruction historiography was understandable, Du Bois contended, as the result of intersectional attraction to a lost cause and a romantic South. But it rested on a bedrock of "propaganda against the Negro since emancipation ... one of the most stupendous efforts the world ever saw to discredit human beings, an effort involving universities, history, science, social life and religion." Such writing demanded counterpropaganda in Du Bois's view, hence the irony in the title of his final chapter, "Propaganda of History".[45]

The idealist in Du Bois prompted him to argue that Reconstruction historiography had "spoiled and misconceived the position of the historian." If history were to be the proper guide for a better future, historians had to distinguish between "fact and desire." In almost the same breath Du Bois made an objectivist demand for the "things that actually happened" and a relativist appeal for the "philosopher and prophet . . . to interpret these facts." These "two functions" of the historian, as Du Bois described them, are precisely the same two he reserved for himself. Confronting a racist historical memory in America could not be accomplished by a mere separation of fact and desire. It demanded contextualism and relativism, the careful chronicler and the moral prophet. Du Bois tried to do both, but in the end, perhaps by necessity and temperament, he chose primarily the latter role.[46]

In the final pages of *Black Reconstruction* Du Bois turned aggressively to art to convey the stakes of contending historical memories. He portrayed the whole of black history from the slave trade through emancipation as a "magnificent drama" and a "tragedy that beggared the Greek." He likened this American epic to the upheavals of the Protestant Reformation and the French Revolution. Black people, he said, had "descended into Hell; and in the third century they arose from the dead, in the finest effort to achieve democracy for the working millions which this world had ever seen." This was a typical Du Boisian flight into hyperbole, but the resurrection imagery frames his angry disavowal of those American historians who had constructed the dominant memory of Reconstruction. So much had been missed; so much had been suppressed. The Civil War, black freedom, and the Reconstruction of the South, Du Bois seemed to be saying, ought to have been the epic of American democracy. "Yet we are blind," he declared, "and led by the blind." Du Bois would have agreed (albeit for different reasons) with Walt Whitman's famous caveat that "the real war will never get into the books." The art of constructing social memory, Du Bois understood, was not a benign process; it thrived on great contention, "with aspiration and art deliberately and elaborately distorted."[47]

The despairing tone of Du Bois's ending in *Black Reconstruction* probably reflected an honest sense of the obstacles this book, and any future revision of Reconstruction history, would face. It also represented

Du Bois's felt need to confront and provoke his fellow historians. He was not writing in 1935 as a typical professor inside the academy; he could not simply take his work to the American Historical Association's annual meetings, which were ironically raging at that time with debates over relativism and objectivity. Du Bois had to contend for American historical memory—for a new vision of the meaning of race and Reconstruction—with the weapons of language. He felt "so futile," he said, in confronting this task. Du Bois viewed the "truer deeper facts of Reconstruction with a deep despair." To him, it seemed an era of great lost opportunity in its own context and great misapprehension in the works of historians. Du Bois waxed nostalgic for the heyday of radical Reconstruction: "those seven mystic years between [President Andrew] Johnson's 'swing around the circle' and the panic of 1873" when Americans allowed themselves to believe in and experiment with racial equality (a yearning, for better or worse, shared by later revisionists during the modern Civil Rights movement). Such a season of hope he then juxtaposed with the "crash of hell" that followed in the late nineteenth century, a period of racial repression and organized forgetting.[48]

Du Bois ended the book with the image of a college teacher in an academic hall somewhere at the turn of the century. The teacher "looks into the upturned face of youth and in him youth sees the gowned shape of wisdom and hears the voice of God." "Cynically," the professor "sneers at 'chinks' and 'niggers.'" Then Du Bois placed the words of the historian John Burgess in the mouth of the teacher. The nation, announced the lecturer, "has changed its views in regard to the political relation of races and has at last virtually accepted the ideas of the South on this subject. The white men of the South need now have no further fear that the Republican party . . . will ever again give themselves over to the vain imagination of the political equality of man."[49] In this metaphoric classroom, with the actual words of a leading Reconstruction historian, Du Bois demonstrated that the real tragedy of Reconstruction was not in the history but in the histories. In this classroom, as in textbooks, in popular culture, and in historiography itself, white supremacy in the present remained secure as long as historical memories were controlled or suppressed. The hope embedded in Du Bois's tragic ending of *Black Reconstruction* is that when the marketplace for the construction of social memories becomes as free and open as possible, while still firmly guided by the rules of scholarship, then the politics of remembering and forgetting might be, here and there, overcome. Whether that was a vain hope or a realized ideal remains the principal challenge of all those seriously interested in American historical consciousness. This is especially true now in a time when public forums, and visual and electronic media, are so susceptible to demagogic leaders who play fast and free with history.

NOTES

This essay was originally delivered as a paper at a 1990 conference on history and memory in African American culture at Bellagio, Italy, and was published in *History and Memory in African-American Culture*, ed. Geneviève Fabre and Robert O'Meally (New York: Oxford University Press, 1994).

1. Martin Luther King Jr., "Honoring Dr. Du Bois," speech delivered at celebration of Du Bois's hundredth birthday, February 23, 1968, Carnegie Hall, New York, sponsored by *Freedomways Magazine*, in *W. E. B. Du Bois Speaks: Speeches and Addresses, 1890–1919*, ed. Philip S. Foner (New York: Pathfinder Press, 1970), 12–13, 15, 17, emphasis added; David Levering Lewis, *W. E. B. Du Bois: Biography of a Race, 1868–1919* (New York: Henry Holt, 1993), 280.

2. Many writers have stressed this dilemma. Among the most interesting works are the essays in *Commemorations: The Politics of National Identity*, ed. John R. Gillis (Princeton: Princeton University Press, 1994); and Charles S. Maier, "A Surfeit of Memory? Reflections on History, Melancholy, and Denial," *History and Memory* 5, no. 2 (fall–winter 1993): 136–51.

3. See *The Invention of Tradition*, ed. Eric Hobsbawm and Terrence Ranger (Cambridge, Eng.: Cambridge University Press, 1983); and Benedict Anderson, *Imagined Communities: Reflections on the Origin and Spread of Nationalism* (New York: Verso, 1991). Many theoretical works discuss historical memory as a process. Among the best are Frances A. Yates, *The Art of Memory* (Chicago: University of Chicago Press, 1966); Maurice Halbwachs, *The Collective Memory*, trans. Francis J. Ditter Jr. and Vida Yazdi Ditter (1950; reprint, New York: Harper and Row, 1980); Friedrich Nietzsche, "The Use and Abuse of History," in *The Use and Abuse of History*, trans. Adrian Collins (New York: Liberal Arts Press, 1949); Michel Foucault, *Language, Counter-Memory, Practice: Selected Essays and Interviews*, trans. and ed. Donald F. Bourchard (Ithaca: Cornell University Press, 1977); Peter Burke, "History as Social Memory," in *Memory: History, Culture, and the Mind*, ed. Thomas Butler (London: Blackwell, 1989), 97–113; *Memory in American History*, ed. David Thelen (Bloomington: Indiana University Press, 1991); Michael Kammen, *Mystic Chords of Memory: The Transformation of Tradition in American Culture* (New York: Knopf, 1991), 3–14; Pierre Nora, "Between Memory and History: Les Lieux de Memoire," *Representations* (spring 1989): 7–25; and Barry Schwartz, "The Social Context of Commemoration: A Study in Collective Memory," *Social Forces* (December 2, 1982): 374–402.

4. W. E. B. Du Bois, *Black Reconstruction in America: An Essay toward a History of the Part Which Black Folk Played in the Attempt to Reconstruct Democracy in America, 1860–1880* (New York: Atheneum, 1935), 725; all citations in this essay are to this

edition unless otherwise noted. On Du Bois, historical imagination, and conceptions of multiculturalism see Anita Haya Goldman, "Negotiating Claims of Race and Rights: Du Bois, Emerson, and the Critique of Liberal Nationalism"; Kathryne V. Lindberg, "W. E. B. Du Bois's *Dusk of Dawn* and James Yates's *Mississippi to Madrid* or What Goes Around Comes Around and Around and Around"; and Brook Thomas, "Schlesinger and Du Bois on the Old New World Order: A Prehistory of the Canon Wars," all in *Massachusetts Review* (summer 1994): 169–201, 283–308, 309–18.

5. Du Bois to Charles Francis Adams, November 23, 1908, and December 15, 1908, emphasis added; and C. F. Adams to Du Bois, November 28, 1908, all in W. E. B. Du Bois Papers, reel 1, University of Massachusetts, Amherst; Lewis, *Du Bois,* 469.

6. Du Bois to Richard Watson Gilder, undated, but collected among the 1909 letters, reel 1, Du Bois Papers.

7. Arnold Rampersad, "W. E. B. Du Bois as a Man of Literature," in *Critical Essays on W. E. B. Du Bois,* ed. William A. Andrews (Boston: G. K. Hall, 1985), 49–66; Arnold Rampersad, *The Art and Imagination of W. E. B. Du Bois* (Cambridge: Harvard University Press, 1976). See also Arnold Rampersad, "Slavery and the Literary Imagination: Du Bois's *The Souls of Black Folk,* " in *Slavery and the Literary Imagination,* ed. Deborah E. McDowell and Arnold Rampersad (Baltimore: Johns Hopkins University Press, 1989), 104–24. On Du Bois's broader literary impact, see Herbert Aptheker, *The Literary Legacy of W. E. B. Du Bois* (White Plains, N.Y.: Kraus International Publications, 1989). Every student of Du Bois is indebted to Aptheker for his compilations, bibliographies, and republications of Du Bois's work. See especially *The Annotated Bibliography of the Published Writings of W. E. B. Du Bois* (Millwood, N.Y.: Kraus-Thompson, 1973). Du Bois's "turn" toward art may also be explained as a persistence of romanticism, apparent from his earliest to some his latest writings. Hence, another way of looking at this change is that it was less a turn than an adaptation.

8. W. E. B. Du Bois, *The Autobiography of W. E. B. Du Bois: A Soliloquy on Viewing My Life from the Last Decade of Its First Century* (New York: International Publishers, 1968), 148; Lewis, *Du Bois,* 47; W. E. B. Du Bois, "My Evolving Program for Negro Freedom," in *What the Negro Wants,* ed. Rayford Logan (Chapel Hill: University of North Carolina Press, 1944), 43, emphasis added.

9. See Rampersad, "Du Bois as a Man of Literature," 62.

10. W. E. B. Du Bois, "Jefferson Davis as a Representative of Civilization," Commencement Address, Harvard University, 1890, in *W. E. B. Du Bois: Writings* (New York: Library of America, 1986), 811–14. On the commencement speech, see Nathan I. Huggins, "W. E. B. Du Bois and Heroes," *Amerikastudien* 34 (1988): 167–74. On Du Bois's race theory and its rootedness in nineteenth-century philosophy, see Anthony Appiah, "The Uncompleted Argument: Du Bois and the Illusion of Race," *Critical Inquiry* 12 (autumn 1985): 21–37; Robert Gooding-Williams, "Philosophy of History and Social Critique in the *Souls of Black Folk,*" *Social Science Information* 26 (1987): 99–114; and Joel Williamson, *Crucible of Race: Black-White Relations in the American South since Emancipation* (New York: Oxford

University Press, 1984), 399–413. It is also worth noting that, given his later stance about black participation in World War I, Du Bois himself also came to "love a soldier." Conversations with Wilson Moses were helpful on this point.

11. See Manning Marable, *W. E. B. Du Bois: Black Radical Democrat* (Boston: Twayne, 1986), 22–23; and Aptheker, *Literary Legacy*, 11–13. On the significance of the Berlin years, see Lewis, *Du Bois*, 117–49.

12. W. E. B. Du Bois, *The Suppression of the African Slave Trade to the United States of America, 1638–1870* (Cambridge: Harvard University Press, 1896), in *W. E. B. Du Bois: Writings*, 193. See James Ford Rhodes, *History of the United States from the Compromise of 1850*, 7 vols. (New York: Harper and Brothers, 1893–1906). Du Bois, *Suppression*, in *W. E. B. Du Bois: Writings*, 194. See also Rampersad, *Art and Imagination*, 68–90. On reconciliation and the rise of the Lost Cause mythology as well as resistance to it, see Paul S. Buck, *The Road to Reunion, 1865–1900* (New York: Little, Brown, 1937); Gaines M. Foster, *Ghosts of the Confederacy: Defeat, the Lost Cause, and the Emergence of the New South* (New York: Oxford University Press, 1987); Charles Reagan Wilson, *Baptized in Blood: The Religion of the Lost Cause, 1865–1920* (Athens: University of Georgia Press, 1980); and David W. Blight, "For Something beyond the Battlefield: Frederick Douglass and the Struggle for the Memory of the Civil War," *Journal of American History* (March 1989): 1156–78.

13. Nathan Irvin Huggins, "The Deforming Mirror of Truth," introduction to *Black Odyssey: The African American Ordeal in Slavery*, reissued ed. (New York: Vintage, 1990), xiii. Du Bois, *Suppression*, in *W. E. B. Du Bois: Writings*, 196–97.

14. W. E. B. Du Bois, *The Souls of Black Folk* (1903; reprint, New York: Signet, 1969), 45. On Du Bois and blacks as historical "outsiders," see Clarence E. Walker, "The American Negro as Historical Outsider, 1836–1935," *Canadian Review of American Studies* (summer 1986): 140–61. For critiques of "double consciousness" see the essays in *Lure and Loathing: Essays on Race, Identity, and the Ambivalence of Assimilation*, ed. Gerald Early (New York: A. Lane, Penguin Press, 1993).

15. Du Bois, *Souls of Black Folk*, 47.

16. John Edgar Wideman, introduction to *The Souls of Black Folk* (New York: Vintage Books, Library of America, 1990), xi, xv–xvi; Du Bois to William James, June 12, 1906, W. E. B. Du Bois Papers, reel 2; Jessie R. Fauset to Du Bois, Ithaca, N.Y., December 26, 1903, in *The Correspondence of W. E. B. Du Bois*, ed. Herbert Aptheker, 3 vols. (Amherst: University of Massachusetts Press, 1973), 1:66. On the reception and reviews of *Souls of Black Folk* across a wide racial and political spectrum, both in the United States and internationally, see Aptheker, *Literary Legacy*, 51–69; Eric J. Sundquist, *To Wake the Nations: Race in the Making of American Literature* (Cambridge: Harvard University Press, 1993), 481–84; and Lewis, *Du Bois*, 265–96. Two very interesting readings of *Souls of Black Folk* are Robert Gooding-Williams, "Du Bois's Counter-Sublime," and Dale E. Peterson, "Notes from the Underworld: Dostoevsky, Du Bois, and the Discovery of Ethnic Soul," both in *Massachusetts Review* (summer 1994): 202–24, 225–48.

17. Du Bois, *Black Reconstruction*, 726.

18. Friedrich Nietzsche, *The Birth of Tragedy* (1874; reprint, Garden City, N.Y.: Doubleday, 1956), 136. On memory in totalitarian societies, see Geoffrey A.

Hosking, "Memory in a Totalitarian Society: The Case of the Soviet Union," in *Memory*, ed. Butler, 115–30. On the importance of words in relation to power, see Vaclav Havel, "Words on Words," *New York Review of Books*, January 18, 1990, 5–8. On the significance of liberation through language in black writing from the slave narratives to the present, see Henry Louis Gates Jr, *Figures in Black: Words, Signs, and the Racial "Self"* (New York: Oxford University Press, 1987), 14–24; Houston A. Baker Jr., *The Journey Back: Issues in Black Literature and Criticism* (Chicago: University of Chicago Press, 1980), 33–46; and Robert B. Stepto, *From Behind the Veil: A Study of Afro-American Narrative* (Urbana: University of Illinois Press, 1979), 16–26. The stakes in debates over social memories are quite real: material resources, political power, and life chances. Language is not life, but it is one major component in how we contend for the meanings of and control over historical memories.

19. Paul Ricoeur, *Time and Narrative*, trans. Kathleen Mc Laughlin and David Pellauer (Chicago: University of Chicago Press, 1984), 1:21, 19; Steven Knapp, "Collective Memory and the Actual Past," *Representations* (special issue, spring 1989): 140; Frederick Douglass, "The Races," speech reprinted in *Douglass Monthly* (August 1859).

20. W. E. B. Du Bois, *The World and Africa: An Inquiry into the Part Which Africa Has Played in World History* (New York: Viking, 1947), 1–2; Du Bois, *Suppression*, in *W. E. B. Du Bois: Writings*, 196–97; W. E. B. Du Bois, *The Negro* (New York: Henry Holt, 1915); and Rampersad, *Art and Imagination*, 235.

21. Lewis, *Du Bois*, 277; Du Bois, *Souls of Black Folk*, xi. "The Conservation of Races" was first delivered for and published by the American Negro Academy, *Occasional Papers*, no. 2, Washington, D.C., American Negro Academy, 1897.

22. Yates, *Art of Memory*, 2–26, 31–36, 129–59, 199–230; Patrick H. Hutton, "The Art of Memory Reconceived: From Rhetoric to Psychoanalysis," *Journal of the History of Ideas* (July–September 1987): 376–92. On the idea of memory palaces or theaters, see Jonathan D. Spence, *The Memory Palace of Matteo Ricci* (New York: Viking, 1983), 1–22.

23. Rampersad, "Du Bois as a Man of Literature," 62; W. E. B. Du Bois, "The Spiritual Strivings of the Negro People," *Atlantic Monthly*, August 1897, 194–98; Du Bois, *Souls of Black Folk*, 250, 258. On Du Bois's writing style generally, see Rampersad, *Art and Imagination*, 33–41.

24. Pierre Nora, "Between Memory and History: Les Lieux de Memoire," *Representations*, no. 26 (spring 1989): 7–25; Du Bois, *Souls of Black Folk*, 96, 102–3.

25. Du Bois, *Souls of Black Folk*, 140, 146, 152, 156, emphasis added. The classic study of slavery at the turn of the century was Ulrich Bonnell Phillips, *American Negro Slavery* (New York: D. Appleton, 1906). On the idea of neoslavery, see Rampersad, "Slavery and the Literary Imagination," 113–14, 121–23.

26. Du Bois, *Souls of Black Folk*, 59.

27. Ibid., 68–69. Du Bois's use of the phrase "no man clasped the hands of these passing figures" is especially interesting because during the 1872 presidential campaign and for a long time thereafter, the slogan, "clasping hands across the bloody chasm" (referring to Union and Confederate veterans) became quite

popular. So far as I can tell, it was first popularized by Horace Greeley and the Liberal Republicans in the election of 1872. See William Gillette, *Retreat from Reconstruction, 1869–1879* (Baton Rouge: Louisiana State University Press, 1979), 56–72.

28. Du Bois, "The Damnation of Women," in *W. E. B. Du Bois: Writings,* 958 (originally published in Du Bois, *Darkwater* [New York: Harcourt Brace, 1920]).

29. Du Bois, *Black Reconstruction.* Edgar H. Webster to Du Bois, November 3. 1930; Du Bois to Webster, November 10, 1930; Du Bois to Harry Laidler, June 10, 1932; Du Bois to F. P. Keppel, Carnegie Corp., November 17, 1934, all in W. E. B. Du Bois Papers, reels 34, 37, 41. Du Bois received a $5,000 grant from the Rosenwald Fund, $1,250 from the Carnegie Foundation, and $500 as an advance from Harcourt, Brace. On Du Bois as historian, I am indebted to Clarence E. Walker, "Black Reconstruction in America: W. E. B. Du Bois' Challenge to the Dark and Bloody Ground of Reconstruction Historiography," a copy in manuscript provided by the author. On the origins, publishing history, and long-term significance of *Black Reconstruction,* see Aptheker, *Literary Legacy,* 211–56; and David Levering Lewis, introduction to Du Bois, *Black Reconstruction* (New York: Maxwell Macmillan, 1992). See also Jessie P. Guzman, "W. E. B. Du Bois—The Historian," *Journal of Negro Education* (fall 1961): 27–46; Ferrucio Gambino, "W. E. B. Du Bois and the Proletariat in Black Reconstruction," in *American Labor and Immigration History, 1877–1920s,* ed. Dirk Hoerder (Urbana: University of Illinois Press, 1983), 43–60; Paul Richards, "W. E. B. Du Bois and American Social History: The Evolution of a Marxist," *Radical History* (1970): 37–65; and Charles H. Wesley, "W. E. B. Du Bois, Historian," *Freedomways* (winter 1965): 59–72. For a discussion of Du Bois as historian that stresses his scholarly "isolation," see August Meier and Elliott Rudwick, *Black History and the Historical Profession, 1915–1980* (Urbana: University of Illinois Press, 1986), 5–6, 70–71, 279–80.

30. Du Bois, *Black Reconstruction,* 9–11. See Stanley Elkins, *Slavery: A Problem in American Intellectual and Institutional Life* (New York: University of Chicago Press, 1959). For an interesting reading of the relationship between Du Bois and Phillips, see John David Smith, "Du Bois and Phillips—Symbolic Antagonists of the Progressive Era," *Centennial Review* (winter 1980): 88–102.

31. Frederick Douglass, as quoted in Du Bois, *Black Reconstruction,* 14–15.

32. Du Bois, *Black Reconstruction,* 13, 715, 14, emphasis added.

33. Ibid., 717, 713.

34. Lewis, introduction to Du Bois, *Black Reconstruction* (1992).

35. Du Bois, *Black Reconstruction,* 124, 126.

36. W. E. B. Du Bois, *The Gift of Black Folk: The Negroes in the Making of America* (Boston: Stratford, 1924), i–ii; Du Bois, *The World and Africa,* 261. Some of the most interesting writing about multiculturalism has been in *Contention: Debates in Society, Culture, and Science.* See essays by David Hollinger, Gary B. Nash, Edward Berenson, Henry Louis Gates Jr., A. E. Barnes, and Todd Gitlin (spring 1992, fall 1992, winter 1993). The ways in which Du Bois's work serves as a model for current debates over multiculturalism is a theme I hope to develop more fully in later work.

37. Du Bois, *Black Reconstruction*, 713–14.

38. Ibid., 715–16. Here Du Bois's historical polemics is apparent. Indeed, it would be difficult for a black historian of his time to acknowledge the Confederate soldier's claim to be fighting for "liberty." But in their 1860s perspective, many southerners saw no contradiction between fighting to preserve a slave economy and for the principles of southern independence or self-determination. Memory is thus demonstrated to be a tricky and deeply political phenomenon.

39. Ibid., 716–17.

40. Ibid., 717. See Rhodes, *History of the United States;* and Claude G. Bowers, *The Tragic Era: The Revolution after Lincoln* (Boston: Houghton Mifflin, 1929).

41. Du Bois, *Black Reconstruction*, 721, 718–19. See John W. Burgess, *Reconstruction and the Constitution, 1866–1876* (New York: C. Scribner's Sons, 1902); and William A. Dunning, *Reconstruction: Political and Economic, 1865–1877* (New York: Harper and Row, 1907).

42. Burke, "History as Social Memory," 106–8; Hosking, "Memory in a Totalitarian Society," 118–19.

43. Du Bois, *Black Reconstruction*, 723.

44. W. E. B. Du Bois, "Confidential Memorandum Regarding the Significance of the Proposed Encyclopedia of the Negro," in *Against Racism: Unpublished Essays, Papers, Addresses, 1887–1961*, ed. Herbert Aptheker (Amherst: University of Massachusetts Press, 1985), 161.

45. Du Bois, *Black Reconstruction*, 727.

46. Ibid., 722. On Du Bois as moral prophet, see Rampersad, *Art and Imagination*, 91–115; and Marable, *W. E. B. Du Bois,* 190–217. On historians' relativism and the idea of historical truth, see Joyce Appleby, Lynn Hunt, and Margaret Jacob, *Telling the Truth about History* (New York: Norton, 1994), esp. 6–9, 241–70; Peter Novick, *That Noble Dream: The "Objectivity Question" and the American Historical Profession* (Cambridge, Eng.: Cambridge University Press, 1988), 164–67, 264–68, 282–91, 387–92; John Higham, with Leonard Krieger and Felix Gilbert, *History: The Development of Historical Studies in the United States* (Englewood Cliffs, N.J.: Prentice-Hall, 1965), 117–31; and Michael Kammen, *Selvages and Biases: The Fabric of History in American Culture* (Ithaca: Cornell University Press, 1987), 3–62.

47. Du Bois, *Black Reconstruction*, 727; Walt Whitman, "Specimen Days," in *Prose Works 1892*, ed. Floyd Stovall, 2 vols. (New York: New York University Press, 1963), 1:117.

48. Du Bois, *Black Reconstruction*, 728, 726. The great irony of Du Bois's despair is that by the 1960s (the "second Reconstruction" in America) the historiography of Reconstruction would come full circle to essentially Du Bois's vision. Inspired in part by Du Bois's work, the revisionists produced an enormous outpouring of "new" history about the Reconstruction era. Led by Kenneth Stampp, Willie Lee Rose, John Hope Franklin, Richard Current, and others, the revisionists reversed virtually every tenet of the traditional "hideous mistake" thesis. They tended to view the radicals as a complex lot who championed human rights but did not brutalize the South. The revisionists persuasively rehabilitated the carpetbaggers, demonstrated the growth of independent black institutions (family, schools, and

churches), illuminated the remarkable growth of black politics, and argued that Reconstruction as a whole was by no means a complete failure, and if it was, they were fond of quoting Du Bois's claim that it had been a "splendid failure" (*Black Reconstruction,* 708). Indeed, no field of American historiography became so active and explosive, and no traditional interpretation was so fundamentally overturned as that of Reconstruction. A half century after the publication of Du Bois's *Black Reconstruction,* Eric Foner portrayed the aftermath of the Civil War as a "massive experiment in interracial democracy without precedent in the history of this or any other country that abolished slavery in the nineteenth century." Foner's monumental effort at a coherent synthesis of this complex era was boldly organized around the theme of "the centrality of the black experience"; see Eric Foner, *Reconstruction: America's Unfinished Revolution* (New York: Harper and Row, 1988), xxiv–xxv. For the most complete collection of revisionist writings, see *Reconstruction: An Anthology of Revisionist Writings,* ed. Kenneth M. Stampp and Leon Litwack (Baton Rouge: Louisiana State University Press, 1969), a book dedicated in part to Du Bois. For two of the best among many historiographical essays on Reconstruction, see Bernard A. Weisberger, "The Dark and Bloody Ground of Reconstruction Historiography," *Journal of Southern History* (November 1959): 427–47; and Eric Foner, "Reconstruction Revisited," *Reviews in American History* (December 1982): 82–88.

49. Du Bois, *Black Reconstruction,* 726–28.

In Retrospect

Nathan Irvin Huggins, the Art of History, and the Irony of the American Dream

I find in the study of history the special discipline which forces me to consider peoples and ages, not my own. . . . It is the most humane of disciplines, and in ways the most humbling. For one cannot ignore those historians of the future who will look back on us in the same way.
—*Nathan Irvin Huggins*
When a boy had come, the friends had said, "now you have a son and a successor." But the son was no successor.
—*Oscar Handlin,* The Uprooted

"Whenever we write history," wrote Nathan Huggins in his final work, "we do so with a sense of transcendent meaning. No matter how limited or particular our study, we assume a broader and grander context in which what we say has meaning and makes a difference."[1] In such assumptions is rooted the maligned but enduring vision of history as art, as human story with emplotment and consequences, as narration that matters.

At heart Huggins was a historiographer in the broadest sense of that term, even a philosopher of history, a meditator on the shape and the meanings of American history. He was also, like his teacher Oscar Handlin, a great narrator. Huggins's storytelling, however, resisted closure and avoided endings, happy or otherwise. He was often perceived as a centrist integrationist on the sensitive issues at the heart of black studies as the field underwent its highly politicized birth and growth from 1970 through the 1980s. But a careful look at his writings reveals a scholar who wrestled in complex ways with the revolution that occurred in the study of Afro-American history and literature from the late 1960s to his death in December 1989. This essay is not a comprehensive appraisal of all Huggins's work; it assesses his historical and artistic vision by examining primarily his most imaginative book, *Black Odyssey: The African American Ordeal in Slavery,* and related essays.

Huggins's first book, a revision of his dissertation, *Protestants against Poverty: Boston's Charities, 1870–1900,* was, like all his later work, rich in irony and paradox, and levied a stern critique at the "moralism and self-indulgent mentality" of late nineteenth-century antipoverty reformers. Although this earliest book did not deal with black history (he avoided, or was urged to avoid, identification with the field early in his career), it did reveal an informed understanding of the social control impulse that motivated "genteel charity reformers." Moreover, *Protestants against Poverty* carefully demonstrated that, historically, poverty in America was a problem of social, not merely personal values, a theme that has remained at the center of our political culture from the Civil Rights era to the present. This work was written as Americans were discovering the "other America" and launching a "war on poverty," the ideas and contexts in which Huggins framed the book. Huggins's essential concern with Americans on the margins, while he consistently sought the nature of national history, would remain his scholarly project throughout his life. His *Slave and Citizen: The Life of Frederick Douglass,* written as a part of Oscar Handlin's Little, Brown series in American biography, was a concise but critical look at the abolitionist turned elder statesman. It richly surveyed the stages of Douglass's life and showed how much the black leader's thought and behavior were rooted, self-consciously, in his own experience—a journey from slavery to freedom to citizenship. Huggins re-created Douglass's story as a reflection of the nation's life in a dramatic era.[2]

Huggins was very much an empirical historian, interested especially in intellectual and social history, but he experimented with forms and style in imaginative ways, insisted on a broad self-consciousness about the craft among fellow historians, and probably enjoyed writing more than research. Huggins was not a historian's historian in the way, for example, John Hope Franklin or August Meier have been in the same field. He did not open new paths of scholarship with innovative methodologies as, for example, Leon Litwack, Lawrence Levine, or Sterling Stuckey did through folklore. His contribution to the new slavery historiography during the 1970s was an epic history aimed at a broad audience, not a major work of scholarship. He shunned ideology and theory, but at the same time he could admire the work of historians who were innovative in their use. With one compelling exception, *Harlem*

Renaissance, he did not produce pioneering monographs that continued to uncover and launch a new field.[3] Huggins entered the field of
African American history with, not before, the crest of revolutions in society and scholarship through which that field found extraordinary new
growth.

Above all, Huggins may have been at his best as a kind of epistemolo-
gist of African American history. He insisted that we could get beyond
race as professional scholars at the same time we probed the depths of
its meaning in American experience. He freely acknowledged that for
black scholars the black experience is often a matter of personal identification, just as in any other group or national experience. But it was the
intersections of multiple experiences that he found the most interesting, and the sheer excitement of history for Huggins may have been the
challenge of discovering just what was knowable or unknowable about
the past. "Black Americans, like the American nation itself," he wrote in
1983, "will be forever searching into the past to provide a sense of legitimacy and historical purpose, forever bound and frustrated in the effort." Huggins believed that American history, as broadly practiced, is
still far too driven by a sense of chosenness, special destiny, or the doctrine of progress. He kept calling for a chastened, more ironic, tragic
view of American history, with the African American story brought to
the center of a new history evolving from the conceptual and social revolutions of Huggins's own time. American dualities, indeed the dual
character of history itself, animated his writing. "We need to know how
and why we use history," he said, "to serve both our needs of personal
and group identity as well as for the more 'scientific' and humanistic
purposes of historical analysis. We should know the differences and not
confound them." That notion of what historians do compares well with
W. E .B. Du Bois's simple but poignant definition of history as "an art using the results of science." It also squares well with R. G. Collingwood's
conception of history as the "science of human nature." Collingwood
warned against the underestimation or misunderstanding of the role of
imagination in history. "The historical imagination . . . is properly not
ornamental but structural," wrote Collingwood. "Without it the historian would have no narrative to adorn. The imagination, that 'blind but
indispensable faculty' without which, as Kant has shown, we could never
perceive the world around us, is indispensable in the same way to history."[4] The structures of historical imagination come from the questions
we ask of the past. Huggins was one of those narrators who eschewed

adornment at the same time he searched for his own voice by exploring into the past. He tried to understand the epic quality of history without being trapped by its formulas.

Huggins loved the big questions. In his 1971 essay "Afro-American History: Myths, Heroes, and Reality," the lead piece in *Key Issues in the Afro-American Experience,* he tried to capture the meaning of that charged and formative moment in the history of this field. After surveying vast changes in American race relations since World War II, and especially during the sixties, he struck the chord of what was happening: "The crisis of the moment has always given rise to new and pressing questions. Thus, in our time, it is not sentiment, liberalism, humanitarianism, nor sudden enlightenment that has compelled historians to take a new look at the American past, but simply the demands of the American present."[5] Thus could Huggins distrust ideology, as I think he always did, and still comprehend its force in relation to events. And thus could he in 1971 denounce history that engages in mere fantasy and superficial mythmaking, and yet six years later write such a self-described "epic" history of the slave experience, a story that could be felt as much as comprehended. In *Black Odyssey* he told a great tale of human, indeed, mythic transcendence over evil, his own vision of the destructive unmaking and yet creative remaking of an African American people, a vision that shares much in outlook with Du Bois and with Ralph Ellison, and was clearly modeled on, and even a provocative response to, Handlin's *The Uprooted,* the epic history of European immigration.[6]

The times were changing, and so were the questions: What did it mean to be a slave? What happens to a culture torn from familiar terrain and ancient values, when it is scattered by an almost unimaginable process of violence into a new epoch? How could something so destructive as slavery produce a "new" people? What did God mean to African American slaves? How do people collectively transcend suffering? How did whole, culturally alive, people walk out of the valley of the dry bones that was slavery? How do we find the right language in our own voices to make sense of such bitter ironies and oppositions? How should the scholar with the desire to write self-consciously "epic" history take the fruits of a historiographical revolution and recast it into a broad narrative that both glides and instructs almost exclusively in his own voice (which is what Huggins attempted in *Black Odyssey*)? How, indeed, can present-day scholars best imagine themselves into the past and understand the "souls" of black folk or any other folk? Where should we locate the ethnic province of black art within the larger provincialism of American art? Is it or should it be an ethnic province at all? What is it about American history and society that has allowed (or compelled) Americans to always believe that they are "coming of age," that they continually must have a "renaissance" of their culture? What makes Americans remake themselves, or at least believe that they are? This was one of Alexis de Tocqueville's great observations; it passionately motivated Walt Whitman; Frederick Douglass couldn't live without the faith that he had remade himself; it informs a great deal of Langston Hughes's poetry; and it was one of the large questions Huggins was trying to test in *Harlem Renaissance*.[7] Big questions.

But there were even more. From the explosion of knowledge, methodology, and particularism of the final four decades of the twentieth century, how do we discern a new picture of the "whole" of American history? Is the whole even knowable anymore? Huggins always answered this question with an emphatic yes. And even broader: What about America as an idea? Is there such a thing? Does—should—America have a "master narrative" of its history? To this, he answered yes, but not with homilies of American exceptionalism. Black history, wrote Huggins in 1983, "is at once distinguishable, yet necessarily within the fabric." He had the boldness to generalize in our age of increasing fragmentation. But he did not want generalizations that would be mere summations or voiceless syntheses. His ambitious hope was that African American history would become one of the "building blocks of a new synthesis, a new American history."[8] Regarding the revolt against the very idea of generalization about America in the 1980s, Huggins seemed to be compelled by the same concern David Hollinger expressed when the latter wrote: "America. If there is such a thing, it would be a shame to miss it." Huggins also seemed to be governed by a maxim that Charles Beard made famous: it is better to risk being wrong about great questions than to be right about trivialities.[9]

If history is a science, Huggins was among those who believed it was a moral science. He distrusted determinism of all kinds, but he surely believed we were bound to levy moral judgments on the past and on ourselves. And he was profoundly concerned about the relationship of past and present, and with the consequences of how we use history. Among the oldest of clichés is that we study the past in order to comprehend the present. In Huggins's work, especially in his essays, one finds the wisdom that the reverse is equally true.

The three essays he published in 1971, 1983, and 1990 serve as a kind of index of the evolution of African American scholarship and especially of his own evolving vision. The 1971 essay ("Myths, Heroes, Reality") had several purposes. He wrote from the position of a scientific historian, describing the craft of history for a general audience, at the same time he tried to introduce a volume *(Key Issues in the Afro-American Experience)* that might open the new teaching field of Afro-American studies. Then he narrowed in on three targets: black cultural nationalism that sought self-esteem through learning about the black experience in isolation; the early 1970s void of teaching materials on black history; and the American mythology of special destiny and progress. Given the context of 1971, and the cycle we now find ourselves in decades later, Huggins's observations about the dangers of national myths of origin and hero-worship, whether fashioned by Homer, George Bancroft, or contestants in today's culture and curriculum wars, are especially telling. But even as he warned against the dangers of historical mythology, he treated the subject seriously and betrayed a personal fascination for it.[10]

"Integrating Afro-American History" acknowledged that the revolution had occurred, and the question was how best to ride its crest into the 1980s. Huggins celebrated the "broad and deep change in American historiography" since the 1960s in relation to the black experience. The 1983 piece joined a preoccupation, indeed virtually a genre, among American historians during the eighties: reflections on the fragmentation of the discipline and calls for a return to "narrative" and "synthesis" in the craft. Such essays, roundtables, and panels at conferences became, and in some ways remain, a staple of historians' increasingly self-conscious introspection about the impact of the new histories. The discipline in crisis, the inaccessibility of the new histories, the loss of audiences: all these issues animated historians' self-examination in the 1980s, and spilled out of their journals into the popular press. We have heard claims about the end of ideology, and more recently, the end of history. But in the eighties the problem facing thoughtful historians was the end of coherence. In 1981 Herbert Gutman lamented in the *Nation* that the understandable "stress on segments" in the new black, women's, or social histories had led to a "disintegration of coherent synthesis." His jeremiad left a striking impression as he invoked T. S. Eliot's *Waste Land* in order to describe American history as a "heap of broken images." In a paper delivered in 1984, and one of the most provocative and widely discussed of such essays, Thomas Bender argued that the way to a new narrative was in imagining a new "plot" for American history, rooted in the study of "public culture." Only this way, argued Bender, would all the newly illuminated "parts" find their way into an understanding of the "whole."[11] The "wholes and parts" debate continues to this day on curriculum committees, school boards, within academic departments, and in national politics. Some postmodernists tell us that the issue of fragmentation does not really matter—all narrative constructions simply struggle against all the others. Some scholars and the public jealously protect their "parts" from the conservative tendencies of synthesis, while many others keep seeking coherence within pluralism, a new way of talking about the whole. Jeremiads have always been easier to express than new covenants are to achieve.

In some ways, this was Huggins's favorite conceptual ground. It allowed him to play with ideas, to provoke from a pedagogical pose, or to speak right from the heart about how he perceived History with a capital H. The 1983 essay was full of historiographical optimism about all the new heterogeneity in American history; at the same time it insisted that we should all, especially African Americanists, imagine a new synthesis. He played with the metaphor of "latent strands" in a larger fabric, and since all these new, previously hidden, threads had come to the surface, the whole tapestry would now look very different. Such a metaphor may reflect the instincts of a cultural historian, and one who had just taken over the chairmanship of the Afro-American Studies Department at Harvard, but it was also precisely—in almost identical language—the same one Handlin employed in his introduction to *The Uprooted*. Writing at the beginning of the age of Reaganism, Huggins recognized that many calls for a return to synthesis were coming from "reactionary impulses," but he demanded that we not flinch, not let a new conservatism control the discourse about multiculturalism, and try, hard as it is, to write about a new whole. In a field forever charged with sensitive questions of agency and racial politics, Huggins left this enduring challenge: "In an important way the story is what history is about. We all need to be calling for a new narrative, a new synthesis taking into account the new history. It is especially important to Afro-American historians, unless we are content merely to work in an eddy of the larger stream." A serious, pluralistic new narrative of American history—one that can fully integrate race, gender, and class, at the same time that it accepts that nations, as political and cultural systems, still have knowable histories—is just what two generations of historians (in America and abroad) have been trying to construct. The 1983 essay, moreover, contained a confession that since his critique of historical mythology in 1971, he had come to "appreciate better how the mythic can suggest itself into the most scholarly work." What followed was a self-critique of *Black Odyssey*, a book he felt was never fully understood or appreciated.[12]

Black Odyssey is a book that cares deeply about the dead. It was a work with which some reviewers at the time did not know quite what to do. Was it history, or was it literature? Or was it something in between? Carl Degler refused to consider the work as history, preferring instead the category "emotional re-creation." Robert L. Harris found the book's lack of scholarly apparatus frustrating but admired its function as a "philosophical . . . excursion into the slaves' interior lives." Lawrence Powell criticized Huggins's lack of concreteness in explicating the dichotomy between tyranny and freedom in American history, but he too admired the author's ability to represent the "emotional truths" of slave experience. In a book so evocatively written, David Donald was, understandably, troubled by the lack of living characters and attention to chronology. Willie Lee Rose, though, admired the way Huggins had found an "honest" place in that marginal land between scholarship and popular history. She honored the way *Black Odyssey* might capture a broad audience at the peak of seventies interest in slavery by asking the "deeper," "harder," "elemental" questions about human bondage.[13] Virtually without quotation or citation, with no scholarly apparatus, Huggins attempted a modern Homeric epic retelling the story of slavery. There are elements of the romantic in the style. The prose is moving and provocative; sometimes it almost sings, and sometimes it is abstract. The story compels attention and reflection, and offers no ultimate resolution or happy ending. He wanted to reach a large reading audience, at the same time he was carefully using the fruits of seventies scholarship in slavery historiography. He wanted to "touch, wherever possible," he said, "the emotional and spiritual essence" of the slaves' experience. His intention was to "reach for the heart of a people whose courage was in their refusal to be brutes, in their insistence on holding themselves together." In such tones one can begin to see the influence of Du Bois on Huggins. Theodore Rosengarten, among others, picked up on this comparison, suggesting that *Black Odyssey* was written like a "meditation," a story "in the spirit of Du Bois, with a grasp for the whole and for the music in the most trying moments of life." Scholars from all disciplines still dispute in which genre or discipline Du Bois's *Souls of Black Folk* best belongs. The critic William Stanley Braithwaite once called *Souls of Black Folk* "a book of tortured dreams woven into the fabric of the sociologist's document." As a historian's document, *Black Odyssey* might be seen in the same light. Moreover, the literary historian Eric Sundquist argued that Du Bois's *Souls* should be understood for its "bardic function," a work of history as poetic remembrance. With differing degrees of success, Huggins, I think, aspired to the same function in *Black Odyssey*.[14]

The prose style and the epic reach of *Black Odyssey* owe much to *Souls of Black Folk*. Du Bois wrote about a different era than the one Huggins sought to re-create. But when Huggins laid out his argument most directly about black collective heroism and psychological transcendence, his writing sounded very much like Du Bois's poetic renderings of a world of "twoness" and racism that made assertions of "true self-consciousness" so difficult. Both books had a similar spirituality. At stake in Du Bois's most famous work and in *Black Odyssey* were the "souls" of people under enormous pressure and on the wrong side of power. Huggins argued that there were three great challenges to the "souls" of slaves: falling victim to "fear" of their oppressors; having their personalities fully compromised by "deception"; or giving in altogether to "hatred." Du Bois, likewise, had identified "tasteless sycophancy," "silent hatred," and in the most oft-quoted passage in Afro-American letters, "double consciousness" as the great risks and possible outcomes of the struggle to be black and American, living either under slavery or with its legacy. The sense of tragedy, the probing for legacies, the quest to know just how powerful the hold of the past is on the present, and the critique of "progress," all of which abound in *Souls of Black Folk,* are also dominant themes in *Black Odyssey.* The souls of slaves survived, Huggins argued, because they fashioned an ethical order out of their own humanity, because they learned how to "manage" fear in an unequal power relationship, and because they created a religion in which they found a home.[15]

Huggins's bold effort to capture a "triumph of the human spirit" over oppression was at once the result of his own research and an attempt to turn George Bancroft, Francis Parkman, the Stanley Elkins thesis, Margaret Mitchell, and a host of others on their heads. "To call our society by its proper name," wrote Huggins in the original introduction, "requires a radical reversal of perspective," a phrase, again, identical to that used by Handlin in the introduction of *The Uprooted.* Preoccupied with and determined to subvert the language of the founding fathers, the proper name Huggins chose for early America was "tyranny." And in his demonstration of the bitter ironies at the root of American history, he chose words used by John C. Calhoun in his defense of slavery to remind us that (in Huggins's words) "a government is no less a tyranny because a majority finds it convenient." Huggins aimed at the heart in more ways than one: *Black Odyssey* is his own attempt to expose and dissolve the central myth of American history, to seize the language of the founding fathers, to reappropriate, revise, indeed rewrite the story through the eyes, feelings, and experiences of African American slaves. The first four chapters of the book end with ironic twists and subtle plays on the language of "founders" and "pursuits of happiness." Huggins's story has no sugarcoating; at times it is a narrative of bleakness and destruction, slave ships without exits—for the slaves or for the readers. But it is a narrative where those excluded from Jefferson's language in the Declaration of Independence manage to take their fate as a material "resource" and convert that very language into their own moral or natural "resource." In Huggins's narrative, slaves become "immigrants" excluded from "the dream" at the founding, but a people irrepressibly at the center of America's "nationmaking."[16] This would not be mere reverse mythmaking or simply a new version of the doctrine of progress, which he had forcefully warned against in 1971. He did, however, take that risk.

Huggins got back to narrative—to words with music and meaning. Here is the ending of chapter 1, where he tries to capture the "rupture" of West Africans from their known world and their forced transplantation into a new universe: "As for those who were torn away to America, none would have willed it so. None, beforehand, could have imagined the awful agony to be endured—the separation from all that they were, the voyage into empty space, the trials of adjustment to a new life. Rudely forced, they were, nevertheless, destined to help create a new world, to become the founding fathers and mothers of a new people." Reaching for the psychological meaning of the African's experience in the slave trade, he tried to give it voice. Personal disasters can simply be part of life, says Huggins. "But what of that catastrophe that spins one outside the orbit of the known universe, that casts one into circumstances where experience provides neither wisdom nor solace? What if the common ground one shared with the sound and the infirm, the rich and the poor, the clever and the dull, the quick and the dead, fell away and one were left isolated in private pain with no known point of reference? Would not then the pain be the slightest of the miseries?" Huggins's notion of the slave trade as the "rupture" of peoples from one world into a new one borrows from and reconfigures Handlin's "disrupted" and "dislocated" immigrants. Handlin's voice near the end of *The Uprooted* makes an instructive comparison to Huggins's. "So Europe watched them go—in less than a century and a half, well over 35 million of them from every part of the continent. In this common flow were gathered up peoples of the most diverse qualities, people whose rulers had for centuries been enemies, people who had not even known of each other's existence. Now they would share each other's future." Huggins's narrative is bleaker; his immigrants are not heading for a "refuge." But both authors write a narrative of loss, stories about peasantries on journeys into "strangeness."[17]

Black Odyssey and *The Uprooted* are stories of migrations and transplantations of peoples on an epic scale. Both are concerned with notions of birthright and liberation, with the severing of Old World ties and the agony of New World beginnings, with dislocation and the alienation between generations, and with the "Americanization" of European and African cultures. In the kind of dialogue between the immigrant father and son with which Handlin concludes *The Uprooted,* one can see at least some of Huggins's inspiration. "America was the land of separated men," Handlin said of his immigrants; they were people both trapped and released by "a cataclysmic plunge into the unknown." Huggins's slaves are forced into a similar plunge, one where questions of degree are the important difference. The immigrant's journey through a sometimes permanent cultural and psychological disorientation becomes the slave's journey through death itself, through hopelessness to survival in a strange new land. The immigrant's fear becomes the slave's terror; the immigrant's "choice" and "opportunity" to venture into the unknown become, for Huggins's slaves, the fate of being "instruments of others' opportunity."[18]

Participants in current public debates over Afrocentric or Eurocentric perspectives on American history might do well to simply begin by reading chapter 1 of *Black Odyssey.* Here they will not find a search for cultural gems of beauty and brilliance to displace an agonizing present, no embrace or invention of roots for their own sake, not even individual heroes or heroines, but a determined attempt to re-create the pastness of the past, a world in which feudalism and pantheism met capitalism and individualism, where ancient tradition and parochialism faced uncontrollable and unimaginable change, worlds being unmade and re-made, a story of cultures smashed in a cruel filter but reforged in new forms, a narrative of social death and sometimes rebirth, hopes and dreams we call American seen through the lens of slavery, an unmistakable *uprooting*. Huggins's narrative is one not of adornment but of structure and plot. It is frustratingly abstract at times; the lack of chronological moorings and the absence of real historical persons and episodes remain bothersome. But as a narrative of migration, and one that tells the story of individual slaves' interior lives in relation to the national meanings of slavery, it reaches for a new "whole" that links the private and public dimensions of history. The story is hard medicine; it is epic and terrible, but romantic only in the form Huggins chose to tell it.

Less dazzling as literature perhaps than the novels set in slavery by Ishmael Reed, Toni Morrison, Shirley Anne Williams, or Charles Johnson, *Black Odyssey* is nevertheless full of literary strategies and instructive metaphors, and it ought to be read with equal care.[19] Today's new narrators would do well to have a look. Huggins's central aim was to represent, or re-create, the psychological and spiritual worldviews of slaves, which were the resources of their survival. And like the great slave narratives, which he was also in some ways rewriting, *Black Odyssey* is a narrative organized around the tragic doubleness of slaves' lives. Like the tales of Frederick Douglass, Harriet Jacobs, or Solomon Northup, Huggins's story juxtaposed destruction and creation, life and death, victory and loss, faith and hypocrisy, numbed resignation and peasant stoicism, victimization and transcendence, Africa and America.

Apart from the ways Handlin's *Uprooted* and Du Bois's *Souls of Black Folk* were models for *Black Odyssey*, there were other influences on the style and substance of Huggins's work. His life itself holds many keys to his approach to American history. Huggins was born in Chicago in 1927, the son of Winston J. Huggins, an African American who worked as a waiter and a railroad worker, and Marie Warsaw, an immigrant Polish American Jew. Huggins later remarked that this mixed racial parentage gave him "a keen sense of race rather early." His father left the family when Nathan was twelve years old. His mother moved the family, including his older sister, Kathryn, to San Francisco, where she died only two years later, leaving the teenage siblings on their own. The young Nathan postponed much of his own early education, working as a porter, warehouseman, and longshoreman to support himself and his sister. When he was drafted into the army near the end of World War II, he had not yet completed high school. He finished school in the service and later went to the University of California at Berkeley on the GI Bill.[20] Once, in a conversation about where, chronologically, one might begin a new course on the Civil Rights movement that he was organizing at Harvard, Huggins broke into wry laughter and told stories of his service in the war. As a guard for German prisoners of war being transported across the country, Huggins had been denied access, as a black man, to the segregated restaurants in which those German prisoners took meals. The black guard stood outside. To this listener, that story sounded like the perfect place to begin such a course, especially for a historian with his sense of irony. Huggins was a master conversationalist, and such was his favorite terrain: the bitterness of racial ironies in America, processed through metaphors of humor.

During the 1940s and 1950s Huggins learned a great deal about black religion and music from his adopted parents, Howard Thurman and Sue Bailey Thurman. Howard Thurman, a black minister and distinguished early scholar of the spirituals, helped the young man, Huggins later recalled, understand why "in those struggles between Good and Evil, Evil, true to life, triumphed more often than not." Huggins acknowledged Sue Bailey Thurman's "profound influence" on his youth, rearing him, he said in the acknowledgments of one of his books, "from the subjunctive to the declarative mood." At Berkeley in the mid-fifties, Huggins encountered Kenneth Stampp at the very time the latter was writing his *Peculiar Institution.* In Stampp's lectures, Huggins claimed, he found his first inspiration that there might be a different way to think about slavery and race in America. From these reminiscences we can get a sense of just how far we have come in the study of slavery since the days when, as a schoolboy, Huggins remembered being taught only a "rather sunny picture of slavery . . . about darkies sitting on a plantation, eating watermelons and singing songs."[21] When we talk about historiographical change, are we not really trying to find ways, as well, to help our students read a book like *Black Odyssey* against such a backdrop as the odyssey of Huggins's own life and that of others like him?

Deep in the well where Huggins gathered his sense of history there remains one further, if more distant, influence: William James. In a piece he wrote for a conference honoring Martin Luther King Jr. at the U.S. capitol in 1986, he asked his fellow historians, as well as the lay public, to take seriously the spiritual power of King's leadership. In assessing King's impact, Huggins wrote, he was struck at how, in our "secular age," scholars are so "poorly equipped to discuss the inner terrain of spirit and mind." In thinking about King, he said, he was "drawn again" to a reading of William James's *Varieties of Religious Experience.* Only by grasping the meaning of King's spiritual appeal and James's argument for why people need spirituality, Huggins concluded, would we understand the meaning of the Civil Rights movement itself. James's lectures on religion were so important, he said (citing three in particular: "The Divided Self," "Conversion," and "Saintliness"), because they do "not assume reason to be the norm, and non-rational experience to be in some sense perverse." Surely this was a guiding sensibility in *Black Odyssey:* in order to truly comprehend the travail of the slaves, in their death and rebirth across time and continents, he may have relied heavily on James's masterful, if agonizing, discussion of the "twice-born" soul, the person whose life and faith have been blinded and then sighted, lost and then found. Along with life itself, and an ever-closer look at African American history, Huggins may have found in James a further understanding of the persistence of evil in human nature, and a comprehension especially of the consequences of denying evil. There were many guides to understanding slave religion, but James may have helped when he wrote that the "completest religions would . . . seem to be those in which the pessimistic elements are best developed," and that "religions of deliverance" are where one finds such development.[22] It was on this level of consciousness that *Black Odyssey* attempted to speak for and about the slaves.

But James may have had an even wider influence on Huggins's thinking about history and pluralism, his love for the play of ideas and the testing of truths, and his insistent claim that no matter how multiple the parts, a whole story must still be told. The essential ingredients of pragmatism—a fierce defense of the freedom of the will; the effort through a kind of critical openness to steer a course somewhere between or around all determinism; and through the study of experience and its consequences, to find not only the links between past and present but also links between nature and the spirit, between science and religion— are all prevalent in Huggins's work.[23] He may have found some inspiration in James that allowed him to write with a realism that was not cynical, and a skepticism that was still spiritual.

In the introduction to the 1990 edition of *Black Odyssey* (the third of Huggins's historiographical essays), one finds perhaps his angriest piece of writing. Written as he was dying, it was a kind of last testament.

Although in some ways an uncompleted argument, the piece is a jeremiad about the whole age of Reaganism, the resurgent racism of the 1980s, and the social despair arising from the intractability of racial and economic problems in what he called the "backwash of the so-called Second Reconstruction." Huggins's final essay makes an interesting comparison to John Hope Franklin's *Color Line: Legacy for the Twenty-first Century,* a book of three essays characterized by a similar angry tone regarding the persistent racism of the 1980s and the roles of national leaders in sanctioning that racism. The new introduction to *Black Odyssey* was, moreover, a final broadside at one of Huggins's favorite targets: American historians' enduring attachment to a "master narrative" of providential destiny. Embedded in the middle of this polemic, however, is one of the clearest appraisals of the slavery historiography of the sixties and seventies, a great service indeed to the student and lay readership he was still eager to capture with this book. The essay directed us to works (Edmund Morgan's *American Slavery, American Freedom,* for example) that truly have amended the Bancroftian narrative, that have demonstrated how "American freedom finds its meaning in American slavery, whiteness and white power found their meaning in the debasement of blacks." Huggins may have underestimated just how much the Bancroftian paradigm has been dislodged. Eric Foner's master narrative of Reconstruction synthesized at least two generations of fundamental revision of a master narrative forged by the Dunning school, *Birth of a Nation, Gone with the Wind,* and decades of textbooks that recycled the tragic legend of the Civil War's aftermath. But as Huggins suggested, master narratives are not easily reshaped, however "deformed." Any new master narrative we may construct, Huggins challenged, must continue to explain the American paradox from the inside out, and not evade it. Furthermore, Huggins explained why the old master narrative continues to satisfy, how it feeds very real needs of national identity formation, why it continues as an abiding mythology of hope in spite of how reality contradicts it. But he will not let anyone off the hook. Nothing of real importance in American history ought be left in isolation, willfully quarantined, or jealously protected. "The challenge of the paradox is that there can be no white history or black history," he wrote, "nor can there be an integrated history that does not begin to comprehend that slavery and freedom, white and black, are joined at the hip."[24] In this idea of a new or different center, produced by contradiction, made by inclusiveness, and appreciative of deep ironies, new narratives and new textbooks are already being written.

The enigmatic title of this final essay, "The Deforming Mirror of Truth," lends itself to a variety of interpretations. But what seems truly deformed in the mirror Huggins constructed is the idea that history itself is going somewhere, that it has some particular end to which it proceeds, that out there on that next hill, just beyond the horizon there may be a national rendezvous at El Dorado. Huggins suggested that the deformed images in the mirror are not the end of mythology or ideology; they are not at all the end of hope either, temporal or spiritual. But they might be images that can help us approach American history as something not only felt, but faced. What he suggested in the unforgettable epilogue of *Black Odyssey* is, in effect, that we need to use our imaginations in order to go back and meet the ghosts of the past, that we should be drawn back to sit in the ugliest corner of the slave ship that landed at Jamestown in 1619 and there read the first two paragraphs of Jefferson's Declaration of Independence. Moreover, in order to understand why generations of immigrants of all colors became attached to something called an American dream, we should read Frederick Douglass on the meaning of the Fourth of July to the slaves. And finally, in order to ultimately find our replacement narrative for the Bancroftian paradigm, we will have to root it in contradiction and irony and not flee from them, and we will have to root it in all the uprooted.[25]

NOTES

This essay was originally delivered at a conference dedicating the Nathan Irvin Huggins Library for American Studies at Palacky University, Olomouc, Czech Republic, March 19–21, 1993, and was published as a retrospective feature in *Reviews in American History* (spring 1994). It is reprinted here with minor revisions. For their criticisms and encouragement, I thank Josef Jarab, rector of Palacky University, Randall Burkett, Christopher Clark, Maria Diedrich, Geneviève Fabre, Jeffrey Ferguson, Henry Louis Gates Jr., Brenda Huggins, Michael Kammen, Stanley Kutler, Lawrence Levine, Leon Litwack, Berndt Ostendorf, Alesandro Portelli, Richard Sewell, and Werner Sollors. I especially thank Werner Sollors for allowing me access to the original manuscript of Huggins's final work, "The Deforming Mirror of Truth," which became the introduction of the new edition of *Black Odyssey*, and Larry Levine and Leon Litwack for their inspiration.

1. Nathan Irvin Huggins, *Black Odyssey: The African American Ordeal in Slavery* (New York: Vintage, 1990), xvi–xvii. All citations in this essay are from the 1990 edition.

2. Nathan Irvin Huggins, *Protestants against Poverty: Boston's Charities, 1870–1900* (New York: Greenwood Press, 1971), 3, 201; and Nathan Irvin Huggins, *Slave and Citizen: The Life of Frederick Douglass* (Boston: Little, Brown, 1980).

Protestants against Poverty was published in the Greenwood series, Contributions in American History, ed. Stanley I. Kutler and intro. Oscar Handlin.

3. Nathan Irvin Huggins, *Harlem Renaissance* (New York: Oxford University Press, 1971). This book is still one of the most original and oft-cited works on that pivotal era in black cultural history. For a critique of *Harlem Renaissance*'s significance, see Lawrence W. Levine, "The Historical Odyssey of Nathan Irvin Huggins," *Radical History Review* 55 (winter 1993): 113–32. Levine's essay was originally delivered as a lecture in the John Hope Franklin Distinguished Lecture series at Adelphi University, February 5, 1992, and is a source of important information for my own essay. Works Huggins edited or coedited include, *Key Issues in the Afro-American Experience*, ed. Huggins, Martin Kilson, and Daniel M. Fox, 2 vols. (New York: Harcourt Brace Jovanovich, 1971); and *Voices from the Harlem Renaissance*, ed. Huggins (New York: Oxford University Press, 1976). Huggins's career and scholarship are also discussed in August Meier and Elliott Rudwick, *Black History and the Historical Profession, 1915–1980* (Urbana: University of Illinois Press, 1986), 124, 127–28, 177, 224, 285; and Peter Novick, *That Noble Dream: The "Objectivity Question" and the American Historical Profession* (Cambridge, Eng.: Cambridge University Press, 1988), 490–91.

4. Nathan Irvin Huggins, "Integrating Afro-American History into American History," in *The State of Afro-American History: Past, Present, and Future*, ed. Darlene Clark Hine (Urbana: University of Illinois Press, 1986), 166; W. E. B. Du Bois, *Black Reconstruction in America, 1860–1880* (New York: Atheneum, 1935), 714; R. G. Collingwood, *The Idea of History* (Oxford: Clarendon Press, 1946), 241. For an essay that shares much in content, argument, and mutual influence with Huggins's critique of the myth of American chosenness and the doctrine of progress, see Leon F. Litwack, "Trouble in Mind: The Bicentennial and the Afro-American Experience," *Journal of American History* 74 (September 1987): 315–36.

5. Nathan I. Huggins, "Afro-American History: Myths, Heroes, Reality," in *Key Issues*, ed. Huggins, Kilson, and Fox, 1:8.

6. Oscar Handlin, *The Uprooted: The Epic Story of the Great Migrations That Made the American People* (Boston: Little, Brown, 1951). For responses to the 1990 edition of *Black Odyssey*, see Peter H. Wood, Peter Dimock, and Barbara Clark Smith, "Three Responses to Nathan Huggins's 'The Deforming Mirror of Truth,'" *Radical History Review* 49 (winter 1991): 49–59; and Levine, "The Historical Odyssey of Nathan Irvin Huggins," 121–23. Wood in particular drew attention to the comparison of *Black Odyssey* to *The Uprooted*. For Ellison's historical vision, see the essays in Ralph Ellison, *Going to the Territory* (New York: Random House, 1986).

7. In the 1979 Festschrift for Oscar Handlin, Richard Bushman commented at length on how Handlin taught through "the power of his questions" and how a book like *The Uprooted* was infused with the idea that "irony lies at the very heart of history and life." However much Huggins may have come to dislike Handlin's growing conservatism over the years, both these notions were surely methods or principles by which he taught and wrote. See *Uprooted Americans: Essays to Honor Oscar Handlin*, ed. Richard L. Bushman et al. (Boston: Little, Brown, 1979), xii–xiii.

8. Huggins, "Integrating Afro-American History into American History," 159.

9. David A. Hollinger, "American Intellectual History: Some Issues for the 1980s," in *In the American Province: Studies in the History and Historiography of Ideas* (Bloomington: Indiana University Press, 1985), 182. Beard is quoted in Michael Kammen, "Vanitas and the Historian's Vocation," in *Reviews in American History* 10 (December 1982): 17. The actual quotation is from a letter, Beard to August C. Krey, January 30, 1934, Krey Papers, University of Minnesota: "It is better to be wrong about something important than right about trivialities." On the whole question of generalization and new synthesis, the literature is huge and scattered. But to begin, especially in relation to cultural history, see Michael Kammen, "Extending the Reach of American Cultural History: A Retrospective Glance and a Prospectus," in *Salvages and Biases: The Fabric of History in American Culture* (Ithaca: Cornell University Press, 1987), 118–53.

10. Huggins, "Afro-American History: Myths, Heroes, Reality," 9–16.

11. Huggins, "Integrating Afro-American History," 157; Herbert G. Gutman, "The Missing Synthesis: Whatever Happened to History?" *Nation*, November 21, 1981, 521, 553–54; Thomas Bender, "Wholes and Parts: The Need for Synthesis in American History," *Journal of American History* 73 (June 1986): 120–36. Discussions of getting back to narrative in the 1980s were many, but see Bernard Bailyn, "The Challenge of Modern Historiography," *American Historical Review* (February 1982): 125; Thomas Bender, "The New History Then and Now," *Reviews in American History* 12 (December 1984): 612–22; Eric H. Monkkonen, "The Dangers of Synthesis," *American Historical Review* (December 1986); "Roundtable on Synthesis," *Journal of American History* (June 1987); "Roundtable: What Has Changed and Not Changed?" *Journal of American History* (September 1989).

12. Huggins, "Integrating Afro-American History," 159–60, 164–65; Handlin, *Uprooted*, 3. That self-critique also included an interesting comparison of *Black Odyssey* to Vincent Harding's *There Is a River: The Black Struggle for Freedom in America* (New York: Harcourt Brace Jovanovich, 1981). On the lack of appreciation for *Black Odyssey*, see Levine, "The Historical Odyssey," 121. Huggins's belief that the book had never been fully understood or appreciated is a point he also made to me in conversations after the 1989 Organization of American Historians meeting in Saint Louis, where he had just delivered a talk in honor of John Hope Franklin's *From Slavery to Freedom*. I once asked him if he had ever been chided or challenged for using a line from F. Scott Fitzgerald's *Great Gatsby* to end *Black Odyssey*, one of the rare quotations in the entire book. He answered simply, "No one ever asked."

13. Carl Degler, "Experiencing Slavery," *Reviews in American History* 6 (September 1978): 277–82; Robert L. Harris, book review, *American Historical Review* 83 (December 1978): 1095–96; Lawrence N. Powell, book review, *Journal of Southern History* 44 (November 1978): 630–31; David Herbert Donald, "A People's Experience," *New York Times Book Review*, December 11, 1977, 10; Willie Lee Rose, "A History of Endurance," *New York Review of Books*, January 26, 1978, 24. In her review, Rose made a point of comparing *Black Odyssey* to *The Uprooted*.

14. Huggins, *Black Odyssey*, lxxii, lxxiv; Theodore Rosengarten, book review,

New Republic, November 5, 1977, 33. For Braithwaite and Sundquist quotations, see Eric J. Sundquist, *To Wake the Nations: Race in the Making of American Literature* (Cambridge: Belknap Press, Harvard University Press, 1993), 482–83.

15. W. E. B. Du Bois, *The Souls of Black Folk* (1903; reprint, Boston: Bedford Books, 1997), 44–45; Huggins, *Black Odyssey,* 180–82.

16. Huggins, *Black Odyssey,* xlv, lxxiii–lxxiv, 24, 56, 84, 113; Handlin, *Uprooted,* 3.

17. Huggins, *Black Odyssey,* 24, 26; Handlin, *Uprooted,* 35–36, 39.

18. Handlin, *Uprooted,* 304–5; Huggins, *Black Odyssey,* 84.

19. Ishmael Reed, *Flight to Canada* (New York: Random House, 1976); Toni Morrison, *Beloved: A Novel* (New York: Knopf, 1987); Sherley Anne Williams, *Dessa Rose* (New York: Morrow, 1986); Charles Johnson, *Oxherding Tale* (Bloomington: Indiana University Press, 1982); and Charles Johnson, *Middle Passage* (New York: Atheneum, 1990). On this trend of black authors to write novels about the slavery period, see *Slavery and the Literary Imagination,* ed. Deborah E. McDowell and Arnold Rampersad (Baltimore: Johns Hopkins University Press, 1989). Critic Henry Louis Gates Jr. has termed this genre the "slave narrative novel." See "The Language of Slavery," introduction to *The Slave's Narrative,* ed. Charles T. Davis and Henry Louis Gates Jr. (New York: Oxford University Press, 1985). In this sense Huggins's *Black Odyssey* might be seen as slave narrative history.

20. The biographical details are taken from George Howe Colt, "Will the Huggins Approach Save Afro-American Studies?" *Harvard Magazine* 43 (September–October 1981): 43–44. On Huggins's biographical background, see also Levine, "The Historical Odyssey," 114–15.

21. Colt, "Will the Huggins Approach Save Afro-American Studies?" 43. Huggins's *Harlem Renaissance* is dedicated to Sue Bailey Thurman. In his bibliography for *Black Odyssey,* Huggins made special mention of Howard Thurman's *Deep River: Reflections on the Religious Insight of Certain Negro Spirituals* (New York: Harper, 1955), *The Negro Spiritual Speaks of Life and Death* (New York: Harper, 1947), and *Jesus and the Disinherited* (New York: Abingdon-Cokesbury, 1949).

22. Nathan I. Huggins, "Martin Luther King, Jr.: Charisma and Leadership," *Journal of American History* 74 (September 1987): 479–80; William James, *The Varieties of Religious Experience* (New York: Library of America, 1990), 154–76.

23. See William James, *Pragmatism,* ed. Bruce Kuklick (Indianapolis: Hacket Publishing, 1981), xii–xiv. Especially important on the question of wholes and parts in history would be William James, "The One and the Many," the fourth lecture on pragmatism, in *Pragmatism,* 61–74.

24. Huggins, *Black Odyssey,* xlviii, xliii, xliv; John Hope Franklin, *The Color Line: Legacy for the Twenty-first Century* (Columbia: University of Missouri Press, 1993); Edmund Morgan, *American Slavery, American Freedom* (New York: Norton, 1975); Eric Foner, *Reconstruction: America's Unfinished Revolution* (New York: Harper and Row, 1988). Huggins's use of the "joined at the hip" metaphor reflects his appreciation of Mark Twain's novel about miscegenation, *Puddin'head Wilson* (1894), a book Huggins insisted belonged in tutorials and introductory courses in Afro-American studies.

25. Huggins, *Black Odyssey*, 243–46. On "The Deforming Mirror of Truth," the introduction to the 1990 edition, see Wood, Dimock, and Smith, "Three Responses," 49–59. Wood insightfully implies that Huggins's challenge in this essay will make postmodernists and conservative defenders of national mythology equally nervous.

Epilogue
The Riddle of Collective Memory and the American Civil War

How do we know a "collective memory" when we meet one? What constitutes a memory community or a memory group? These are elusive, but essential, questions in understanding history's relationship to memory. Svetlana Boym, a scholar of nostalgia, aptly called collective memory "a messy, unsystematic concept." It is nevertheless indispensable to understanding how people comprehend themselves in time. Collective memories, Boym wrote, provide the "common landmarks of everyday life." Instinctively and empirically, we know that memory has a powerful social dimension; contending social memories explode in our faces nearly every day somewhere in the world, on the streets in unstable countries, or in debates over commemorative sites and the creation of new museums in nations at relative peace with themselves. Historians ignore the social power of memory at their peril. Pierre Nora defined collective memory as "what remains of the past in the lived reality of groups, or what these groups make of the past." That process of *making* collective memories goes on every day in all societies. Individual memory is much easier to discern, and even seems more reliable. But as a historian of the memory of World War I, Jay Winter argued that collective memory should be seen as the "heart of a matrix," a set of practices and ideas embedded in a culture, members of which learn how to decode such practices and ideas and use them to forge identities. Winter warned that national memory and collective memory are not the same thing. "Nations do not remember," he wrote, "groups of people do. Their work is never singular and is never fixed."[1] Indeed, the collective memory of any community, especially in democratic societies, is always contested and in transition. Collective memories may be troublesome and multiple, and the plots and narratives they foster are contradictory. But they are the cultural frameworks, conscious or not, that give shape and meaning to our lives.

Such has surely been the case with America's struggle to forge collective memories of the Civil War. Nations may not remember, but they are the evolving creations of high stakes contests between groups that do remember and contend to define the past, present, and future of national cultures. Is the United States the nation that preserved itself in the War between the States, or the republic that reinvented itself in a war that destroyed racial slavery and expanded freedom and equality? Was the war a terrible bloodletting on the way to a better, more unified nation ready to play its appointed role in world affairs? Or was the war a deep national tragedy, the meaning of which is embedded in many different group memories—those of defeated white southerners, victorious white northerners, black former slaves, the descendants of free blacks, or European immigrant groups who made up significant percentages of the Union armies? Indeed, who owns the memory of the Civil War? Is it those who wish to preserve the sacred ground of battlefield parks for the telling of a heroic narrative of shared military glory on all sides? Or is it professional historians with academic training, determined to broaden the public interpretation of Civil War sites to include slavery, social history, women, and home fronts? Should the master narrative of the American Civil War be an essentially reconciliationist story of mutual sacrifice by noble men and women who believed in their equal versions of the right? Or should that master narrative be a complex, pluralistic story of sections and races deeply divided over the future of slavery, free labor, and the character and breadth of American liberty? If everyone fought for "liberty" in the Civil War, then whose collective memory of the struggle should have a privileged place in textbooks, films, and on the landscape of memorialization? Indeed, whose claims to "liberty" prevailed?

Just by asking these questions we see how contested the memory of the Civil War can be. Answers to such questions depend, of course, on historical contexts, on shifting historical interpretations, and on who controls the mediums and access to historical memory. Collective memories are instruments of power in all modern societies. They are wielded for political ends, to shape social policy, and for control of the historical narratives in which people understand themselves. As the southern poet Robert Penn Warren suggested on the occasion of the Civil War centennial in 1961, "the Civil War draws us as an oracle, darkly unriddled and portentous, of personal, as well as national fate."[2] As it was in 1961, so it is in 2001: our fates are still linked to how we remember and interpret the Civil War. To understand the riddle of history's fascinating confluence with memory and with Americans' recurring encounter with the meaning of their most divisive event, we should continue to make memory that power we think *about* as much as *with*. And we should preserve, visit, and study our Civil War battlefields. Then we should lift our vision above the horizon, beyond those alluring landscapes, and ponder all the unfinished questions of healing and justice, of causes and consequences, of racial disharmony that still bedevil our society and our historical imagination.

NOTES

1. Svetlana Boym, *The Future of Nostalgia* (New York: Basic Books, 2001), 53–54; Pierre Nora, quoted in Jacques Le Goff, *History and Memory*, trans. Steven Rendall and Elizabeth Claman (New York: Columbia University Press, 1992), 95; and Jay Winter, "Film and the Matrix of Memory," *American Historical Review* 106 (June 2001): 863–64.

2. Robert Penn Warren, *The Legacy of the Civil War* (1961; reprint, Cambridge: Harvard University Press, 1983), 102.

Index

Aitken, Alexander, 62
Alexander, Edward Porter, 178
Allen, George, Jr., 154
Allen, Richard, 202
American Anti-Slavery Society (New York City), 39
American Historical Association, 250
American Revolution (Civil War as second), 29, 37–38, 48–49, 79–84, 93, 98, 113, 133, 139, 157, 187, 188
American Slavery, American Freedom (Morgan), 272
Amherst College, 246
amnesia. *See* forgetting
Anderson, Benedict, 126, 224–25
Anderson, Robert, 184, 185
Andersonville, 109
Andrews, William, 15, 26n. 5, 45
The Annals of the American Academy of Political and Social Science, 199
Anthony, Andrew, 19
Antietam battle, 55
antislavery movement. *See* abolitionism
apartheid. *See* Jim Crow
Appeal to the Colored Citizens of the World (Walker), 31
Appomattox (Virginia), 185; South's surrender at, 121, 162, 173, 217
Aptheker, Herbert, 252n. 7
Arlington National Cemetery, 96
Armstead, Mary D., 37
Armstrong, Samuel, 178
Army of the Potomac, 55, 72n. 5, 73n. 21, 140
art. *See* films; language
Arthur, Chester A., 106
"Ashokan Farewell" (song), 212–13
Association for the Study of Negro Life and History, 193
Atlanta (Georgia), 82, 110, 174, 204, 227
Atlanta Constitution, 145–46
Atlanta News, 194

Atlanta University Studies, 230
Attucks, Crispus, 205
Augusta (Georgia), 194
Augustine (saint), 2, 13
Auld, Sophia, 20
Auld, Thomas, 19, 21
Auld house (Saint Michaels, Maryland), 11
autobiography: accuracy vs. truth in, 13; Americans' fascination with, 13, 16; Douglass's, 11–27, 97, 241; Du Bois's, 227; as historical sources, 17–19; James Weldon Johnson's, 195–96. *See also* slave narratives
Autobiography of an Ex-Colored Man (Johnson), 195–96, 207

Bachelder, John, 177
Bailey, Betsy, 11, 12
Bailey, Frederick, 11. *See also* Douglass, Frederick
Bailey, Harriet, 11
Baker, Ray Stannard, 199
Baldwin, James, 13, 120
Ball, Charles, 47
Ballou, Mrs. Sullivan, 216
Baltimore (Maryland), 12, 20, 23, 48
Baltimore Afro-American Ledger, 143
Bancroft, George, 263, 266, 272, 273
Barnes, Mrs. James, 54
Barringer, Paul B., 131–32
Battery Wagner. *See* Fort Wagner
battlefields, 70, 71, 279; mapping of, 177, 178; and problems of Civil War memory, 170–90. *See also* Blue-Gray reunions; *specific battlefields*
Beard, Charles, 240, 262
Beasley, David, 153–54
Beauvoir, Simone de, 13
Beckwith, Mrs. S. C., 187
Beecher, Henry Ward, 184

Beer, Thomas, 156

Bellows, Barbara L., 102

Beloved (Morrison), 13, 14, 104–5

Bender, Thomas, 264

Ben Hur (Wallace), 180

Benjamin, Walter, 3

Bennett, A. G., 183

Bibb, Henry, 31, 35

Bible, 46–47, 113, 187, 243

Bierce, Ambrose, 53, 63

Bingham, Caleb, 77

biography, 76–90, 212. *See also* autobiography

Birth of a Nation (film), 128, 218,
272

Black, J. C. C., 194

black degeneration. *See* freedom: ex-
slaves as unable to cope with

Black Odyssey (Huggins), 259, 261,
265–73

Black Reconstruction in America (Du
Bois), 112–13, 145–46, 157,
225–26, 239–51

blacks. *See* African Americans

black studies, 258, 263, 264

"The Black Worker" (Du Bois), 240

Blaine, James G., 69

Blake, Walter H., 136, 137

Blight, David W., ix

"Blow Ye the Trumpet, Blow" (song),
200

Blue-Gray reunions, 103; African
Americans' place at, 127, 136–37,
141, 150n. 25, 181–82; alternatives
to, 237–38; black responses to,
142–44, 182–83; Brewster's attendance at, 70; in Burns's Civil War
documentary, 121–23, 125, 217; as
ritual of national reconciliation,
127, 134–46, 161, 177–83. *See also*
reconciliation

Blyden, Edward, 93

Boritt, Gabor, 216

Boston (Massachusetts): abolitionism
in, 39; and Boston Massacre, 40;

Bunker Hill centennial in, 178;
Emancipation Day in, 200; fugitive
slave rescues in, 36; monuments to
Robert Shaw and Fifty-fourth Massachusetts in, 151n. 38, 153–69. *See
also* Camp Meigs

Boston Daily Evening Traveler, 176–77

"Boston Hymn" (Emerson), 200

Boston Massacre, 40

Bowers, Claude, 128, 246

Boym, Svetlana, 278

Boy Scouts of America, 137

Bradley, David, 117n. 19

Braithwaite, William Stanley, 266

bravery. *See* courage and honor

Brewster, Charles Harvey, 53–75

Brewster, Harvey, 55

Brewster, Martha (Charles Harvey
Brewster's sister), 55–56, 62, 70

Brewster, Martha Russell (Charles
Harvey Brewster's mother), 55–57,
59, 60–61, 66, 67, 70

Brewster, Mary (Charles Harvey Brewster's sister), 55–58, 62, 70

Brewster, Mary Katherine (Charles
Harvey Brewster's daughter), 70

Briggs, George N., 54–55

Briggs, Henry S., 54

Bristow Station battle, 55

Brooklyn Daily Eagle, 142

Brown, John, 200, 233; Harpers Ferry
raid of, 37, 42, 43–44, 47, 82, 129,
205. *See also* "John Brown's Body"
(song)

Brown, Tom, 167n. 2

Brown, William Wells, 31

Brown vs. Board of Education, 134

Bruce, Blanche K., 93

Buck, Paul H., 100, 144–45, 190n. 29

Bunker Hill centennial, 178

Burgess, John W., 246–47, 250

Burns, Anthony, 36

Burns, John, 175

Burns, Ken, 121–24, 182, 211–20

Burroughs, Charles, 205

Douglass, Frederick, 40, 200, 205, 232, 262, 273; on antebellum fears, 48; autobiographical art of, 11–27, 269; banquets in honor of, 93–95; biographies of, 259; in Burns's Civil War documentary, 124; busts of, 202; and Crummell, 127, 128–29, 132–33, 144; Du Bois on, 241; on emigration, 41; as fugitive slave, 31, 133; Lincoln's relationship with, ix, 76–90; on the meaning of the Civil War, x, 30, 48–49, 93–119, 155, 159, 171, 187–88, 245; on memory, 11; newspaper of, 96; on racism, 86, 95, 98, 102, 106, 107–8, 130–31, 233; on resistance to slavery, 33, 38; shoe company named for, 202; and Underground Railroad, 50n. 12. *See also specific works by*

Douglass, Lewis, 133

draft laws, 59

Dred Scott decision (1857), 32, 39–40, 47

Du Bois, W. E. B., ix, 129, 149n. 22, 157, 161, 199–201, 261, 266; and American historical memory, 223–57; "double consciousness" concept of, 202, 230–32, 266, 269; on emancipation observances, 197, 198, 204–8; historical sources used by, 242–43; on history, 145–46, 260; as influence on Huggins, 265–66, 269; King on, 223; on Lincoln, 78, 82; on the meaning of the Civil War, 28, 93, 112–13, 151n. 38; pageants written by, 152n. 41, 205–6; on race problem, 125, 174, 191; satires by, 207–8. *See also specific works by*

Dunbar, Paul Laurence, 153, 166

Dunning, William A, 246, 247, 272

dysentery. *See* disease

Early, Jubal, 102

"Easter-Emancipation, 1863–1913" (Du Bois), 206

Easton (Maryland), 11

Edwards, Thomas, 199

Egypt, 47

"1883 Civil Rights Cases," 95

Eliot, T. S., 263

Elkins, Stanley, 240, 266

Ellison, Ralph, 17, 67, 128, 223, 261

emancipation (of African American slaves), ix; Burns on, 124; Douglass on, 24, 49, 84–88, 94, 98, 100, 106, 111–12; Du Bois on, 249; emergence of, during Civil War, 30, 65, 78–79, 81, 82, 87–88, 111, 146, 200; Frémont's proposal for, in Missouri, 74n. 28, 80; interpreting Civil War through the story of, 158, 165, 183–87, 218; invisibility of, in American narratives, 112, 174, 181; Lincoln on, 34, 67–68; as a national blunder, 130–31, 144, 164, 182, 239; as part of America's unmastered past, 193; as seized as well as given, 29, 111; semicentennial of, 193–210. *See also* Emancipation Proclamation; freedom

Emancipation Proclamation, 80, 200; anniversaries of, 84, 93–95, 101, 152n. 41, 194–95; ignoring of, at Blue-Gray reunions, 136, 146

Emerson, Ralph Waldo, 13, 15, 200, 232

emigration (as a possible solution to slavery), 33, 39, 40–41, 80, 132

Encyclopedia of the Negro (Du Bois's proposed work), 247

epic: Civil War depicted as, 122, 124, 159, 211, 213–15; Du Bois's attempt to write historical, 235–37, 249; Huggins's history as, 259, 261, 265–66, 268–69. *See also* tragedy

ethnicity. *See* African Americans; iden-

tity; immigrants; pluralism
evil, 261, 270, 271
"Ex-Confederate Association of
    Chicago," 179

Fair Oaks battle, 56, 61, 63
Faulkner, William, 121
Fauset, Jessie, 232
Fells Point (Baltimore, Maryland), 12
Fields, Barbara, 121, 214
Fifteenth Amendment (to U.S. Con-
    stitution), 132, 173
Fifty-fifth Massachusetts regiment,
    163
Fifty-fourth Massachusetts regiment,
    132–33, 151n. 38, 153, 154,
    157–59, 161–63, 165, 177, 187
"Fifty Years" (Johnson), 203
films: on Civil War, 55, 121–24,
    151n. 40, 182, 211–20, 272; on
    World War II, 6n. 4
First South Carolina Volunteers, 166
Fischer, David Hackett, 191
Fisk University (Nashville), 195
Fitzgerald, F. Scott, 276n. 12
Fitzpatrick, Sarah, 43
flags: Confederate, over South Car-
    olina statehouse, 153–54, 156; con-
    tention over return of, 177–79;
    Union regimental, 54–55
Florence (Massachusetts), 54
Floyd, Silas X., 194–95
Foner, Eric, 33, 216–17, 257n. 48,
    272
Foote, Shelby, 121, 214, 216
Ford's Theater (Washington, D.C.),
    170, 184
forgetting, 227; as part of politics of
    memory, 2–3, 63, 98, 106, 108–10,
    125, 126, 129–31, 138–42, 171,
    180–83, 191–92, 247–48, 250–51
Forrest, Nathan Bedford, 124
"For the Union Dead" (Lowell), 163
Fort Mill (South Carolina), 163
Fortress Monroe (Virginia), 65

Fort Sumter, 48–49, 54, 184
Fortune, T. Thomas, 93
Fort Wagner battle, 80, 156, 157, 159,
    163, 165, 176–77
Fosters, Gaines, 102
Fourteenth Amendment (to U.S. Con-
    stitution), 95, 132, 173
Fourth Corps (Army of the Potomac),
    72n. 5
Fourth of July speeches (Douglass's),
    127–28, 241, 273
Franklin, Benjamin, 13
Franklin, John Hope, 128, 153,
    193–94, 243, 256n. 48, 259, 272,
    275n. 12
Frederick Douglass Shoe Company
    (Lynn, Massachusetts), 202
Fredericksburg battle, 55, 61, 70, 178
Fredrickson, George, 132
Freedmen's Bureau, 234, 237–39
Freedmen's Memorial Monument
    (Washington, D.C.), 84–85, 101–2
Freedmen's Relief Committee of
    Philadelphia, 204
freedom: Brewster's view of, 58, 67;
    ex-slaves as unable to cope with,
    130, 131–32; images of, 16–17, 47,
    48–49, 77; meaning of, to Doug-
    lass, 14–15, 49, 98; New Year's
    Day as day of, for ex-slaves, 76;
    postwar celebrations of, by blacks,
    184; purchase of Douglass's, 20;
    slavery as threat to all Americans',
    34, 45, 67–68, 203, 272. *See also*
    emancipation; Emancipation
    Proclamation
Freeland, William, 11, 19
Free-Soil party, 38
Frémont, John C., 43, 74n. 28, 80, 81
From Slavery to Freedom (Franklin),
    276n. 12
Fugitive Slave Act (1850), 32, 34–36.
    See also slaves: fugitive
Fuller, Margaret, 15
Fussell, Paul, 53, 62, 73n. 18

future: America's orientation toward, 108; forgetting as key to, 63, 110, 129, 130, 142; history's role in, 4; slaves' concern about whether they had a, 15, 29, 33, 39, 41, 45–46, 48, 88, 156; slaves' projection of, 47. *See also* jeremiads

Gallagher, Gary, 215–16
GAR (Grand Army of the Republic), 69, 128, 137, 178. *See also* veterans
Garfield, James A., 106, 178
Garner, Cornelius, 76
Garnet, Henry Highland, 31, 38, 41, 79
Garrison, William Lloyd, 32, 106, 184, 198, 200, 205
Garvey, Marcus, 133, 134
Gates, Henry Louis, Jr., 277n. 19
gender: as division in war, 60–61; Du Bois's use of, 238–39; and portrayals of reconciliation, 125; and reception of Douglass's autobiography, 21; of recipients of Brewster's Civil War letters, 55–56, 60–62, 64, 67, 70, 71. *See also* men; women
Georgia: Blue-Gray reunions in, 178; Civil War devastation in, 174, 237; fears about slave revolts in, 43–45; sharecroppers in, 236–37. *See also* specific towns and cities in
Gettysburg battle, 55, 102, 123; Bierce on, 63; Blue-Gray reunions at, 70, 121–23, 125, 127, 134–46, 178–79, 181–83, 217; Burns on, 215, 216; Lincoln's speech on, 80, 82, 139, 140; mapping of, 177, 178; visits to site of, 175
Ghost Dance, 102
ghosts: in black writers' works, 104–5; at Blue-Gray reunions, 142
GI Bill, 270
Gilded Age, 69, 123; historical consciousness in, 97, 108, 112, 113, 178

Gilder, Richard Watson, 226
Gillis, John, 120
Gillmore, Quincy A., 184
Gilmore, James S., III, 154
Glatthaar, Joseph, 65
Goethe, Johann Wolfgang von, 93
Gone With the Wind (Mitchell), 151n. 40, 272
Goodbye Darkness (Manchester), 61
Gooding-Williams, Robert, 148n. 14
Gordon, John Brown, 195
Gore, Orson ("Austin"), 19, 21
Gorsuch, Edward, 36
Grand Army of the Republic. *See* GAR
"Granny" (former slave), 200–201
Grant, Ulysses S., 84, 101, 106, 107, 121, 217
Great Admiral (ship), 70
Great Britain, 6n. 4, 20
The Great Gatsby (Fitzgerald), 276n. 12
"Great House farm." *See* Wye plantation
The Great War in Modern Memory (Fussell), 73n. 18
Greeley, Horace, 255n. 27
Greener, Richard T., 93
Griffith, D. W., 128, 218
Grimke, Archibald, 149n. 22, 151n. 38
Gurganus, Allan, 156
Guthrie, Woody, 203
Gutman, Herbert, 263

Haiti, 41, 107
Haitian Emigration Bureau, 41
Halbwachs, Maurice, 3, 191
Halleck, Henry W., 65
Hampshire College, 212
Hampton, Wade, 180
Hampton Institute, 178
Hampton Park (Charleston), 185, 187
Handlin, Oscar, 258, 259, 261, 264, 266, 268, 269, 274n. 7
Hanley, Lynne, 73n. 18
Harcourt, Brace (publishers), 255n. 28

Harlan, John Marshall, 95, 162

Harlem Renaissance (Huggins), 259–60, 262

Harper, Francis Ellen Watkins, 31, 39

Harpers Ferry: John Brown's raid at, 37, 42, 43–44, 47, 82, 129, 205; Storer College in, 129, 133

Harris, Robert L., 265

Hart, Albert Bushnell, 227

Harvard University, 161, 227, 228–29, 264

Harvard University Press, 18, 229

Hayden, Lewis, 36

Haydenville (Massachusetts), 54

Hayes, Rutherford B., 106, 107

Henry, Patrick, 37

heritage. *See* identity

Heritage Preservation Association (Virginia), 154

Higginson, Henry Lee, 161–62

Higginson, Thomas Wentworth, 166

Hill, John H., 37

historian(s): academic, ix, 1–2, 211–20, 246–47, 250, 258–77, 279; as custodians of the past, 1–7; Du Bois as, 223–57; Huggins as, 258–77; need for trained, 211–20, 225; public, ix, 2. *See also* African American history; history; memory (historical)

history: African-American, within fabric of American history as a whole, 29, 97, 101–2, 134, 156, 201–3, 226, 231–32, 234–51, 258–77; as art, 258–77; audiences for, 1, 121, 124, 153, 215, 216, 259, 263, 265; Burns's lack of training in, 212–13; defined, 1–2; Douglass's interest in, 96, 97, 114, 115n. 2; vs. film, 211–20; master narrative of, 192, 230, 262–64, 267–68, 271–72, 279; of memory, 1–7, 193; military, x, 124–25, 159–60, 172–73, 176, 177; as moral discourse, 243, 244, 262, 266; official, 145, 225, 232, 233, 247, 250; pluralistic approaches to, 224; public, ix, 2; as a science, 145, 233, 248, 260, 262–63; social, 2, 53, 124, 191, 213; sources for, 17–19; uses of, 2, 4, 97, 113, 120–21, 126, 128, 134, 145, 153, 191, 224–25, 228, 239–51, 260, 262. *See also* African American history; epic; interpretations; memory (historical); myth(s); nostalgia; progress; tragedy

History of the United States from the Compromise of 1850 (Rhodes), 246

Hobsbawm, Eric, 192, 193, 225

Hollinger, David, 262

Holly, James T., 41

Holmes, Oliver Wendell, Jr., 99, 100, 120, 138–39, 165

"home": in Brewster's letters, 56; in slave songs, 46

Homer, 213, 216, 219, 263, 265. *See also* epic

honor. *See* courage and honor

Horton, James, 167n. 2

Horwitz, Tony, 175

Hosking, Geoffrey, 247

Howe, Julia Ward, 200

Howells, William Dean, 123, 157

Huckleberry Finn (Twain), 67

Huggins, Kathryn, 269

Huggins, Nathan Irvin, ix, 47, 146, 230, 258–77

Huggins, Winston J., 269

Hughes, Langston, 203, 262

Hutton, Patrick, 234

identity (and memory), 2, 4, 120–24, 224, 272

Illinois, 41, 204. *See also* towns and cities in

Imagined Communities (Anderson), 126

immigrants: and American dream, 273; slaves as, 267–69; as Union soldiers, 216

Indians, 102, 228

individualism, 13, 108–9, 142, 228

"Integrating Afro-American History" (Huggins), 263–66

interior lives: in autobiography, 17, 19; Huggins's examination of slaves', 265, 269; in slave narratives, 13–14, 22–24

Inter-Ocean (newspaper), 180

interpretations: of Civil War through the story of emancipation, 158, 165, 183–87, 218; and collective memory, 2, 120–25, 130–31, 134, 144–46, 191–93, 223–25, 278–80; history's link to, 2, 154, 213–14, 217–19; and racism, 156–57, 193–94, 223–57. *See also* epic; history: master narrative of; myth(s); progress; tragedy

"Irrepressible Conflict" (Seward's speech), 46

Israel, 47, 48

Jackson, Giles B., 197

Jackson, Stonewall, 124, 195

Jacobs, Harriet, 18–19, 269

James, William, 160, 223, 227, 232, 270–71

Jamestown (Virginia), 273

Jefferson, Thomas, 103, 267, 273

"Jefferson Davis as a Representative of Civilization" (Du Bois's speech), 228–29

jeremiads: commemorative moments as opportunities for, 202, 206–8; Douglass's, 113; Du Bois's, 234, 249–50; Gutman's, 263–64; Huggins's, 272; nineteenth century popularity of, 16; slave narratives as, 45

Jim Crow (apartheid; segregation): Du Bois on, 235–36, 242–48; in federal government, 143–44, 182–83; resistance to, 35; in southern archives, 243; triumph of, after

Reconstruction, 95, 109, 112, 114, 127, 131, 139, 141, 143–45, 160–61, 182, 198; during World War II, 270. *See also* disfranchisement; white supremacy

Joe Turner's Come and Gone (Wilson), 104

"John Brown's Body" (song), 158, 184, 186

Johnson, Andrew, 250

Johnson, Bradley T., 164

Johnson, Charles, 269

Johnson, James Weldon, 195–96, 203, 207, 208

Johnston, Joseph E., 121, 195, 217

Johnston, Mary, 173–74

Journal of American History, 212

Kammen, Michael, 3–4, 145, 200

Kansas-Nebraska Act (1854), 32

Kant, Immanuel, 260

Keckley, Elizabeth, 79

Keegan, John, 63

Kennesaw Mountain battle, 178

Key Issues in the Afro-American Experience (ed. Huggins, Kilson, and Fox), 261, 263

The Killer Angels (Shaara), 216

Kilmer, George, 178

King, Martin Luther, Jr., 134, 223, 270–71

Knapp, Steven, 233

Ladies Memorial Association of Charleston, 187

Ladies Memorial Society (Richmond), 164

Lafayette, Marquis de, 137

Laidler, Harry, 240

language (literacy), 199; Douglass's mastery of, 13, 14–15, 17–18, 20, 76, 77, 81, 85; of founding fathers, 267; of historians, 211–13; Lincoln's mastery of, 76, 81, 87; as unable to communicate the horrors of war, 62–63; as a weapon, 33, 44–46, 85, 232–33, 250, 254n. 18. *See also* history; myth(s); slave narratives

Lazarus (Biblical figure), 113

Lee, Fitzhugh, 180

Lee, Robert E., 124, 173, 195; Burns's portrayal of, 215; veneration of, 102, 105, 155

Lee, Stephen D., 180

Leeds (Massachusetts), 54

Legacy of the Civil War (Warren), 171

letters (as historical source), 53–71

Levine, Lawrence, 46, 259

Lewis, David Levering, 223, 226, 227, 234, 243

Liberia, 40, 129, 132, 133

Liberty party, 38

Lichtenberger, J. P., 199

lieux de memoire, 235

The Life and Times of Frederick Douglass (Douglass), 23–25, 200

"Life Pictures" (Douglass's speech), 25

Lincoln, Abraham, 69, 106, 123, 124, 143; assassination of, 24, 79, 83, 87, 88, 170, 185; on black Union soldiers, 48; Brewster as supporter of, 64; Douglass's relationship with, ix, 76–90; and emancipation of slaves in Missouri, 74n. 28; and Emancipation Proclamation, 200, 205; ex-slaves' memories of, 201; Freedman's Memorial monument to, 84–85, 101–2; Gettysburg Address of, 80, 82, 139, 140; on significance of emancipation, 34, 67–68; on slavery as the cause of the Civil War, 28. *See also* emancipation

Lincoln, Mary Todd, 79, 184

Lincoln, Robert, 194

Lincoln League, 194

Lincoln Park (Washington, D.C.), 84

Linderman, Gerald, 60

literacy. *See* language

literature, 112; black degeneration portrayed in, 131–32; jeremiads in black, 45, 113, 206–8, 234, 249–50, 272; by "local colorists," 102, 103; plantation school of, 127, 128, 151n. 40, 163–64, 173, 201, 236; and "slave narrative novel," 276n. 19. *See also* autobiography; biography; epic; slave narratives; *titles of specific works*

Little, Brown (publishers), 259

Litwack, Leon, 216, 217–18, 259

Liverpool (England), 35–36

Livingstone College (Salisbury, North Carolina), 162

"local color" writers, 102, 103

Locke, Alain, 126

Loewen, James, 168n. 15

Logan, Rayford, 227

Loggins, Vernon, 16

London *Times*, 141

Longstreet, Helen D. (Mrs. James), 140–41

Longstreet, James, 102, 140, 180

The Lost Cause (Pollard), 159

Lost Cause mythology, 140, 142, 197–98; in Burns's documentary, 215; Du Bois's challenges to, 225, 236, 237; in 1880s, 128; in 1890s, 155, 164; in 1914, 197–98; rise of, 98, 102–6, 173, 174

Louisville Courier-Journal, 138, 182

Lowell, Robert, 115, 160, 163

Lukacs, John, 1

lynching, 114, 132, 143, 162–63, 182, 229, 238, 247; Douglass on, 87, 108

Lynn (Massachusetts), 202

Macaulay, Thomas, 213

Macon (Georgia), 44, 195

Manchester, William, 61

manhood. *See* manliness

manliness: in the Civil War, 55–63, 68, 69, 71, 138–39, 141–42, 156–58,

manliness (*continued*)
166; Douglass on, 15, 21; and sectional reconciliation, 125, 137–39, 178; standards of, for black troops, 68, 156–58, 166. *See also* courage and honor

Mann, William Hodges, 137–39, 181

mapping (of battlefields), 177, 178

marriage (intersectional), 125, 176

The Marrow of Tradition (Chesnutt), 162

Marshall, Thurgood, 134

Martin, J. Sella, 39

Martin, Thomas, 197

Maryland, 11–12. *See also* cities and towns in

masculinity. *See* manliness

Massachusetts State College, 61

"Master Andrew," 19

McClellan, George B., 65, 214, 219

McCullough, David, 122, 214

McDowell, Deborah, 21

McDowell, James, 42

McHenry, Jerry, 36

Medford (Massachusetts), 54

Meier, August, 259

Melville, Herman, 15

Memorial Day (Decoration Day): blacks' founding of, 183–87; Douglass's thoughts on, 96, 98, 99, 111, 113, 114, 129, 130, 159; Union and Confederate veterans recognized on, 161

memories: defined, 1; idealizing of, 71; individual vs. collective, 2–3; repression of, in order to survive, 63, 110, 129, 130, 142. *See also* forgetting; memory (historical); nostalgia

memory (historical): author's interest in, ix–x; black writers' portrayal of, 104–5; collective, 1, 2–3, 121–24, 191–92, 223–57, 278–80; defined, 2; Du Bois's attempts to forge an alternative, 223–57; emotional

power of, 234–35; evolution of, 120–21; history of, 193; literature on, 5n. 2; national, 84, 192, 224, 242, 278–80; official, 3, 232, 247, 250; as owned, 2, 4, 279; politics of, 2–3, 120–21, 125, 129–31, 134, 153–54, 165–66, 172, 191, 223–27, 250–51, 256n. 38, 278–80; and power, 1–2, 154, 234–35, 278–80; as the prize in struggle between rival versions of the past, 95–98, 105; vs. recollection, 129; selective, 60, 111, 128, 233; social (*see* memory: collective); studies of, as subfield in American history, ix. *See also* forgetting; history; interpretations

memory palaces, 234–35

men: relations among, in war, 58–60; war as separating women from, 60–61. *See also* courage and honor; manliness; *names of specific men*

Metropolitan A. M. E. Church (Washington, D.C.), 133

migration, 267–69. *See also* emigration

"A Mild Suggestion" (Du Bois), 207–8

Miller, Kelly, 199

Milliken's Bend battle, 80

Minkins, Shadrach, 36

minstrel shows, 247

"The Mission of the War" (Douglass's speech), 81, 160, 187–88

Missouri, 74n. 28, 80

Mitchell, Charles, 163

Mitchell, Margaret, 151n. 40, 236, 266

"A Modest Proposal" (Swift), 207

Mohr, Clarence, 43

monuments and museums: to Confederates, 164, 179–80, 245; to freedmen, 84–85, 101–2; and memory, 2, 142, 278; need for, in Charleston, 187; to regiments, 151n. 38, 153–69, 177; to southern slave in South Carolina, 163–64. *See also* battlefields; Blue-

Nicolay, John G., 184
Nietzsche, Friedrich, 6n. 2, 110, 145, 191, 233
Niger Valley Exploring Party, 40
Nora, Pierre, 2, 235, 278
Norfolk (Virginia), 68, 76
North: black abolitionism in, 32–36; black responses to Civil War outbreak in, 48–49; interest of, in southern battlefields, 175–76; racial caste in, 30; sympathy of, for Lost Cause, 109; version of Civil War story told in, 98. *See also* nationalism; reconciliation; sectionalism; white supremacy
Northampton (Massachusetts), 53–54, 56, 59, 64, 68, 69
North Carolina, 161, 162, 179, 198, 245
Northrup, Solomon, 45, 269
nostalgia (sentimentalism): in Blue-Gray reunions, 70, 134, 142, 144–45; Brewster's, for army life, 60; about Civil War, 121–27, 159–60, 172–75, 217–18; and Du Bois, 228, 237, 250; in neoabolitionism, 200; post-Cold War absorption with, 192–93

Oakwood Cemetery (Chicago), 179–80
Oates, W. C., 180–81
Odum, Howard, 199
O'Ferrall, Charles, 164
"Of Our Spiritual Strivings" (Du Bois), 235
"O Freedom" (song), 205
"Of the Black Belt" (Du Bois), 236–37
"Of the Dawn of Freedom" (Du Bois), 234, 237–39
"Of the Meaning of Progress" (Du Bois), 235
One Hundred and Fourth U.S. Colored Troops, 187

Oneida Institute, 129
opium, 63
Outlook, 141
Ovington, Mary White, 200–201
Oxford University Press, 219n. 3
Ozick, Cynthia, 4

Page, Thomas Nelson, 103, 163, 201
pageants, 152n. 41, 205–6
Palmer (Massachusetts), 54
Parkman, Francis, 266
Parsons, Henry W., 58–59
Parsons, Joseph B., 55
Patriotic Association, 186
PBS (Burns's Civil War documentary on), 121–24, 182, 211–20
Peculiar Institution (Stampp), 270
Peninsula campaign, 55, 56, 63
Pennington, James W. C., 31
Pennsylvania: commission for Blue-Gray reunions in, 134–37, 150n. 25; and emancipation observances, 204
Petersburg (Virginia), 73n. 21, 187
Philadelphia (Pennsylvania), 37, 179; emancipation observance in, 204, 205; fugitive slave rescues in, 35
Philadelphia Brigade, 179
Philadelphia Inquirer, 136
The Philadelphia Negro (Du Bois), 230
Phillips, Ulrich B., 18, 240, 254n. 25
Phillips, Wendell, 200
Pickett's Charge (Gettysburg battle), 136, 138, 179, 182
Pierce, Franklin, 36
Pinckney, Daryl, 15, 23
Pine and Palm (newspaper), 41
"plantation legend," 18, 130. *See also* slaves: as contented and loyal
"plantation school" of literature, 127, 128, 151n. 40, 163–64, 173, 201, 236
Planter (steamer), 184
Plessy vs. Ferguson, 131, 161, 162

pluralism (in the U.S.), 192, 223, 224, 243–44, 279; concerns about emphasis on, 263–64; Du Bois on, 226

politics: of forgetting, 2–3, 63, 98, 106, 108–10, 125, 126, 129–31, 138–42, 171, 180–83, 191–92, 247–48, 250–51; of historical memory, 2–3, 120–21, 125, 129–31, 134, 153–54, 165–66, 172, 191, 223–27, 250–51, 256n. 38, 278–80

Pollard, Edward A., 159

Populist movement, 161

Port Hudson battle, 80

poverty, 259

Powell, Lawrence, 265

Powell, William P., 35–36

power (and memory), 1–2, 154, 234–35, 278–80. *See also* history; memory (historical); myth(s)

pragmatism, 271

"presentism," 191–93

Preston, Dickson, 11–12

Price, Joseph, 162

Principles of Scientific Management (Taylor), 136

prison farms, 236–37

progress: Americans' belief in, in history, 146, 157, 230, 260, 266, 267, 272; of blacks, 31, 197, 198–99, 202–6; in Burns's Civil War documentary, 123, 213–14, 219; Douglass's belief in doctrine of, 98; Du Bois's challenge to theory of, 234, 235–36, 244, 266

Progressive era, 126–27, 139–40, 198–200, 204–6

"The Propaganda of History" (Du Bois), 225, 240

protest. *See* resistance

Protestants against Poverty (Huggins), 259

Providence (Rhode Island), 35

Provincial Freeman (newspaper), 40

Pryor, Sara, 103

Puddin'head Wilson (Twain), 276n. 24

Puritans, 13

Purvis, Robert, 35, 39

Quarles, Benjamin, 18, 29, 38

Quincy (Illinois), 204

Raboteau, Albert, 47

race: author's interest in historical significance of, ix–x; disharmony based on, as continuing issue, 280; Du Bois's conception of, 225, 234; eliding of, in post-Civil War reconciliation talk, 100, 123–28, 132, 134–46, 156, 172–74, 180, 181, 217, 245; increasing division by, following Civil War, 125–52, 173, 217; memory often invoked in name of, 4; Southern mentalities on, 196–98. *See also* African Americans; emancipation; Jim Crow; pluralism; racism; slavery; white supremacy

racism: within abolitionist movement, 32, 64–66, 71; as barrier to self-improvement among blacks, 31; Brewster's, 64–65; Douglass on, 86, 95, 98, 102, 106, 107–8, 130–31, 233; in historical interpretations, 156–57, 193–94, 223–57; scientific, 225. *See also* Jim Crow; white supremacy

Rampersad, Arnold, 227, 234, 235

Ranke, Otto von, 3

rape, 108. *See also* lynching; slaveholders

Rappahannock Station battle, 55

Reagan, John H., 165

Reagan, Ronald, 264, 272

reconciliation (post-Civil War sectional): battlefields used for, 170–71; Blue-Gray reunions as rituals of national, 127, 134–46, 161, 177–83; depiction of, as reconciliation (post-Civil War sectional), (*continued*)

"clasping hands across the bloody chasm," 161, 254n. 27; Douglass on, 100, 105–6, 109, 113–14, 245; Du Bois on, 228, 236; as obscuring race and other central issues of the war, 100, 123–28, 132–46, 155, 156, 160–62, 171–74, 180, 181, 214, 217, 239, 245; portrayal of, through gender and imagery, 125; and view of Civil War as between brothers rather than nation-states, 126, 138, 161–62, 178, 181, 183, 217, 229, 279; Washington on, 181. *See also* Blue-Gray reunions; nationalism; veterans; white supremacy

Reconstruction, 79, 84, 96, 98, 105–7, 109–11, 117n. 22; in Burns's Civil War documentary, 121, 123, 214, 217, 218; Du Bois on, 223, 225–27, 237–39, 244–50; as a failure, 132, 144, 155, 182, 223, 242, 245–47, 256n. 48, 272; goals of, 172; Jim Crow's triumph after, 95, 109, 112, 114, 127, 131, 139, 141, 143–45, 160–61, 182, 198; legacy of, 162, 237–38; "new" history of, in 1960s, 256n. 48, 272; and reconciliation, 179, 181. *See also* Jim Crow

Red Badge of Courage (Crane), 61

Red Cross, 136

Redpath, James, 41, 185, 187, 190n. 29

Reed, Ishmael, 269

regeneration. *See* Civil War: as second American Revolution

religion: African Americans' uses of, 22, 46–47, 129, 132, 133, 201, 206, 231, 266, 270–71; civil, 84, 101, 102, 155; memory often invoked in name of, 4. *See also* Bible

Remond, Sarah Parker, 31

Renan, Ernest, 138

reparations (for slavery), 193

Republican party, 155, 250; antislavery (free labor) stance of, 34, 43, 44, 64, 87; blacks' relationship to, in 1850s, 38; Brewster's support for, 64, 69; Douglass's support for, 106–7, 111; Frémont's challenge to Lincoln in, 81; Longstreet as postwar supporter of, 140

resistance: Douglass's, 16, 21; as a right, 15; as a tactic against slavery, 33–40, 42–45, 79–80. *See also* Underground Railroad

reunions. *See* Blue-Gray reunions; reconciliation

Rhodes, Elisha Hunt, 55

Rhodes, James Ford, 229, 246

Richmond (Indiana), 204

Richmond (Virginia), 63, 164, 176, 197

Richmond Examiner, 159

Ricoeur, Paul, 233

The Rise of American Civilization (Beard), 240

Road to Reunion (Buck), 144–45, 190n. 29

"Robert Gould Shaw" (Dunbar), 166

Rochester (New York): Douglass's home in, 50n. 12, 88; Douglass's speeches in, 110–11, 113–14, 130; reactions to Lincoln's assassination in, 24, 88

Rock, John, 39–40

Rodgers, Daniel, 199

romanticism (Douglass's), 21

Rome (Georgia), 44, 45

Roosevelt, Theodore, 99

Rose, Willie Lee, 256n. 48, 265

Rosengarten, Theodore, 265

Rosenwald Fund, 255n. 28

Rowell, James, 70

Royce, Josiah, 227

Ruggles, David, 35, 37

runaway slaves. *See* slaves: fugitive

Ryan, Abram, 174

slavery (*continued*)

as a sin, 161–62; South as having fought for, 96, 114, 164, 194, 245; sprit of, in Jim Crow, 95. *See also* abolitionism; emancipation; freedom; slave narratives; slaves; Underground Railroad

slaves: auctions of, 76; concerns of, over their future in America, 15, 29, 33, 39, 41, 45–46, 48, 88, 156; as contented and loyal, 15, 18, 103, 130, 154, 163–64, 197–98, 201, 240; as "contraband of war," 65, 66–68; fugitive, activists among, 41; fugitive, as heroes, 241; fugitive, Douglass as, 18, 21, 25, 31; fugitive, in Union army, 65, 66–68, 76, 82; fugitive, rescues of, 34–36, 108; fugitive, return to owners of, 80; memories of, 200–201; monuments to, 163–64; number of, who fled to Canada, 34, 36, 37; role of, in causing the Civil War, 42–44; self-emancipation of, 111, 246; as serving in Confederate army, 136, 154; songs of, 22–23, 46–47; trade in, 32, 267–68. *See also* emancipation

Slotkin, Richard, 98, 123

Smalls, Robert, 93, 184

Smith, Gerrit, 38, 96

Smith, James McCune, 32, 41, 48

social Darwinism, 131–32

Soldiers' Home (Lincoln family retreat), 86

Somme battle, 62

songs (of slaves), 22–23, 46–47. *See also specific song titles*

Sons of Confederate Veterans, 154, 218

The Souls of Black Folk (Du Bois), 161, 201, 227, 231–32, 234–39, 242, 266, 269

South: Appomattox surrender of, 121, 162, 173, 217; blacks serving on side of, 136, 154; Civil War ruins in, 174, 176–77; as having fought for slavery, 96, 114, 164, 194, 245; influence of, after Civil War, 143, 161, 180; neo-Confederates in, 167n. 2; New, 103, 117n. 22, 125, 155, 173; Old, 103, 125, 173, 201, 240; presidents from, 103, 138–40, 182; race and Civil War memory in, 195–98; slavery in, 30, 132; version of Civil War story told in, 96, 98, 100, 102–4, 155, 163–65. *See also* Confederates; Jim Crow; lynching; reconciliation; Reconstruction; sectionalism; white supremacy

The South: A Tour of Its Battlefields and Ruined Cities (Trowbridge), 175–77

South America, 40

South Carolina, 153–54

Soviet Union, 6n. 4

Spanish-American War, 103, 123, 134

Spotsylvania battle, 55, 63–64, 70, 71

Springfield (Massachusetts), 54, 72n. 6

Stampp, Kenneth, 30, 256n. 48, 270

Starn, Randolph, 121

"The Star of Ethiopia" (Du Bois's pageant), 152n. 41, 205–6

Stearns, George Luther, 200

Stephens, Alexander H., 174

Stevenson, Adlai, 180

Stewart, Maria, 32

Still, William, 35, 37, 48

Storer College (Harpers Ferry, West Virginia), 129, 133

Stowe, Harriet Beecher, 34–35, 47

Stuckey, Sterling, 259

suffragists. *See* women: supporters of rights of

Sumner, Charles, 106

Sundquist, Eric, 266

The Suppression of the African Slave Trade to the United States, 1638–1970 (Du Bois's thesis), 229–31

Supreme Court. *See* U.S. Supreme Court

Swift, Jonathan, 207, 208

Symington, James, 217
Syracuse (New York), 36, 108

Taft, William Howard, 194
Taney, Roger B., 39, 47
Tanner, Benjamin T., 93, 160
Taylor, Frederick W., 136, 199
Taylor Society, 136
tenant farmers, 236–37
Tenth Massachusetts Volunteers,
    53–71, 73n. 21
Texas, 44
Thelen, David, 212, 220n. 4
"There Is a Holy City" (song), 47
Thirty-fifth U.S. Colored Troops, 187
Thirty-sixth New York, 55
Thirty Years War, 122
Thompson, Samuel, 137
Thoreau, Henry David, 13, 15
Thurman, Howard, 270
Thurman, Sue Bailey, 270
Tillman, Ben, 197
Time and Narrative (Ricoeur), 233
"To a Historian" (Whitman), 4–5
Tocqueville, Alexis de, 108, 109, 262
Tomb of the Unknown Soldier (Ar-
    lington National Cemetery), 96
Topeka Capital, 204
Toplin, Robert Brent, 212, 214–15,
    219n. 3
Tourgee, Albion, 99–100, 155
tradition. See myth(s): vs. tradition
tragedy: in American history, 239,
    242–43, 249, 260, 266; Americans'
    love of, with a happy ending, 123,
    157; Americans' reluctance to view
    Civil War as, 157–58, 182, 215,
    279; Civil War remembered as,
    leading to national unity, 140, 146,
    181, 193, 217, 219; of Lincoln's
    assassination, 170, 184. See also epic
The Tragic Era (Bowers), 128, 246
Trowbridge, John T., 175–77
Truth, Sojourner, 31, 47, 205
Tubman, Harriet, 31, 202–3, 231

Tuckahoe Creek (Maryland), 11, 12
Turner, Henry McNeal, 149n. 22
Turner, Nat, 39, 42, 205
Twain, Mark, 67, 232, 276n. 24
Twelfth Regiment Armory (New York
    City), 204
Twenty-first U.S. Colored Infantry,
    183

Uncle Tom's Cabin (Stowe), 35
Underground Railroad, 35; leaders of,
    31, 37, 48, 202; legacy of, 203; pro-
    posal for government-sponsored,
    82
Underwood, John C., 179–80
Union soldiers: African Americans as,
    40, 48, 65, 68–69, 76, 80, 82, 109,
    132–33, 143, 158–59, 161–63, 165,
    166, 177, 183–84, 205, 245–46;
    cemeteries for, 185–86; immigrants
    as, 216; letters of, 53–75; racism
    among white, 64–69, 80; standards
    of manliness for black, 68, 156–58,
    166. See also Blue-Gray reunions; na-
    tionalism; reconciliation; sectional-
    ism; veterans
United Confederate Veterans,
    164–65, 194. See also veterans
United Daughters of the Confederacy,
    164, 187
United Nations, 224
United States: centennial of, 127,
    137; central issues of Civil War still
    alive in, 122–23, 280; individual-
    ism in, 13, 108–9, 142, 228; orien-
    tation of, toward future, 108; plu-
    ralism of, 192, 223, 224, 226,
    243–44, 263–64, 279; re-inventing
    oneself as theme in, 13, 20, 24–25,
    133, 262; slavery as demonstrating
    limits to democracy in, 240–42;
    World War II films in, 6n. 4. See
    also Civil War; individualism; Jim
    Crow; progress; race; slavery;
    tragedy

U.S. Congress, 164; blacks in, 161; Blue-Gray reunions funded by, 135, 181; and emancipation, 65, 84, 152n. 41, 197–98

U.S. Constitution, 38, 39, 95, 98, 106, 111, 125, 132, 162, 173

U.S. Post Office, 143

U.S. Supreme Court: and civil rights, 95; Dred Scott decision of, 32, 39–40, 47; on *Plessy vs. Ferguson*, 131, 161, 162; and school desegregation, 134

U.S. Treasury Department, 143

United States v. Stanley ("1883 Civil Rights Cases"), 95

U.S. War Department, 135

"universal" (search for), 15–16, 21. *See also* pluralism

University of Berlin (Germany), 229

University of California at Berkeley, 270

University of Munich (Germany), 122

University of Virginia, 131–32

The Unwritten War (Aaron), 112

The Uprooted (Handlin), 261, 264, 266, 268, 269, 274n. 7

Urbana (Ohio), 163

"The Use and Abuse of History" (Nietzsche), 191

valor. *See* courage

Vardaman, James, 197

Varieties of Religious Experience (James), 271

Vesey, Denmark, 184

veterans: African Americans as Union army, 40, 48, 65, 68–69, 76, 80, 82, 109, 132–33, 143, 158–59, 161–63, 165, 166, 177, 183–84, 205, 245–46; black, at Blue-Gray reunions, 127, 136–37, 141, 150n. 25, 181–82; black, at Shaw/Fifty-fourth Massachusetts monument unveiling, 158–59, 165; and Lost Cause mythology, 102–3, 140, 198; occupational anxieties of, 60; selective

memories of, 60. *See also* Blue-Gray reunions; Confederates; GAR; manliness; Union soldiers; United Confederate Veterans

Vietnam War, 214

vigilance committees, 35, 37

Villard, Fanny Garrison, 200

Villard, Oswald Garrison, 151n. 38, 198–99

violence. *See* resistance; war; *names of specific wars*

Virginia, 179; Blue-Gray reunions in, 178; Civil War devastation in, 174, 176; Confederate History Month in, 154; in Lost Cause mythology, 103. *See also* names of places and battles in

voting. *See* disfranchisement

Wade, Benjamin Franklin, 106

Walden (Thoreau), 13

Walker, Clarence E., 255n. 28

Walker, David, 31, 38, 205

Wallace, Lew, 180

war: Anglo-Saxons' love of, 228; history buffs more interested in battles than in causes of, 124–25, 159–60, 172–73, 176, 177; relations between men in, 58–60; as separating men from women, 60–61; as villain in Burns's Civil War documentary, 214. *See also specific wars*

Ward, Geoffrey, 217, 218

Ward, Samuel Ringgold, 31, 33–34, 40

Warren, Robert Penn, 95, 111, 171, 173, 211, 279

Warsaw, Marie, 269

Washington, Booker T., 129, 134, 144, 149n. 22, 156, 181, 198, 199, 241–42; and emancipation observances, 202–3

Washington, D.C.: Douglass's house in, 12, 87; Douglass's official roles in, 107; emancipation observance

DAVID W. BLIGHT

*is Class of 1959 Professor of History and Black Studies at Amherst
College. He is the author of* Frederick Douglass' Civil War:
Keeping Faith in Jubilee *(1989); and* Race and Reunion: The
Civil War in American Memory *(2001), which won seven book
awards, including the Bancroft, Abraham Lincoln,
Frederick Douglass, and Merle Curti prizes.*